EUGENE BARDACH

Getting Agencies to Work Together

The Practice and Theory of Managerial Craftsmanship

BROOKINGS INSTITUTION PRESS

Washington, D.C.

Copyright © 1998

THE BROOKINGS INSTITUTION
1775 Massachusetts Avenue, N.W.
Washington, D.C. 20036
www.brook.edu

Library of Congress Cataloging-in-Publication data

Bardach, Eugene.
   Getting agencies to work together : The practice and theory of managerial craftsmanship / Eugene Bardach.
      p.   cm.
   Includes bibliographical references and index.
   ISBN 0-8157-0798-3 (alk. paper)
   ISBN 0-8157-0797-5 (pbk. : alk. paper)
      1. administrative agencies—United States–Management.   2. Public administration—United States.   3. Intergovernmental cooperation—United States.   I. Title.
   JF1601 .B37 1998   98-25467
   352.2'6'0973—ddc21   CIP

9 8 7 6 5 4 3 2 1

The paper used in this publication meets the minimum requirements of the American National Standard for Information Sciences—Permanence of Paper for Printed Library Materials, ANSI Z39.48-1984.

Typeset in Palatino

Composition by R. Lynn Rivenbark
Macon, Georgia

Printed by R. R. Donnelley and Sons
Harrisonburg, Virginia

Getting Agencies to Work Together

Preface

THIS BOOK ORIGINATED as an idea for a study of the more ambitious and innovative forms of interagency collaboration in American state and local government. Since I began studying policy and program implementation in the early 1970s I have considered difficult interagency working relationships, which are usually strained if not absent, a significant but surmountable barrier to effective implementation. So have many other people, though with varying degrees of skepticism and hopefulness. Harold Seidman, a distinguished scholar of public administration, once mocked "interagency coordination" as a public administrator's—and academic's—philosophers' stone.

Nonetheless, a bit more interagency collaboration is probably going on these days. In its most interesting manifestations it goes beyond traditional cost sharing in order to achieve economies of scale. It extends to the creation of joint-production capabilities, both in service delivery and in regulatory enforcement. My interest in the phenomenon was shared by the Innovations in American Government Program of the Ford Foundation and the Kennedy School of Government at Harvard, which have generously provided the principal support for this book. Interagency collaboration is often a needed platform for product innovations. A surprisingly large number of product innovations (or at least those found among the innovations program award winners) appear to require interagency collaboration of some kind to get them up and keep them running. In a sample of forty-six Ford Foundation innovations program award winners between 1986, when the program started, and 1994, I counted about half that fit this description.

Moreover, interagency collaboration in joint-production activities is in an important sense an innovation per se, albeit a process rather than a product innovation. I have often found a remarkable enthusiasm for the process among people engaged in it, a belief that they were doing something new and remarkable, even heroic. The collaborators say they often have to learn a new way of thinking, a new way of doing business, to put results ahead of procedures, capacity building above turf protection, trust ahead of suspicion, joint problem solving ahead of accepted, time-worn methods.

I hope that the book makes a contribution to the understanding of innovation in the ways I had originally imagined it would. I have grander hopes as well. As my research progressed I came to see an even more important connection between interagency collaboration and innovation. Both are special cases of a broader phenomenon—namely, creativity in public management, or perhaps more precisely, the creation of new things out of old materials.

The existing literature, both in government and in the private sector, sheds some light on this phenomenon, but not much. What is missing is something even more fundamental than an understanding of managerial creativity: It is a conceptual framework for understanding purposive activity altogether—what I eventually came to call craftsmanship activity. The conceptual problem is in making space for purposive activity in the more or less deterministic worldview of workaday social science. I realized that if I was going to be able to understand interagency collaboration, I would need to do some work at this basic level first.

I welcomed the prospect. I have long felt that the study of public management and public administration could not make further progress until this basic problem has been solved—or, if not "solved," then at least softened up. Interagency collaboration would be, I thought, a medium through which I might explore more fundamental issues.

Whether I have succeeded at all in softening up the basic conceptual problem is for readers to judge. I can only say that I have enjoyed the challenge and have been deeply grateful to the many people and institutions who have offered one or another form of support. Over the years I have benefited from discussions about many issues dealt with in this book with friends and colleagues: Rebecca J. Bardach, Michael Barzelay, Robert D. Behn, Jon Brock, David K. Cohen, John Ellwood, Richard F. Elmore, Jane E. Fountain, Judith E. Gruber, Meredith I. Honig, Judith E. Innes, Robert A. Kagan, David L. Kirp, Todd R. LaPorte, Cara Lesser, Leo Levenson, Martin A. Levin, Frank Levy, Laurence E. Lynn Jr., Lawrence M. Mead, H. Brinton Milward,

Lawrence B. Mohr, Mark H. Moore, Michael O'Hare, Ellen Schall, Eugene Smolensky, David L. Weimer, and Mark Yessian. I received valuable comments on the manuscript, in addition to more general intellectual guidance, from Robert Agranoff, Alan A. Altshuler, Edith D. Balbach, Hector Cardenas, Xavier Castaner, Stephen Page, Bill Parent, Beryl A. Radin, Craig W. Thomas, Marc D. Zegans, and anonymous reviewers. Hector Cardenas and Cara Lesser did admirable work as research assistants for part of the project. In addition to principal financial support from the Ford Foundation/Kennedy School of Government Innovations in American Government Program, I also received support from the Center for the Study of Law and Society and the Committee on Research of the University of California at Berkeley.

Deborah Hardin edited the manuscript; Inge Lockwood proofread the pages; and Robert Elwood prepared the index. Nancy Davidson, acquisitions editor for Brookings Institution Press, offered excellent editorial advice.

Hundreds of informants and interviewees contributed time and goodwill, too many to thank by name. I am most grateful to them. To some of them I doubtless owe an apology as well. Some will feel that the level of rated collaborative success I bestowed in chapter 3 is either higher or lower than I do. Many might also think that, in my treatment of their sites in subsequent chapters, their talents and importance have been underappreciated. Some will feel that their rivals have been appreciated excessively. And some will feel that they are being criticized unfairly or invidiously. Although I did my best, within the limits of my resources and my abilities, I am prepared to plead guilty. As I explain in chapter 1, the objectives of this study were primarily conceptual. I was not aiming for justice, which, if achievable at all, would have required vastly more research effort than I could possibly have invested. My aims were to create a conceptual framework and to advance some hypotheses that could guide future research. Justice will have to be sought from a different quarter.

Finally, I wish to thank my wife, Nancy Bardach, for her irrational encouragement and her world-class proofreading skills.

Contents

Tables

Figures

1

Creating Value through Collaboration

In 1969 the New York City Health Department was ready to attack the problem of lead poisoning in young children. Gordon Chase, newly appointed by Mayor John Lindsay as the department director, was to mobilize administrative and budgetary resources for this program. Chase created a new Bureau of Lead Poisoning Control and assembled previously disparate functions related to the problem. With the mayor's implicit support and sanctioned by attention from the city's liberal political elite, Chase persuaded the City Bureau of the Budget to allocate an extra $3 million to address lead poisoning. He put pressure on hospitals to accept cases for treatment and also created a more focused system of field inspector responsibility for case-finding.

In some respects Chase's system appeared to have worked well. It broke down when it came to recidivism, however: Children who had been treated successfully turned up months later with high levels of lead in their blood again. Flaking lead paint in old tenement apartments, which would find its way into children's mouths and ultimately their blood streams, was the source of the problem. After several months it became obvious that a permanent solution would require the paint source to be removed or effectively covered. To accomplish this task, the New York City Housing and Development Administration had to agree to collaborate by substantially upgrading its emergency repair program. This would have entailed spending money and finding ways to put pressure on landlords to clean up the apartments. The agency did not do so. Even Chase, whose can-do style of public management has made him a minor hero in the eyes of students of public management, was unable to persuade Housing to cooperate.

It is not clear why Housing did not cooperate.[1] It is easy to speculate about what the head of the housing agency might have said to Chase when the possibility of collaboration was broached: "We would really like to help, but . . .

—. . . we have our own housing-related health issues to deal with, such as vermin and heating-system breakdowns in the middle of winter."

—. . . our housing inspectors aren't trained to recognize lead paint problems, and we aren't set up to test paint samples in-house or to send them out for testing."

—. . . citizens complain to us about clogged toilets, vermin, unsafe stairways, heating and air conditioning breakdowns. We don't hear from them about the quality of the interior paint."

—. . . we'd need a club to threaten the landlords, and the city council has already shown its reluctance to give it to us."

—. . . What? You are proposing to have your own field people take on the job of inspecting apartments and getting the paint removed? It's out of the question to have anyone but our own people going into apartments and negotiating with landlords. They would just compete with what our own people are doing, foul communications with landlords, and upset the tenants."

—. . . What? Avoid competing with our people and fouling relations with landlords by having your people work on teams with our people? Not so fast. Which agency would be responsible for organizing their work schedules and supervising what these field people do? Suppose your field guy only takes a half hour in a building and our guy needs to spend an hour? What would happen if the team members disagreed? Suppose landlords come running to *us* about problems caused by *your* inspector?"

Perhaps unspoken, but real enough, would have been another list of "answers," maybe even unconscious ones:

— "If we do this, who knows what other bright ideas Health might soon have for taking control of my resources?"

— "I dare not say no outright; so we can let this be 'studied' forever by an interagency task force."

1. Rosenthal (1973).

— "This fellow Chase is on an ego trip, and I won't help pay for it."

One approach Chase might have taken would have been to find a common superior, someone with authority over both agencies and who was in a position to order collaboration outright. For instance, rather than going directly to the director of the Housing and Development Administration, Chase might have first appealed to the mayor's office. But assuming the mayor would have approved of the plan, his order to Housing to cooperate would have been empty without constant follow-up to see that it was being carried out and without at least some continuing efforts to remove unexpected constraints and influence the supply of unexpectedly needed resources. The mayor would likely have said, "Great idea, Gordon, we'll tell the Housing director to be sure to cooperate on this, and then the two of you just work out the details." Once it became apparent that the Housing director could stall forever over the details, however, it would have also become apparent to the mayor (and assistants) that their scarce time and energy would be needed to make the order stick and, very likely, that they could not allow this issue to displace issues perceived to be of greater substance.

A less obvious tactic would have been for Chase to work from the bottom up rather than the top down. He could have instructed his staff to find a middle manager in Housing who was personally interested in the lead poisoning problem, possibly an individual who lived in one of the neighborhoods most at risk or who personally knew a family that had been affected. If this person could have been turned into an ally and could have helped find other allies in the Housing department, preliminary analyses of some of the technical issues might have been accomplished before Chase had had his first conversations with either the director or the mayor's office. However, these mid-level allies in Housing might have been risking trouble if their contacts with outsiders were to have become construed as acts of disloyalty or irresponsibility.

Even if motivation, and hence resources, would have been forthcoming, Housing and Health still would have had to work out the operational details of how housing inspections and abatement actions would actually be coordinated with the case management process. What actions in one agency would trigger what actions in the other agency? Who would be assigned to the inspection and abatement tasks? Would there be joint Housing-Health inspection teams? Who would supervise them? Would Health personnel be delegated as Housing's enforcement powers and vice versa? Once the agencies got down to this nitty-gritty level of issues, would they actually be able to solve the problems they implied? At what cost in money and in possible performance degradation of the other programs for which Housing and Health were responsible?

The difficulties of designing an effective and efficient operating system for the collaborative effort likely was not solved if an interpersonal culture of trust and pragmatism was not established, along with a system for building and maintaining consensus at the executive, or policy, level. Trust, a problem-solving ethos, and consensus-building processes do not just appear, however. It takes time, effort, skill, a mix of constructive personalities who are around long enough to build effective relationships. Is government able to supply such talent? Is it able to create the conditions that make it possible for the talented individuals to do what they have to do? What can some subset of these talented individuals do to help create the right conditions?

Furthermore, whatever they do has to be done over a long period of time, because effective collaboration is a state that emerges relatively slowly. Hence we must also ask whether such individuals can energize and guide a complex developmental process that will take place over a long time period, a period in which disruptive political and fiscal shifts might possibly occur. Possibly they could if they were to stay in their agency positions and roles. But turnover happens, and it tears at the fabric of personal relationships that is essential for collaboration to work.

A New Optimism

For many years I taught this case in graduate classes with only casual attention to Chase's problem with the housing agency. His likely failure in those quarters seemed so obvious that it was hardly worth discussing. Agencies cooperate? Of course not! As one of my colleagues quipped when I told her I was writing a book about interagency cooperation, "Short book, huh?"[2] If Chase were alive today and working on the housing agency problem, I believe it might prove more tractable than it was in the past. Survey responses from nearly 1,000 cities and counties even in 1984 found a new management style in local government service delivery: "planning and developing interjurisdictional

2. Suzanne Scotchmer, an economist on the Goldman School faculty.

policies and programs; forging adaptive program responses that rapidly respond to change; working in the thicket of interjurisdictional networks, politics, and problem solving; and leveraging, contracting, and finding new technical solutions to social problems."[3]

Today it helps that reform of American public administration is now much talked about. *The New Public Management* is a term of art among students of the subject.[4] Osborne and Gaebler's *Reinventing Government* has become a field manual for reformers.[5] I estimate that every public sector manager I interviewed in the course of my research for this book knew of *Reinventing Government* and its general message. The central message, in my view if not necessarily that of everyone I discussed it with, is to manage for results, not simply in an effort to go through the expected motions. One of the important results should be to satisfy one's "customers." Slightly less central are the prescriptions about the most effective means to these ends: Find ways to measure results and pay attention to what the measures say; give more power to low-level employees; take advantage of private sector pressures toward efficiency by contracting out for actual service delivery rather than having government in the direct service-delivery business.[6]

Osborne and Gaebler were drawing to a large degree on a stock of reform ideas current in the private sector, most famously expressed by Tom Peters and Robert Waterman in *In Search of Excellence*,[7] and in the doctrines of the Total Quality Management (TQM) movement.[8] Although these ideas have not been rigorously tested, they often enough conform to intuition and common sense, and they travel in company with supportive studies of some aspects of the doctrine and many persuasive anecdotes.[9] The central ideas that have had the most appeal to practitioners of public administration, to judge by a recent book reporting on some successful TQM applications in government, are the customer focus, employee involvement in the improvement of work

3. Agranoff and Pattakos (1989, p. 82).

4. See Borins (1996) and, for a critique, Savoie (1996).

5. Osborne and Gaebler (1992). One could also count the new governance ideas about replacing hierarchy with collaboration in intergovernmental relations (Radin and others, 1996, pp. 3–4).

6. Even less central, in my view, are their prescriptions for private-public partnerships and paying managers for performance.

7. Peters and Waterman (1982).

8. Creech (1994).

9. Hackman and Wageman (1995).

processes, closer collaboration with suppliers "to ensure that the supplies utilized in work processes are well designed and fit for use," continuous employee analysis of work processes, and close communication with customers to identify and understand what they want and how they define quality.[10]

Thus as large-scale administrative reform has come to draw more than a yawn among policymakers and policy intellectuals, I have begun to think more deeply about the causes behind Chase's interagency collaboration problem and others like it and to see what might be done to abolish or circumvent them.

Craftsmanship Theory

This book seeks to develop the conceptual tools that make it easier to do the causal analysis that such reform requires. It is clear that whatever else might help explain success in the collaborative process, the effort and creativity of what I call *purposive practitioners* is an essential explanatory ingredient. The pages of this book are populated by leaders inspiring a sense of novel possibility; by line workers looking for ways to do their jobs better; by middle managers rising to the technical challenges of coordinating interagency operations and resource flows; by top executives looking to further their conception of the public interest; by politicians and community advocates stirring the pot, delivering threats, handing out plaudits. Every effort at interagency collaboration involves a veritable ecosystem of people proposing to one another that they do things differently and better—and of course disagreeing profoundly, often bitterly, about what "better" means and whether or not the other person's better might actually be worse.

Public management and public administration have no theory about what evokes purposiveness—a combination of public spiritedness and creativity—in some situations but not in others or what form it takes when it is invoked. It is not that the academic literature on public management and public administration ignores purposive practitioners or the creative process. Far from it. A great deal of the literature describes the work of seemingly purposive practitioners (and occasionally that of inept or dull practitioners), and a good deal of it offers advice about

10. Cohen and Eimicke (1995).

what practitioners should do. Some of this literature is extremely insightful. However, as a whole it is theoretically weak or, more precisely, atheoretical.[11] It is atheoretical in that managerial purposiveness is assumed implicitly to be a phenomenon that is prior to, or perhaps beyond, the reach of causality and therefore in no need of theoretical understanding—something like God to an eighteenth-century deist, an Unmoved Mover. It is simply there, doing its high-minded work. Or it is a manifestation of will—about which nothing further needs to be—or can be—said.

There is some truth in this, but not enough to allow it to stand as the whole story. The analytic problem is in understanding purposiveness not as a product of individual will alone but as a product of the *interaction* between individual will and certain conditions in the surrounding environment. In particular, the technical possibility of creating something new and better, the opportunity to create public value, as Mark H. Moore has put it, will evoke a preexisting purposiveness in some people, provided the opportunity is perceived.[12] Moreover, the process evolves over a long time period and contains political dimensions. The technical possibility of creating new value, in successful cases, must be attractive enough to spark at least some collective hopefulness and enthusiasm. Such growing interest and attention in its turn must create a new political possibility. Out of this new political and technical situation grow still more technical and political possibilities—and creative actions—in an ongoing developmental process. I try to capture this interaction between an evolving medium of linked possibilities and purposive interventions through the master metaphor of craftsmanship.

I explicate the basic concepts of craftsmanship theory in chapter 2. The substantive elements of the collaborative process, such as consensus formation and negotiation over resource contributions, will be taken up in chapters 4 through 8. Chapter 3 contains a brief overview of some nineteen cases of interagency collaboration, drawn from a variety of policy domains, that I intensively mine for examples throughout the book. In the balance of this chapter I discuss the nature of the problems to be found in the U.S. policy landscape for which collaboration is potentially a value-creating solution.

11. Lynn (1996).
12. Moore (1996).

Collaboration Defined

I define *collaboration* as any joint activity by two or more agencies that is intended to increase public value by their working together rather than separately. This definition requires some elaboration.

WORKING TOGETHER. The nature of the work agencies do together can be quite varied. It includes everything from, say, operating hundreds of joint field enforcement teams over a long period of time and a large geographical area to occasional meetings at the middle-management level to tidy up an existing division of labor between the agencies.[13] Whether the work is resisted much or little is not relevant. Nor is the particular means of collaboration relevant—for example, whether it is carried on self-consciously or with special cognitive effort or skill.[14]

PUBLIC VALUE. Managers in the for-profit sector commonly ask about how some organizational unit or process adds value to their firms. By this they mean something like enhancing productivity and thereby profitability. Tax collectors in European countries with a value-added tax might ask how much value a firm adds to a raw material that it processes and then sells in the marketplace. Public value is analogous. The principal author of the term, Mark Moore, wrote about it as follows:

> Managerial success in the public sector [amounts to] initiating and reshaping public sector enterprises in ways that increase their value to the public in both the short and the long run. . . . Sometimes this means increasing efficiency, effectiveness, or fairness in currently defined missions. Other times it means introducing programs that respond to a new political aspiration or

13. This latter sort of activity is in a sense the reverse of what some people might mean by collaboration, because it could amount to an agreement to stay out of one another's way. However, as I shall explain, if staying out of one another's way is done properly, this is a way of increasing value, and working together to manage this certainly must count as collaboration.

14. By way of contrast, Gray defined collaboration as "a process through which parties who see different aspects of a problem can constructively explore their differences and search for solutions that go beyond their own limited vision of what is possible" (Gray, 1989, p. 5). In a work two years later, with Wood, the definition is more specific still about the means used. "Collaboration occurs when a group of autonomous stakeholders of a problem domain engage in an interactive process, using shared rules, norms, and structures, to act or decide on issues related to that domain" (Gray and Wood, 1991, p. 146).

meet a new need in the organization's task environment so that its old capabilities can be used more responsively and effectively. On occasion it means reducing the claims that government organizations make on taxpayers and reclaiming the resources now committed to the organizations for alternative public or private uses.[15]

It is not necessary to assume that collaboration is *motivated* by managers' interest in creating public value. Indeed, careerist and bureaucratic motivations are often quite important sources of collaborative effort. There is an inescapable element of subjectivity in deciding what constitutes *public value* or *the public interest*, its near synonym. I explain how I deal with the subjectivity in chapter 6.

JOINT ACTIVITY. Jointness creates several possible sources of new value. In general, they are the same sources that we see when any two or more social entities work together rather than separately, whether they are bees manufacturing honey, children playing on a teeter-totter, or businesses collaborating on a project. These are the economic gains realized by trading partners, the economies of scale that arise from pooling resources, the complementarities in production that arise when specialized competencies are blended in the right way, and the creation of social capital, such as a common language or a culture of trust.[16] All of these turn up at some point in this book, although scale economies make only a cameo appearance.

INCREASE PUBLIC VALUE. If the joint activity posited by collaboration is to increase public value, we must recognize that, from a purely technical point of view, this is not necessarily easy to achieve. If collaboration creates social value, so do its counterparts, differentiation and specialization. In fact, specialization is almost certainly the much greater engine of value creation. It is the division of labor based on the principle of comparative advantage that furnishes the raw materials that Adam Smith's invisible hand so marvelously allocates. Furthermore, in the context of large corporate bureaucracies, the fact that subunits might never have to interact with one another is a sign of health,

---

15. Moore (1996, p. 10).
16. See Putnam (1993) and chapter 7.

not sickness. It shows that the organizational division of labor is working. Specialization is going on where it should be, within subunits. A lot of working together across subunits might suggest that specialized tasks have been organized inefficiently, or that formal units specializing in integrating the work of other units have not been properly designed,[17] or that a lot of wasteful politicking is going on.[18] However, because formal communication channels are often less effective and efficient than informal channels for the purpose of integrating work, it is clear that some informal collaboration across subunit boundaries is a sign of organizational health rather than pathology.

The optimal combination of specialization and integration must be achieved by some blend of intelligent structural differentiation among subunits, formal hierarchical coordination, and informal working relationships. Needless to say, it is not easy to find the right blend or to keep adjusting it according to changing circumstances. In light of this fact, any attempt to try to increase value by improving collaborative working relationships might, for technical reasons alone, prove ineffective or even counterproductive.

Departures from the Technical Optimum

This is the case, at any rate, in the private sector, in which theory leads us to expect that firms facing competition are continually, if intermittently and imperfectly, making adjustments on all these fronts. In the public sector, however, in which the pressures to adjust continually toward superior design and process solutions are less, the utility of collaborative solutions to the underlying technical problem is much more general.[19] When adjustments do occur, organizational domain definitions and formal integrating mechanisms are much less likely to be influenced by technical than by political and bureaucratic considerations.

It is impossible to say exactly how much public value is being lost by departures from some technical optimum, however different observers might choose to define this. Economic theory and a wealth of available

17. Galbraith (1977); March and Simon (1968); Williamson (1986, 1991).
18. However, Gresov and Stephens studied influence attempts among subunits of a large private firm and found no support for this hypothesis (Gresov and Stephens, 1993).
19. Elmore (1986).

data can be used to approximate optimal performance and cost benchmarks in competitive markets dominated by informed consumers. For instance, if government should, for some reason, undertake to supply goods and services on its own for which such benchmarks exist, then it is possible to assess quantitatively just how government performance and cost compare to these benchmarks.[20] In general, no private sector benchmarks comparable to these exist to define the optimal blend of differentiation and integration; nor are there clear-cut benchmarks derived from any other source—for example, careful measurements of performance and cost across various public sector cases. My hypothesis that substantial public value is being lost to insufficient collaboration in the public sector is supported mostly by common sense and by the existence of two obvious facts: Political and institutional pressures on public sector agencies in general push for differentiation rather than integration, and the basis for differentiation is typically political rather than technical. I call this the pluralism problem. Furthermore, even if the basis for differentiation is technically optimal at the time agencies and their missions are created, changes in the nature of problems and the availability of solutions—or perhaps changes in our understanding if not necessarily in the realities—make the older pattern of differentiation obsolete. I call this the obsolescence problem.

The Pluralism Problem

The American ethos of pluralist democracy, and the institutions that it has spawned and that in turn have nurtured it, regard differentiation with a generally benign eye. For instance, the American tradition of localism entails that geographically adjacent communities will operate to some degree from specialized, mutually exclusive, and jealously protected tax bases. They worry a great deal about protecting their own communities' agency budgets from social costs imposed by their neighbors. They also worry about protecting their local service beneficiaries from the possibility of different priorities in service mix or in targeting that might occur if neighboring jurisdictions started to take a hand in policy decisions. Although regional consolidation of small local police departments might effect economies of scale, these small units are often

20. Donahue (1989).

preferred because of their greater controllability by small communities or neighborhoods.

If economies of scale are to be realized, then collaborative efforts across such local boundaries may be one way to do so.[21] In the domain of emergency services, for instance, cities often enter into mutual aid agreements, which allow for resource pooling under extraordinary circumstances. Small cities sometimes contract with surrounding counties to manage their bill collections. The most common solution to the diseconomies of small scale, however, is to refrain from providing the relevant services through the public sector at all and to contract with private sector firms that can operate at the appropriate scale in a larger regional market unconstrained by jurisdictional boundaries.

Furthermore, the institutions of American federalism create many niches that are believed to warrant either political protection or attack, depending on one's point of view. A state and a federal agency both involved in the same technical function, regulating workplace safety, let us say, approach their tasks in the context of the quite possibly different political constituencies whose influences prevail in these typically different arenas of political action. In general, state workplace safety regulators are thought to be more responsive to employer interests than are their federal counterparts. Hence interagency collaboration that is premised on purely technical grounds would also work to facilitate communication among individuals with different policy biases. One could surmise that, in general, the result would be wiser policy and implementation, although the widespread experience of having to compromise with ideologically unpalatable partners might make many doubt it.

Nor is it just geographically based niches that are to be protected. Public sector agencies are created to execute faithfully whatever specialized mission has been assigned to them by a historical legislative mandate and by the legislative overseers of the budget and expenditure

---

21. At a more mundane level simple economies of scale may be available to agencies in the same government for simple services such as photocopying and mail processing. One study found substantial cost savings (Master, 1992). However, the study says nothing about the loss of productivity that might have accompanied the greater bureaucratization and centralization of these simple services.

process. Governmental organization at any given moment is to some important extent an expression of the theory relied on by some previous coalition of legislative victors attempting to embody its victory in institutions that will survive possible future reversals of fortune.[22] That theory normally has prescribed defining a program structure, a set of budget categories, and a legislatively enshrined mission that could resist political tampering. Unfortunately, this is a prescription for resisting adaptation to changing circumstances of any kind.

In the human services the multiplication of specialized programs addressed to narrowly defined populations, needs, or service approaches—the so-called categorical programs—means that a single citizen eligible for service from several such programs must fill out many forms and shuttle from office to office, perhaps over a wide geographical area. The counterparts on the regulatory side of government are agencies that impose redundant reporting requirements on regulated parties and engage in compliance enforcement in isolation from one another. The regulated party is left to deal with multiple reporting forms, multiple deadlines, and multiple visits from inspectors and auditors. A study of business licensing in New York City found that a business with ten workers planning to double its production and invest $300,000 in infrastructure would need to go to seven agencies and twenty-one departments, could spend up to $8,175 for up to forty-five permits and licenses—and that the time required to accomplish this was some six to ninety-one weeks.[23] Occasionally the compliance requirements of the several agencies are in conflict, thereby imposing uncertainty on the regulated party.

The same forces of political pluralism that have created relatively specialized agency structures—structures that call out for adaptation through collaboration—also make collaboration difficult. From a narrow, constituency standpoint, collaboration is distinctly undesirable because it threatens to blur an agency's mission and the agency's political accountability for pursuing it. This sort of narrow constituency-driven accountability tends to draw force from more general good-government norms of accountability—for example, through the close monitoring of agency expenditures.

22. Horn (1995); Moe (1989).
23. Acosta and others (1994, pp. 34–35).

The Obsolescence Problem

Institutional divisions also serve as barriers to thinking creatively—some critics would say thinking realistically—about the systemic, or holistic, nature of certain problems and appropriately systemic solutions. Policies are fragmented by outmoded thinking enshrined in outmoded programs, say the critics, our attention misdirected, and our resources deployed inefficiently and sometimes ineffectively. It often takes heroic efforts to overcome such fragmentation, efforts sufficient to merit recognition by the Ford Foundation and Kennedy School of Government Innovations in American Government program. Sandford Borins analyzed the applications of 217 programs that achieved at least semifinalist status in the period 1984–92. He found some sort of holism in 61 percent of the applicant self-descriptions.[24]

In one policy domain after another there are allegations that policy mistakenly ignores

—ecosystem effects. This happens when policy aims to protect species rather than an ecological community of which the species is a part or to protect species habitat that is too small to prove viable in the long run. It also happens when resources such as timber are managed without taking account of the effect on other resources such as soil and water.

—the systemic unity of environmental media as a sink for wastes. "It's got to go somewhere," said critics of the early approach to environmental regulation that dealt separately with air, water, and land.

—family-system processes in favor of looking at particular individuals, such as the unemployed mother or the abused daughter, whose troubles happen to have come to the attention of the best funded or most politically responsive social agency. Instead, say the family-system theorists, an individual's troubles should be interpreted as the problems of a whole family that happen to be manifested in one individual, perhaps because that individual is unusually susceptible or because others have in effect ganged up on him or her. Proper treatment would require attention to all the relevant family members as individuals and also to their interactions with one another.

—the whole person by treating one problem at a time and doing so in the context of a separate program and profession for each. Although this may work for individuals who need only one or two services, the

24. Borins (1998, p. 20). The name of the program was changed from State and Local Innovations to Innovations in American Government.

minority who need many services would benefit from a more integrated approach—for example, low-skill, poorly educated welfare recipients who also have drug dependency problems and no friends or relations who will provide child care while they improve their basic literacy and arithmetic skills. The whole-person approach is also believed to be more humane and therefore ethically preferable.

—natural systems of prevention as opposed to remediation. The system in question is an organism that carries forward strengths and weaknesses acquired at an earlier time into some later period, often compounded by natural developmental processes. An example is a regimen of exercise and healthy nutrition that would reduce vulnerability to disease in the future. This sort of systems logic is claimed to apply in many areas—for example, preventing welfare dependency by supplying adequate education, preventing delinquency by providing recreational opportunities.

—system assets as opposed to deficits. We are all given to dwelling more on what is wrong with a person, family, community, or organization than what is right. This has a surprising effect on how we design our intervention strategies to "fix" what is wrong. It causes us to locate the source of the remedy outside the system. The implicit model is calling the plumber to fix the broken faucet. Unlike plumbing systems, however, organic systems often have the ability to repair and otherwise improve themselves. Strengthening this ability is often thought to be a more effective and a more respectful way to approach the problem than the plumbing-repair approach. However, because most of our public systems of intervention have been set up to respond to political pressures to fix some community or family or individual problem that is spilling over onto others, they are set up on the plumbing model.

Once the hard structure of budget and personnel categories and agency turf is in place, the conceptual models follow suit. They, too, focus on the deficits of systems rather than on their natural assets. These conceptual systems take on a life of their own. They tend to focus on those fragments of the problem that fit with the hard structure and to exclude more asset-based ways of thinking.

Reorganizing Versus Collaborating

If the organizational division of labor in U.S. public administration is not optimal at any given moment, what is to be done? The solution I explore in this book is collaboration across agency lines. It is behavioral and process oriented; it is not structural—that is, it is not looking to formal reorganization. A word ought to be said about why not.

Osborne and Gaebler do not attend more than in passing to the question of what their reform agenda implies for how agencies might better work together. But to the extent that they do attend to it, they focus entirely on reorganization. "Reorganize along mission not turf," they write. They give the example of George Latimer, who when he became mayor of St. Paul, saw the Port Authority, the Office of City Planning, the Community Development Office, and the Planning Commission all "charg[ing] off in different directions." Latimer reorganized and "left three agencies each focused on a specific mission and each extraordinarily effective in pursuing that mission."[25] But if there is one proposition on which consensus among students of public administration is firm and widespread, it is that reorganization normally produces little of value at a very high cost in time, energy, and personal anxiety.[26] Rarely are old organizational units and identities abolished. The boxes on the organizational chart are simply renamed and moved around. One result is that the old loyalties and fears persist, and people find a way to act on them, despite counterforces brought to bear by the new organizational arrangements.

Furthermore, because the supposedly inferior logic of the old arrangements—a geographically based way of managing a health services system, for instance—did after all contain a certain logic, the superior logic of the new arrangements—perhaps a disease- or functionally based scheme—will not succeed without paying tribute to the older logic. This continuing tribute will be afflicted by some of the same frictions and miscommunications that plagued the older system. Finally, the social dynamism that causes old logics to decay is permanent and inescapable. Even were reorganizations to be entirely successful for a period, that period is likely to be very brief. Like the newest and most authoritative dictionary of a living language, the ink has not dried before its authority has eroded to some extent.

25. Osborne and Gaebler (1992, p. 132).

26. Thomas (1993). Lynn (1980) did find that a major reorganization of the human services system in Florida, though almost destroyed by a rocky transition period, survived intact and in principle at least was able to embark on a less fragmented course of service delivery.

One implication is that a serious administrative reform agenda must contemplate the importance of altering the working relationships among organizations without substantially altering their organizational identities. I say "contemplate" advisedly because, even when collaboration is the better bet than reorganization, it is not always a good idea. Noncollaborative business as usual might sometimes be even better. Collaboration should be valued only if it produces better organizational performance or lower costs than can be had without it. We should not be impressed by the idea of collaboration per se. That collaboration is nicer sounding than indifference, conflict, or competition is beside the point. So, too, is the fact that collaboration often makes people feel better than conflict or competition. I do not want to oversell the benefits of interagency collaboration. The political struggle to develop collaborative capacity can be time consuming and divisive. But even if no such struggle were to ensue, the benefits of collaboration are necessarily limited.

Considering collaboration on its own terms, we should not expect even the best of interagency working relationships to overcome the difficulties faced by any activity in American government that requires new funds. Although collaboration does not always require new moneys, when it does it necessarily suffers from the processes of incremental budgeting, which keeps money where it always has been, and from the constraints of the public sector fiscal environment. More important, collaboration cannot eradicate underlying conflicts that occur because the agencies represent different citizen constituencies, whether these constituencies are formed around ideology, tax base, or interests in receiving service or escaping the burdens of regulation. Collaborative processes can correct misperceptions about the magnitude and scope of conflicts and can often stake out common ground that had hitherto not been realized. But because these basic conflicts exist, there will always be a limit to how much any of the parties will be—and sometimes should be—willing to sacrifice for the sake of further collaboration.

Summary

Interagency collaboration is defined as activities by agencies intended to increase public value by having the agencies working together rather than separately. Although I cannot prove—and do not attempt to—that unexploited opportunities to create value in this way are abundant, many institutional features of our policymaking system suggest this is the case. The process of trying to exploit such opportunities involves, at a minimum, leveraging personnel and financial resources for collaborative purposes, designing and managing an effective operating system, reaching and maintaining consensus on basic goals and on trade-offs among relevant subgoals, creating an effective culture or ethos of interpersonal working relationships, and securing the implicit or explicit consent of elected officials. It is a complex developmental process that unfolds over a long time period.

This book aims to explain how this process works and to make available ideas to activists and practitioners of public management interested in furthering interagency collaboration. To do this I have had to develop a conceptual framework that permits social scientists to achieve a more realistic and methodologically defensible conceptualization of the creative process in public management than we have had. I base this conceptualization on ideas about craftsmanship, particularly ideas about the varied purposes of those who are engaged in the process and about the medium in which they work.

2

Craftsmanship Theory

This chapter discusses the major concepts and arguments of craftsmanship theory. It begins with the dependent variable in interagency collaboration—that is, the state of affairs that craftsmanship is alleged to produce. This I conceptualize as interagency collaborative capacity. I review two theories purporting to explain the conditions under which interagency collaborative capacity develops, and I show their limitations. I then turn to explicating basic concepts of craftsmanship theory using examples from a craft activity in the physical world: building a house. I also sketch the relevant analogies between building a house and building interagency collaborative capacity. I conclude the chapter by noting that craftsmanship theory permits two different and complementary forms of causal analysis. One is explaining variation in the degree of success across a number of cases. The other is the qualitative understanding of various aspects of craft materials, the craft process, and the product of that process. I argue that effective qualitative understanding is a precondition for the sort of causal analysis that seeks to explain variation.

Capacity as the Dependent Variable

The commonsense approach to talking about collaboration, and the conventional social science approach to explaining it, is to think of it as a set of acts or activities.[1] These are activities such as three agencies reviewing the problems and service plan of a troubled family, or two

---

1. This is the approach of Gans and Horton (1975), one of the classic studies, and of many others. See also the synthesis of studies by Mattessich and Monsey (1992), which takes a similar approach.

park districts coordinating the hiring of a private goatherd to crop the grass as part of the same contract, or five environmental enforcement agencies coordinating a predawn strike on a metal plater dumping cyanide residues into the city sewers. Collaborative acts would also include such activities as individuals from different agencies exchanging business cards, sitting through planning meetings, and objecting to the terms of a draft memorandum of understanding. However, in the context of social science, collaboration considered as activity does not make for a convenient dependent variable. Nor, in respect to craftsmanship theory, does it make for an end product that craftsmen might be aiming to produce.

First, not all collaborative activities are equal. Some are preparatory to others rather than useful themselves, and any conceptual scheme that took activities as the crucial outcome variable would be obliged to weight these different sorts of activities relative to one another. But doing so presents insurmountable difficulties. For instance, although it might seem that productive activities should be counted more heavily than preparatory activities, this is not always correct. The biggest barrier to organizing cooperation might occur, let us say, at the point at which agencies must reconfigure their geographic service boundaries; and once they have done so, we should take note that a major milestone has been reached, even though it is a purely preparatory act.

Furthermore, in some cases the preparation may be more socially valuable than the activities. In emergency services, for instance, the understandings whereby neighboring fire departments would render mutual aid are of value every day that they are not invoked, whereas the acts of mutual aid are of value only on the one day in ten or twenty years when conditions require them. The same applies to most environmental enforcement functions performed by agencies acting collaboratively in that the actuality of detecting and punishing offenders is generally not as valuable as a deterrent capacity that potential violators fear to test.

To generalize from these examples, it is the potential to engage in collaborative activities rather than the activities themselves that is what we really care about when we talk about interagency collaboration. I call this potential interagency collaborative capacity, or ICC. It has an objective and a subjective component. The objective component includes formal agreements at the executive level; personnel, budgetary, equipment, and space resources assigned to collaborative tasks;

delegation and accountability relationships that pertain to those tasks; the various administrative services that support all this collaborative work. Chapters 4 and 5 go into more detail about the nature of the objective components and about the challenges entailed in acquiring them. The subjective component is mainly the relevant individuals' expectations of others' availability for, and competency at, performing particular collaborative tasks. These expectations, in turn, are often built around beliefs in the legitimacy and desirability of collaborative action directed at certain goals, the readiness to act on this belief, and trust in the other persons whose cooperation must be relied on for success. Chapters 6 and 7 elaborate on the subjective components of capacity.[2]

In some important ways interorganizational collaborative capacity is very much like an organization in its own right. What are organizations, after all, if not capacities for the joint productive work of many separate individuals?[3] With only a bit of oversimplification, one might say that interagency collaborative capacities differ from more conventional organizational capacities mainly by virtue of their component parts having thicker boundaries and more powerful sources of environmental influence than average. Indeed, I find it analytically convenient to speak of interagency collaborative capacity as though it were an agency itself, with conventional agency systems inside it—an operating system, an overhead and control system, a decisionmaking system. Often I will refer to a particular identifiable case of interagency collaborative capacity as *an* ICC or *the* ICC.[4]

The capacity concept has many virtues. One is that it is developmental. We can imagine an ICC starting small and growing larger—or declining from some peak to an intermediate or very low level. We can also imagine that it might obey certain discernible regularities in

2. Agranoff and McGuire (1998) noted the conceptual confusion surrounding the capacity concept in public management and public administration. They said, "the concepts of capacity and capacity building have come to be used in rhetorical rather than scientific terms. Capacity remains a mysterious concept to scholars; we know it exists but we do not know what it is" (pp. 85–86). I suspect that the conceptual problem is solved to a large extent by explicitly including the psychological component, as I have done. However, as I point out later, this does create serious measurement problems.

3. Barnard (1938).

4. Some of the practitioner literature on interagency collaboration adopts this usage also, generally referring to collaboratives—for examples, Melaville and Blank (1993); Wagner (1994). There is also a similarity to what Arnold Meltsner and Christopher Bellavita (Meltsner and Bellavita, 1983) once called a policy organization.

development—and that, if it did not, this, too, would count as a worth-while discovery, of interest to practitioners and social scientists alike. For instance, as I shall show in chapter 8, the subjective and the objective components of ICC are not necessarily correlated developmentally at any moment in time. The subjective component may be very powerful but may be lacking budgetary resources or crucial data management systems. Alternatively, the objective components may be in place, but mistrust and miscommunication among executives or field personnel may prevent them from being used. In addition, we may note that an informal and highly subjective set of working relationships across organizational boundaries may operate effectively without any formal or objective recognition at all.[5]

Second, the concept of capacity is general. The exact nature of capacity could vary somewhat depending on the tasks, the agencies, or the purposes in question, but it would fit a multitude of cases without stretching linguistic conventions. An example of such use appeared in a paper on educational reform: "Within the context of systemic reform [in education] , capacity is the ability of the education system to help all students meet more challenging standards . . . capacity may be increased by improving performance of workers (e.g., individual teachers); by adding such resources as personnel, material, or technology; by restructuring how work is organized; and/or by restructuring how services are delivered."[6]

Third, the concept of capacity is flexible. A set of would-be collaborators can start by developing the capacity to reorganize their division of labor, under some circumstances a fairly easy task, but then move on to more challenging tasks such as pooling their resources to achieve complementarities in production.

Fourth, capacity is the sort of concept that several researchers have shrewdly intuited would be analytically useful to understand authority in transorganizational systems.[7] This is advantageous because we often

5. Chisholm (1989).

6. O'Day, Goertz, and Floden (1995, p. 1).

7. Agranoff (1991, pp. 540–41). Three earlier candidates as transorganizational governance concepts are the interorganizational field (Warren, 1967), the implementation structure (Hjern and Porter, 1981), and program structure (Mandell, 1994). The last two efforts are heroic but, in my view, ultimately not satisfying. One also might count as a transorganizational concept the interorganizational problem domain (Wood and Gray, 1991,

need to ask questions that pertain to groups or sets of agencies—for example, will some agency in this set of agencies perceive the latent opportunity for value-creation and take pains to mobilize others? Can the agencies collectively generate the minimum level of resources needed for cost-effective operations? What are the dynamics of governing the collaborative group in the public interest?

Fifth, and most important, capacity implies both quantity and quality. One can ask both "How much?" and "How good?" Most of the previous social science literature on interagency collaboration, which I shall discuss later, addresses the first question but neglects the second. That is, the literature is concerned mainly with the question of whether collaboration exists, and on what scale, but not with whether the collaboration is productive. This book, to the contrary, is much more concerned with issues of productive quality.

One of the disadvantages of the capacity concept is that it is hard to empirically estimate interorganizational collaborative capacity. Given the importance of the subjective component, one might say that interagency collaborative capacity is mostly a state of minds. It is hard for an outside observer to know what is in such minds. Moreover, the state of such minds is always changing, as are the identities of the players who own the minds. I shall return to these matters in chapter 3, where I try to assess the degree of collaborative capacity in several ICCs I have studied firsthand.

Previous Theories

Although previous theories of interagency collaboration have aimed to explain collaborative behavior rather than capacity, it is nevertheless possible to make use of their concepts and empirical findings.

Resource Dependence

Resource dependence theory holds that although agencies in general value autonomy and therefore eschew cooperation, if a focal agency's

---

pp. 140–41); it is more successful, though its ambitions do not stretch to governance matters. And as I indicate later, "network," a current favorite, enters into my theory, though not with the same degree of primacy that others give it.

resource base depends on some other agency, the focal agency will be willing to cooperate with the other agency.[8] Thus cooperation is the quid pro quo for, say, service contracts or a stream of referrals that might bring payments or social legitimacy.[9] Although countering "dependence" is a misleading and narrow characterization of an agency's propensity to seek revenues and customers that is motivated by much besides the desire to protect against dependence, this propensity is reasonably well documented and comports with common sense.[10] Pursuing clients, revenues, and legitimacy, after all, can serve value-creating and agency-protecting goals simultaneously.[11] In addition, these actions can serve the goal of creating organizational slack that managers can use for a broad range of purposes.

Resource dependence theory is limited, however. It aims to predict whether the focal agency is willing to try to collaborate with some other agency. It does not try to predict whether the efforts will succeed or what the agencies will define as success, nor does it say which other agencies a focal agency will turn to when it has a choice of plausible collaborators. In fact, agency managers often have a great deal of latitude with respect to such matters, and if we are concerned with the creation of value-creating collaborative capacity rather than simply with the surface activity of collaboration, we must attend to these questions. Even in its own terms, resource dependence theory is constrained by the fact that public sector agencies are not able to move very rapidly to buffer dependency-associated risks, through collaboration or through any other means, no matter how much their managers may wish to do so.

Finally, on those infrequent but important occasions when agency managers are seeking to develop value-creating capacity, resource dependence may *follow* collaboration rather than the other way around. Many of the cases I discuss in this book are of this type. This sort of

8. Alexander (1995); Pfeffer and Salancik (1978).

9. Van de Ven and Walker (1984).

10. A study by Oliver (1991) of 389 voluntary social service agencies in Toronto failed to confirm the predictions of dependence theory. However, the operational measure for the dependent variable may not be valid.

11. An interesting case in point is the essay by Hal Beder (1984) in which he aims to persuade the adult education professional community of the value of collaboration of a variety of other campus units and off-campus institutions and private firms. The arguments range unselfconsciously across both value-creating and institution-protecting motives.

process is likely to proceed along several dimensions at once, with the mutual contribution of resources being contingent on the emergence of some sort of common vision, a climate of mutual trust, and a technical capacity to make use of mutually contributed resources to good effect. In such a process, the participating organizations are extremely aware of their mutual vulnerabilities and resource interdependencies, but their managers proceed to structure the relationships so that all of the participants can recognize that, in some sense, they are better off, or at least not worse off, with the relationships in place than they would be otherwise.

Network Theory

The resulting set of relationships is construed by many researchers as some sort of network, and a large body of theory and research about interorganizational networks now exists to try to explain how the relationships emerge, are sustained, and create value for the participants and, in some cases, for the society. Throughout this book I make use of a network concept and the corresponding literature. I find it useful mainly as a way to describe a certain kind of communications capacity (a set of relations among actors' agencies or individuals) that facilitates efficient communication among them for some particular purpose—delivering services to citizens, organizing for political advocacy,[12] socializing with individuals of similar status and taste, seeking out partners with complementary assets for completing a production value chain from product discovery to marketplace.[13] In a citywide network of lawyers linked mainly for commercial purposes, for instance, the actors are able quickly and easily to identify other actors in the network whose productive capacities would likely be useful to them; and actors who want their capacities to be discovered make use of the networks to have them discovered.

A particularly interesting generic type of network involves complex production relationships that benefit from being able to form and dissolve quickly. The participants therefore wish to protect themselves against opportunistic exploitation by their partners without having to suffer the delays and costs of formal contracting. This generally means

12. See Knoke (1990).
13. On this last point see Powell (1996).

that there is some element of trust in the relationships so that post-transaction adjustments to meet the parties' needs and interests can be made quickly and with minimal interpersonal friction.[14]

The prototypical examples of production networks are high-technology firms in Silicon Valley in California, the biotechnology industry, and regional manufacturing districts such as Prado and Modena in Italy.[15] Some of the sociological literature that has done so well to describe such networks is misleading on the underlying rationale for creating and maintaining network relationships, however. It emphasizes the existence of underlying social bonds among the participants, the shared culture, the level of trust that permits the participants to reach understandings quickly. The literature downplays the motivational role in network dynamics of the prospects of commercial gain, however, which is usually a central concern to the network participants.[16]

Because network relationships differ substantially depending on the type of purposes served by the network, it is always necessary to be clear about the type of network under discussion. In ICC operations there are two main kinds: the implementing network and the interagency production network.[17]

An implementing network is a set of individuals who design or operate the machinery that makes for smooth day-to-day operations within the constraints set by the various partner agencies.[18] The manifestations of such networks are extremely varied. One type looks like a formal working group, the sort that meets monthly, has a fairly continuous membership of middle managers or supervisors, and allocates budgets and assigns personnel and creates schedules. Another is completely disembodied, perhaps consisting only of intermittent telephone calls between two or three people who talk only to troubleshoot breakdowns

14. See Williamson (1986, 1991).

15. Barley, Freeman, and Hybels (1992); Powell (1990, 1996); Powell and Brantley (1992); Saxenian (1994).

16. For instance, Powell (1990), though by the time he published his 1996 paper on the biotechnology industry, the commercial motivation had become much more prominent. For the sociological approach more generally, see Nohria and Eccles (1992).

17. Radin and others implicitly, but clearly, conceive of the interagency networks they studied as productive entities: "Networks span organizations to do what matrices do within organizations. They are unbounded or bounded clusters of organizations that are nonhierarchical collectives of separate units." (1996, p. 151).

18. Morgan and others (1996).

in arrangements that are already fairly well coordinated. A third type, which is most apparent when rapid organizational change is foreseen, involves up-front planning together with creating the systems that will directly support operations.

The actors in an interagency production network are organizations, not individuals. One category of production relationships involves sellers and buyers, producers and customers, service providers and clients for service. Another involves the sharing of expertise, information, and authority to do better case management. In the private sector, network relationships are typically mediated by money. In the public and nonprofit sectors, they often are not. Relations can be structured by formal instruments such as contracts or memorandums of understanding, or they can be based on tradition or implicit personal commitments by organizational leaders.

In a geographically based network of human services agencies collaborating on matching clients to an appropriate portfolio of services, the communications processes among the participants are embedded in interpersonal relationships and also in an infrastructure of various connection mechanisms such as an informal readiness to initiate or to accept referrals, formal contracts and memorandums of understanding, the location of personnel in a common site to facilitate access by customers or clients, and the use of a common information system. These connection mechanisms, which enable the participants to hold down transaction costs on an ad hoc basis, usually will have been created by costly prior investments by the parties in attaining mutual understanding about their respective capacities, resources, objectives, constraints, and the terms under which they are willing to do business.

The mere existence of an efficient communications network does not guarantee that it will perform well in a productive sense any more than does access to 100 television channels guarantee that that the viewer will find anything worth watching. The actors in the network also have to be, at minimum, both competent and motivated to produce. In interagency production networks, as we shall see, some sort of leadership role is often critical. So, too, are peer monitoring and coordinating roles. The networks literature does not say much about such role differentiation within a network. It is generally so enthusiastic about networks functioning as an *alternative* to hierarchy as well as to markets that it neglects the useful aspects of hierarchy, such as the division of labor and role differentiation, that are often functional for network performance.[19] An important exception to this is the widely cited book by Christine Alter and Gerald Hage, *Organizations Working Together*.[20] In this book the authors claim that centralization and hierarchy produce better results. Their theory is not persuasive, however, and their evidence, according to my interpretation, is more consistent with a preference for decentralization and flattening than with the opposite.[21]

Craftsmanship in Practitioner Writings

Some insightful and articulate veterans of interagency collaborative work have written excellent how-to manuals about their craft, and I have made much use of some of them, especially *Together We Can: A Guide for Crafting a Profamily System of Education and Human Services*, by Atelia I. Melaville and Martin J. Blank.[22] I attempt to go beyond the discussion in this book by analyzing in a more explicit and systematic way the nature of the problems to which their prescriptions are addressed—for example, the natural pluralism of our political institutions described in chapter 1.

19. See Powell (1990); Radin and others (1996, p. 17).

20. Alter and Hage (1993, pp. 184–85).

21. Alter and Hage's empirical base is 158 human service agencies organized into fifteen networks in "Fulton" County, Iowa, and "Farnam" County, Illinois. Their theoretical orientation is technological, in the sense that the nature of the network's technical tasks ought to determine the overall structure of the network and the nature of the interpersonal interactions within it. Given this orientation, they attempt to characterize provider networks in terms of global dimensions such as degree of complexity, differentiation, centrality, size, and connectivity. Tasks are assessed in terms of scope, duration, intensity, volume, and uncertainty. For environmental and operational process variables in their causal schema, see the useful figure on p. 103. (Alter and Hage, 1993).

Their theoretical argument is unclear, however, and the empirical analysis does not help to clarify the matter. The argument's shortcomings begin with neglecting to demonstrate that the several networks being analyzed are actually coordinated or integrated. In the absence of such benchmark information, it is not possible to believe in, or indeed to make much sense of, the welter of correlation and regression coefficients purporting to explain how the supposed coordination occurs. In fact, given the known prevalence of breakdowns in the extent and quality of services integration, one must suppose, at the very least, that the degree of coordination across each of the fifteen networks was highly variable.

22. Melaville and Blank (1993).

Explaining Success and Failure

A cadre of agency managers, advocates, and others trying to build an ICC is like a polyglot crew of laborers constructing a house out of misshapen, fragile, and costly lumber on a muddy hillside swept by periodic storms. In both the metaphor and the reality, the raw materials and the environmental conditions are full of challenges, but smart and dedicated craftsmen using intelligent craft practices may be able to overcome them.

A theory aiming to explain variations in success with regard to interagency capacity building should therefore begin by taking account of variations in the following:

—the quality of the human and social material available to would-be collaborators;

—the efficacy of what I call the *smart practices* used by aspiring collaborators to work with the available materials;

—the availability of critical skills and abilities within the community of potential collaborators; of special importance are improvisational, adaptive, and leadership skills, and the ability to understand the nature of collaboration as a dynamic developmental process;

—the vulnerability of the emerging ICC structure to hostile forces in the environment, and the skill of the builders in protecting the ICC against these.

Materials

Any craft involves the skillful manipulation of materials. In the case of public management, these materials are comprehensive and diverse. They include human nature, group dynamics, bureaucratic loyalty and disloyalty, legal and administrative rules, and economic and career incentives. They include both the generic and the particular: human nature and Lee, the assistant secretary for enforcement. It is impossible to supply a comprehensive list.

New materials are created over the course of a craft process, and old ones destroyed or transformed. Timber becomes lumber, lumber becomes framing, framing becomes a wall, and many walls together create an enclosure. As we shall see in chapter 8, understanding how this developmental process occurs is central to understanding how an ICC emerges.

OPPORTUNITY. Opportunity is a particularly important type of material for the ICC process. Consider the house-building analogy. Bring together the right materials, do a bit of framing, sawing, and hammering following the blueprints for a house, and suddenly, before your eyes, there is first the apparent shape of a house, and very quickly thereafter a completed house. What caused the transformation?

Integration, one might say. But this cannot be the principal explanation, because integrating just any set of materials in any haphazard manner would cause either no transformation or a different sort of transformation. Integration had to have been operating on various elements—the materials and the architectural design, to simplify the case—that had the latent potential to be combined fruitfully. Latent potentials to create value on the cheap, whether through integration or through any of a host of other means, I call *opportunities*. One might say that opportunity is the potential to get something for nothing.

In the physical and biological world such opportunities are quite familiar. An engineer might exploit the insulating properties of some material or the propensity of certain bacteria to digest garbage and convert it into water and carbon dioxide within the confines of a wastewater treatment plant. The bacteria work without wages and never go on strike. That sanitation engineers have managed to recruit such a work force is testimony to a certain spirit of ingenuity, a cleverness about getting something for nothing.

Is it possible and worthwhile for public management to emulate the engineers' spirit of wresting free gifts from nature? The managerial world of human purposes, relationships, expectations, symbols, and the like does not present itself as coherently and unambiguously as does the world of physical materials and spatially definable designs. Nevertheless, some simple examples suggest that "something for nothing" is a good motto for public management as well. The idea of gains from trade, for instance, suggests that voluntary exchanges can produce dividends for both parties, be they individuals or organizations, virtually out of thin air. The same can often be said about clearer communications, inspiring workers to take a broader view of their work than is required by their narrow bureaucratic assignment, and sequencing the tasks in a campaign of organizational change in such a way as to create momentum or bandwagon effects.

Opportunities include these and other such something-for-nothing potentialities.

Such potentialities are an important ingredient of creative public management and public policy, even though not always recognized as such by actors or commentators. More light can be shed on the opportunity concept by examining a sample of public sector innovations, where exploiting opportunities is a key to what makes these innovations in the first place.[23] Consider the sample of forty-six state and local innovations awards winners between 1986, when the program started, and 1994, which I mentioned in the preface.

Nineteen of these, the largest single cluster by far, spotted opportunity in the shape of a more holistic view of an entity—a family, a community, a rape victim, an innercity schoolchild—than was usual in the service provider or funder communities. In nine of these nineteen cases, there appears to have been a significant element of interagency collaboration as well. The second-largest cluster, with ten cases, used technology, particularly computer technology, in a way that was not usual in government programs—for instance, a program in Arizona called QuickCourt permitted state residents to handle many common legal matters without an attorney and to produce documents for use in many situations. In nine cases the government recognized an opportunity to remedy what economists would call market imperfections—for example, by offering official opinions to property owners on a fee-for-service basis about the technical and legal quality of their contractors' hazardous waste cleanup plans, by stimulating an insurance pool for small nonprofit service providers, and by linking medicaid-type insurance with private insurance for long-term nursing care. Five cases fell in a category, following Levin and Sanger, that I think of as using old stuff in new ways—using the dead time of youths in detention for the delivery of social and support services, for example.[24]

23. It is not the only key. Novelty I take to be the other major attribute (Altshuler and Zegans, 1997, pp. 74–75). For some innovation award winners novelty also entails actively overthrowing old habits of mind (Moore, Sparrow, and Spelman, 1997).

24. Levin and Sanger (1994, chap. 3) interpret all the innovations as being essentially "using old stuff in new ways." I do not disagree, but there is more than that to what makes them innovative. The remaining three of the forty-six cases did not reflect the seizing of any evident technical opportunity but were presumably thought "innovative" because they aggressively promoted certain values or attached legitimacy to a more expansionary conception of an agency's or a government's role.

In twenty-two of the forty-six cases, existing institutions redefined organizational roles and missions to better exploit the potential inherent in their resources, particularly their human resources. For instance, a police department and local hospitals deploy nurses to gather forensic information from rape victims in nonhospital settings; a network of black clergy and churches cooperates with the state social services agency to encourage members of each congregation to adopt at least one black child; schools are hosts to social and health services for their students; an environmental regulatory agency barters permits in exchange for an oil company's creating new endangered species habitat. In other cases, the role redefinition went beyond the agency to the government as a whole—for example, New York City helping to develop an insurance arrangement that makes low-cost liability coverage available to nonprofit service providers doing business with the city; Fairfax County, Virginia, creating a network of insurers and health care providers to supply coverage for poor children in the county.[25]

A list of generic opportunities commonly found in policy design and program management and published in an earlier work of mine are provided in the appendix to this chapter.[26]

In the ICC context, six principal types of opportunity are usually relevant:

—the political and budgetary climate that leads agency managers to see bureaucratic benefits in collaboration;

—the potential value-creating synergy that comes from agencies doing their work collaboratively rather than separately;

—the problem-solving potential of frontline worker teams that comes from their superior access to information;

—the climate of confidence once a critical mass of potential collaborators has signaled its readiness to help or at least not to obstruct;

25. The particular type of role redefinition of interest to the Ford Foundation judges is evidently an expansionary one, consistent with the foundation board's broad humanistic and liberal social values. Agencies and governments are innovative if they do more, not less. A conservative foundation might expand the definition of what counts as an innovation to include tax cuts intended to stimulate private investment or spending caps that preclude government from controlling more of the citizenry's wealth. Its judges would be promoting different values, endorsing a different role definition, and therefore perceiving a different set of technical opportunities that might be exploited.

26. Bardach (1996, pp. 67–68).

—the culture of pragmatism about bureaucratic structure and process that might be used to nourish cross-agency collaboration;

—the extra boost that comes from sequencing steps in a long development process according to an underlying technical or political logic.

CRAFTSMAN AND MATERIAL ARE ROLES, NOT PEOPLE. In any management process, and especially in the process of ICC development, the manipulation of materials is multilateral. That is, any craftsman in the process is, from another craftsman's point of view, a part of his or her set of materials. Conversely, anyone who appears to be the materials being manipulated by someone else's craftsmanship has the potential for turnabout: The someone else becomes materials to be manipulated by the actor's own craftsmanship.

This is not mere wordplay. There are important analytical implications. Consider leadership: As we shall see in chapters 6, 7, and 8, leadership functions are often critical to ICC success, and when someone or some cadre arises to perform these functions, the leader manipulates her followers as a craftsman would manipulate her materials—eliciting common goals, creating an atmosphere of trust, brokering the contribution of agency and personal resources to the common venture, deploying their energies in accord with some strategic plan. But manipulation also runs from the followers toward the leaders. In the ICC environment, it is not guaranteed that anyone will arise to perform leadership functions at all, or perform them effectively if leadership does arise. Leadership in an ICC is a difficult and sometimes dangerous job, often without adequate compensation and unsupported by staff or other resources. If the potential followers want the job done well, they may have to use their own craftsmanship skills to manipulate potential leaders, who in this context act as the followers' own materials. They may, for instance, have to offer inducements of status and moderate power to the potential leaders of their choice and to manipulate them in other ways.

To put it another way, *craftsman* and *material* are roles in a system of strategic interactions, not personal attributes, talents, or conditions of individuals. Who plays these roles shifts over time; and everyone plays both roles at one time or another and sometimes simultaneously in different relationships.

PURPOSES. I divide into three broad categories the array of possible purposes that move actors in the potential ICC development process: careerist, bureaucratic, and value-creating.

—*Careerist purposes* benefit the actor in his or her capacity as a private individual aspiring to ease, security, income, prestige, and power in the work setting.

—*Bureaucratic purposes* aim to protect or enhance the resources, broadly construed, of the organization in which the actor is employed.

—*Value-creating purposes*, as I suggested in chapter 1, aim to improve the effectiveness or productivity of a program or agency in regard to its espoused mission of benefiting the public or to some broader mission that encompasses it.

The conventional view is that careerist purposes and bureaucratic purposes, operating either independently or in concert, consistently overwhelm those value-creating purposes that, in a better world, would animate ICC development.[27] This is indeed the common scenario, and I shall analyze its powerful sources at length in chapter 5. But there are other possibilities as well.

First, bureaucratic and careerist purposes sometimes favor ICC development. Legislative masters, or perhaps an elected chief executive, may push for the appearance of cost savings and an end to apparent redundancy or fragmentation and back the demand with threats of budgetary sanctions or other controls. As I noted in chapter 1, because interagency collaboration is often associated with innovation, and innovation is usually positively valued, collaborative efforts, or at least their appearance, may be career enhancing. In addition, in certain rare cases, a classically imperialist attempt to expand bureaucratic turf by sweeping other agencies into a nominally collaborative arrangement might actually succeed, though I did not observe such effort in the course of my research.

Second, at the level of the individual actor, when they are opposed value-creating purposes sometimes compete successfully with careerist and bureaucratic purposes.[28] The dynamics of such a competition are no

27. Perhaps I should say that this is one important conventional view. Another, which looks to exchange to motivate collaboration and by implication social improvement, assumes that the purposes that motivate exchange are some unspecified combination of value-creating and bureaucratic purposes—for example, countering resource dependence. See the earlier discussion of resource dependence theory.

28. Provan and Milward (1991).

doubt complicated and are certainly beyond the scope of this book. For the sake of simplicity I rely on Howard Margolis's model of human motivation that makes room for both selfish and altruistic motivations and predicts that whichever set of motivations has been best satisfied most recently will yield to the other set.[29] Individuals whose careerist purposes are temporarily fulfilled may therefore choose to follow, for a time at least, a more rewarding value-creating purpose. This would also apply to individuals whose career purposes are involuntarily fulfilled because their careers have reached a plateau that it is unlikely that they can leave.

Third, an important and often overlooked dynamic involves the emergence or destruction of value-creating purpose in response to emergent or disappearing political opportunity. Hence it is not just that purposes shape the changing political environment; the changing political environment also shapes purpose. Bureaucracies, their leaders, and their field staff might pursue narrow missions in unimaginative ways for years, until a few changes in the objective political or resource environment suddenly catalyze dramatic new opportunities for creating value in different ways. When this happens, value-creating purposes may compete effectively for effort and personal creativity with bureaucratic or careerist purposes. Moreover, value-creating opportunities may suddenly loom that draw leadership into ICC development and away from some more traditional value-creating enterprise that the actors perceive as less productive or inspiring. Following such a dynamic, the possibilities of mobilization for ICC development grow bandwagon-style as a function of their own success. At the individual level, moreover, the growing prospect of success for an individual's value-creating purposes make an investment in the altruistic side of the individual's utilitarian account more attractive relative to investment in the selfish side.

Smart Practices

Opportunities are only latent potentialities for producing value. To be worth anything in a practical sense, they must be exploited by some means. Taking my cue from the widespread concern with identifying

29. Margolis (1982). On the idea of separate motivational budgets, see also Dawes (1988, p. 59) summarizing the work of economist Richard Thaler.

and disseminating *best practice*, I call such means *smart practices*. As a matter of definition, a *practice* is a specifiable method of interacting with a situation that is intended to produce some result; what makes a practice smart is that the method also involves taking advantage of some latent opportunity for creating value on the cheap.

The point is most easily understood by referencing the world of engineering technologies and a wastewater treatment plant. Although the garbage-eating bacteria constitute the opportunity, the design of the entire rest of the plant—the part that feeds garbage in one end, mixes it with the garbage-eating bugs for just long enough to allow the bugs to do their work, and discharges the end product of clean water plus carbon dioxide into some natural body of water—is an example of smart practice. Operating the plant efficiently also involves smart practices. By merely adjusting the balance of bugs, garbage, and treatment time cleverly the cost of operations and the risk of destabilization can be minimized. The bugs need to be fed enough garbage frequently enough to survive in sufficient numbers, but not so much or so often that they are suffocated. Here are some examples of smart practice from the domain of interagency collaboration:

—Teams of service providers from different agencies in the human services areas can exploit production complementarities. Training them to work well together enhances those complementarities. Provided the training can be done cheaply, it counts as a smart practice.

—An analogous complementarity in regard to planning can be exploited by middle managers from different agencies meeting regularly to exchange information, planning for the efficient use of their respective resources, and gathering feedback about the effectiveness of the ICC's work. A smart practice would be to give these managers the flexibility to make significant decisions on their own authority.

—Opportunities for fruitful exchange may be enriched by a facilitator who shuttles between agencies smoothing communication flows and providing reassurances about what potential partners are doing. As this process continues, the facilitator improves his skills, increases the legitimacy of his personal intervention, and sets the stage for his possible emergence as a low-key sort of leader. Hence one practice exploits three opportunities simultaneously, making it a very smart practice indeed.

—Building an interagency database exploits technical complementarity. If done early in the ICC development process, this task can encourage the collaborators to take on more politically sensitive challenges later, thus exploiting a developmental opportunity as well.

Smart practices can vary from the simple to the complex. At the simple pole of the continuum is something like building an interagency database. At the complex pole is the entire ICC itself, a virtual organization created to take advantage of some collaborative opportunity and incorporating a great many lesser smart practices into its design—in other words, those having to do with the acquisition of resources, creating a culture of trust, and so on.

Smart practices can be about process as well as product. That is, we can talk about the smart practices of building a house and not just designing a finished structure that incorporates smart practices of design, choice of materials, and so on. In the case of process, smart practices look like what are usually called strategies. Here are two candidates for smart practice status from the process of ICC development:

—The executive-level leadership of an ICC decides to try to take advantage of the problem-solving expertise of middle managers to help design the contemplated operating system of the ICC. The leadership's strategy is to establish informal lines of communication between themselves and the middle managers and to facilitate the frequent exchange of ideas and information among the middle managers.

—An amorphous group of agency executives engaged in a protracted and frustrating dialogue over the possibilities of fruitful collaboration sees the potential for improving the process by inventing a coordinating mechanism. Their strategy is to take advantage of the availability of a community foundation leader whom all parties trust (within limits) and whose foundation role rewards her for serving as a coordinator in such situations.

CHALLENGES. Implementing smart practices or any other sort of putatively helpful measure is often beset by challenges. It is essential to grasp the nature of these challenges, and in particular to distinguish between those that exist because the implementation setting specifically involves interagency collaboration and those that are attributable to less specific conditions—for example, operating in the public sector or working on sensitive matters with a group of strangers.

One might think of challenges arising from less specific conditions as inconvenient confounding influences that prevent us from seeing clearly what is distinctively difficult about interagency collaboration. In that case we would try to imagine them away with the aid of statistical tools were the data available to permit doing so. My own approach, however, is to assume that there are always challenges when individuals or agencies try to accomplish a complex task, and that the most intellectually satisfying analytical strategy is to ask whether and how the specific interagency dimension of the relationship aggravates—or in rare cases ameliorates—the challenges that exist for other reasons.

Furthermore, to perceive these latter challenges also requires looking through comparative lenses. That is, the ICC context aggravates challenges that are themselves more complex versions of other, more fundamental, challenges. I focused mainly on the relatively more complex challenges organizations face when they are public and bureaucratic. I also considered managing coordination processes among actors in multiple agencies rather than in a single agency, and managing coordination among organizations rather than among individuals. Not every lens was helpful in every case. But running through the list was often a useful, and relatively easy, exercise.

RISKS, COSTS, AND VULNERABILITIES.   The overall value of a smart practice represents the net difference between the value of the opportunity itself and the costs, risks, and vulnerabilities of the practice that exploits it.[30] Vulnerabilities are of special interest. Every smart practice has its particular vulnerabilities to collapse, perversion, abuse, or cost escalation. For instance, if privatizing certain municipal service functions is a smart practice when carried out correctly, it might become a dumb practice if carried out incorrectly—for example, if the would-be contractor is a profit-maximizing monopoly, if the bidding process is corrupted, if inappropriate performance measures are stipulated in the contract, or if the municipal contract management procedures are overly rigid or overly lax.[31]

Here are some common and significant sources of ICC vulnerability that will be discussed in subsequent chapters:

30. Smart practices come in two basic flavors: "cheap," offering relatively modest net gains for very low costs and risks; and "pricey," where very large gains are to be had from modest or relatively large risks and costs. In the normal course of events, which is to say the day-to-day flow of managerial activities, cheap smart practices probably predominate. Leadership frequently moves managers to a situation in which they are involved with pricey smart practices, however. As we shall see, this applies to leaders in the ICC context as well, whose contributions are often critical to success.

31. Donahue (1989).

—natural and elections-induced turnover in the personnel involved in the capacity-building process;[32] these are magnified by the slow pace of ICC development (chapter 8);

—the failures of competent, trusted, and hard-working leaders to step forward (chapter 7);

—an unusually high degree of turf protectiveness on the part of top managers in an agency whose cooperation is indispensable to the overall success of the ICC (chapter 5).

Prudent and insightful designers or implementers of a smart practice know its generic vulnerabilities and can take pains, in particular circumstances, to try to protect against the most serious ones. This is always something of a guessing game, and typically actors face a tradeoff between the risks of continuing vulnerability and the costs of protection. Furthermore, some vulnerabilities are strategically chosen and in that sense welcome. Strategic vulnerability represents a deliberate choice to increase vulnerability on a particular dimension in the hopes of improving one's position in regard to other values—for example, quality of opportunity, resource costs, or other dimensions of vulnerability. An example is accepting the vulnerabilities of slower paced ICC development to spend more time negotiating with stakeholders whose possible opposition is in the balance.[33]

IMPORTANCE OF MEASUREMENT. My analysis of smart practices is almost entirely theoretical. Although in some cases I have been able to cite supportive research literature, usually the empirical grounding for my arguments amounts to adducing one or more actual examples of practices that appear to take advantage of a something-for-nothing sort of opportunity and trying to explain how the practice works. This sort of qualitative understanding of the nature of a smart practice—its internal logic, so to speak—is generally not enough to establish it as a practice worthy of widespread or even limited adoption. The positive strength of the practice might prove slight except under specialized

32. On the low survival rate of programmatic innovations as a result of such changes, see Light (1994).

33. Mark Moore (1996, pp. 273–74) described the top management strategy of embracing public accountability in order to add external pressures to management's own internal pressures. Top managers thus adopt a calculated strategy of making themselves and the entire organization vulnerable to criticism for failure. This is discussed later in the chapter and again in chapter 5.

conditions. Even when positive strength is great, there may be more than offsetting costs and vulnerabilities. In most cases only a great deal of empirical assessment can establish, even roughly, just how smart a practice is or delineate the conditions under which it is so or is not. Because I do not, in most cases, provide such an assessment, one should think of the smart practices I discuss as candidates for smart-practice status rather than as sure winners.

IMPORTANCE OF INSIGHT. One of the common, and correct, criticisms of what is known in public management studies as the best practice research (BPR) literature is that the real value of the alleged best practice is not always established by extensive empirical testing. Its value is asserted simply on the basis of one or two seemingly successful cases, good anecdotes, and savvy showmanship.[34] I lament the absence of empirical assessment, but I believe the deeper criticism of the BPR literature is that it is not sufficiently attentive to the qualitative strengths of the practice. It shows too little insight into the nature of the opportunities of which the practice tries to take advantage. Best practice research should begin by explaining *how* a particular best practice manages to be *good*, or *best*—or, in my terms, *smart*.

One should think of best practice research or smart practice analysis as a sort of reverse engineering that in its simplest form finds an amazing gizmo, takes it apart, and tries to figure out the clever trick that makes it work so well. This can involve a complex process of theoretical reasoning. One has to theorize about how the design, or the operational processes, of the gizmo somehow takes advantage of basic forces, basic properties of materials, and basic geometries. One has to bring to bear a sophisticated understanding of fundamental laws of nature, such as conservation of matter and of energy.[35] One does not simply look at the gizmo and note that framjus has been connected to hoojit and assume that that constitutes the piece of cleverness, the useful trick, inherent in the gizmo.

Smart practice analysis lacks the capacity to break down and reconstitute the gizmo that is ordinarily available to engineers trying to test hypotheses about exactly how the useful trick works. Nor does it have access to the body of scientific and technical knowledge that permits

---

34. Overman and Boyd (1994, pp. 78–79); Lynn (1996, pp. 97–100).
35. Denn (1986).

engineers to arrive at a realistic understanding. Furthermore, assuming some clever design or operational logic does in fact wait to be discerned in the specimen of the gizmo being analyzed—and that one can achieve a reasonably correct understanding of what it is—for an engineer to generalize beyond the specimen at hand is often straightforward. A physically embodied technology will usually reproduce its performance in any environment that does not differ drastically from the environment in which the original specimen was seen to perform so well. In contrast, social and behavioral technologies of the sort smart practice analysis usually aims to find are different in degree if not in kind. They do not ordinarily have such hard edges and tight internal logics. Organizations cannot be broken down and reconstituted. There is but a small stock of high quality "knowledge" about basic social and behavioral processes.[36] However, there is little point in worrying about these limitations until the effort has been made to use clever thought experiments in lieu of actual physical experimentation and to use what knowledge, or at least reasonable conjectures, we do have.

36. In addition, the language one uses even to characterize what the practice actually is can prove treacherous. This is demonstrated by what I take to be the mistakes made by those who study the replication process—explaining whether and how the replication of some exemplary program "model" occurs in other sites. Craig H. Blakely and his colleagues (Blakely and others, 1987) examined seven innovative programs in education and criminal justice adopted in at least twenty sites nationally. They followed a procedure developed at the University of Texas Research and Development Center for Teacher Education in 1981. This procedure "conceptualized social programs as consisting of a finite number of components or parts. Program fidelity could then be defined as the number or proportion of finite program components that were implemented." Components were observable activities, materials, or facilities and had to be verifiable through interviews with staff members and clients of the implementing organization. Each component was also to be "logically discrete from other components" and, if not discrete, then it "should not depend on the implementation of another component" (p. 260).

The degree of presence of each component was rated as ideal, acceptable, or unacceptable (p. 258). The authors found a .38 correlation between fidelity of replication and effectiveness. This finding does not necessarily show that fidelity increases effectiveness, however. It is possible that components were sacrificed not because implementers were in any sense unfaithful to the original model but simply because they were constrained by circumstances to implement what they realized was a regrettably imperfect, but it was hoped acceptable, version of the model. The .38 correlation shows that more of something increases effectiveness, but it is not clear that the something is the model. The essence of the model is the clever trick for taking advantage of some latent potential, or opportunity, for extracting value on the cheap. Counting the number of implemented components is no way to characterize how well the model was implemented.

Skills and Abilities

My focus is less on the personal skills of craftsmen than it is on the nature of craft materials and on the nature of craft practice: I focus on lumber and the ways to choose it rather than on architects and builders, to return to the home-building analogy. But I need to discuss craft skills and abilities to some extent, because they are obviously integral to the whole craft process.

GROPING ALONG. The best craftsmen are skilled at perceiving opportunities in the materials at hand and surveying the array of possible smart practices that might be used to exploit them. Some of this is done through pure rational and self-conscious planning, but more is done experimentally, through trial and error, in a process Robert D. Behn has called "groping along."[37]

Behn's principal specimen of groping along is Ira Jackson, a young and inexperienced appointee as Commissioner of Revenue in Massachusetts in 1983. Behn accepted Jackson's self-deprecating description of himself as a person without ideas, without a strategy—just someone who experimented and retained what worked as he transformed the Department of Revenue from a laughingstock into an apparently successful tax collection agency. In the end Jackson was able to fashion a crisp slogan and a smart strategic idea for the agency: "honest, firm, and fair revenue collection."[38] But this was not an idea that Jackson grasped at the beginning of his tenure. He groped his way into it.

Jackson was groping not just at the level of ideas but at the level of action as well, a point Behn was less definite about, preferring to call it "trying . . . numerous things. Some work. Some do not. Some are partially productive and are modified to see if they can be improved. Finally, what works best takes hold."[39] It was at this level that Jackson was most successful: Once he had accumulated enough successes it was not too difficult to examine them with a view toward conceptualizing the common thread.

Valuable as the groping along metaphor is, its use by Behn and others in the subsequent literature tends to underestimate the role of cer-

---

37. Behn (1988).
38. Behn (1988, p. 644). The full, and very interesting, details of Jackson's successful turnaround efforts are described in Behn (1987).
39. Behn (1988, p. 645).

tain kinds of craft materials in affording a kind of tactile guidance to the actors doing the groping—the latent potential, one might say, of certain materials to signal "hotter" and "colder." In the revenue collection case Jackson was groping within a well-structured domain of potential strategies and tactics. He instituted a series of tough, well-publicized enforcement actions against tax evaders. This is a strategy that must have occurred to every tax collector since the pharaohs. At the same time he added a twist that made this strategy suitable for a liberal democracy: He represented his increased pressure on tax evaders as a form of *service* to "the hundreds of thousands of honest taxpayers in Massachusetts."[40] At relatively low levels of tax compliance, people who pay through continual collections at the source are at risk of feeling like suckers relative to those who can avoid the tax collector's grasp by means of once-a-year self-assessment. It was part of Jackson's shrewdness to appreciate that the majority could be induced to support tougher action against a seemingly unworthy minority even if this tougher action might spill over to everyone else as well. As it happened, there were many domains and many classes of tax evaders—from restaurants that pocketed customers' meal taxes to yacht owners who dishonestly declared out-of-state addresses for their crafts—that could be targeted in this way.

In the ICC case, groping along occurs first in a typically lengthy, complex, multiparty discussion process in which participants signal one another about their degree of interest in collaborating on some range of projects whose blurry definition is clarified as the discussion proceeds.[41] The groping is facilitated to the extent that the participants are mutually intelligible to one another and willing to be reasonably honest. These two conditions are often hard to meet simultaneously. At the individual level much of the groping is done by actors trying to conceal their true interests or to hang on to their professional and bureaucratic paraphernalia even while testing to see how far they might go in disclosure without incurring too much risk and cost for their agencies and themselves. This is true even of actors motivated by value-creating purposes. A

40. Quoted in Behn (1987, p. 17). Jackson said he was trying to prevent "a new social disease. It has become the 'in' thing to cheat on taxes rather than the wong thing." One of his favorite slogans was that tax cheating was not a victimless crime (p. 17).

41. One might say that in the ICC arena planning occurs through groping along, thereby reconciling the two seemingly opposite modes of innovation analyzed by Golden (1990).

considerable level of craftsmanship skill is often needed to move the collective discussion in expeditious and constructive channels. Some of these skills, such as good listening, need to be distributed widely among the participants, and others, such as those involved in fashioning creative methods for holding down unnecessary costs and risks of collaborative action, need to exist only in a few individuals—provided those individuals are allowed to exercise their skills.

COMPENSATING. One of the hallmarks of craftsmanship is the ability to find functional substitutes of near equivalency, as when a chef, lacking the required zucchini, substitutes eggplant in her standard casserole recipe, or an architect substitutes plastic for wood when the owner insists on lowering total project costs. Interagency collaborators do the same when they shift goals in the light of emerging difficulties or compensate for the defection of, say, a county agency by bringing into the fold a nonprofit service provider. How do such compensatory adjustments occur?

Compensatory adjustment can be explained in two mutually compatible ways. One is to see actors making choices. Explaining why they do one thing rather than another would then entail describing their objectives, their preference functions, their levels of information, their degree of risk aversiveness, and the like. This is a familiar explanatory paradigm. The other explanatory strategy highlights the nature of the raw materials that structure choices in the first place. In the ICC case the range of choices is often constrained by the institutional and political system in which the craftsmen do their work—for example, periodic elections, doctrines of legislative supremacy in appropriations, and line-item budgeting. But the particular mix of options within the range is as likely to be expanded as constrained by the jumble of personalities, perceptions and misperceptions, competing priorities, and shifting attentions within the pool of relatively attentive potential participants in the ICC development process. Craftsmanlike improvisation is always possible, and the shifting jumble of various raw materials can increase its scope.

What are the limits of improvisation? Both in craft process and in craft product some functions must be performed. Note that the idea of functional substitutes, mentioned previously, implies a prior assumption that there is some system to which the functions pertain. This assumption of system for the craft process makes sense, although the nature of the system and the functions and structures it integrates can be conceptualized in different ways. Looking at a physical process such as building a house, one might say that it is the systematic integration of materials, purposes, skills, tools, and designs. In the ICC case I choose to focus on four components that are integrated into an ICC: an operating system, resources contributed by the participating agencies and others, a steering process more or less designed by the ICC partners, and a culture of pragmatism and trust that facilitates joint problem solving at all hierarchical levels of the ICC.

In a system of functionally interdependent components it improves our understanding of their relationships if we can think about the components both as complements and as partial substitutes. If they are seen as complements, all are required to complete the whole craft enterprise, and the failure of one is fatal no matter how abundant or high quality the remaining elements might be. No resources, no ICC; no trust, no ICC; no steering, no ICC; no operating system, no ICC. These are basic functional elements in an overall system, one might say, and a working system requires that all of them be supplied. In this sense the system components are complements.

But once the basic requirements for each of the functions have been supplied, the component elements of the system can work as partial substitutes for one another. For instance, although a minimally effective design and set of building materials are complements in a house, once these minimum requirements have been met, a better design can substitute for the architect's first-choice building materials if these prove to be unavailable or too costly. In the ICC context, if trust is relatively poor in middle management, it may be possible to compensate by having more resources and a very high-quality steering process. Or if mutual intelligibility proves to be elusive, actors simply might invest more time and effort in overcoming the resulting barriers.[42]

Qualities Analysis and Explanation of Variation

The analysis of craftsmanship that appears in chapters 4 through 8 is essentially the sort of analytic understanding one gets from a

42. There is no assumption, it should be emphasized, that any such substitutions will occur, or that required functions will be carried out at all. In an a priori sense, collapse of the whole craft enterprise is no less a possibility than success.

manual on carpentry for the home craftsman. In general, each chapter or main chapter division begins by explicating the nature of some potential challenge or problem that besets ICC construction. It then reviews the practices that might be available to deal with such challenges, highlighting the ones that I take to be candidates for smart-practice status and explaining the nature of the opportunity that it aims to exploit.

Potentialities

When I refer to the *nature* of challenges, problems, and opportunities, I have in mind a certain meaning of that term. I think of challenges, problems, and opportunities, along with the evolving capacity of an ICC and the vulnerabilities of ICCs and of smart practices, as potentialities in the world that exert some causal influence on actions and events. By the standards of conventional social scientists, who construe causality in terms of weaker and stronger forces, potentialities are a seemingly alien and unscientific construct. In truth, it is alien, but it is not unscientific.

Two questions are pertinent to its scientific status. First, are such potentialities real, particularly if they are unnoticed, unexploited, or for other reasons never actually materialize? Second, assuming the answer is yes, can we test for their causal efficacy, in principle if not always so readily in practice?

Consider a sugar cube. If it is seen to dissolve in water, most people would probably agree that the water alone is not the cause of the cube's dissolution. So, too, is the solubility of the sugar, even though as a latent potential and as a very silent partner in the causal process, it admittedly does have a slightly mysterious ontological status.[43] Even if the sugar cube sits undissolved forever, most people would still agree that its solubility is a real property.

In the physical sciences potential is treated as though it were real and measurable. There is potential thermal energy in a chemical bond, and more of it in a complex hydrocarbon molecule than in a water mol-

43. Wherever they come out on the ontological question, professional philosophers have a category—modality— for states of the world described by verbs such as "might" and "may" and by the adjectival suffix "—ility," as in "solubility" (Mondadori and Morton, 1979).

ecule. There is potential kinetic energy in a stone poised to roll down a hillside, and more of it in a large stone than in a small one. Engineers distinguish between the effective and the theoretical—one could say potential—production capacity of some system, and this distinction has found its way as well into the leading textbook on managing government operations.[44] Reference to latent potentials is not wholly absent in the social sciences either. In some corners of psychology there is talk of individual developmental potential. Economics talks about potential gains from trade. At a more practical level, investors look for the profit potential in a business or in a deal; there is every reason to suppose that they are talking about something real, even if very hard to measure.

Testing the Causal Efficacy of Potentialities

By conventional social scientific interpretation, what counts as a proper understanding or explanation is a lawlike statement about the forces that underlie hypothesized regularities. The value of such a statement is typically tested by massing observations on independent variables to explain the variance in observations in dependent variables around some central statistical tendency.

Up to a point, the same procedures can be used to test hypotheses about potentialities. This is so because potentialities vary in magnitude, and their causal effects in many cases will vary as a function of their magnitude. An opportunity to create value through collaboration can be large or small. The same is true of the potential for a bandwagon effect, the vulnerability of an ICC, the probable effectiveness of a smart practice, the abilities of an ICC leader to improvise and adapt should the need or opportunity arise, and so on.[45] Like the profit potential of a business enterprise, such qualities might be hard to measure. But to the extent that rough estimates can be made, they would lend themselves to a perfectly standard sort of variance analysis. In subsequent chapters I shall look through variance-explanation lenses at three

44. Rosenthal (1982, p. 56).

45. There are limits, however, to the reliability of a test carried out in this way. The causal effects of potentialities cannot be observed unless people happen to exploit them, intentionally or otherwise. Moreover, the full strength of any given potential will not be evident if the people exploiting it act with little skill or determination.

potentialities that bear on ICC success: (1) the relative clarity of technical means–ends relationships across policy domains, because clarity facilitates conflict resolution and the definition of a common purpose; (2) the strength of political and financial incentives to collaborate; and (3) a favorable cultural climate regarding bureaucratic flexibility.[46] I will also look at a fourth independent variable, the quality of leadership, which, as I shall explain in chapters 6 through 8, is indirectly related to potentiality.

Qualities Analysis

To understand what craftsmen perceive, anticipate, and sometimes act on, one must first understand the nature of the potentialities that are available to them.[47] Because these potentialities are qualities of the world, I refer to the effort to achieve this type of understanding as *qualities analysis*.[48] (*Qualitative analysis* would be a more felicitous description, but that term is already in use to describe a type of data and an approach to data collection and interpretation.)[49]

Note that before variance analysis can be performed, one must have in hand a good qualities analysis: Otherwise one does not know what magnitudes to be concerned about. This is one reason why I emphasize qualities analysis rather than variance analysis. Another is that I wish to lean against the pervasive social scientific culture that has tended to reify "variation," to make it into a phenomenon worthy of understanding per se, even though it is, in most contexts, a mere artifact of our own processes of observation, comparison, and hypothesis test-

---

46. It is not obvious that incentives should be considered a type of latent potentiality. However, incentives do no effective causal work until some actor notices them and responds to them. In this regard they are no different than the solubility of a sugar cube, which must await immersion before its causal power is manifest.

47. Furthermore, in order to understand whether a given potentiality will be actualized, one must understand the craftsmen that are available to act on it.

48. It often makes sense to say that the central idea of causality is the *causal mechanism* that translates cause into effect. See King, Keohane, and Verba (1994, pp. 85–87). This metaphor, though narrow, does convey the right spirit of trying to grasp *how* the translation process occurs. The actualization of potentiality and, more generally, the activation of causal qualities might be called an *activation* type of the process that translates cause into effect. See King, Keohane, and Verba (1994, chap. 3).

49. See, for instance, Strauss and Corbin (1990).

ing.[50] I instead wish to pull social scientific attention back to certain qualitative aspects of the world that are important but, as with potentialities and the smart practices based on potentialities, elude easy understanding. Finally, I wish to produce the kind of analysis that would be of use to practitioners as well as to social scientists, and I believe qualities analysis fulfills that objective at least as well as variance analysis.

Summary

Interagency collaborative capacity (ICC) or sometimes "an ICC" when it is considered a virtual organization, is created by a process analogous to that of one or more craftsmen building a house. This craft metaphor is intended to emphasize that the process is integrative, creative, and purposive. The craft metaphor also suggests a number of craft-related concepts that will have an important role in my theoretical development and that are explicated in this chapter: materials, opportunity, purpose, smart practice, challenges, the vulnerability of the ICC and of various smart practices, craft skill and ability, and compensation and adaptation. Success in ICC construction is a function of the skill and purposiveness of craftsmen interacting with the quality of available materials and the craftsmen's ability to fashion protections against potentially destructive environmental forces such as personnel turnover and the erosion of political alliances.

The analysis in this book emphasizes the causal qualities in the world, especially those that exist as latent potentialities that operate only if they are properly actualized. It downplays analysis that aims to discover causal forces. It also shows only passing interest in the sort of causal explanation—often with only a limited theoretical grounding—that aims to explain observed variation in some dependent variable.

---

50. A derivative error is to suppose that a good theoretical understanding of a phenomenon is equivalent to a listing of correctly identified necessary and sufficient conditions for its occurrence or for variations in its observed manifestations. This is like having a formula to predict the trajectory of a thrown baseball—an admittedly desirable intellectual feat—but not understanding that the ball is subject to a qualitative force in nature called gravity.

Appendix:
Some Generic Opportunities in
Policy Design and Management

By-products of personal aspirations. It is possible to structure new incentives or create new opportunities for personal advantage or satisfaction that indirectly can result in social benefit—for example, offering to share the benefits of cost-reducing innovations with public sector employees who conceive them and implement them.

Complementarity. Two or more activities can be joined so that each might make the other more productive—for example, public works construction and combating unemployment.

Development. A sequence of activities or operations may have the potential to be arranged to take advantage of a developmental process— for example, assessing welfare clients for employability and vocational interest before, rather than after, sending them out for job search.

Exchange. There are unrealized possibilities for exchange that would increase social value. We typically design policies to exploit these that simulate marketlike arrangements—for example, pollution permit auctions, arrangements to reimburse an agency for services it renders another agency's clients or customers, and so on.

Multiple functions. A system can be designed so that one feature can be used to perform two or more functions—for example, when a tax administrator dramatizes an enforcement case in such a way as both to deter potential violators and reassure nonviolators that they are not being made into suckers for their honesty.

Nontraditional participants. Line-level employees of public agencies often have knowledge of potential program improvements that could be incorporated usefully into the agencies' policies and operations. The same is true of the agencies' customers, clients, or the parties whom they regulate.

Rationalization. Purely technical rationalization of a system is possible— for example, shortening lines by deliberate spacing of arrival times or creating contracts to solidify informal agreements that are vulnerable to decay and misunderstanding.

Rummaging. By rummaging mentally one might discover novel uses in seemingly improbable but readily available materials—for example, using the automobile registration system as a vehicle for carrying out voter registration as well.

Underutilized capacity. Examples, in many communities, are school facilities that are used for relatively limited purposes for only part of the day and for only part of the year—although school officials would be quick to warn that tapping into this capacity without harming school functions is not always easy.

3

Methods and Cases

In this chapter I describe my strategies of data collection and interpretation and introduce nineteen cases of ICC development. The case introductions serve two purposes. The main purpose is to provide background for the examples I adduce in later chapters about challenges and smart practices in the ICC development process. The other purpose is to support an assessment of the degree of success that collaborative efforts achieved in each case. These assessments will be put to use at several points in later chapters in which I attempt some variance analysis, with degree of success as the dependent variable.

I group the material in major sections by policy domain and begin each section with a discussion of the principal value-creating opportunities that interagency collaboration is thought—either by veteran observers or by myself—to afford in that policy domain. I then turn to collaborative efforts observed in particular sites and provide a sketch of the general political context for the efforts and their history.

The level of detail varies somewhat across cases. There are many reasons for this. Some policy areas are more complex than others. Some, such as fire prevention in the urban–wildland intermix zone, I assume will be much less familiar to readers than others and therefore will need more explanation. I will describe only the cases that I or my students or assistants looked at with more than passing interest. This means that we spent at least two days interviewing, in person or on the telephone, individuals involved in the collaborative process. Normally we spent much more time than this.

Choosing the Cases

Because my principal objectives in this study were conceptual more than empirical, I needed to find collaborative efforts that promised to be conceptually helpful. Unfortunately, there is a chicken-and-egg problem: The more conceptual help one needs from one's study sites, the less able one is to know where such promise might lie. Accepting the inevitability of gambling, I placed my bets using the following reasoning.

First, I reasoned that there was no point in studying situations in which collaboration, though potentially value creating, was hardly attempted. Such situations are legion and reflect an equilibrium dictated by a great many forces, many of which are well understood. Noncollaboration is overdetermined, as mathematicians might say, and a few more empirical examples of it would add nothing to my understanding of its causes. I therefore concentrated on cases in which at least moderate efforts to break free of this equilibrium had occurred.

Second, I thought it would make sense to search in policy domains in which the latent opportunities for creating social value through interagency collaboration were high—for example, ecosystem management, welfare-to-work programs for multiproblem individuals, and children and family services, as I mentioned in chapter 1.

Third, given my circa-1995 hunches about the nature of craftsmanship and qualitative analysis—recently refined, polished, and put on display in chapter 2—I reasoned that, based on site reputations or observable characteristics, I should identify sites in which there were

—an unusually challenging and qualitatively clear set of problems;

—a history of having faced and then overcome a sequence of problems over a long time period. I would be able to look for ideas about process and development as well as for ideas about smart practices;

—conditions that would suggest some limit on the efficacy of one or more smart practices, a limit determined by the workings of our political system;

—individuals of known creativity, energy, and skill, who might be an unusually rich source of smart and innovative practices;

—substantive results that appear to be successful. In these cases I might be able to reason backwards to the craft materials or smart practices that made success possible;

—an ICC development process that the participants regarded as particularly creative in terms of their own local experience.

I was also interested in collecting an ensemble of cases that might show how the same generic smart practice would deal with the problems presented by a variety of technical contexts—for example, social service delivery as opposed to environmental regulation or public works.

Not all cases with apparent promise turned out to be fruitful. As if to compensate, some cases yielded very interesting material about three or four dimensions.

Collecting Data: Informants' Reports

It is one thing to locate potentially interesting cases and another to extract useful information from them. The important elements in the ICC development process do not leave traces in physical artifacts or written records. To find out what happened and how it was (or was not) achieved, there is no substitute for asking participants who were directly involved or who learned about events or people's perceptions of events in some reliable fashion. This means finding knowledgeable informants who are willing to be interviewed and who are willing to provide a relatively complete and impartial report. In this less than ideal world, however, it usually has meant sacrificing impartiality for knowledgeability and accessibility and trying to preserve impartiality in the emerging record by, first, using my own knowledge and common sense to apply counterbiasing interpretations and, second, by comparing one informant's account with another's on the other side of the issue.[1]

In some cases I was interested in learning about the motivations and purposes—value creating, bureaucratic, and careerist—of the individuals I was interviewing. I often asked them for self-reports. How hard I worked to probe for the darker truths about such matters—the truths about which interviewees might prefer not to speak—depended on many factors. I often reasoned that it would have been simply futile to probe at all and hoped that I would be able to learn the darker truths

---

1. My approach (Bardach, 1996, pp. 84–126) has something in common with that of a nosy journalist.

from asking others. In other cases I found that some gentle encouragement was sufficient to elicit quite a lot of apparent candor.

A more difficult problem of interpreting informant reports concerns their
assessment of broad currents of opinion among some subcommunities—
for example, line workers in an organization or the aggregate of firms
subject to some regulatory program. Because such opinion currents are
often germane to the probable costs, risks, and effectiveness of some strategy or tactic, it is important to know about them. They are often without
any simple or obvious indicators. Furthermore, they are often change-
able and, indeed, changing. Although informant reports concerning these
opinion currents are often better than having no information at all, they
are still likely to be imperfect. I assumed that informant reports tended to
overhomogenize opinions and to perceive them as being closer to their
own point of view than they actually were.

It is sometimes very important to assess magnitudes as finely as possible. It may make a big difference if an actor thinks that, say, some collaborative development will prove to be bureaucratically "very" costly
or only "moderately" costly. One perception might motivate active
resistance; the other, a wait-and-see stance. It can matter a great deal if
an actor is intensely committed to pursuing some purpose or only luke-
warmly so, or if she perceives a particular risk as employment threatening or merely mission threatening. As an interviewer, my own
approach to assessing such magnitudes was often to ask about them
directly and to listen carefully to the exact words and phrases informants used in response. Because I tape-recorded many interviews, in
this and the chapters that follow I frequently quote the exact words of
my informants to convey to the reader impressions similar to the ones
that I received.[2]

Strategies for Conceptualization

Because the main goal of this study was conceptual, I tried to be self-
conscious about my approach to using empirical materials, particularly

---

2. My sample of cases, from a statistical point of view, is merely opportunistic, and my
measurement procedures of only modest reliability and validity. Hence my data are
unsuitable for a serious effort to explain variance across the cases. However, as I said at
the conclusion of chapter 2, my main objective is qualities analysis, which is to a large
extent conceptual. For this purpose even rough data can supply interesting specimens.

my interviews, to aid the process of concept formation. Although I wanted to conceptualize the objective aspects of a craft environment that a craft practitioner might wish, or need, to work with, these could be accessed only by talking to practitioners. First, the right practitioners can function as knowledgeable informants. Second, in many cases practitioner purposes, calculations, and perceptions are an integral part of what a smart practice actually is.

The principal social science methodological literature that speaks to the use of field interviewing to support concept formation in organizational analysis comes from sociologists using the approach of grounded theory.[3] The approach originates in a research tradition concerned with interpersonal transactions, with the way people respond to events, and with the meanings that individuals attribute to others or to situations. If such are one's research objectives, the literature has much to offer. But I was concerned with phenomena that were much less social-psychological, much more external and objective. I wanted information from my informants about the nature of change strategies and how well they seemed to work. Their subjective experience of these things was important to me, but I needed to structure interviews to guide the informants toward being, in effect, my partners in analysis and not just a source of data about their own experiences or feelings or thoughts.

When I began my work, I thought not in terms of smart practice but in terms of best practice, and I was acutely aware of the controversy over the methodology of BPR. E. Sam Overman and Kathy J. Boyd, two of the most trenchant methodological critics of BPR in the field of public management, wrote in a 1994 paper that it is atheoretical, unsystematic, generalizes beyond the instant case without warrant, and disregards tough questions about whether even in the instant case the alleged best practice is really responsible for any observed successes.[4] This line of criticism had (and has) much merit.[5] In my view the most damning element of the anti-BPR critique is that it is atheoretical. More careful theorizing about the nature of a putative best practice could mitigate to a large extent the problems associated with haphazard sampling.

To this end, one should seek inspiration in reverse engineering, discussed in the previous chapter. If one is looking for a useful trick that

---

3. Glaser and Strauss (1967), Strauss and Corbin (1990, esp. chap. 10).
4. Overman and Boyd (1994).
5. A subsequent, equally trenchant, critique is Lynn (1996).

one can replicate to one's own advantage, then high performance or innovative design is a tip-off about where to look. BPR practitioners have got this part of the procedure right. As I suggested in chapter 2, it is in the analytic process that BPR fails.

My own strategy for reverse engineering what appears to be a smart practice is to ask about how it exploits an opportunity—that is, how it tries to extract value on the cheap. I try out the sentence, "The practice X appears to be trying to take advantage of the fact that Y," and I try to characterize X and Y in such a way that one can see how value might indeed be produced on the cheap. For example, "Empowering front-line service teams permits an ICC to take advantage of the fact that frontline personnel have more information about the technical problems they face jointly and about the possible joint solutions they might create than do their supervisors or higher level managers." I then ask if there are possible side effects of the practice that might off-set the inferred advantages. To continue the example, "Undesirable side effects might include an erosion of accountability, undesirable inconsistencies across service teams, and the like."

I was also interested in variants of the generic smart practice, that is, different ways of implementing the smart practice that get slightly different results and serve as a menu of options for actors working in different contexts, e.g., a wastewater treatment plant using a continuous or an intermittent approach to aerating the mix of garbage and bugs.[6] In the ICC case, for instance, I examine in chapter 6 the generic smart practice of "leadership" and define two variants, which differ in how they deal with the fears that agency partners typically have that leaders might somehow favor other partners at their own expense. One variant deals with these fears by projecting a very low profile, the other, by doing the exact opposite. Of course, it may sometimes be debatable what is essential to the definition of the generic smart practice—say, of "empowering front-line service teams"—and what ought to be counted as an element in some context-specific variants, such as a specific means of enforcing accountability.

Typically, a variant appears in—or is purposively and strategically selected for—a context in which it is somehow more suitable than alternative variants. These different contexts could be defined in many different ways. The most important variations in context have to do with

6. Denn (1986, p. 102).

key actors' willingness to accept certain side-effects, run certain risks, or achieve certain subsidiary goals; the fiscal and partisan constraints on action; the career aspirations and personality characteristics of key individuals who are implementing the smart practice; and the degree of competency or incompetency of relevant organizational units.

Because this was to be primarily a conceptual study, I did not systematically attempt to find, analyze, and classify many variants of generic smart practices. I hope this is a task for future researchers. But the specimen-finding step in smart practice research is only the first. It can help identify the qualities of opportunities and associated smart practices that produce something for nothing. In most cases, though, one must look to magnitudes as well: The size of the something-for-nothing advantage is critical if the range of possible side effects is large and varied and if some proportions of these are themselves substantial. In the end, there is no substitute for empirical research, though the most useful sort might aim to uncover those portions of the range in which the alleged smart practice is not a good bet rather than to look only for reassuring central tendencies.[7]

Rating ICC "Success" and Other Attributes

In the heading of the discussion of each study site I include a high–medium–low rating of success assessed at the time my observations ceased[8] or the ICC was killed off by circumstances beyond the control of its major actors.[9] I offer these ratings despite some serious technical and conceptual concerns.[10]

Subjective States Problem

As I said in chapter 2, the subjective component of interagency collaborative capacity is particularly important. To simplify matters for the

7. Conversely, practices that are not "smart" on average might turn out to be so in certain restricted domains.

8. Usually this was mid-1997. The exceptions are Riverside, 1993; antitobacco education, 1994; Oregon welfare, 1995; memorandum of understanding on biodiversity, 1996; Tennessee, mid-1996.

9. New York state contract administration reform when Governor George Pataki took office in 1995.

10. Many of these concerns are present for the ratings of cases on the independent variables too, discussed in subsequent chapters.

purposes of rating ICC success, I treat it as the only important component, reasoning that the objective component eventually will catch up with the subjective component, if it is not already matched.

However, it is obviously very difficult for an observer such as myself to know other people's true dispositions to collaborate, including their anxieties about the risks of collaboration and the terms on which they might be prepared to collaborate. Even if one has some estimate of these at the individual level, there are difficulties in aggregating these states across individuals into a single-capacity rating for the collaborative community as a whole. My rough-and-ready approach to this problem is to allow my informants to make these assessments on my behalf to the extent possible.

Appearances Problem

I was occasionally prepared to override informants' judgments, because it is easy to be misled by surface appearances. As I point out in chapter 7, for instance, stalemate and the threat of breakdown are often needed to catalyze a new willingness to overcome barriers that looked insurmountable before. Some of my informants, seeing such phenomena, might underestimate real progress. I was also prepared to discount informants' assessments when I thought they were engaging in wishful thinking—or unduly cynical thinking—about the extent of collaborative capacity.

Baseline Problem

The principal conceptual issue concerns the appropriate baseline against which success is to be measured. One measure of current success would be the percentage of the distance traversed by the parties in their capacity-building efforts between a hypothetical starting point of zero progress toward achieving full collaborative potential and an end point of 100 percent. An even better measure would discount this proportion-of-potential-progress measure by the costs, risks, and delays involved in achieving it.[11] From a conceptual standpoint, at least, this is the principal measure of success I use in this book.

---

11. I speak of the broad category of social costs, only some of which are described by financial transactions.

There are a number of difficulties with making this conception of success fully intelligible, never mind operational:

—It is often difficult to know what the technically optimal level really is. Moreover, different people will construe different technical optimums, each bringing his or her own values to the task. I deal with this problem by working from what I take to be a consensus-level of aspiration in the relevant community of collaborators and in some cases making some adjustments of my own to that consensus.

—It is not clear where in time it is most analytically helpful to locate the beginning of the collaborative efforts. In the East Bay fire prevention case discussed later, one could plausibly see the beginning of the process just after the 1923 fire, the 1980 fire, or the 1991 fire. Unless otherwise specified, I take the beginning of the history to be where informants say or imply it was.

—It is hard to know how large a discount factor to apply to achieved success in the light of observed or inferred costs. Because ICCs often require coordinator time and energy, there is certainly reason to believe that the incremental costs of collaborative production are higher than the costs of autonomous production. In general, though, I ignore such incremental costs. One reason is that in most cases they are probably not very large relative to all the other costs of interest. Another reason is that, in some cases, the higher incremental costs should decline over time as agencies and people settle into new ways of doing business and learn how to trim them.[12]

—It is also hard to know how large a discount factor to apply to achieved success given what appears to be substantial delay, or conversely how much extra credit to allow for apparent speed. On the surface, at least, the more complex and ambitious the objectives of the participants in a development process, the longer it should take to begin to see the benefits of collaboration. We should have a standard of normal speed that takes account of scope and complexity. It should also take account of the normal delays built into any public sector or bureaucratic process. However, it is hard to gauge what is normal—and, indeed, many of my informants told me that nearly everyone, including them-

12. Furthermore, some of the cases in my sample are intended as demonstration projects (the community organizing sites, the Coordinated Youth Services Council, the New York master contract, and the Elkhorn Slough), wherein the value of production is not just the ordinary product of the agencies' work but information or inspiration as well. In such cases one should be prepared to incur higher costs.

selves, underestimated the time it would take to produce results. My own approach to this problem has been (1) to look for unusual levels of criticism of delay as reported by participants, and (2) in the case of what I took to be substantial and preventable delay, to downgrade a high or medium success score to the category just below it. I treated four of nineteen cases in this manner. [13]

Multibranch Problem

I had to make an analytical decision about how to treat multibranch cases—that is, where the ICC includes a center and multiple sites on a periphery, such as a state-financed and state-guided but locally administered welfare-to-work program. Even if one grants that it is reasonable to talk, as I do, of "an ICC" in a single site among a well-defined group of agencies, one could question whether it makes sense to speak of a single ICC at all in these more complex cases. I do so for essentially the same reason that I am usually willing to speak of "the" California State Department of Health as a single organization even though it has many geographical branches and several functional divisions, all of which are only loosely integrated bureaucratically and professionally. Even though it does not always make sense to treat multibranch organizations as a single organization, sometimes it does, and I like to keep the latter option open.

This does not mean that one has to treat these cases exactly alike for all purposes. In four of these multibranch cases I have essentially assessed the capacity at the center, but considered in doing so the ability of the center to induce collaboration in sites at the periphery. These cases are the Tennessee Children's Plan, the memorandum of understanding on biodiversity, military base environmental cleanup, and the Maryland Systems Reform Initiative. In the case of California's Healthy Start, I omit consideration of the center (state agencies) altogether. In the cases of military base redevelopment, California's state and local efforts at antitobacco education, New Jersey School-Based Youth Services, Oregon welfare-to-work, and Oregon Integrated Children and Family Services, I attempted to encompass the whole of the system, averaging what I took to be the characteristics in the peripheral sites and then folding in

---

13. The four cases are: Coordinated Youth Services Council, Denver Family Opportunities Program, Del Paso Heights, and the Tennessee Children's Plan.

Figure 3-1. *Cases of Interagency Collaboration, by Policy Domain*

School-linked services
Healthy Start (multiple sites in California)
New Jersey School-Based Youth Services

Children, family, and youth services
Coordinated Youth Services Council (Marin County, California)
Maryland Systems Reform Initiative
Tennessee Children's Plan
Oregon Integrated Services

Community organizing
Del Paso Heights (Sacramento County, California)
Prescott Project (Oakland, California)

Welfare-to-work programs
Riverside County, California
Oregon
Denver Family Opportunity

Antitobacco education (California)

Preventing fires in the East Bay hills (California)

Regulation
New York state contract administration
Multimedia environmental enforcement

Natural resources and ecosystem management
Elkhorn Slough (California)
Memorandum of understanding on biodiversity (Pacific Northwest and
    Northern California)

Military base closure and reuse (national)
Economic redevelopment
Environmental cleanup

the interagency characteristics at the center along with the characteristics
of the relationships between center and periphery.[14] (See figure 3-1 for a
list of the nineteen cases discussed.)

My reasons for treating the cases differently had mostly to do with
how much confidence I had in my impressions about different aspects

14. All the cases are so complex and multifaceted that it almost seems preposterous to
assign them a global characterization. The problem is even worse when we turn to rating
ICCs with regard to independent variables—for example, "Oregon welfare-to-work ICC
high on pragmatic attitude toward bureaucracy." However, this sort of heroic characteri-

of the various cases. For instance, in the California Healthy Start case the results available from systematic evaluative studies gave me more confidence about the sites at the periphery than in any other case, but I had no such source for other cases. In many cases I have had to make an educated guess about how to characterize an ICC on some dimension—for example, guessing about the aggregate of local situations in Maryland based perhaps on some combination of stray remarks picked up in interviews, inferences derived from their collective political action, inferences from state–local relations in Maryland more generally, and the like.

School-Linked Services

School-linked health and social services for children typically are provided at the school site for children attending that school. The services are usually provided not by the school personnel themselves but by providers outstationed at the school site sent by other public and sometimes nonprofit agencies.[15] The services are often conceptualized as part of a broad strategy of services integration to the child's larger family, although the focus also may be much narrower.[16] The provision of these services in the school setting is justified partly as a way to improve students' academic performance: A child who is constantly hungry and sleep deprived cannot learn. But even if there were no impact on learning, improving children's (and their families') physical and emotional health would be a good thing.

The technical logic of school-linked services is strong. Teachers will have access to specialists who will help them deal with disruptive behavior and with other problems that interfere with their students'

---

zation of heterogeneous systems and cultures is standard practice in comparative politics, although often accompanied by more cautious measurement procedures than I have been able to apply—for example, Putnam (1993)—and it can make sense if the heterogeneity within the system or culture, however great it may be in some sense, is nevertheless smaller than the heterogeneity across those that are being compared.

15. Center for the Future of Children (1992, p. 7).

16. In the early part of this century school-linked services were part of a campaign to prevent the spread of infectious diseases and to help assimilate immigrant families into the dominant culture (Tyack, 1992). One might say that the campaign objectives are still the same except that the "diseases" have more to do with poverty and the relevant "culture" is not American but middle-class, because the target schools today are those attended by large numbers of "high-risk" children.

learning. Further, schools are places in which children are accessible to service providers (case finding and case management), and providers are accessible to children and their families. Finally, through the children service providers might find a way of accessing the family as a whole.[17]

An evaluation by Palo Alto–based SRI International of California's school-linked services program (Healthy Start; see later discussion) recorded improvements on many dimensions, although many of these were small. One of the most impressive was increases of 25 to 50 percent in access to health care services for core clients—those who would receive intensive, extended services—who lacked them at the time of admittance.[18] Another was the reduction in mobility on the part of these clients. High mobility leads to gaps in course work and curriculum coverage, disruptions in relations with teachers and friends, and a general increase in stress. More than one-third of core students had changed schools at least once in the year before Healthy Start intake. This proportion dropped to 23 percent after participating in the program.[19]

Healthy Start (Medium)

In 1991 the California legislature passed the Healthy Start Support Services for Children Act, intended to provide health, mental health,

---

17. The technical logic is not entirely clear-cut, however. There is the risk that the nonacademic objectives of the health and social service providers will compete in an untoward way with the academic objectives of the school, perhaps by taking up too much student time, or school space, or school district funds. In an earlier period, the outside professionals were sometimes critics of the educational institutions that, in their view, alienated their clients (Tyack, 1992, p. 25), and the same relationship sometimes occurs today (as I observed in one of my field visits). Also, some advocates of community development hold that community centers (along the model of settlement houses) rather than schools would be more congenial settings for many of the services to take place, and that such centers should not be deprived of the service offerings that might attract families to the centers and so help these centers thrive in a more diffuse way (Chaskin and Richman, 1992). Finally, in inner-city settings, the level of health and social services to be coordinated may simply be too low to be worth bothering about (Crowson and Boyd, 1993, p. 156).

18. Wagner, Newman, and Golan (1996, p. 4-8, exh. 4-3). Three quarters of the staff thought that accessibility of services had increased during the past year and attributed this increase to Healthy Start (p. 4-14). Changes of a comparable magnitude were observed in core families reporting a need for food, clothing, and emergency funds (p. 4-3, exh. 4-1).

19. Wagner, Newman, and Golan (1996, p. 4-23, exh. 4-13). However, absenteeism was no better (if not slightly worse). Student grades were slightly better and principals reported that the incidence of violent actions in their schools and the proportion of students who were suspended or expelled decreased marginally after two years of involvement of their schools in Healthy Start (pp. 4-25–4-27).

and social services to children and their families in schools serving relatively high-risk populations. The program had bipartisan support. It also had the commitment of Pete Wilson, the recently elected Republican governor and a relative fiscal conservative who was also facing a staggering state budget deficit. Healthy Start was one of only a handful of new expenditures that Wilson proposed. At the same time a number of foundations in the state were meeting to discuss their funding strategies in the area of school-linked services and the opportunities to influence state policymaking for children and families.[20] In early 1992 the governor, the state superintendent of public instruction (an elected official and a Democrat), and representatives of the foundations signed an agreement in principle to collaborate on the overall effort. The state Department of Education, the state Department of Health Services, and the federal Health Care Financing Administration subsequently arranged for medicaid funds to reimburse local education authorities for providing services to eligible students.[21]

Under Healthy Start the state made planning grants and, in a majority of cases, subsequent operational grants to schools of up to $450,000 for a three-year period. Between 1992 and 1995, the state made 149 operational grants to communities involving 469 schools.[22]

I rated success in this case as medium rather than high because relatively little had been done in most sites to try to connect the work of noneducational professionals in the schools to the work of teachers in their classrooms and because, as of April 1997, it appeared that the prospects for sustaining funding when the state seed monies ran out were relatively mixed.[23]

New Jersey School-Based Youth Services (High)

The School-Based Youth Services program in New Jersey, begun in 1988, targets high schools in poor urban and rural areas. It was funded primarily by a $6 million appropriation from the state to a local entity, usually a school district, a city or county agency, an existing nonprofit

---

20. Wagner and others (1994a, p. 1-2).
21. Wagner and others (1994b, pp. 5-1, 5-2).
22. Golan and others (1996, p. 1-2).
23. California State Department of Education, "Healthy Start: Status of Sustaining Sites," 1997.

agency, or a specially created nonprofit corporation.[24] Its local programs are also successful at attracting other sources of funds and becoming magnets for other grants and programs. The program won an Innovations in State and Local Government award in 1991. I visited several sites in 1994, heard much praise from students who used program services, and met many enthusiastic program managers and frontline staff. As of 1994 it was operating in thirty sites throughout all of New Jersey's twenty-one counties. Although somewhat varied to suit local preferences, the program essentially locates youth counselors and social services workers on school grounds and creates an inviting, nonjudgmental atmosphere that encourages students to share their troubles—and their triumphs—with competent, friendly adults who can help them gain access to various community and governmental resources.

Although School-Based is focused more on youth in trouble than on youth in general, it shares a philosophy known loosely as youth development, which looks at teenagers as whole individuals at a certain stage in the life course rather than as carriers or victims of pathology, as so many programs do. Such pathology as there may be ought to be dealt with, to the extent possible, by helping teenagers to strengthen their own capacities. In some cases this means supplementing the work that the family is already doing, but in others it means acting as a replacement for the family.

School-Based has had strong support from a Republican and then a Democractic governor (Thomas Kean and then James Florio) and has not been cut by Republican Christine Todd Whitman. Although the parent agency of School-Based, the Department of Social Services, took a hefty budget cut, the legislature preserved School-Based intact.

Children, Family, and Youth Services

As I said in chapter 1, the critics of currently "fragmented" government programs in the area of children, family, and youth services argue that several related types of opportunity are being ignored: the greater remediability of problems when conceived in their natural family-systems and whole-person configurations; the greater efficacy and the lower cost of prevention as opposed to remediation; and the existence

24. Best (1992).

of families' and individuals' assets as opposed to deficits. These opportunities are invisible or, if visible, not readily exploited owing to the jumble of specialized agencies, missions, programs, line-item budget categories, professions, personnel categories, and the problem-centered ideologies that thrive in such overgrown turf.

A major problem in the area of children and family services as perceived by program managers and professional service providers is that the funding for most current programs is narrowly targeted toward some specific population, problem, or intervention strategy. A 1987 report of California's Little Hoover Commission estimated that, exclusive of K–12 education, at least forty-seven programs in thirteen agencies were administering programs for children at a cost of $5.9 billion a year in California.[25] In the early 1990s one study reported seventy-two federal categorical programs for children.[26] This funding approach permits legislators and interest groups to use the budgeting and auditing systems of government to ensure that monies are spent approximately in ways that these overseers desire.

Program managers often strain to find ways to patch funds together to provide the package of services they think would make sense in individual cases. But this can take a lot of time and energy; and critics of the current system have abundant anecdotes to suggest that many children and families simply fall through the cracks.[27] When it is done on a broader basis—for example, managing afterschool programs for youth to integrate, say, funds for anti-drug-abuse education, recreation, and parenting education, the service provider will ordinarily need to maintain a documentation trail that convinces auditors that money has not been misspent. This is costly and risks disallowance for reimbursement by auditors who may be skeptical, narrowly focused on technical compliance issues, or reluctant to avoid blame should some subsequent audit question their actions.

One antidote to this and other causes of service fragmentation is often called, naturally enough, *services integration*, the core objective of which is that the client, whether an individual or a family-like unit,

---

25. Presentation by Grantland Johnson, president, Sacramento County board of supervisors, in Zellerbach Family Fund (1990, p. 10).

26. Kagan and others (1995, p. 5, citing unpublished papers by Sid Gardner).

27. Unfortunately, it is hard to assess how much of the problem is a result of a shortage of resources rather than of the mismanagement of existing resources.

should receive timely, high-quality, individual services in such a way that they complement one another.[28] For example, Gwen, an adolescent unmarried mother, should receive parenting training, on-site child care in her high school, perinatal and well-child medical care, and counseling. Given Gwen's objective hardships and her level of stress, all these complementary services must be available at the same point in time, or synchronously, in order to permit her (and her child) to attain a functional level of maturity and eventual economic self-sufficiency. It would further mean that as Gwen matures or "improves," she moves along a continuum of services: There are appropriate and timely handoffs from one service provider to the next in the continuum.[29]

Just as school-linked services can be seen as part of a larger strategy of offering services and supports to families, so the strategy of serving families can be seen as a strategy for developing communities—which in turn can be seen as a way of strengthening supports for families. The community, viewed through this lens, is a refuge for emotional support, a reservoir of potential surrogate grandparents and other informal child care providers, a panoply of eyes and ears (and mouths) enforcing norms and preventing crimes, a source of casual and entry-level jobs for "our" kids, a communications channel for public health or social services outreach, and an object of prideful identification.

But before families can be enriched by communities, the communities themselves may need to be enriched. This may be accomplished in various ways. A community center in the style of a settlement house is a possible beginning. It might have collocated public and private services, classes, opportunities for sociability, counseling in informal settings, activities that bring generations together, and so on. Another step is to provide activities that originate in the community center and also create environmental

28. The banner of services integration is flown in the human services domain in general. A report of success in the rehabilitation area is found in Rogers, Anthon, and Danley (1989), who compared counties in Vermont with regard to placement in competitive employment. Positive results are also reported for mental health by Provan and Milward (1995).

29. One of the best how to manuals concerning approaches for would-be developers of interagency collaborative capacity in *any* policy domain, *Together We Can*, by Atelia I. Melaville and Martin J. Blank (1993), was produced with children and family services in mind and was sponsored jointly by Health and Human Services and the U.S. Department of Education.

amenities that can be enjoyed by the community at large—for example, park maintenance, security patrols, community gardens.

Coordinated Youth Services Council (Low)

At the height of its powers and prestige, in 1993–94, the Coordinated Youth Services Council (CYSC) of Marin County, California, was in some ways the very model of a family-serving collaborative. Its core function was to manage the cases of some sixty-five multiproblem families a year who were being seen by at least two public agencies (or by one public and one private agency) and who presented unusually complex problems. It relied on a technique it called *parallel case review*, which took place in a roundtable meeting of all the line staff from the several agencies involved with the case. This might mean representatives from the county agencies on mental health, social services (usually child protective services), probation, public health, and a school. In some cases, private psychologists and family therapists could also be involved. The group would hear reports from the various professionals and would consensually design a service or treatment plan. A lead case manager would be appointed, and the others present in effect would be part of a continuing treatment team. There might also be progress reports and follow-up reviews with approximately the same group or some subset. In theory, each of the agencies involved in the case would make available treatment staff, funds, or other resources.

The CYSC was itself a nonprofit organization made up of the five major public family-serving agencies and sixteen private service providers in Marin County. The CYSC had its own executive director, clinical director, two- to three-person staff of counselors, therapists, and so on, and a number of clinical interns. It also deployed five professional staff from public health, social services, mental health, probation, and the county school office, most of whom worked on a part-time basis for the CYSC, who were collocated at the CYSC facility, and who CYSC conjointly supervised along with the employing agencies. It had a budget of about $600,000, which included a discretionary fund of $100,000 that case managers could use to fill in service gaps for clients (though in fact they spent little of it). The relatively wealthy Marin Community Foundation contributed nearly the entire budget.

In 1994 CYSC staff estimated that the program had saved $3 million in public monies over a two-year period by preventing group home placements.[30] A 1993 evaluation found that the staff, though overworked, had high morale.[31] Had I rated its ICC capacity at that point, I would have judged it high. By the end of 1994, however, the CYSC, which had been riding high, had fallen to earth. Staff members were feeling overwhelmed with responsibilities. Managers discovered that dissemination of the CYSC's parallel case review model to the other agencies was often resented and was not even working very well at the CYSC. The Marin Community Foundation was threatening to terminate its funding. "We have learned some very humbling lessons over the past few years, very humbling lessons," the executive director said in June 1997.

Maryland Systems Reform Initiative (High)

Unlike California, which has strong county government and a tradition of county management of children and family services, in Maryland it has been the state that has dominated this program area. Hence the push to increase interagency collaboration in Maryland, as in many other states, has had to move along a second front, namely increasing devolution to localities. This complicates the process considerably in that a credible local administrative apparatus has to be created to make the ICC concept feasible. This apparatus may or may not be able to make use of local governmental institutions. Similarly, there may or may not be strong locally based offices of the state service agencies.

As in most other states in which the reform of service delivery to families, youth, and children has taken hold, Maryland was suffering from an explosion in the cost of out-of-home placements for its high-risk families. Between 1987 and 1990 the overall cost of placement had increased 64 percent.[32] Some 600 children were costing the state $50,000

---

30. 1994 report, attach. 4, app. B.

31. One case manager was quoted in an evaluator's report as saying CYSC had an "extremely dedicated and energetic group of people, able to apply professionalism in a practical way to produce good client outcomes. Able to bring in resources not normally available to providers doing case management services. Provides a forum for effective MDT [multidisciplinary team] case management services that has not been provided in this county to date. Very happy with the management of the project." (Appendix, "CYSC Key Informant Interview Results-Case Review Process," p. 1.) See Arnett (1993).

32. Lundberg (1991, pp. 11–12).

to $100,000 each. Maryland also faced the political embarrassment of having to export its most troubled or endangered children to homes outside the state. Geographic separation would make reintegration with families more difficult. The providers would not be regulated by Maryland public agencies, and the state economy would not benefit from spending on a local industry. The cost was very high: $45 million in fiscal year 1992.[33]

System reform efforts in Maryland flowed in several different channels, all of which eventually joined in the Office for Children and Youth, created by Governor Donald Schaefer and headed by the governor's close ally, Nancy Grasmick. The most significant was a foundation-funded demonstration of the family preservation strategy in Prince George's County.[34] In the spring of 1991 Grasmick's office also pushed a bill in the state legislature that aimed to create the Department for Children, Youth, and Families. This new entity was to absorb the Department of Juvenile Services and all foster care and child protective services from the Department of Human Resources, though not the Department of Education or the children's programs of the Department of Health and Mental Hygiene.[35]

What emerged from all this reform activity was primarily the Systems Reform Initiative, or SRI, that was built on the family preservation model and was to be extended beyond the demonstration program in Prince George's County. In 1990 legislation was passed requiring local jurisdictions to create local planning entities (later renamed local management boards) to implement interagency services in all counties and in Baltimore. These entities were to have 50 percent private sector membership and were charged with developing an interagency system of direct services and planning to fill existing gaps in service. They could

33. Maryland Subcabinet for Children, Youth, and Families. 1994. "Status of Systems Reform Fiscal Year 1993," p. 3.

34. This strategy entails intense, virtually round-the-clock social services provided over a relatively brief period—for example, six weeks—to families with children who are being abused or are likely to be abused and so are at high risk of being placed in foster care or some other protective institutional arrangement. The somewhat controversial assumptions behind the strategy are that even the most disturbed families often "want to do right for their kids" and that foster care or other institutional arrangements are often psychologically detrimental (Schuerman, Rzepnicki, and Littell, 1994, p. 5). The theory of intervention emphasizes family-centeredness, family empowerment, a community orientation, use of the home as the primary service site, and the opportunity that crisis presents to promote positive change (p. 19).

35. Lundberg (1991, p. 14).

deliver services directly or contract out. Of the state funds deemed saved by avoiding out-of-home placements, 75 percent were to be turned over to these local entities for the purpose of developing community-based services. The other 25 percent were to be retained by state agencies and used for prevention. The Systems Reform Initiative office, which had already emerged within the governor's Office for Children, Youth, and Families, undertook to promote the aims of the legislation.

Whether or not the family preservation strategy contributed to the result, out of state placements decreased in the July to October 1992 period by 51 percent relative to the same period a year earlier.[36] In fiscal year 1993, 39 percent fewer children entered out of state placement, and $1.14 million was returned to the local planning entities for local capacity building.[37]

Progress was slow, however. During the course of hammering out the fiscal 1997 state budget, a variety of interests expressed the feeling that system reform was not proceeding rapidly enough. Despite the legislative mandate, a substantial minority of counties had not yet created an official local management board. The performance and potential of some existing boards were seen as inadequate.[38] A task force chaired by the lieutenant governor was created to review the entire process. It recommended a new state Commission on Children and Families made up of diverse stakeholders with substantial powers—for example, setting reimbursement rates for providers, conducting program audits of state agencies and local service systems, and recommending to the governor which individual, state agency, nonprofit organization, or for-profit organization would negotiate annual funding agreements with the localities. Neither the governor nor the legislature officially accepted the report's recommendations, however.

Tennessee Children's Plan (Medium)

The reforming discourse in Tennessee in the late 1980s and early 1990s was not so much about the evils of fragmentation as it was about

36. Maryland Subcabinet for Children, Youth, and Families. 1994. "Status of Systems Reform Fiscal Year 1993," p. 3.

37. Maryland Subcabinet for Children, Youth, and Families. 1994. "Status of Systems Reform Fiscal Year 1994," p. 23.

38. I rated this Maryland case as a high success. However, I simply felt unable to judge whether the delay for a project of this scale was or was not within the bounds of "normalcy." I decided to err on the side of tolerance.

the excesses, both humanitarian and fiscal, of having too many children in custody and of treating them poorly while they were in custody. Between fiscal years 1985 and 1989, commitments grew by 28 percent, and a 1989 study by the state Department of Finance and Administration found that 31 percent of those children in custody were in an overly restrictive placement, only 12 percent of the need for family preservation services was being met, and only 31 percent of the need for family mental health therapy was being met.[39]

The director of Finance and Administration who instigated the study, David Manning, was a personal friend of the Republican governor and had strong ties to leaders of the Democrat-controlled legislature as well. He is said to be a man of great intelligence, drive, and charisma. From his position at Finance and Administration controlling the state's dollars, and in conjunction with allies at the top of the state Health Department, he created TennCare, a medicaid-managed care plan, one of the first in the nation. Manning decided to make almost as big a revolution in children's services. He called it the Children's Plan and in February 1991 presented it to the legislature's Select Committee on Children and Youth.

The logic of managed care was to be exported, to the extent possible, to this client population as well. Funds hitherto used by the separate departments for custodial services would be pooled into a single account. Interdisciplinary Assessment and Care Coordination Teams (ACCTs) were to manage the cases of each child, and they would use the account to purchase services, if necessary, from any of a variety of private sector vendors.[40] The key managerial component in the whole system was to be the twelve regional Community Health Agencies (CHAs), which had been created in October 1989 as part of the TennCare initiative to develop community-based health resources.

By early 1995, although it was not clear that service quality was improving, the system was able to demonstrate average daily costs declining: Whereas in mid-1991 approximately 18 to 22 percent of first admissions were to private psychiatric hospitals, by 1995 these were down to 2 percent.[41]

39. Tennessee State Department of Finance and Administration (1990, pp. iii–v).

40. In the long run, Manning wanted to subject the public agencies to the same competitive discipline as the private providers.

41. "Tennessee Children's Plan Review: February, 1995, Suggestions for Responsible Cost Reduction." Internal document.

Interagency relationships at the line level varied a great deal among the twelve CHA regions. In some cases they worked together reasonably smoothly, and in others there was animosity verging on strife. In several regions the situation was colored by what turned out to be a shortage of beds—the influx of additional federal funds notwithstanding—so that ACCTs could hardly manage cases, so involved were they with simply finding a child a bed for the night (and not always in the same geographic locale from which he or she had come.) Juvenile court judges, who are, in effect, key line staff in the case-management process, had not been consulted about the system changes and in many cases refused to cooperate with the ACCTs. The ACCTs also began operating with very little training and, according to one observer, "were completely overwhelmed by the enormity of their responsibilities."[42]

At the top management level in Nashville, chaos was more the norm than the exception. Manning had conceptualized the desired system well but had not detailed the steps needed to move it there. Committees and meetings proliferated. Manning's attention shifted to other matters, and the process of redesigning the new system turned into a fiasco.[43]

By late 1994 a combination of fiscal pressure—with cuts on the order of 5 to 10 percent in state funds for the children's services agencies—and dissatisfaction with the administrative structure at the state level led policymakers to consider the possibility of creating a new Department of Children's Services. A year later this was an accomplished fact, and throughout 1996 a simultaneously creative and focused but—inevitably—chaotic effort was under way to make the transition. One of the most significant changes was a conversion of all the child-serving agencies' line staff into generic family service workers.

Considered as a six- or seven-year process, the reorganization of children's services in Tennessee is a success. Observers that I interviewed disagree over whether a less rocky road to the same outcome was available. Those who think so hold that the process should have been more gradual, more given to technical problem solving, more respectful of orderly decision procedures, and more reliant on informal consensus building without the pressure of arbitrary deadlines and top-down

42. Maloy (1994, p. 25), quoting an interviewee. Problems between Department of Youth Development staff and ACCT staff were also documented in an internal November 1994 report, Paul DeMuro, "DYD and The Children's Plan: Confusion, Competition, or Cooperation?"
43. Maloy (1994).

domineering by Manning and his allies. Those who believe otherwise argue that there was so much latent resistance in the agencies' turf protectionism and in the general lethargy of government that Manning's management-by-chaos approach was the only workable one. These latter observers argue that the only real choice was between a little more or a little less chaos. I am inclined to side with this latter camp; but as I shall argue in chapter 6, it is possible that a great deal less chaos might have ensued had Manning—or someone as respected and as effective but more able to implement details—led the reorganizing process during 1991 and thereafter.[44] I downgraded the success rating from high to medium to take account of the fact that substantial delay did occur and that probably at least some of it was preventable.

Oregon Integrated Services (High)

Because Oregon is a large state with diverse subpopulations, local self-governance is a dominant value. County government is strong. The field offices of state agencies located far from Salem often retain a local flavor. It was only natural that when state policymakers began to think about services integration, they thought first about how the idea could be made to work at the local—indeed, the grass-roots—level. In July 1991 the director of the Department of Human Resources, Kevin Concannon, an executive who commanded great respect in and out of government, held a series of townhall meetings across the state. These meetings elicited complaints about access to services, barriers to receiving services that address multiple problems, and duplication of services. In April 1992 a draft plan and supporting concept paper were distributed to state and county employees, consumers, advocates, and providers. The distribution effort was consciously targeted beyond a narrow Human Resources constituency and included schools, housing, the correctional system, transportation agencies, churches, and community service agencies.

The result was "an invitation to communities throughout the state to join DHR in redesigning and integrating their local human services delivery systems."[45] This invitation was reissued in four subsequent years as well. Each project was supposed to be justified in terms of both

44. Whether it would actually have been possible to find such a person in 1991, or who it might have been, I do not know.
45. Oregon Department of Human Resources, 1994. "Service Integration: Evaluation Report on 1992 Department of Human Resources, Service Integration Project."

local goals and some subset of the 259 Oregon so-called benchmarks that had been adopted by the legislature in 1991, an array of quantitatively specified societal goals.[46] Although the invitation was backed by a promise of only $500 and a commitment to a Human Resources liaison who would, in addition to offering technical assistance, act as an advocate for the project in Salem, the local response was enthusiastic. These liaisons came to be known as "barrier busters." They did what they could—and it was often quite a lot—to see to it that Human Resources made whatever adjustments were needed to endow the local project with the flexibility needed by the locals. By December 1994 there were thirty-nine local projects. Each one was overseen by a local planning committee composed of a broad range of local partners.

A parallel effort to that of Human Resources, focused on education, was undertaken by the state Department of Education. It reached conclusions favorable to the idea of promoting school-linked health and social services. The two state agencies, Human Resources and Education, themselves became natural partners. A result was that many of the local projects had a school or education component. In the state legislature, one of the strong advocates of the benchmarks and of services integration, Senator Bev Stein, successfully promoted a bill to require Human Resources to initiate a number of interagency human investment service projects on a demonstration basis; shortly thereafter, eight were begun around the state.

In 1994 and 1995 I visited five sites at which local services integration activities were taking place.[47] I will attempt in brief to convey the important facts about three of them.

GLENDALE–AZALEA. The decline of the timber and forest products industries in this rural community left many people unemployed and without skills easily marketable in the larger economy. Alcoholism was high. So were the rates of child abuse and neglect. The school district superintendent championed the development of a skill center in which a broad range of services and activities would be available. It was also to be the site of social gatherings. In 1992 the school board hired a dynamic social worker with community-organizing skills, Shaun Brink. A local lumber company donated an abandoned office site. The com-

46. Altshuler (1997, pp. 60–62).
47. Some started up without having been prompted first by the Human Resources service integration initiative. See p. 173.

pany promised to employ, and to promote, many of the individuals who obtained a GED or acquired certain proficiencies. Umpqua Community College became a major partner, and all the state human service agencies have been eager to outstation workers in the center. Counseling in a wide range of areas, from teenage support to employability to alcohol and drug abuse, has been an important component of the center.

By mid-1997, though Brink was still in place, the original program champion, the superintendent, had left and his replacement was reported to be showing considerably less enthusiasm. The program was still functioning well, but the founders' original vision of spreading the model throughout the county had stalled.

BRENTWOOD–DARLINGTON. Portland Impact, a citywide community action agency that said its hallmark is "fostering self-sufficiency in those we serve," began in 1991 to run a neighborhood family center in this low-income and semirural neighborhood of southeast Portland. It also was the destination for recent waves of Southeast Asian and Russian immigrants. When I visited the center in 1995, it was bustling with a variety of people and activities, from old people eating lunch and socializing to young men looking for employment counseling. I met with an ensemble of center-affiliated service staff ranging from a welfare worker to a public health nurse to the principal of the nearby middle school. Their enthusiasm for the neighborhood, the center, and their co-workers from the participating public and private agencies was palpable. By 1997 the project, flourishing more than ever, had moved into a new community center, built for itself and some community partners.

UPPER ROGUE FAMILY CENTER. The center is based in White City, a small town in southern Oregon, not far from Medford. It was started in 1991 by the county health director, a school principal, and a district director of the Oregon Adult and Family Services Agency, Oregon's name for the state welfare department. In 1994, when I visited, it had been in operation for three years. It had evolved from a site that simply collocated staff who interacted on a limited basis into a relatively cohesive, high-morale team in which staff from different agencies had become comfortable performing one another's functions and treating one another as extended family. Indeed, on a few occasions when they were facing internal tensions, they assembled and acted out the sort of "family unity" meeting that they had taught their troubled clients.[48]

Community Organizing

Some versions of community development also include a large component of community organizing. Community organizing carries diffuse overtones of political mobilization and community self-governance. According to this view, the community is a set of potential resources not just in relation to itself but as a means to leverage resources from the larger world outside the community. It may be a pressure group on local government for more public resources or an advocate to public agency managers for doing business in the community in a different sort of way—for example, in a more collaborative way. The community may even be a substitute source of governance authority relative to the institutions of traditional local government. In some cases, the successes of a local community at increasing its power and autonomy vis-à-vis the outside world may also be a source of community pride and the confidence necessary to reach for even more.

In cases in which the community stands in an adversarial relationship to local government, a self-governance agenda looks particularly attractive. One difficulty, however, is wresting governance from the institutions that currently govern. Another, less obvious but more subtle and daunting, is crafting for the community a new system of governance. The history of experiments in what the ancient Greeks would have called constitution making contains far more failures than successes. The relatively successful U.S. experience with the design of governance institutions at the federal, state, and local levels is the exception.

48. The strategic idea behind this model is to empower families to take the lead in planning their own treatment program, in consultation with professionals and in conjunction with a variety of neighbors, fellow employees, and the like (those whom the family wishes to participate and who also agree to do so). The philosophy is oriented to the family's assets rather than its deficits. The language and attitudes of the professional staff are of great concern. This is suggested in a piece of literature for professional guidance distributed by the Oregon Department of Human Resources: "Families accept 'issues of concern' terminology much better than 'problem' terminology. Concerns are not the same as problems. 'Concerns' personalize and take ownership. . . . Problems do not resolve anything. Strengths are what resolve issues of concern. . . . Options are preferable to advice. Advice is disrespectful."

Del Paso Heights (Medium)

Arthur Bolton, trained in the 1950s as a social worker and community organizer, in 1962 began a long and successful career as a staff member in the California state legislature and as a Sacramento-based private consultant to the legislature and other clients. In 1992, following three years of networking with policymakers in Sacramento and with a large number of California and some national foundations, he was named to direct the newly created Center for Integrated Services to Families and Neighborhoods (CISFAN). CISFAN was intended as an administrative shell to permit Bolton to do community development work with a community self-governance slant in several carefully chosen neighborhoods. The plan was to get to work in several local communities to establish "neighborhood family service organizations" in a settlement-house style, governed by locally constituted boards of directors, that would deliver, in a complementary fashion, a wide range of services to neighborhood residents. Bolton also arranged for allies in the legislature to submit bills permitting such entities to exercise an array of fiscal and administrative powers.[49]

Grantland Johnson, president of the Sacramento County Board of Supervisors, was eager to have a CISFAN-type pilot project implemented in his neighborhood, Del Paso Heights. This desire dovetailed with a more general desire to reorganize and decentralize human services in the county. In March 1993 the Neighborhood Services Agency (NSA) opened its doors, aiming to serve a low-income neighborhood with fairly well demarcated boundaries and a clear historical identity. This was a loosely organized collection of some fifteen line staff from several county agencies, most of them volunteers. The target population of about 11,000 was about one-third African American and also had a large bloc of Hmong and other southeast Asian immigrants.

The start was rocky. The first site coordinator proved inadequate and was forced out after seven months by a combination of pressures from

49. Among many other reasons that I chose to look at the work of CISFAN and the several sites in which it operated was my long-time acquaintance with the talents of Bolton. He was the principal protagonist of my first book (and doctoral dissertation), *The Skill Factor in Politics: Repealing the Mental Commitment Laws in California* (Bardach, 1972). I had thought him extremely skillful when I watched him at close range in the mid-1960s. I was curious to see if the bold strategies and tactics he had perfected in legislative work would prove helpful in the much more complex and fragmented, but equally political, context of project implementation.

below and above. The position was then vacant for six months, during which time the site staff in effect managed themselves. This was a period of high morale but also confusion and an apparent lack of productivity. However, despite complaints about lack of support from home agencies, excessive workloads, stress from learning how to work together across agency and professional lines, and anxieties over professional status issues, most of the staff liked working in the interagency context and were overwhelmingly ready to recommend to other communities that they try something like the NSA.[50]

Alongside the NSA service delivery system was a community self-help organization called the Mutual Assistance Network (MAN). The MAN was a separately incorporated nonprofit organization (until May 1994 operating through CISFAN and thereafter as a community development corporation) able to receive and spend funds on its own. Observers consider the MAN the preeminently successful feature of the Del Paso Heights experiment. It started two community gardens (one of which did not survive for long), a parent support group, a grandparent support group for persons raising their children's children, a block-grandparents program to combat juvenile delinquency, and several youth recreation and development programs. As of June 1997 it had an annual budget of more than $1 million and had created some forty-five jobs. Together with the Sacramento County Housing and Redevelopment Agency, it was planning a resident-built neighborhood center, for which it had received one of eight nationally awarded Housing and Urban Development grants.

I would have rated Del Paso Heights high except for the delay of approximately two years in sorting out its problems with the county and its relatively belated discovery of the opportunities presented by the MAN.

Prescott Project (Low)

Just after World War II the Prescott neighborhood of West Oakland, California, was a thriving center of African American community life. It was known as the jazz center of the Bay Area. By the early 1990s, however, its 6,000 residents (70 percent African American, 15 percent Hispanic ancestry) were living on the margin, with 47 percent on some

50. Minnicucci Associates (1995, pp. 31–32).

form of public assistance, the neighborhood divided by freeways, and very few local jobs. In early 1992 Bolton and some colleagues gathered commitments in the form of official resolutions from the Oakland City Council, the Oakland Board of Education, and the Alameda County Board of Supervisors to participate in a joint venture to design, establish, and test an alternative, family-centered, neighborhood-based system of human services in the Prescott neighborhood. The mayor of Oakland was also on record in support of the project.

A year passed in meetings with community groups and other collaboratives (Oakland is home to a great many) and in exploring potential organizational commitments by various county agencies. These agencies were proving more skittish than their nominal superiors on the elected boards might have anticipated. Bolton and his associates also drafted a neighborhood self-governance plan, which would have created a joint powers authority under California law, with the contracting jurisdictions being Alameda County, the city of Oakland, the Oakland Housing Authority, and the Oakland Unified School District. In June 1993 an organizer was hired. CISFAN arranged a series of site visits for agency staff to Del Paso Heights and to two apparently model school-linked services programs in Southern California. A decision was then made to try to create a neighborhood-based family services center on the campus of Prescott Elementary School. Despite lukewarm assurances of cooperation, the school principal proved reluctant in the end to provide space either in the school or on the grounds.

CISFAN had some small successes organizing the residents of a nearby public housing project and helping the Prescott school and its parents to obtain a state Healthy Start grant. However, it failed to interest its foundation funders in supporting a move to establish itself as a federally recognized community development corporation, because one was already operating nearby.

In July 1995 Bolton wrote a letter to the center steering committee that declared the Prescott project "not successful" and in effect at an end. He diagnosed as the main reasons for failure that Alameda County did not fulfill its promises of three years earlier; that "aggressive leadership" from elected officials was not forthcoming; that the project organizers did not manage to give neighborhood residents "a big stake in the revitalization effort," such as jobs; that "we had no visible base in the neighborhood" nor enough connection "to any indigenous organization with a strong neighborhood base"; and that the organizers were "easily ignored or conned" by local actors playing sophisticated political games. "Oakland is a difficult place," he wrote.

Even though the CISFAN operation closed down in Prescott, as of June 1997 the Healthy Start activity had taken shape and had become a good focus for subsequent community development. A family life resource center is now located in the community, though not on the school grounds, and it is reinforcing the successful work of a federal Healthy Start project in the same community that the Alameda County Public Health Department had started in 1991. Observers think there may have been some slight carryover from the CISFAN efforts to those of the state Healthy Start, but probably not much.

Welfare to Work

Many welfare-to-work programs involve collaborative relationships among the local social services agency, adult schools, community colleges, state employment agencies, community-based training organizations, and substance abuse programs. An ideally functioning system to serve welfare-to-work clients would integrate services for a client at a single point in time and also over the course of the client's participation in the service delivery system.

The technology of moving welfare recipients into the labor force and then into jobs is moderately complicated. Recipients are quite heterogeneous. In the early 1990s, during the era of the federal–state JOBS programs, some 40 percent were short-term program users, down on their luck but reasonably able and willing to find and hold employment. Almost another 25 percent were relatively long-term users who faced physical or social or psychological barriers to work that could be considered insuperable.[51] Without immense luck, most of these would never be job-ready. The remaining recipients would have constituted the obvious target group in any reasonable system of triage. Almost but not quite job-ready, they would have presented various challenges to the JOBS program managers and line workers.

Program theorists were divided between two models. One, labor force attachment, held that the most important route to success for the almost-but-not-quite job-ready population was through teaching atti-

---

51. Gueron (1996). Gueron said "probably less than 25%" who "cannot work, or who could work only with special support" (p. 555).

tudes, behaviors, and skills that would encourage rapid entry into the labor force. The human capital model held that the best route was through the longer term process of attaining a bundle of marketable skills.

In 1991 and 1992 I worked on a study of how to improve agency productivity in the JOBS program for the Manpower Demonstration Research Corporation of New York City. I visited sites in California, Oregon, Oklahoma, and Michigan. The most interesting of these was in Riverside County, California. For this book, I revisited the two sites in Oregon and added a third. I also spent a week in Denver in 1994, learning about the Denver Family Opportunity (DFO) welfare-to-work program.

Riverside County (Medium)

The Riverside County, California, program was a relatively pure expression of the labor force–attachment model.[52] It was also a highly successful program in terms of getting clients into jobs and off the welfare rolls.[53] The prevailing slogan, directed at case managers as well as clients, was "any job is a good job," because a job would provide immediate income, socialization in the world of work, self-knowledge about one's skills and career preferences, and potential contacts to search for the next job. Moreover, it aimed to boost the self-esteem of JOBS participants (called Greater Avenues for Independence, or GAIN in California) and sent the strong message that the participants could—and should—expect a lot from themselves, not just in the way of job search but in terms of a broader human experience. The county welfare department director was the indefatigable, and some would say visionary, promoter of the program, which proved to be strikingly successful. Another important element in the success of the program was the transformation of the GAIN organization into a high-involvement organization (see chapter 4).

Riverside GAIN developed virtually no working relationship with the state's employment development department, which GAIN managers took to be wholly uninterested in serving welfare clients. It relied to some degree on Job Training Partnership Act (JTPA) organizations for

---

52. See Bardach (1993).
53. Riccio, Friedlander, and Freedman (1994).

training services and subsequent job placement, but a lot on its own in-house job developers, who were teamed with small groups of case managers (employment counselors). Most interesting were its relations with adult schools: The GAIN program negotiated careful contracts with these providers and paid them on a tightly calibrated performance basis—for example, $X for every tested grade-level improvement for each client.

I rated collaborative success medium in this case because the successful relations between the Department of Social Services and the schools are balanced by the weak relationships between the employment and training agencies and Social Services. However, the overall programmatic success of the Riverside GAIN program is a useful reminder that collaboration is only one road to producing value, and that other roads may sometimes be even more effective and efficient.

Oregon (High)

Early in the JOBS program, top management in the state Adult and Family Service (AFS) agency decided on an aggressive strategy of collaborating with three other large institutional players in Oregon: the community colleges, the JOBS Council, and the Employment Division. At the same time or not long thereafter, AFS top management also decided to devolve considerably more power and responsibility to its district-level offices, numbering about fifteen around the state, and to line staff.[54] One could profitably view the interagency collaborative effort and the intraagency reinvention effort as parallel, indeed complementary, strategies in the same war. Moreover, these were executed in tandem with the benchmarks campaign described previously. By 1995 the statewide system had turned into a relatively high performing operation. Even while the state legislature was chopping other agencies' budgets in the midst of a general fiscal crisis, brought on in part by a tax-limitation measure passed in 1990 and phased in over several years, it maintained the AFS budget. For fiscal year 1995 it did this in exchange for a promise to reduce the welfare caseload by more than enough to offset the expenditures. The AFS—and a growing state economy—delivered, decreasing the caseload by 9.4 percent for the fiscal year.

54. The exact number varied over time with consolidations and other such changes.

As in the integrated services program, the state welfare-to-work program operated through local collaboratives. There were fifteen service districts, and the collaborative in each one would deliver services under a contract with AFS that monitored performance fairly closely. At the local level relations among the various service providers in each collaborative were generally good, though there was great variation. At the low end—for example, in the Medford district in the early 1990s—relations were so poor that professional mediation services were sought.[55]

Denver Family Opportunity (Medium)

The Denver Family Opportunity Program (DFO) was a community-wide public–private partnership dedicated to improving the life prospects of families receiving benefits of aid to families with dependent children. Its centerpiece was client employability, employment, and eventual self-sufficiency, but it also attended to family needs for housing, mental health counseling, child care, health, and the like. I interpreted the dominant philosophy of the DFO as based on a version of the human capital model that included the capacity to fulfill child care and other needs as being nearly as important as strictly educational capital. It was started by then Denver mayor Federico Peña in 1988 as a sort of community forum that commissioned six advisory task forces on aspects of self-sufficiency programming; by 1994, when I spent a week interviewing, its managerial core was the DFO/JOBS unit in the Denver (County) Department of Social Services, which managed the cases of approximately 2,000 clients and maintained working relationships with about forty partners in the community. These partners ranged from public entities such as the Denver public schools to the Mile High Child Care Association to a nonprofit training group, Colorado Women's Employment and Education.

The DFO had a staff of four to six professionals, accountable to an executive committee drawn from representatives of the most actively involved sponsor agencies. A smaller steering committee of about fifteen persons, which included the professional staff, met every other month. Planning and outreach work was divided among six task forces covering areas such as youth services, health, employment and training, and housing. Chair of the council and the executive committee was the

---

55. See Bardach (1993).

president of the Community College of Denver, which was a major provider of education and training services to DFO clients. A client advisory board met monthly, with an average attendance of eight to ten persons.[56] About half the costs of staffing the partnership were contributed by the Colorado Trust, a local philanthropic organization. The rest came from government agency budgets.

Not all DFO partners subscribed to the dominant program philosophy. For a period, at least, the mayor's Office of Employment and Training (the JTPA agency of Denver) had rocky relations with the DFO when I visited in 1994, though they steadily improved. By mid-1997 Employment had established a one-stop career center, with some funding assistance from the DFO, and the DFO also ran in another location what was in effect a satellite unit of the career center. Between 1994 and 1997 the DFO also worked out access links for its clients with the Department of Labor job bank.

For whatever reasons, DFO clients did not leave welfare for work at a very high rate. In the three-month period of March to May 1994, the average caseload was about 1,400, and only seventy-three clients entered employment. One can assume that many of these would have entered employment even without the benefit of the JOBS program.[57] During this period the economy in Denver was strong and unemployment was just above 4 percent. Because even a very high performing welfare-to-work program such as Riverside GAIN has trouble adding more than 15 or 20 percent to the base rate of clients exiting welfare to employment on their own, it is unlikely that more than a dozen of these cases ought to have been credited to the exertions of the DFO/JOBS agency and the rest of the DFO partnership. Of course, there could have been many non–employment-related benefits produced by the DFO partnership. But by mid-1994 the DFO had done no internal evaluation of either its employment or its non–employment-related impact.

After federal welfare reform passed in mid-1996, Colorado devolved substantial administrative prerogative to the county level. Alone among Colorado's sixty-three counties, Denver City and County are coexten-

56. East (1993, p. 18).

57. It is interesting to note that, according to one case worker I interviewed in mid-1994, the DFO had become progressively *more* employment-oriented in the five years he had been with the program.

sive. Despite some uncertainty about what roles the city council and the mayor were entitled to assume under the new state welfare law, Mayor Wellington E. Webb appointed a welfare reform task force. Many of the DFO players shifted their energies to the task force, and DFO as an organization went into slow decline. By mid-1997 caseloads had fallen by 50 percent relative to 1993—a result in part of a very hot local economy and in part of a mix of still not understood factors—leaving a residual caseload of extremely hard-to-serve recipients. The DFO/ Social Services concern with housing and health issues for welfare clients took a backseat to acculturating welfare clients to basic expectations about the workplace and to various barriers to employability. The program still did not have in place what its managers regarded as an adequate evaluation system.

I would have rated DFO as a high-success case had it not taken so long to develop the internal capacity to evaluate its own performance and to realize that, in terms of its professed employability goals at least, it was not performing satisfactorily.

Antitobacco Education (Medium)

Health education professionals in public health departments see in the schools an opportunity to reach a large and very important target group: students. And school personnel see in health departments an opportunity to get resources and expertise for a variety of health education activities. This perception of complementarity may be strained, however, by the rather different theories held by health educators in schools and in health departments of how programs should be designed and delivered. (More details are provided in chapter 4.)

In 1988 California voters approved a ballot initiative increasing cigarette taxes by 25 cents a pack and earmarking 20 percent of the revenues for health education or for the prevention of tobacco use. Subsequent implementing legislation assigned programming responsibility jointly to the state Department of Education and the state Department of Health Services. These departments in turn made grants to county health departments based on population and, on an attendance-formula basis, to school districts. Local health department officials in turn often made grants to community-based organizations. By the fall of 1992 it was estimated that 565 paid employees were working on tobacco-related projects at the state, county, and community levels.[58] More than $100 million annually was being spent on the tobacco education prevention program.[59]

Although access to school sites was critical to health department staff fulfilling their mandate to carry out antitobacco education programming for children and youth, nothing in the governance or funding structure guaranteed health department officials access to school sites. Access had to be negotiated through the district and through individual principals and teachers.[60]

At the state level relations between the two lead agencies were generally poor. However, at the local level relations were often better. Balbach studied collaborative results and processes in eight counties. She rated them collaborative, as of 1993, if key staff "believed that they had a good working relationship with the other agency" and if they reported mounting jointly at least five of sixteen designated programming activities, at least three of which were "major activities requiring multiple contacts to plan and execute and often resulting in an on-going program." Three of the counties met this standard. The others she called cooperative, because although "there was not generally hostility between the offices," the respondents "did not believe they had a working relationship" and had done at most three of the sixteen activities.[61] In one county a collaborative pattern in 1991 had degraded to cooperative in 1993.

Preventing Fires (High)

A new type of fire hazard has come into existence in the last fifty to sixty years, the urban–wildland intermix. This is the blend of residences and dense vegetation that puts many lives and much valuable property associated with urban living patterns in the way of fires that spread in the fast-running manner associated with wildland zones. The intermix zone presents particularly difficult problems for firefighters. Although there are fire hydrants, water volume and water pressure are not reli-

58. Balbach (1994, p. 87). Unless otherwise indicated, all the information in this section is drawn from a doctoral dissertation by Edith DeWitt Balbach, which I chaired. I have also benefited from personal conversations with her.

59. Balbach (1994, p. 122).

60. Balbach (1994, p. 93).

61. Balbach (1994, p. 157).

able. Access to fire engines is restricted by steep, winding, narrow roads often constricted by cars parked on the shoulders. Backfires that could be used in the wildland zone are precluded because they endanger people and property. The same holds for aerial drops of drum-encased retardants. Human activity in the intermix zone increases the risks of ignition relative to what it would be in a wildland zone and, owing to inadequate safety precautions—for example, in the placement of power lines—relative to at least some of the risks in urban areas as well.

Because a rapidly spreading fire is no respecter of jurisdictions, this situation creates a new need (opportunity) for constructive cooperation among various public agencies and private parties, for example, in regard to response plans, incident management systems, training, and standardization of equipment. Once structures are in place, prevention is largely a matter of reducing the presence of fuels, particularly vegetation, both on private and on public lands.[62] Because one needs to surpass certain threshold levels before vegetation reduction does any good, coordinated efforts are needed in this domain as well. Furthermore, it makes sense to finance certain public activities cooperatively—for example, a weather-sensing station that serves all jurisdictions.

On October 20, 1991, a twenty-four-hour conflagration in the Oakland–Berkeley hills in California destroyed 3,469 residences and killed twenty-five people. Property damage was estimated at $1.7 billion. This was not the first such conflagration in the East Bay hills, however. A combination of low humidity, high temperature, and a strong Diablo wind sweeping in from the east and gusting down the leeward side of the coastal range caused fifteen very large fires between 1923 and 1991, although usually with less destruction of life and property. In the 1923 fire 584 buildings were burned, largely in North Berkeley.[63] In 1982 a blue ribbon committee constituted after another major fire in 1980 recommended a joint powers authority, a special assessment district, a fuel break along the East Bay hills, and special fire-hazard-mitigation zoning. Although the Parks District and other agencies implemented some of the recommendations on their own, none of the projects that depended on collaboration were implemented.

62. Replacing old wood roofs with less flammable materials is also of some importance.
63. Tidrick (1992). I rated success in this case as high because I counted the beginning of ICC development from 1991. I would have downgraded performance in the East Bay fire case two category levels had I decided to count its beginning from the fire of 1980 or earlier.

Nevertheless, in the 1991 fire interagency cooperation was universally regarded as inadequate. Only half the fire trucks that showed up had adapters to connect hoses to Oakland's nonstandard hydrants. At least one mutual aid engine company was not given an assignment for more than twenty-four hours after arrival, and many reported three- to nine-hour waits.[64] The Oakland Parks and Recreation Department had "thirty guys with chain saws who could fell trees and interrupt the tree canopy," said Tony Acosta, an assistant director, but these were not called into action. No overall incident command system was in place. At the Oakland–Berkeley border, Oakland police were forbidding Berkeley residents from retrieving belongings even though this was permitted under Berkeley policy. Less obvious than these response problems was an even worse failure of prevention: There had been no efforts to curb the fuel load on public and private properties.

In the aftermath, state legislators from the East Bay threatened to draft a bill requiring local governments to create a joint powers authority (JPA) that would somehow deal with the fire problem. A JPA has authority to enforce policy decisions and to collect financial contributions from the signatory agencies. Seeking what they took to be a less cumbersome, and possibly a more autonomy-protecting, arrangement, local fire chiefs constituted the Hills Emergency Forum (HEF), a six-partner interagency group dedicated to exploring avenues for cooperation in the face of these novel threats: the cities of Oakland and Berkeley, the East Bay Municipal Utility District (which managed thousands of acres of watershed land), the East Bay Regional Park District, the University of California at Berkeley (UCB), and the Berkeley Laboratory (a federal research facility operated by UCB). A disused interjurisdictional committee of fire chiefs was reinvigorated under the HEF aegis, as well as a Vegetation Management Consortium whose mission was to reduce the fuel load and apply other vegetation management practices. The HEF received a planning grant to hire staff and consultants from the Federal Emergency Management Agency.

By 1996 the HEF had adopted a widely praised fuel management plan and most of the participating agencies had endorsed it, even though formal adoption was delayed in some cases because of requirements for environmental review under the California Environmental Quality Act. The plan identified priority areas for work and described appropriate

64. California Governor's Office of Emergency Services. 1992. "The East Bay Hills Fire Report to Elihu Harris Mayor of Oakland and Loni Hancock Mayor of Berkeley."

management practices for each major vegetation type. It designated 3,900 acres as high fire hazard. A number of other collaborative actions had also taken place over the previous years. Partners had

—created an incident command system;

—introduced a program of controlled burns for training and fuel management purposes, accompanied by public education to accept the practice;

—adopted formal mutual aid agreements between the partners and also included some outside agencies as well—for example, the cities of El Cerrito and Richmond;

—with funds donated by the Park District built a remote automated weather system to determine the occurrence of local red flag (extreme) fire danger conditions;

—developed an extensive geographic information system database for simulating potential fire behavior in the East Bay;

—promoted local hazard abatement programs targeted at home owners;

—conducted various public education efforts.

The central and most difficult part of the whole interagency effort was leveraging resources for the vegetation management work. There were disparities between the partners. The Parks District and the Utility District had large budgets for such work already, although by some standards not large enough: according to retired Berkeley fire captain Rex Dietderich, only 50 to 100 acres of the 3,900 high-hazard acres in the East Bay Regional Park District had been adequately managed. Although it might be difficult to increase the number of acres judged to be properly managed to the level desired by the plan, at least the staff and the boards understood exactly how this fit in with their organizational missions. At the other extreme was UCB. In the early 1990s UCB was absorbing budget cuts and downsizing its faculty by encouraging early retirement. Its leaders were not eager to expand what looked like peripheral activities, at great expense, to the greater detriment of its core research and teaching functions. Moreover, some of the UCB-controlled vegetation management areas were also home to faculty and graduate student ecological research projects.

Vegetation, of course, is also habitat for wildlife. Environmentalists initially raised objections about what they feared might be severe habitat reductions, although eventually many environmentalists softened their criticism. These objections coincided with aesthetic concerns that vegetation management would denude the landscape and that fire breaks would leave enormous scars on the terrain. Home owners' desires to protect the rustic ambience that came with dense growth on their property or in their neighborhoods also weighed heavily with policymakers. A tendency to block out discomfiting thoughts about a perhaps distant future harm might have eroded support as well. In any case, the voters residing in the Oakland Fire Assessment District, which had been created just after the 1991 fire, voted by 55 to 45 percent to end their special $50 assessment. The city council of Berkeley was so sure that a comparable vote in Berkeley would lose that they did not even put the question to the voters.[65]

Regulation

In some policy domains, because regulated parties are overseen by two or more regulatory agencies, there is room for interagency collaboration on a number of counts: Reducing the transaction costs and delays in applying for permits by collocating permitting agencies or by assigning one agency authority to broker the process on behalf of the applicant ("one-stop shopping"); reducing the need for regulated parties to host a multiplicity of inspectors or submit duplicative reports by consolidating inspections at the regulated party's site of business; eliminating cross-program incompatibilities in regulatory requirements; increasing appropriate compliance pressure on regulated parties or tightening the net of criminal deterrence; through joint workshops educating regulators about how to do their jobs better; through teaming motivating regulators to higher quality performance; reducing enforcement costs by consolidating compliance functions or activities; and coordinating subsidy programs to help defray compliance costs with more pressure-oriented compliance programs.

65. In addition, the vote would have been linked with a referendum on a larger, $6 million, parks appropriation, which the council did not wish to jeopardize. The $50 annual assessment was not the only cost imposed by the municipalities on residents. Almost two-thirds of the funds were spent on residential inspection activities. Killing the assessments was also a way of killing the residential inspection staff that was telling homeowners to cut trees and remove shrubs. The average compliance costs (mostly one-time costs, however) were about $500. One public agency representative to the Vegetation Management Consortium observed that "the private landowners like to think the whole problem would go away if the public landowners would just do their jobs."

In many cases another sort of collaborative possibility attaches to regulation as well. This is the collaboration between regulatory agency and regulated party. The underlying potential for realizing joint gains differs by policy area. In the area of worker health a firm's managers have some interest in investing in illness prevention and exposure reduction if their employees know about the risks and value the risk reduction. Any regulatory agency that helped the employer do this and also reassured the workers that the firm was doing what it claimed to be doing would be welcomed by the firm provided it restricted its enforcement activities to tasks with these features. Within these limits (and perhaps broader ones if management was altruistically concerned with the well-being of the workers), the firm would also be inclined to be cooperative with the agency. In my terms they would have a small, limited-purpose ICC.

At the most potentially collaborative end of the regulatory spectrum we have contract management in all its aspects, especially in human services, from contract design to the auditing of contract compliance by the contracting agency. Though typically we expect some tensions in the contracting process over how much money is paid and received and for what precise purposes, we also expect the tension to be mitigated by the fact that both parties share a value-based interest in the contractor's high-quality performance.[66]

At the most oppositional end of the regulatory spectrum we have much environmental regulation. The regulated entity pays all the costs of compliance (except those that can be passed on to customers or workers), whereas the benefits of regulation are enjoyed by citizens at large. Except for encouraging the regulators to be more "reasonable"—no small matter in many cases!—the firm's and the regulator's (narrow) interests do not overlap sufficiently to provide for joint gains.[67] In such cases the two-entity ICC is likely to have limited purposes indeed.

The potential value of interagency collaboration may be greater in the environmental area than in other areas of social (noneconomic) regulation simply because there are so many different bases of specialization— that is, by medium (air, water, soil), by geographical locale, by type of

---

66. That I construe contract management for the present purposes as a form of "regulation" is admittedly unconventional.
67. Bardach and Kagan (1982).

hazard (toxic, nontoxic), by regulatory program or law (Superfund sites), by type of contaminant (lead paint), by type of site (industrial, residential); and by function (prevention, enforcement, permitting). Also, federal, state, and local regulators may independently regulate the same entities.[68]

New York State Contract Administration (High)

The New York State Office of the State Comptroller occupies its own thirty-plus-story building in Albany. As of November 1994, when I conducted a week of site interviews, its staff scrutinized every procurement contract and required the contract-administering agencies to superintend their contractors with a gimlet eye. It insisted on expenditure breakdowns into literally hundreds of statistical subobjects such as automobile tires and oil. It audited the agencies frequently and in an adversarial spirit. The Office of the Comptroller originates in the state constitution, and the comptroller is independently elected.

The burdens on contractors were substantial, particularly those with multiple state contracts. In 1990 there were more than 100 contractors in New York state drawing funds from five or more state contracts. The Door, a comprehensive youth services provider in lower Manhattan that in 1991 served some 6,000 adolescents, had seven contracts with three agencies for $1.4 million and filed eighty-four expenditure reports annually. When the state, in a demonstration program to streamline contract administration (described later), subsequently folded the seven contracts into a single master contract and reduced to four the number of expenditure reports, The Door was able to let go some three to five professional accountancy and bookkeeping staff.[69]

Rigid expenditure controls also impaired the contractor's ability to deliver high-quality programming. The Door's budget officer gave this example: If a mental health counselor funded by a counseling grant were to leave in the middle of the year, under the master contract The Door "could probably throw in . . . a milieu counselor or a sexual health counselor or even a teacher, somebody who is giving direct services to the client. [But] before that we would have to submit a modification request and go through a whole rigamarole. But we would not do that

68. See Fontaine (1993) and Scott and Barzelay (1993).
69. The Door was downsizing for other reasons too, so it is not certain exactly how much of the staff reduction is attributable to the change in contracting procedures.

because it takes too long and it is too much work, and if it is more than halfway through the contract year, then it may take three months before we hear from them [and the year is just about over]."

Running for reelection in 1990, Governor Mario Cuomo responded to the organized complaints of the nonprofit contracting community by promising to reduce such burdens. The task fell to the staff of the governor's Council on Children and Families (CCF), an entity created in 1977 by Governor Hugh Carey to help coordinate policy among the main child- and family-serving departments and to act as a source of innovative policy and program ideas.

A 1989 concept paper written by The Door staff proposed a multiyear master contract with the state that would "serve as a 'platform' guaranteeing support for The Door's operations and allowing it to enter into categorical contracts where it and a State agency see the need for specific funding for specific needs." The CCF staff considered platform funding politically infeasible, but they were eager to support the master contract concept.

Although the concept was simple, the details were not. One challenge was to write a set of performance specifications that would meet the minimal needs for control and accountability perceived by the participating agencies. They had to put something else in place of the detailed and input-oriented contracts, contracting not for a host of different provider agency actions and staff time but for a set of measureable results and some general complement of staff to deliver them. They had to alleviate the anxieties of the program agencies about giving up control and the anxieties of the overhead agencies that the shift could lead to abuse, corruption, or illegality. They also had to solve a managerial design problem: How would one actually administer the new process well—and which agency or system would do it?

After some fifteen months of discussions and negotiations with five or six program agencies (first fiscal and then programmatic staff) and with representatives of the comptroller's office and the Office of the State Attorney General, the master contract was completed. It took effect on January 1, 1992. The Office of Alcoholism and Substance Abuse Services (OASAS), the Division for Youth, and the Department of Health were the state participants. As lead agency, OASAS, which provided 55 percent of the funds to The Door, was to manage the relationship. This meant that OASAS was to handle all the paperwork, though much reduced, and was to be the sole conduit for communications on fiscal—but not programmatic—matters between the state and The Door.

The master contract had a single boilerplate suitable for all the agencies with provisions for multiyear contracting and simplified annual renewal. It placed greater emphasis on outcome measures. It created a uniform budget format combining categorical state funds into one funding stream, prescribed a coordinated audit approach, created a single definition of allowable costs, and set up a consolidated payment and reporting system. It also replaced the cumbersome and delay-ridden reimbursement system with a quarterly cash advance system, thereby greatly improving The Door's cash flow.

When I interviewed OASAS contract administrators and Door managers three years after the process had been in place, everyone expressed general satisfaction. The drive to manage by reference to measurable results was welcomed by all, except that some of the paperwork required by the old system still burdened line-staff under the new system, which imposed its own additional paperwork.

In November 1994 Republican George Pataki upset Democrat Mario Cuomo in the race for governor. This event disrupted CCF plans to extend the master contract concept to other sites. Although the CCF, a small and low-budget office in state government, survived the new governor's downsizing, budget cutting, and general house cleaning, it found it prudent to keep a lower profile. Gubernatorial support for its work could not always be counted on. The two principal staff in the office who had been working on the master contract effort, Susan Lepler and Rob Rosenkranz, left the office in May 1995 to set up their own consulting firm.[70]

Multimedia Enforcement (High)

Environmental regulation has traditionally been organized by medium, that is, soil, air, or water. Yet regulatory resources devoted to one such medium, particularly inspectors and information systems, might in many cases be advantageously deployed with respect to other media as well. Such multimedia enforcement efforts were among the

70. Their first assignment was with Monroe County, whose health department director was familiar with their work with The Door. The result was a master contract consolidating $3.5 million from nine funding streams for six programs.

collaborative possibilities envisioned when California, in 1990, placed five hitherto separate state environmental regulatory entities under one coordinating umbrella, the Environmental Protection Agency (Cal/EPA).[71] These were

— The Air Resources Board (ARB). The ARB directly regulates auto and truck pollution (mobile sources) and oversees, and provides technical assistance to, the state's thirty-four local air-quality management districts, which have direct responsibility for stationary sources. The ARB is headed by an eleven-member board appointed by the governor.

—The Water Resources Control Board. The state Water Board, created in 1967, deals with issues of water rights and water quality. Its water quality efforts are carried out through a discharge-permitting process that is largely devolved to nine regional water-quality control boards whose boundaries roughly correspond to watersheds. The regional boards are autonomous from one another and from the state water board.

—The Integrated Waste Management Board. The Waste Board was created in 1989 to promote waste reduction and recovery statewide and, more particularly, to reach waste diversion goals of 25 percent by 1995 and 50 percent by 2000. It also oversees the pollution abatement efforts of the local enforcement agencies that have primary responsibility for regulating landfills, transfer stations, and the like. The enforcement agencies are typically environmental health units of local government. Landfills present potential problems of litter, odors, combustible methane, air-quality degradation, and the leaching of contaminants into groundwater or streams.

—The Department of Toxic Substances Control (DTSC). Unlike the Waste Board, the Water Board, and the ARB, the DTSC is an agency accountable to a single director. The chain of command runs through the director of Cal/EPA to the governor. The DTSC deals with hazardous wastes under state and federal laws, particularly the federal Superfund (Comprehensive Environmental Response, Compensation and Liability Act,[72] or CERCLA), which governs closed or abandoned hazardous

71. Cal/EPA also included a sixth entity, the Office of Environmental Health Hazard and Assessment. This office is responsible only for providing scientific, technical, and public health expertise regarding the human health risks of chemicals in the environment. It does not promulgate or enforce regulations.

72. 42 U.S.C. §§ 9601–9615, 9631–9633, 9641, 9651–9657 (1980).

waste sites, the federal Resource Conservation and Recovery Act (RCRA),[73] which covers active sites, and their state-level counterparts.

—The Department of Pesticide Regulation. Pesticide regulation is primarily in the hands of county agricultural commissioners, though Pesticides exercises oversight and sometimes conducts its own enforcement actions. The department is also responsible for implementing the state Safe Drinking Water and Toxic Enforcement Act,[74] passed by a controversial ballot initiative in 1986. In the creation of Cal/EPA, Pesticides was removed from the Department of Food and Agriculture, where some critics thought it was too much under the control of agricultural interests.

Governor Pete Wilson, who early in his first term championed the creation of Cal/EPA, appointed as his first administrator of the new agency James Strock, then the assistant administrator for enforcement in the U.S. EPA and a person widely respected by environmentalists and businesspersons alike. Strock was willing to take a hard enforcement line against clear environmental violators. He saw no contradiction between being a friend of business in general and being an antagonist of particular businesses that, by flouting environmental laws, caused harm to public health and the environment. In 1992 he named as agency counsel and one of his key assistant secretaries Bill Carter, who was just concluding a seven-year stint as a deputy Los Angeles County district attorney and was a key member of the Los Angeles Toxic Waste Strike Force. During 1990–92 he had also been a special assistant U.S. attorney in the central district of California and a member of the state/federal environmental crimes task force. During his two years at Cal/EPA, Carter became the in-house champion of multimedia enforcement. He was admired, liked, and respected, and he inspired, coaxed, and cajoled resources out of the turf-protective agencies and boards that made up Cal/EPA. His extensive network of professional contacts in district attorneys' offices throughout the state added local enforcement resources to those he was able to shake loose from the state agencies. One result, according to his chosen (though not immediate) successor, Gerald Johnston, was "hundreds" of multimedia enforcement actions.

Within Cal/EPA Carter chaired an enforcement coordination group whose members included the chief counsel and lead enforcement per-

73. 42 U.S.C. §§ 6901–6991i (1982).
74. Health and Safety Code, sec. 25249 et seq.

sonnel of the constituent boards and departments. The group was also supposed to coordinate enforcement priorities, develop an integrated database, standardize enforcement and case referral protocols, and promote the cross-training of Cal/EPA enforcement personnel. A major objective of the cross-training was to increase the number of eyes and ears in the field. A pilot project was begun on landfills, which present a rich array of multimedia issues, under the leadership of the Integrated Waste Management Board.

One of Carter's legacies as multimedia enforcement champion was an annual four-day cross-media enforcement symposium to train 200 to 300 managers and line staff from the Cal/EPA agencies. Local environmental regulators and law enforcement officials also attended, along with a smattering of attendees from industry and from other states. Attendees were encouraged to think of enforcement and the threat of enforcement as valuable complements in the toolbox for increasing compliance and improving the environment. They learned how to recognize potential violations in program areas other than their own and to whom to report violations. They also learned to appreciate the value of good investigative techniques and documentation. I watched the videotapes of the 1994 symposium and attended the one in 1995. The symposium was organized by the ARB, whose training division enjoyed a national reputation. The attendees were clearly enthusiastic about the training. Exactly how much impact it had is another matter, however. The executive director of the ARB guessed that his agency received only ten to fifteen tips a year that resulted from the training. But he cautioned that one should see the training as only one step in a long process of creating an organizational culture that encourages thinking about environmental problems and solutions more multidimensionally and smoothes the way toward more cross-agency cooperation.

Carter left in mid-1994 for a position as assistant U.S. attorney in Los Angeles. During the following year, two individuals filled in on an interim basis. During this period, almost no new multimedia enforcement actions were initiated at the state level. In June 1995 Johnston was appointed on a more permanent basis. Johnston had spent the previous six years as a deputy district attorney for Orange County and head of the strike force aimed at criminal violators of the hazardous waste laws. Johnston revived and expanded the capacity for multimedia enforcement by promoting environmental enforcement task forces at the local level. Like Carter, Johnston was liked and respected professionally, and he was endowed with an extensive network of local allies. The local task forces were intended to take the initiative in finding and selecting cases and enforcing restrictions. Johnston cast the state in the role of junior partner to the locals, supplying funds, enforcement staffpower, technical assistance, and encouragement, but not taking the lead. In two years, thirty such task forces were up and running.

Although Cal/EPA had no data that could directly prove the efficacy of the multimedia and local task force approach, Johnston said in a May 1997 interview that the numbers of criminal and civil environmental enforcement cases being pursued in California were "way up—just over a hundred in the past year where the state got called in—[and] in the last eighteen months there has been a huge up-tick of coordinated enforcement cases," and that multimedia cases were three-fourths of the enforcement cases in which Cal/EPA was involved (as opposed to the case handled by constituent agencies and boards).[75]

Natural Resources and Ecosystems Management

Consider soil. It is a valuable resource for agriculture. It is a noxious raw material for constituting harbor-clogging silt and road-clogging landslides. It is a medium of transportation for fertilizer and pesticide residues on their way to polluting streams and bays. It is a habitat for flora and fauna that can invigorate (or injure) a terraqueous ecosystem. It is an incidental covering for land that in some cases is destined to be bulldozed for housing, roads, or shopping malls. In some areas it is also a source of dust particles that can impair human health and damage equipment.

Any action intended to manage soil may affect many natural and manmade systems. Furthermore, the array of actions that manage soil is varied—stabilizing, removing, cleansing, barricading, covering, to name just a few—and may take place many miles from where one desires to have an impact. The actions themselves are varied and are sometimes not even intended as actions that bear on soil management—for example, siting a housing development or logging a stand of trees. It is not

75. As indicated previously, I rated success in this case as high. Even though there was a delay of a year in multimedia enforcement between the end of Carter's tenure and the beginning of Johnston's, I did not count this against the performance of the ICC because progress under Carter and Johnston seemed sufficiently rapid that it offset the delay.

surprising, then, that many public agencies and private parties are potentially involved in managing any given acre of soil.

However, with some few obvious exceptions such as the Soil Conservation Service, renamed the Natural Resources Conservation Service (NRCS) in 1994, almost no agency whose actions bear on soil management is set up to give soil management as high a priority as some other task that it is given. Nor is the NRCS necessarily concerned with *all* the systems that are affected by its own soil management programs, inasmuch as it is focused on soil as a resource for agriculture and not soil as a medium for transporting fertilizer residues.

What is true of soil is true of other natural resources. Both complexity and constituency politics stand in the way of optimal management.

It is doubly difficult to manage resources with an eye to their interrelationships in an ecosystem or their joint contribution to the genetic biodiversity that ecological scientists so value. The multiplicity of necessary partners is daunting, and figuring out how to coordinate them operationally presents purely technical challenges more difficult than those that pertain to any other policy domain I discuss in this book. The currently dominant tool for motivating ecosystem management is the Endangered Species Act,[76] which manages simultaneously to be overly broad, with regard to the range of animal species, and overly narrow, being unconcerned with biodiversity as an objective. It is also too reliant on clumsy and heavy-handed regulation as its primary programmatic method. Almost no agency has as its primary mandate improvement of the ecosystem; and even if some small office buried in the EPA or the Fish and Wildlife Service or the National Oceanic and Atmospheric Agency takes ecosystem management as its special mission, it is often forced to rely for political protection on advocacy groups that have as many enemies as friends.

Elkhorn Slough (High)

The Elkhorn Slough is one of the most biologically productive estuaries in California. Its 44,000-acre watershed drains into the Monterey Bay just south of Santa Cruz. At least ten colleges and universities use the slough area for research. An area of great natural beauty, it also

76. P.L. No. 93-205, 87 Stat. 884 (1973).

attracts hikers and kayakers. It is partially contained in the Monterey Bay National Marine Sanctuary. Much of the slough's wetlands have been designated natural preserve and have been purchased by the Nature Conservancy and the California Department of Fish and Game. A privately funded Elkhorn Slough Foundation has been set up to encourage research and promote conservation.

About 25 percent of the acreage is devoted to agriculture, with strawberries by far the most dominant single crop (about 35 percent of the total).[77] In the short run the ecological health of the slough is threatened primarily by sediment and pesticides draining from adjacent farmland.[78] The rate of soil erosion is one of the highest in the United States, a result to some degree of the presence of slopes-based agriculture.[79] Strawberry fields alone contribute two-thirds of the total erosion.

The NRCS and other agencies have been trying to educate growers to adopt erosion control measures. However, despite the NRCS public estimates to the contrary and an NRCS program to subsidize private erosion prevention, further investment in erosion prevention would not have been financially beneficial to the average farmer under the subsidy terms offered in 1994.[80] Traversing a cultural gap has also proven difficult, particularly in regard to the Mexican population, who work 10 to 15 percent of the acreage. So even had there been no economic barriers, not many farmers would have been interested in adopting better erosion control measures. Of those interviewed, 60 to 70 percent said that, even if they had unlimited time and money, they would not manage erosion differently than they already did. Among the Mexican growers, 88 percent said they did not believe there were off-site impacts of erosion.

Nor have threat-oriented regulatory approaches been helpful. Because the sources of most erosion are diffuse and hard to monitor, the EPA and the Regional Water Board have been effectively impotent. The California Coastal Commission and the Monterey County Planning Department have jurisdiction over new agricultural enterprises but have no authority to control existing practices. The Monterey County Department of Public Works could have fined landowners who permitted erosion that caused traffic safety, road damage, or flooding problems. In practice they rarely did so, and in any case, erosion that caused

77. Belden and others (1994, p. 9).
78. In the long run erosion by tidal action also presents a threat.
79. Belden and others (1994, p. 6).
80. Belden and others (1994, pp. 32–33).

such effects was a small percentage of all the relevant erosion. Furthermore, Public Works itself has occasionally violated county ordinances by consolidating dirt in such a manner that the pile was subject to erosion. One county building inspector was assigned (part-time) to drive county roads, look for erosion, and warn or cite violators of a county erosion control ordinance. The inspector had an informal arrangement to refer most violators to the NRCS, which might then offer the violator the benefit of its education and subsidy programs.[81]

Since the early 1990s new sources of funds were being made available for erosion prevention from the EPA and the Water Board. "They're all trying to find someone to receive that money and implement projects," Daniel Mountjoy of the NRCS said when I interviewed him in April 1995, but the problems of coordination were much more evident than the solutions. "Everybody here wants to collaborate," he said. "There's no lack of desire to collaborate. I think we're all just searching for what's the best model for it. How can we do this, without feeling we're reinventing . . . spending all our days talking about it, and not doing it."

Since that time a general consensus has emerged among the concerned agencies that, compared to compliance-oriented regulation, focuses on education, financial incentives, and jointly planned capital investment projects as the preferred strategy. Mountjoy and his main ally, Lynn Dwyer of the foundation-supported Sustainable Conservation in San Francisco, hit on a strategy of helping farmers in the slough watershed undertake relatively small conservation projects of whatever kinds made sense to them given their needs. The help would come in the form of providing federal cost-sharing grants in the range of $2,000 to $10,000, customized consultation, and expediting the permitting process with the half dozen or so agencies that had regulatory responsibilities in the watershed: the Army Corps of Engineers, the regional Water Board, the U.S. Fish and Wildlife Service, the California Department of Fish and Game, the California Coastal Commission, and the county Planning Department.

The regulatory barriers were large. The permit fees alone could run $2,000 to $4,000, and it was easy for farmers to run afoul of inconsistent

81. This referral had to come in lieu of a citation, and not in tandem with one, because the federal subsidy was not available to lawbreakers. The building inspection office liked the warning–referral solution because, among other reasons, it minimized work for them. One constraint on the warning–referral solution was political opposition from some Anglo landowners who saw that it implied a leniency bias toward Mexicans.

requirements across agencies. Mountjoy and Dwyer approached each agency for the functional equivalent of a watershed-wide permit that would serve as an umbrella for each separate project. The NRCS, acting through Mountjoy, would get the right to pass on the individual project's acceptability under the umbrella permit. Dwyer undertook the legwork of negotiating the terms of each agency's umbrella permit. For the first funding cycle, ending in July 1997, the NRCS made $177,000 worth of cost-sharing agreements, and the umbrella permits were almost, but not quite, completed.

The intent of Mountjoy and Dwyer was to have this process in Elkhorn Slough serve as a model and inspiration for other watersheds. They profess great optimism that farmers and officials in nearby Salinas Valley, a large watershed, will be interested in replicating the Elkhorn model.

Memorandum of Understanding on Biodiversity (Medium)

In May 1991 a federal district court judge enjoined the U.S. Forest Service from holding timber sales in forest areas lying within the range of habitat of the northern spotted owl, an endangered species. The judge found that the Forest Service had violated the Endangered Species Act by not providing for the owl's habitat in Forest Service logging plans. Timber harvests on 23 million acres of Forest Service and 2.4 million acres of Bureau of Land Management land all but stopped in California, Oregon, and Washington for the next three years until a plan was provisionally accepted by the judge.[82] Logging and milling communities were devastated. Jobs disappeared, as did annual revenue-sharing funds that the Forest Service remitted to the counties. Communities that were normally the backbone of the Forest Service's political constituency were infuriated that their reliable patron and protector had let them down.

Other resource management agencies observed the humiliation of the Forest Service and shuddered. To some, particularly to Ed Hastey, the California state director of the Bureau of Land Management (BLM), the handwriting on the wall was particularly ominous. BLM acreage in

82. Thomas (1997a, pp. 283–85). Unless otherwise indicated, all the information in this section is drawn from a doctoral thesis by Craig Thomas (Thomas, 1997a). I was a member of the supervising committee. I have also benefited from personal conversations with Thomas.

California was geographically distributed in patchwork style. Any plan for endangered species habitat would almost certainly involve the BLM with many adjacent landowners, both private and public. It would be far easier to deal with other public land managers than with private landowners.

Hastey's concern for protecting the bureau's traditional multiple-use policies of land management dovetailed with the biodiversity concerns of environmental scientists and ecologically minded resource managers in the BLM and in a number of federal and state agencies. By 1991 this professional ecologist community had established a fairly strong communications network across the relevant agencies. In 1983 three federal regional offices and three state agencies had created an Interagency Natural Areas Coordinating Committee that committed them, in principle, to a "vaguely defined process" for identifying natural areas and recommending management alternatives.[83] The plan languished for six years but was given a new life in 1989 when a revised agreement was signed, this time with the forceful support of Hastey, almost alone among agency directors.

Also in 1989 the California state legislature directed the California Resources Agency to improve interagency coordination on wildlife and timberland management. This agency housed both the Department of Fish and Game and the Department of Forestry and Fire Protection. The agency convened the Timberland Task Force, composed of high-level representatives of five state agencies, four federal regional offices, and two private organizations. It was assisted by a technical committee. Progress was slow, however—too slow for Hastey, who successfully persuaded the task force chair to establish an ad hoc committee to the task force, which he hoped would come to grips with the problem of planning and managerial fragmentation in, at least initially, the key timberland province of concern to the BLM: the Klamath. This ad hoc committee brought together a wide range of professional ecologists and some ecologically minded resource managers from the several agencies.

The result of the ad hoc committee's efforts was a memorandum of understanding (MOU) on biodiversity signed in mid-1991 by ten state and federal agency directors; within the next year it was signed by another sixteen agencies. The signers "agree to make the maintenance and enhancement of biological diversity a preeminent goal in their

83. Thomas (1997a, p. 128).

protection and management policies. . . . The basic means of implementing the strategy are to be improved coordination, information exchange, conflict resolution, and collaboration among the signatory parties. . . . [The] tools may include the establishment of mitigation and development banks, planning and zoning authorities, land and reserve acquisition, incentives, alternative land management practices, restoration, and fees and regulation."[84]

The BLM conception of best practices in resources management entailed heavy reliance on the voluntary cooperation of local parties, private and public. Along with the Soil Conservation Service, BLM had been a heavy user of the coordinated resource management and planning process (CRMP, or "crimp") developed in the 1950s in Oregon and Nevada to resolve multijurisdiction problems on western rangelands. Hastey and others saw to it that the MOU on biodiversity, therefore, had a clear commitment to involving local interests in all aspects of planning and implementation.

As an exercise in interagency cooperation the memorandum subsequently proved to be a great success. In terms of promoting actual biodiversity, however, it has been a seeming failure, at least in the short run. Apart from pooling data—admittedly no small matter—very little collaboration on biodiversity planning or joint implementation has actually occurred as a result. The reason is simple: Politically, biodiversity has too many enemies and not enough friends. The commitment to localism packed the policymaking arena with county supervisors, most of whom had no use whatever for biodiversity, ecological thinking, or the Endangered Species Act. As it turned out, CRMPs were a misleading forerunner, inasmuch as the implementers of the system rarely asked local interests to forgo as much prospect of private wealth as the MOU on biodiversity would normally have implied. Also, not all the relevant agency directors believed their agencies were subject to possible lawsuits of the type that had undone the Forest Service and that clearly threatened the BLM. Moreover, even those who were more concerned, such as Hastey, were unable to convince their middle managers that biodiversity was itself desirable or that lawsuits were actually waiting in the wings.

In the longer run, the MOU may have a significant effect. It has raised awareness of biodiversity as a value, legitimated the use of eco-

---

84. Thomas (1997a, pp. 586–87).

logical rhetoric and analytical models, and given lower-level staff and managers a certain mandate, albeit an imprecise and contestable one, to use agency resources, within limits that must usually be strenuously negotiated, for the purposes of protecting biodiversity. Although many ecologists are disappointed in the results, it is probable that their community and their ideals are today in much better shape with the memorandum in place than they would have been otherwise.

Military Base Closure and Reuse

Since 1988 the Department of Defense (DOD) has closed approximately 130 military bases in the United States in four separate rounds.[85] Unlike earlier base closure efforts, the task of designating the bases was given to a special commission. The commission was to name its list for each round, and the Congress and the president would accept or reject the whole list. The intention was to minimize the veto points that local opponents of closure might be able to manipulate politically. These closures were also to be different in that each community affected by closure would be given a chance to create a Local Reuse Authority (LRA) that would plan for the reuse of the property and to purchase or lease the property for its own purposes. The military was to defer to local desires as expressed in the plan. The DOD Office of Economic Adjustment was to make grants to the LRA to help the members plan, and it would assign staff members to act as liaisons among the LRA, the military services, and the DOD. Congress hoped that these procedures would soften the impact on the local economies.

Many of the bases are severely contaminated. In the aggregate, the cost of environmental cleanup on closing bases could run into the tens of billions of dollars and last until 2010 or longer. Negotiations over how much cleanup is appropriate at any site and what remedies ought to be chosen are often difficult, but they are probably no more so than in

85. For a time during 1995–97 I was consulting to an MIT team studying base closure and local redevelopment under contract to the U.S. Economic Development Administration with additional contract management by the Office of Economic Adjustment of the Department of Defense. I conducted hundreds of interviews with actors playing many roles in the process and attended a large number of public or semipublic meetings. All my interpretations of the collaborative process are mine alone and do not necessarily reflect the views of the contract funders or the MIT team. My account of events and processes in the base closure and reuse case is intended to be valid only up until early 1997.

the private sector. The process is complicated greatly, however, by the fact that the money for the cleanup ultimately comes from the federal government and is therefore subject to the politics of the federal budget process.

I treat base economic redevelopment and base environmental cleanup as two separate cases within the overall base closure and reuse process. Each of these cases involves its own large constellation of different agencies and groups. Although the two constellations do overlap substantially, the collaborative processes in the redevelopment and the cleanup spheres differ in very interesting ways.

Base Redevelopment (Low)

Unlike the other cases described in this chapter, with regard to redevelopment the relationships among the military services and the local communities are almost entirely those of business partners. There is no question here—or there ought not to be—of professional or bureaucratic paternalism that looks after troubled children or biodiversity or residents of a high fire-hazard zone. The parties have interests and assuming that they are all equally informed about the objects of their negotiations, they are able to bargain with one another on the basis of those interests. In some respects their interests are at odds with one another. Much of the business they transact has to do with how much each party should pay the other, or put at risk, in exchange for what. However, as with most business transactions, by bargaining intelligently and structuring their deals creatively, the parties can emerge with both of them better off.[86] *Interagency collaboration* in this case means implicit and explicit efforts to enlarge the pie before dividing it.

As partners in enlarging the pie, the military services, though continually improving, have not done very well. Real estate disposal is not likely to be a high priority for a military organization whose *raison d'être* and self-image are sustained by winning or preventing wars. Nor, indeed, is the disposal process, when done correctly, as orderly as the military culture, with its overlay of bureaucratic culture, would favor. Done correctly, disposal is really a matter of satisfying the unsettled wants of diverse, and possibly conflicting, users. Using market-driven disposal procedures can simplify the process to some degree, but local

86. Or at least one can be made better off while not making the other less well off.

community interests, expressed in sometimes unpredictable political ways, always unsettle the process to some degree.

The process of transferring base property from military to civilian control is, to an outsider, quite complex. Tensions between the military department that owns the base and the LRA can arise over many issues—for instance, how (and whether) to bundle the base utilities into the more general transfer process; the use of leasing as an alternative to or a preliminary to conveyance by sale; the appropriate maintenance of base facilities during what can be a protracted transfer process; the determination of a final sale price; and the appropriate procedures for resolving differences over the sale price.

LRA advocates have generally found much to complain about in the whole process. However, the current shortcomings are only a fraction of what they would have been had a great many people over the past ten years not invested in adjusting the framework legislation, White House priorities, DOD policy and procedures, and the mode of communication among the partners, all in order to speed economic redevelopment and to create the conditions for better collaboration. The highlight of the adjustment process was President Bill Clinton's five-point plan announced in 1993, which implicitly gave the highest priority to community economic development relative to maximizing property sales revenues to the federal treasury. The following year Congress created the Economic Development Conveyance, a vehicle for conveying base property to the LRA at less than fair-market value, provided the LRA intended to use the property to promote local economic redevelopment.

It is a long way from presidential pronouncements and laws written in statute books to effective implementation on the ground by complex hierarchical institutions and the humans who work in them. Acknowledging the difficulty of generalizing about such matters across several civilian units of the DOD, three quite different military branches, hundreds of varied district and regional personnel, hundreds of base-level officials, thousands of environmental regulatory officials and community environmental advocates, and many thousands of individuals acting on behalf of the LRAs, most observers agree that, although the capacity of the partners in the base closure and reuse for constructive collaboration has steadily improved over the past ten years, it falls far short of where it ought to be and that the process has been very slow.

To take one example, negotiations over final sales prices can take up to two years. Officially, the procedures that govern them do not, in most cases, cast them as negotiations at all—much less real estate deal making, which would put the most collaborative spin on the process—but as a process in which the LRA submits an application for a conveyance that is then reviewed for acceptability by the owning service. In some cases the service has denied the application without making a counterproposal or explaining how the next application could be significantly improved.

Environmental Cleanup (High)

Given the conflictual nature of environmental cleanup issues, the chief goal of interagency collaborative capacity building should be improved communications among the parties to the conflict. Even though LRAs, environmental regulators at the state and federal level, and environmental advocates have not always agreed among themselves or with DOD policy on cleanup standards in general or on the resolution of site-specific issues, the capacity of the parties to communicate clearly and efficiently has evolved to a remarkable degree.[87]

COMMUNICATIONS AT THE LOCAL LEVEL. Relationships among the cleanup partners at the local level vary widely. Some are relatively frictionless and use everyone's talents for finding value-enhancing solutions to cleanup problems. Others feature distrust (occasionally outright betrayal), delay, and value-diminishing solutions. The main issues typically are these:

—How should the cleanup sites on a base be prioritized so that they fit the priorities required for reuse? The military service has an incentive to group sites to achieve economies of scale in cleanup, whereas the LRA would prefer sites higher in reuse potential.

—What should be the level of cleanup at a site? Local land use plans to some extent determine the cleanup standard selected for a site: A planned wildlife refuge does not require as much—as costly—cleanup as a site where residential use is planned. Industrial use falls in between.

---

87. Once again, I remind the reader of the ambiguities inherent in choosing a baseline against which to measure success, discussed previously.

—What cleanup remedies should be selected? At the site level, if institutional controls, such as deed restrictions, are in place, will future problems, caused either by land use changes or by any other process, undermine their effectiveness?

President Clinton's five-point plan also called for fast-track environmental cleanup, which created base cleanup teams (BCTs) that included state and federal environmental regulators along with a base environmental coordinator (BEC) designated by the military department. The general opinion among my informants was that, although the BCTs and the BEC had not made the cleanup track any faster, they had considerably improved communications and hence the ability of the various parties to work cooperatively.

COMMUNICATIONS ABOVE THE BASE LEVEL. Collaboration issues exist above the site level too. State and federal regulators are often present on the same sites enforcing laws that are partially redundant: Superfund and Resource Recovery and Conservation Act. National policy-level issues are complex and involve a large number of participants, including the Environmental Protection Agency, the LRAs, state attorneys general, environmental advocacy groups, cleanup contractors, various units within the DOD, and the military departments. The most important are the following:

—How should the cleanups at the several bases be prioritized so that they fit the priorities for community reuse activities? To integrate the cleanup process and the reuse process on the entire national chessboard of bases and sites requires resolving certain policy questions—such as what would constitute equitable treatment of the competing community claimants—and also designing a system to obtain reliable information about the status of reuse activities at the various bases.

—If all the cleanup is done in the present, the federal government pays. If future land use changes to a use requiring a higher level of cleanup, however, the federal government might not pay—*will not* pay, if current DOD policy holds—a policy the LRAs are protesting.

—At the national level, what should be the budget for reuse-related cleanup in any given year and over a longer term? Predictability of funding over the long term helps ensure that communities with low-priority claims today can have reasonable assurance that their reuse needs will be met in a known, albeit elongated, time frame. The federal government some ten years ago committed itself to a very ambitious cleanup goal, but as the true—enormous—costs of this goal have come more clearly into focus, there has been backpedaling, with the LRAs feeling somewhat betrayed and uncertain.

In distinct contrast to the economic development side of the base reuse process, the partners on the cleanup side have been engaged in a constructive dialogue over all these and other matters of policy and implementation. One of the most visible and collaborative aspects of that process has been the work of the Federal Facilities Environmental Restoration Dialogue Committee. Its origins go back to the first half of 1989, when ten governors and forty-nine attorneys general, along with many other policymakers and concerned citizens, urged that the U.S. Department of Energy establish a system for setting priorities for conducting environmental cleanup. A professional facilitator organization, the Keystone Group, was hired to organize and convene the interested participants, and the first meeting of what came to be called the Dialogue Group occurred in June 1991. A second was held in October 1991, and an interim report was published in February 1993. During regional briefings, concerns were raised that local government and the environmental justice community had not been adequately included. The group was expanded on two occasions to meet these concerns, the total reaching fifty persons by January 1995. A final report was issued in April 1996. It conceptualized a scheme for prioritizing cleanup objectives, and it asserted the principle of full disclosure for any budget-building shortfall that would preclude achieving near-term cleanup milestones or undercut previously negotiated schedules.[88]

The DOD also maintains a continuing advisory committee, the Defense Environmental Remediation Task Force, that has dealt with a number of issues, the most important being the question of appropriate future liability for the DOD if land use were to change and contamination standards were to become more demanding.

88. The dialogue group went so far as to propose that "the regulated agency should prepare and make publicly available in a timely manner supplemental reports that will accompany the cleanup budgets that the agency submits from the facility level through the successive levels of its organizational structure (if they exist) up to its headquarters, and from its headquarters to" the Office of Management and Budget, Federal Facilities Environmental Restoration Dialogue Committee (1996, p. 92).

The DOD also participates actively in environmental cleanup discussions and related activities in excellent forums for discussion and for the oversight of work groups outside those of its own creation—for example, the California Military Environmental Coordinating Committee. Good lines of communication exist between the office of Sherri Goodman, the deputy undersecretary for environmental security, and the U.S. EPA. These also extend to environmental advocacy networks, such as the Pacific Studies Center, a private nonprofit organization that maintains a running dialogue on the Internet in which DOD personnel occasionally participate along with community-based advocates, representatives of the offices of state attorneys general, the U.S. EPA and its regional offices, and so on. It is an indication of the openness of the office of the deputy undersecretary of defense for environmental security that a well-known leader of the environmental activist community, Lenny Siegel, acknowledged them as accessible and trustworthy (and sometimes even "our friends"), even though he said he often disagrees with their policies.

Other forums and networks exist through which local and state representatives debate environmental cleanup policy ideas and exchange war stories, technical information, and political advice—for example, the National Association of Attorneys General, the International City and County Management Association, the Association of State and Territorial Waste Management Officials, and the National Association of Installation Developers. In all cases, federal policymakers are also plugged into these. Besides future land use, the most important issues that have been raised in all such forums and networks have concerned early transfers; institutional controls; and the problem of handling unexploded ordinance.

Summary

My top priorities in collecting empirical materials were to help me develop and refine the concepts of craftsmanship theory as they would apply to the building of interagency collaborative capacity. These priorities had implications for the way I selected cases and conducted interviews. In many respects these methods were unconventional, but they were arguably much better suited to the objectives than more conventional methods.

I provided brief introductions to nineteen cases of ICC development that I studied firsthand and that furnish the preponderance of examples of smart practices, opportunities, and craft problems that appear in the next five chapters. I also rated the degree of success of these nineteen ICCs, despite technical and conceptual limitations. I rated three as low, seven as medium, and nine as high. The relatively large proportion of high ratings occurs because my method of case selection prescribed looking in sites where I had reason to believe collaboration was going well.

4

The Operating System

Most ICCs at some point in their development create and manage an operating system—the system that transforms physical or symbolic material into something different and, presumably, more highly valued. For most of the ICCs discussed in this book, this material is some sort of case that needs to be managed somehow. In the human services programs, the cases are generally individuals, sometimes families or neighborhoods, who are supposed to be helped to move from one status to another. In environmental enforcement the cases are typically regulated firms, their property, and their equipment that need to be kept in, or brought into, compliance. In base reuse and fire prevention the cases are properties. All these characterizations, admittedly incomplete, are of course vast simplifications and fuzzy at the edges, but the fuzziness permits us to fill in specific details that vary with context.

I take the essence of the collaborative case management process to be communicating in a certain way about the management of the case—intelligently, responsibly, professionally, creatively, practically—and to be making optimal use of the diverse talents, authority, and material resources that the partners bring to the process. With this subject matter in mind, I focus the discussion in this chapter on five design challenges for the operating system of an ICC that is to be capable of high-quality performance:

—supporting the flexibility of thought and action required to deal with novel or unanticipated opportunities and problems,

—motivating lower-level staff,

—increasing mutual intelligibility and trust across agency-professional roles and boundaries,

—maintaining accountability and making it serve the broader aims of high-quality thought and action,

—exploiting financial exchanges among partner agencies as an opportunity to induce high-quality performance.

I limit the focus to issues that are generic to ICCs across policy domains. Hence I do not deal with admittedly vexing but domain-specific problems such as those that confidentiality requirements pose for the design of accountability systems in the integration of services to children and families.

Flexibility

An ICC confronts more novelty and variety than the governmental organizations that contribute to it. Why should this be so? First, it is created explicitly in order to look at social problems through different lenses and to look at a broader menu of solutions than have been attempted by the existing set of organizations. Second, it has to deal with not just a broader menu of solutions but also a more complicated one in that the involvement of other organizations almost always guarantees new constraints, which the ICC will have to learn to overcome. Third, its first efforts are bound to be full of mistakes. It must operate in a trial-and-error mode. Hence it is its own source of novelty and variety. Fourth, although an ICC is not by definition new—in principle, an ICC can become just as institutionalized and venerable as a veteran governmental organization—I happen to be concerned, for the purposes of this book, primarily with ICCs in their start-up period.

An ICC should be designed to operate in ways that are appropriate to this relatively unusual task environment. This means, first, instilling the spirit of teamwork into the line-level workers who manage the ICC cases and into the participants in the interpersonal implementation network.[1] Second, it means, whenever possible, loosening controls such as narrow categorical restrictions on budgeted expenditures and on agency-level reprogramming authority. Third, it means giving an unusual degree of flexibility to the line-level staff and to the implementing network. Balbach surveyed staff in eight counties implementing the California tobacco education program and received fairly consistent answers: "The administrative level can hurt a program but

1. For a definition, see chapter 2.

cannot get positive action going. The staff level . . . 'the worker bees,' need to take responsibility for forging the working-level links."[2]

In safety and environmental regulatory programs, the needed flexibility must come from looking at the programs not mainly as instruments of coercion in a righteous cause but as implements that must be deployed intelligently and self-consciously in order to solve problems. This means learning how to focus on the problems rather than on the compliance and review apparatus that typically comes to dominate regulatory programs. A remarkable experiment in the air force suggests the value of such a shift. A process called *variable oversight*, intended to reduce multiparty reviews, delays, and excessive paperwork in base environmental cleanup, was developed and tested at Langley Air Force Base in Virginia. It substitutes brief memorandums and tables, more frequent and less formal communication, and more focused problem-solving efforts for the cumbersome and legalistic procedures in conventional use. Program managers calculated that variable oversight could reduce the process from twenty-seven to sixteen steps (documents) and reduce review on four of the sixteen remaining documents. Cost savings to the air force could be 15 percent, and the EPA could save as much as 40 percent.[3]

Devolution and Empowerment

None of this necessarily implies that lower-level flexibility is needed. However, it is unlikely that centralized and hierarchical management, especially of the sort usually seen in the public sector, will be able to do the job very well. In addition, line workers need to have the freedom to organize themselves into teams.

By *team* I mean a set of individuals (1) whose agencies' contributions are thought to be mutually complementary in their productive capacities and (2) whose individual characteristics—including such matters as their knowledge and skills, their access to resources and to status within their home agencies, their aspirations and beliefs, their personal strengths and weaknesses—are taken into account by those, including the team members themselves, who organize their respective activities.

---

2. Balbach (1994, p. 173).
3. Versar (1995, p. 8-5). The Versar Report does not offer any estimate of the reductions in delay in months or years.

Examples are a Cal/EPA strike force targeting a major polluter violating many laws at once in several overlapping jurisdictions and a team in a welfare-to-work program consisting of a case manager, a job developer, an eligibility worker, and a secretary–receptionist who work on clients in the case manager's caseload (though not necessarily exclusively on these).[4] In ICCs we probably see more teams at the field-worker level than at the middle management or higher levels.

The degree of formality and self-consciousness in a team varies. At one extreme a team appears on an organization chart; at the other it is simply an aggregation of individuals from different agencies that habitually engage in teamwork to do their jobs well.

SELF-MANAGING TEAMS. At the line level, operatives from the collaborating organization need to work out ways of taking advantage of one another's expertise, access to their home agencies' resources, and whatever else it is about the collaborative that stimulated the emergence of the ICC in the first place. The more they can do this for themselves, the more likely they are to come up with good solutions.

There is probably no ideal internal organization of such a team. Self-management is touted in the literature on teams in the business sector, and it will often make sense in the public sector as well. In Oregon, for instance, I interviewed participants in a welfare-to-work team of some six

4. My definition says nothing about how well the members actually work together or feel bound to do so. I prefer to leave such matters to empirical study rather than to definition. But Jon R. Katzenbach and Douglas K. Smith, in *The Wisdom of Teams*, define a team as a "small number of people with complementary skills who are equally committed to a common purpose, goals, and working approach for which they hold themselves mutually accountable" (1993, p. 92, emphasis deleted). A *real team* lies near one end of a continuum anchored at the other end by a *working group*, whose members interact "primarily to share information, best practices, or perspectives and to make decisions to help each individual perform within his or her area of responsibility" (p. 91). In between lie the *pseudo team* and the *potential team*, both of which, like the working group, do not aspire as much as a real team to improve the group impact on organizational performance. (Beyond the real team is the *high performance team*, which is like a real team and then some: Its members "are also deeply committed to one another's personal growth and success" [p. 92, emphasis deleted].) For the purposes of my discussion I make only the weakest assumptions about the degree of commitment in team members, commonality of purpose, and level of mutual accountability. True, some minimum of all these must exist before it makes sense to speak of a team at all. But, as we shall see, in the public sector there are many political and bureaucratic barriers to frontline workers or middle managers from different agencies working as a real team. Much of my discussion in this chapter concerns the problems of getting teamlike productivity out of the team participants despite these barriers.

to ten persons drawn from four different agencies who collectively decided on the frequency of their meetings (once every week or two), their location, duration, and, of course, their agenda. But a self-managing team may still require centralized internal coordination and therefore some degree of hierarchy—principles I heard emphasized by individuals who worked on interagency teams making site-level environmental inspection visits. In the context of a regulatory action there is an obvious logic to speaking with one voice to the representative of the regulated entity, who is, correspondingly, aiming to speak with one voice to the site visitors. This logic applies to interagency fiscal and program audit teams as well, such as the one sent to evaluate The Door.

As the regulatory example suggests, the substantive nature of the team's work will have some bearing on how a team manages its internal division of labor, its membership, the permeability of its boundaries, its mix of skills, the expectations imposed on its members, and the like. As teams work together, moreover, they learn from experience. In the case of The Door, the funding agencies conducting the site visit had prepared a single evaluation instrument that coordinated their work on site, consolidated their overlapping concerns into a single set of questions, and made sure that their separate and special concerns were all acceptably represented in the instrument. The work of the team on site was thus greatly facilitated by the instrument that had been created for their use—by a team of instrument designers partially made up of some of those who were on the site visit—well before the site-visit team was obliged to assemble at The Door and do its work. The team's efforts were also facilitated by the advance preparation made by staff of The Door, not just filling out forms and assembling data but also meeting to take stock of their agency's objectives, strategies, and performance. The site visit actually took less time and produced more in the way of mutual understanding than could have been anticipated.

Who ought to be the team convener, facilitator, or coordinator? Many attributes are relevant, ranging from the representative of the most important agency in the collaborative (the person from the Office of Alcoholism and Substance Abuse Services in the case of The Door) to the person with the most obvious seniority or experience or the most skill at suppressing troublemakers. The ability to stimulate group effort and improve the quality of interpersonal work dynamics is also important. Raising someone to be first among equals or even a bit higher can be a reward for past effort, an inducement to future effort, and a model for other team members. Local environmental enforcement actions "are built around people with a commitment to making it work," according to Gerald Johnston of the Cal/EPA. "For the most part these are people who give out their home phones, who are willing to get calls at two in the morning. You have to have somebody there who is an inspirer." Who such people are, he said, emerges from the group process. "Some people just sit back . . . [But] you almost always have one personality that emerges as a leader. Because it's a lot of work to make these things happen, every one else is happy to let that person do it."

When a frontline worker with a collaborative assignment is out-stationed to some identifiable site, he or she will typically be involved in a *matrix accountability system*, reporting to a home agency supervisor and also having some sort of responsibility to whoever plays a leadership role on the site. This means that the site leader and each of the several agency supervisors and middle managers who are responsible for the various team members themselves become, in effect, a team, albeit a loose one. I learned very little about how such supervisory-level teams function. I heard few complaints about them, but my impression is that the supervisors rarely talked with one another about the work of their respective line workers.

IMPLEMENTING NETWORKS. Allowing working relationships among frontline workers to evolve in accordance with the natural logic of the task is not ordinarily threatening to the host organizations, at least not so long as the frontline workers act in rough conformity with the procedures and priorities of their home agencies. But at the level of the implementing network, those individuals who oversee the deployment of staff, space, funds, and so on, the stakes for the home agencies go up. The implementing network could make embarrassing mistakes. It could spend too much money, commit the wrong staff, permit troublesome precedents, make overly ambitious promises. The home agencies will almost certainly want to keep more control over the middle-management implementing network within the ICC than over its field-level teams. This will be especially true when the home agency directors are uncertain about the degree to which they want to commit their organizations to support the ICC. The need for flexibility and the fear of flexibility are mixed in nearly equal proportions.

One solution is for the implementing network to maintain a low profile, to act informally, quietly, unself-consciously. This solution permits conflict or failure in any portion of the network to be isolated and resolved without jeopardizing the functionality or the political standing of the rest of the network. Chisholm's study of Bay Area transit organizations found that coordinating networks of this type were able to work out assistance relationships during emergencies, locations of bus stops, signage, and routing. Bay Area Rapid Transit managers were even able to pick up an informal mediation role when two other transit systems fell to fighting over the use of bus pads at one of BART's stations.[5]

Another solution is for the implementing network to build credibility slowly but steadily, by succeeding at tasks that are within the acknowledged scope of its authority, flagging their successes and getting credit for them, and thereby earning an incremental expansion of their authority. The middle-manager implementing network of the welfare-to-work collaborative in Medford, Oregon, came into its own when the agencies' senior managers fell to bitter and seemingly irreconcilable quarreling. Emboldened by the fact that they could hardly do worse than their superiors, they began by solving the easy problems, such as stabilizing and publishing a schedule of community college life skills classes and inducing the college to consolidate JOBS-related programming responsibilities in a single individual. They also induced the Adult and Family Services (AFS) district manager to accept this concept, which she had resisted on the grounds that a community college coordinator might jeopardize AFS caseworker accountability for, and control over, the client. By virtue of these and other such small successes, their legitimation by outsiders as the operations group, and also their self-conscious management of intragroup dynamics, the group created an atmosphere of mutual trust and a conception of group identity.[6]

To Control and Protect

However valued flexibility might be by those trying to make an interagency collaborative work well, flexibility gets no boost from our governmental institutions. Indeed, these enshrine all the opposing virtues of specificity, stability, predictability, and accountability.[7] These

---

5. Chisholm (1989, pp. 105–06).
6. For more detail on the events, see Bardach (1993, chap. 3).
7. Altshuler (1997, p. 39).

virtues then come to mask the less commendable goals of protecting special interests.

The problem begins with the public's reasonable demand for efficient controls against waste, fraud, and abuse. These reasonable demands are transformed into unreasonable demands when it is revealed that the controls have prevented less than 100 percent of such waste—as all genuinely efficient controls must inevitably do. Demand then grows for more stringent, though in an overall sense less efficient, controls to eliminate the last remnants of waste, fraud, and abuse. This occurs in part for the sake of community symbolism. Antigovernment sentiment, always latent within some large proportion of the public and eager for a cover to carry on its own campaign, feeds the demands.

Flexibility has no ally in interest group politics either, which leads to the creation of agencies, the appointment of agency personnel, and the construction of narrowly targeted expenditure categories that protect a variety of special interests, ranging from sugar beet growers to plumbers to psychiatrists to residents of Mineola and Missoula. Some of these special interests are both worthy and in need of protection from forces that could readily undercut them in the implementation process. However, the worthy and the unworthy alike are harmed by the fragmented policy thinking and the administrative rigidities of the protectionist system.

Intragovernmental rivalry further strengthens the system, because the legislative branch feels that it is one of those weak but worthy interests. It needs protection from the executive branch, or so it feels. Because it reasons that the executive will be able to gain an advantage by manipulating the procedures and personnel of the agencies, it retaliates by amplifying its traditional authority over budgets and expenditure categories and by intensifying its oversight of how funds are spent.

The protectionist system of budget categories is one of the most severe limits on the possible scope of interagency collaboration.[8] It is what helped create the fragmentation that now motivates ICC development efforts, and it is also what blocks those efforts from succeeding. Whether those efforts are always bound to be successful is, of course, very much in question. To the great surprise of many observers, the regulatory barriers to entry in freight transportation, air passenger service,

8. Chuck Alston, "Call to Fuse Federal Programs Greeted Skeptically on Hill." *Congressional Quarterly*, March 2, 1991, pp. 540–44.

and telecommunications have crumbled in the past twenty years. Of course, legislative bodies' institutional stakes in regulation are generally not as high as they are in budget categories and expenditures.

A string of control agencies, such as personnel, budget and finance, audit, procurement, and contract compliance exist to implement procedures aimed at waste, fraud, and abuse and to guard the protectionist systems that the public and the legislature have put in place. Interagency collaborative work often brings the partner program agencies into the path of these control agencies, for these agencies must often approve contracts, new job descriptions involving unconventional interagency activity, and budget expenditures on unconventional or unplanned objectives. If these agencies were always reasonable and public spirited, their involvement would present no special difficulties. However, they are no more immune to the diseases of bureaucracy than any of the program agencies whose activities they oversee. Their objectives become too narrow, their concern for turf too pressing, their methods too rigidified, their accessibility to reasoned argument too attenuated. Before collaboration can move ahead, therefore, the control agencies must somehow be dealt with. They must be educated, domesticated, or reinvented. None of these approaches is certain, easy, or quick.

One smart practice is to export program management functions from public sector to private sector organizations, thereby removing these functions to some degree from the purview of the control agencies. The original champion and long-time director of School-Based programming argues on the basis of experience that nonprofit organizations are generally better as the local managers of such programming than school districts. The exportation strategy is not always possible, of course, and even when it is, the local managers always have to deal with the control agencies to some extent.

If the essence of reinvention is to shift an agency's orientation from inputs and procedures to results and a solicitude for customers, the control agencies present an unusual problem. If results are defined narrowly as preventing waste, fraud, and abuse, then it is often the case that they can achieve these only by making their customers—that is, the program agencies with whom they deal—unhappy, assuming that the customers are interested in performance. Reinventing a control agency then becomes a matter of redefining the agency's objective—as cost-effective program agency performance perhaps, rather than simply preventing waste, fraud, and abuse—or finding artful ways to satisfy agency performance objectives without harming the anti-waste objective. That this in fact can be done has been demonstrated in Minnesota and well documented by Michael Barzelay in *Breaking through Bureaucracy.*[9]

Less grand than reinvention is the case-by-case adjustment of control agency practices in a way that leaves their fundamental spirit unaltered, or even enhances it somewhat, but better satisfies the program agencies at the same time. A good example of this is the invention of the master contract in New York State. Such a strategy is greatly assisted if it is possible for managers in the program agencies to develop informal relationships with sympathetic allies who are well-placed within the control agencies. State JOBS managers in Oregon told me they had received valuable help designing a system for choosing district-level prime contractors to manage the JOBS program from a creative person in the attorney general's office.

Because the excesses of control agencies are to some extent the product of political forces, political forces can sometimes be mobilized to counter them. Given the prominence of legislatures in the push for excessive control, elected chief executives and their political appointees are the most obvious candidates to push back. They too can claim the mandate of "the people"—the mandate in this case to have government produce results and not just red tape. In Oregon this claim can be backed by pointing to the benchmarks program and everything it represents. In the case of the Oregon Human Resources efforts to promote the collocation aspect of services integration, it also helped that the Human Resources agencies owned many of their own physical facilities and furnishings. The Human Resources director, Kevin Concannon, was able to push not just the program managers of the several departments toward services integration but the departments' property overseers as well. He created an interagency facilities council and gave each agency a mandate that any new leases, acquisitions, and renovations should "consider the needs of other agencies and of community partners," and he assigned one of his staff to hold the council member accountable for results. One informant told me that, after all this, getting the agencies to cooperate "was not hard."

9. Barzelay (1992).

Buying Flexibility

Up to a point, flexibility is for sale. School districts, principals, social service agencies, and community-based organizations could all be brought into collaborative arrangements by the $6 million that the state of New Jersey put up for School-Based Youth Services. This was new money, money not taken from someone else's budget and leaving resentments in its wake. Nor was it old money being used in new ways, ways that would have to be justified to skeptical auditors or budget analysts.

Paying for a whole new collaborative program is an expensive way to buy flexibility, however. Retargeting existing funds with just a bit of new money may be almost as effective. Foundations, which are often the source of such new money, like to think of these as catalytic funds. The Marin Community Foundation gave CYSC a budget of $100,000 a year to spend filling in gaps in a client's service package that were left after the public agencies had finished rummaging in their own cupboards. A consortium of foundations backed Arthur Bolton and his CISFAN staff to act as catalysts for public sector agencies. Cal/EPA planned to donate four circuit prosecutors to serve environmental enforcement task forces in some six to eight rural counties. Gerald Johnston got the idea when the Lake County district attorney told him that, although they could assemble a lot of other staff power for the task force, they did not have the prosecutorial staff to fill out the complement of needed expertise. Johnston's hope was that a three-year grant from Cal/EPA would enable the local task forces to get up and running and to develop enough momentum so that after the grant funds ran out they would be willing to find money from local sources.

As a smart practice, catalytic funding aims to exploit a powerful opportunity. I believe it is often difficult to execute, however. Recipients may fail to deliver what the donors, and perhaps even the recipients themselves, anticipated delivering. This may have occurred with regard to the Prescott project for instance, when Alameda County agency heads did not fulfill their promises to relocate services in the neighborhood. It is also vulnerable to strategies by fund recipients who may try to substitute the donor's contributions for their own, a standard problem in the design of all grant-in-aid funding mechanisms. One way of protecting against this vulnerability is to supply resources in kind rather than in cash, as the Cal/EPA offer of circuit-riding prosecutors does. However, it takes a fair amount of honest discussion and careful planning for both donor and donee to hit on in-kind contributions that will act as effective catalysts.

Motivating Lower-Level Staff

Flattening hierarchy and loosening overhead controls in the name of increasing flexibility is also consistent with motivating staff effort to achieve higher quality results. In this latter context the term in common use is job enrichment. It is a central element in what Edward E. Lawler III calls a "high-involvement organization."[10]

Job enrichment is a well-documented way to improve the motivation, performance, and satisfaction of relatively skilled and internally motivated workers in private business, and there is every reason to think it would also work with the kind of professional or semiprofessional line workers and middle managers of special concern in this book. These sorts of individuals are motivated by having meaningful work, autonomy to do the job the way they feel is best, and feedback on their performance.[11] If work is "enriched"—that is, designed to be motivating in these ways—quality improves. Lawler, one of the most astute and prolific contemporary students of organizational behavior, wrote,

> When individuals are responsible for the work they perform, that is, when they psychologically own it, they seem to be more motivated to turn out a high quality product. . . . Quality may also be improved because employees have a broader perspective on the work process and as a result can catch errors and make corrections that might have gone undetected in a more traditional work design. . . . And because they have autonomy to make ongoing improvements, employees can also fine tune and make adjustments in the work process as they become increasingly knowledgeable about how their work can best be done. . . . Furthermore, employees who have a history of learning to work autonomously and creatively are better able to take on new tasks, meet new challenges.[12]

10. Lawler (1992, chap. 3).
11. Lawler (1992, pp. 81–82).
12. Lawler (1992, pp. 85–87). See also Appelbaum and Batt (1994, pp. 137–39).

Lawler noted that working in teams can often enrich the job experience and as a result, quality. Specialists can join forces to create a sense that the team has responsibility for a whole job. For individuals who enjoy the social interaction, teamwork can add a valued dimension to work life. It can also provide a chance to learn from the ideas and expertise of others.[13]

Besides enriching the job experience, teamwork can also lead to quality improvements per se. The cross-training of employees enables them to help each other. This can sometimes eliminate the need for supervision and support. Moreover, when groups are cohesive, peer pressure improves quality.

Valued social rewards, such as praise from other members of the group and acceptance by the group, depend on satisfactory individual performance. Similarly punishments are sometimes administered when individuals do not perform well. Groups may be more effective at giving rewards and punishments than are supervisors. Often the reaction from peers is more critical to employees than the reaction from bosses, but perhaps more important, often peers are constantly present and able to give continuous reinforcement while bosses are not always present."[14]

All this applies clearly in the ICC context to line staff. Managing a case in its entirety, and in cooperation with trusted peers, is what a meaningful work experience would normally entail. This would be true whether the case involved a troubled family, a polluting facility, an endangered species habitat, or a vegetation management area. Although not every line worker relishes a "meaningful work experience," many do; and many more come to relish it once they have had the experience. Harm Wilkinson, a welfare-eligibility and welfare-to-work staff member at the Del Paso Heights Neighborhood Services Agency is representative of many line workers:

A lot of us have had to really gear back from our [community] involvement recently. Our other work was beginning to suffer. . . .

---

13. Lawler (1992, pp. 89, 95–96). Empowerment is hard on the supervisory level (Walton and Schlesinger, 1979). But this is a transitional problem for organizations.

14. Lawler (1992, pp. 98–99). See the fuller discussion of peer accountability on pp. 144–46.

This job creates a continuous paper trail, and there is never enough time to keep up. . . . At the time I came over here, I didn't know that it was more work. It seemed like, you get a reduced case load and, being . . . honest, that was attractive. . . . [But] your own personal level of involvement is what really gets you in trouble. You don't know how much enjoyment and how much satisfaction you're going to get out of it. And when that starts happening, it's easy to start to get more and more involved. . . .[15]

At the level of the implementing network, the causal connections between job enrichment and quality and between teamwork and quality would still hold, and it is easy to see how the implementing task lends itself to creating a team spirit. It is harder, though, to see how the implementation task fills the bill as an "enriched" job unless the upper management in the collaborating agencies makes the implementing network feel responsible for the success of the various cases and teams that in effect it services.[16] The Medford JOBS implementing network is almost certainly the exception that proves the rule. In most settings, its level of esprit would not be likely. Why not? Those drafted for coordinating work would normally be responsible for a variety of coordinating functions in their home agencies besides those being dealt with by the ICC. In these more usual cases, the special handling required by ICC functions would disrupt their more encompassing routines—for example, if they oversaw field inspections in their agency that were normally organized geographically but had to allocate staff to the ICC line teams based on nongeographic principles, or special data files had to be created that could be jointly accessed by staff from one's partner agencies. Unless top management creates, or allows to develop, the special conditions that would make interagency implementation work job-enriching, middle managers are likely to view ICC functions simply as adding to their headaches and their overall workload. It is perhaps for this reason more than any other that middle managers are often thought to be more likely to resist interagency collaboration than are line workers and top executives.[17]

15. For further support from Del Paso Heights staff, see Minnicucci Associates (1995, p. 32).
16. Galbraith reported—some twenty-five years ago, to be sure—that participation in interagency projects ranked last among twenty tasks rated by managers (Galbraith, 1973, p. 54).
17. Allio (1993, p. 20); Thomas (1997a, pp. 346–56).

Job enrichment at the line level does not just happen. In fact, given that a shift to interagency teamwork is like many other types of organizational change, which may be especially difficult in the public sector, it may be hard to get the new tasks performed at all. Change on this order requires the intelligent effort of many individuals up and down the agency hierarchy. Such effort is not always forthcoming. I discuss outright resistance in the next chapter. I mention here only those deficiencies of effort that arise from more innocent causes, such as lack of foresight and poor communication skills across organizational levels. Innocent or not, however, such deficiencies can leave line workers without needed material supplies, without the taste for autonomy or the interpersonal skills needed for effective teamwork, without the certain mandate they require before they will exercise their discretion, and without a clear and effective channel of communications that permits them to pursue needed remedies.

It is somewhat telling that the Del Paso Heights Neighborhood Services Agency (NSA), which had the nominal support of the president of the board of supervisors, the county executive, and the director of the Human Assistance Department, first had an overworked and poor site coordinator and then for seven months no site coordinator at all. Throughout the first two and a half years the site coordinator reported through a bureau chief to a division chief who reported to a deputy director of Human Assistance.[18] Partly as a result of the NSA's organizational as well as physical isolation, in the first few years case information among managers was not adequately shared, morale was erratic, productivity was poor, and project evaluation was nonexistent.

This was a somewhat extreme set of complaints. Much more common was the complaint that collaboration increased paperwork and reporting responsibilities for line workers. In the case of the master contract with The Door, for instance, paperwork decreased for the top-level staff at The Door but, in the first few years at least, increased for the line workers. The paperwork problem was relatively severe at the Coordinated Youth Services Council and was said to have been partly responsible for line-worker burnout. The most ubiquitous complaint for outstationed workers was that fellow workers back in the home office and sometimes supervisors thought they were loafing. All occupations and professions differentiate "real work" from everything else. Real

---

18. Minnicucci Associates (1995, pp. 42–43).

work in government bureaucracies seems to occur while seated at one's desk. Being at a meeting elsewhere in the building may be almost as real. Being out in the field is a poor excuse for work altogether.[19]

It almost certainly helps a lot if interagency collaboration, self-managing teams at the front line, and job enrichment are all part of a larger strategy of bureaucratic reform. A successful example is the Oregon Adult and Family Services agency. The AFS was transforming itself vertically—flattening itself—at the same time as it was making itself more porous horizontally, that is, more open to relationships across the boundaries dividing it from other agencies. Its director, Steve Minnich, cut the size of the top executive team from fourteen to seven, recruited four of the seven from the private sector, consolidated three middle-management levels in the field into two, held lots of retreats with large numbers of staff, brought in trainers and organizational development consultants,[20] created high-performance work team demonstrations in two large counties, decentralized the budget preparation process, began to experiment with a way to let districts keep some of the welfare savings for their own programming, and made operations managers at the local level into integral members of the case management teams.

Mutual Intelligibility and Trust

Giving line-worker teams discretion and flexibility does not ensure that they will function productively. The individual members must be able and willing to work together effectively. This means helping them to overcome the training and socialization in the agency-professional roles they have hitherto occupied.

By an agency-professional I mean a person (1) whose work entails some serious risk to society if it is not performed well; (2) who, because he or she cannot be monitored effectively by those who bear the consequences of his or her actions, must act with a sense of fiduciary responsibility; (3) who uses specialized technical tools for doing his or her work; and (4) who is employed by an agency that partially (but not completely) monitors his or her performance.

Under this definition many frontline workers in government agencies are to some degree agency-professionals. Sometimes society recog-

19. Sims (1986, p. 29).
20. I received mixed reviews about the number and variety of trainers and consultants.

nizes them as such—physicians, planners, engineers, lawyers—because they are traditional professionals. In other cases, frontline workers function as traditional professionals even though they are not accorded the status. Many field enforcement officials fall into this latter category—for example, those responsible for air pollution compliance or for enforcing the building code. Typically they must have some measure of both technical and legal knowledge and must be able to relate to the complying party with a calculated blend of legal pressure, partial forbearance, and technical assistance. Some service agency personnel—job developers for employment programs, contracts managers for social service agencies that contract out a lot of their work to nonprofits—also fall into this category.

Collaborative Challenges

Working relationships at all levels are improved by staff from collaborating agencies getting to understand one anothers' agency-professional worldviews. The process takes time and experience.[21] This is often not easy. Differences in perspective cause them to focus on different aspects of a problem and to rely on different intervention strategies. Differences of linguistic usage, often unremarked at first, can grow, for a time at least, into a lethal source of misunderstanding and frustration. There may also be differences in regard to social values. At bottom, the problems of mutual unintelligibility, misunderstanding, misperception, and mistrust are wound together in one knot, the strands of which, though often distinguishable and even capable of being disentangled, are mutually reinforcing. Here is a sample of how they manifest themselves.

—A social worker in Maryland who worked with multiproblem families said, "The substance abuse [counselor] feels that if people relapse into drugs sometimes, that can be okay. But if you are concerned about children, well you just can't allow that."

—Public health nursing and child welfare agencies regard home visits and aggressive outreach to families as good professional practice. Substance abuse staff regard such practices as "coddling," because their idea of good practice is to induce the client to "make the statement that they have a problem and step forward for treatment."[22]

21. Radin and others (1996, p. 161).
22. Minnicucci Associates (1995, p. 40).

—A social worker and community organizer in Oregon noted the conflict among line-worker team members about how much of a "rescuer" to be in working with families. Working with teachers, there was distrust over their commitment to confidentiality: "We've had to educate teachers not to chat in the lunch room."

—An Oregon community college counselor working with the JOBS program recalled the early days of collaboration in her office among herself, adult and family services case workers, and Job Training Partnership Act (JTPA) staff when they used to fight over whether to call people "participants" or "students" or "clients." Eventually they brought in an outside facilitator. They had "an ugly meeting, a whole bucketload of people, a wild meeting over something really stupid. . . . [The facilitator] did this diagram on the blackboard and said 'You're all three saying the same thing, these three factions.' And I don't think we had a clue as to what was going on. . . . 'Stop and hear,' [the facilitator said]."

—The same staff group had heated disagreements over the meaning of "job ready" and therefore over whom it was, or was not, appropriate to refer for JTPA services. In the end the JTPA agency relaxed some of its restrictions and everyone agreed that the appropriate standard for referral ought to be "job-search ready."

—The public health community based its approach to antitobacco education on the National Cancer Institute environmental model of tobacco use and cessation, which targeted various channels and environments such as vending machines, public-space smoking restrictions, advertisements, and work sites. The education model, by contrast, focused on individual children and the risk factors in their lives that made them vulnerable not only to the use of tobacco but of other drugs as well and, indeed, to engaging in all manner of risky behaviors.

Such problems can degrade ICC performance. Line-level staff with incompatible views of agency professionalism will find ways to avoid making the called-for referrals or accepting the proffered advice on how to manage a case. Communications will slow down and become less candid. At best, such problems will consume lots of time and energy as staff members from different agencies struggle to make themselves understood across large gaps in meaning and belief. Those who operate implementing networks will put out less effort to coordinate schedules, create mutually useable information systems, assign high-performing personnel to ICC functions, and so on.

The nature and scope of the communications problem varies considerably by policy domain. The more technical the nature of the task—that is, based on predictable cause-effect relationships and free of contested value issues—the more constricted is the likely scope of trouble. The resource managers and fire fighting professionals who served on the vegetation management consortium were focused on removing potential fuel from the environment in which wildfires might start and spread. The language for characterizing their collective problem and describing their options was relatively precise and mutually intelligible. Their ideas about how to resolve disputes among themselves were relatively congruent—that is, appeals to evidence and science. Although in practice they were often hampered by technical uncertainties, they were not hampered by ambiguities in what they were talking about. This situation stood in contrast to that among the human services professionals.

I characterized each of my nineteen cases described in chapter 3 as high, medium, or low with respect to what I judged to be the relative technical clarity of the tasks. I took account of financial and administrative issues also in making this assessment and for this reason considered the problems of the Maryland Systems Reform Initiative murkier than those of Oregon Integrated Services, for instance. The results are shown in table 4-1. Although, of course, the number of cases is small and the quality of measurement on both the independent and the dependent variable, degree of success, is extremely crude, a weak positive relationship is evident.

Miscommunications may be better than no communications, however. At least the former contain the seeds of their potential remediation. Despite the facts that the military-civilian partnership regarding the economic development side of base reuse was troubled regarding a host of issues and that it probably would have been possible to create simple forums to air these issues and find useful cooperative solutions, the military did not offer to help create such forums, and the civilians were too disorganized, confused, or intimidated to make their own proposals. I attended one meeting between army personnel and representatives of perhaps twenty LRAs in which the LRA representatives fumed and stormed over various problems in their own communities and the army

Table 4-1. *Technical Clarity Helps* ·

Technical clarity of tasks	ICC success level[a]		
	High	*Medium*	*Low*
High	Fire prevention New York contract administration Multimedia environ- mental enforcement Base cleanup New Jersey School- Based Youth Services	Healthy Start	Base redevelopment
Medium	Oregon Integrated Services Oregon welfare	Denver Family Opportunity Antitobacco education Riverside GAIN	
Low	Elkhorn Slough Maryland Systems Reform Initiative	Del Paso Heights Tennessee Children's Plan Memorandum of understanding on biodiversity	Marin County Coordinated Youth Services Council Prescott Project

a. See chapter 3.

spokespersons, though attentive and courteous, responded with little more than "check" and "so noted."

Some Smart Practices

All in all, there are good reasons for ICC promoters to want to try to solve problems of mutual unintelligibility and potential mistrust. What might qualify as smart practices for doing so?

USING DISAGREEMENT TO IMPROVE DIALOGUE. If the objectives are clear and the task relatively technical, then sharp differences in perspective could even be *helpful* to the team's work, provided the participants learn how to make good use of dialogue.[23] Environmental enforcement task forces, made up of prosecuting attorneys, regulators, and investigators, often do this. Knowing the prosecutors, according to Gerald Johnston of the Cal/EPA multimedia enforcement project, the regulators are less likely to withhold information from "those aggressive jerks in the DA's office," and the prosecutors will be able to explain that "there is an ethical duty for them not to take cases you don't think you can prevail on." Moreover, because the prosecutors' resources are limited, they will encourage regulators to settle by the administrative route if possible. "I have a lot of faith that the more review these cases get by entities with different perspectives, the better [the] decisions [that] will be made."

LETTING HUMAN NATURE TAKE OVER. Human nature inclines people toward reciprocity and toward liking and trusting the people with whom they have to work on a routine basis.[24] Furthermore, over time they will discover their areas of agreement and find ways to work within them—probably enlarging them as trust and understanding grow over time, nurtured by successful experiences. Johnston observed,

> Initially, when you have task forces starting, you have everybody staring at one another thinking, "I'm not sure why I'm here." For a task force to mature into an entity that really can deal with environmental problems, it takes a couple of years. . . . The key component is cross-education. Other agencies can't help you until they understand your mission and your jurisdiction. That takes quite a while. You have to make lots of presentations and have people interested in learning.

Success in this mutual education endeavor explains why line workers, even from agencies whose top managers routinely mistrust the competency and motives of their partner agencies, can manage to trust one another when their bosses cannot. Katherine Armstrong, who worked closely with services integration teams in Contra Costa County, California, said, "That's why I push for these *teams* of people who are at a scale of face-to-face-ness, where you can have a conversation over a

23. Brett (1991); Kelman (1992).
24. The classic study in support of this proposition is Festinger and Carlsmith (1959).

period of time, and people can kind of gravitate to a happy medium—not so much [around] the department assignment as [around] their talents, what they uniquely are strong at. Then they come together around the family, around those things, which . . . [otherwise would have been seen] as, 'Oh, this is my department's responsibility.'"[25]

What does it take to make this strategy of gravitating to a happy medium work? In general, staff turnover needs to be minimized, unless turnover occurs in the service of replacing people who cannot function well in a team setting with those who can, and top managers (and program evaluators) must learn to see early failures as inevitable stages of a developmental process. Also, it might help to put staff in a situation that both forces and allows them to rise to the challenge. In the Upper Rogue Family Center in Oregon the staff was out-stationed at some physical distance from their agencies' home offices, supervision on site was loose, and they were given a broad mandate to invent something effective. It was not easy at first. People were reticent and cautious. But the dynamics of the situation eventually took over. A line worker from the employment department gave this account:

> We're very fortunate. We've got a real good mix of people. We haven't had a lot of confrontation, if any. . . . [But] people said, 'Okay, well, we're the mental health element, that's what we do, don't try to mess with us.' And then we had CSD. CSD said, 'we deal with children.' And then we had the manager who said, 'Okay, we're the Employment Department, we've got rules and regulations, and this is the way we do things.' [But] somewhere down the line there was a catalyst that kind of overlapped these agencies and brought them together, so that a lot of people, a lot of managers in there said, 'Okay, if we have to work with it, we'll give it a whirl. Sounds like a good idea.' And then that way, common sense and being idealistic kind of reigned supreme, I guess. And we didn't have to hold onto our manuals as our bibles and say, 'Oh, can't do that, says right here in this manual.'

25. Mutual liking helps, but mutual professional regard may often be enough to compensate for difficulties at the personal level. One informant also told about the public health nurse who disliked others on the service integration team and was disliked by them. But the nurse loved the work and did not want to leave the team, and the other team members did not want her to leave.

INCREASING SELF-AWARENESS. Self-awareness is cheap and can go a long way, especially in such simple forms as denying one's self the luxury and pleasure of using bureaucratic jargon without bothering to try to educate others who are not likely to understand it. A bit more costly strategy involves going out of one's way to try to learn the professional and bureaucratic language and worldview of one's counterparts.

More costly still—to some people, though perhaps not to others—is a strategy of forcing people to confront their stereotypes and so, with luck, to rise above them. On two occasions I have heard Felicia Marcus, the Region IX director of the EPA, tell of her difficulties in getting other agency representatives to get beyond their stereotype of the EPA as a deaf, stubborn, unreasonable agency. Marcus was a Chinese history major in college with some Chinese language training under her belt, but when visiting China she discovered that of two native speakers listening to her talk, one would understand perfectly well and the other would not. She was advised by an American friend who had lived for several years in China that she too had suffered this not uncommon problem. "Some people," she explained, "see a white face and simply do not believe that the person behind it is speaking Chinese." The solution? "Stand directly in front of them, look them in the eye, and say 'I am now speaking Chinese.'" Applied to her own situation, Marcus said she had adopted the practice, in difficult situations, of saying, "I am from the EPA, but I am now being reasonable."

DISCOVERING A COMMON IDENTITY. Group members that have jointly and creatively solved a challenging collective problem feel more bonded to one another, and to the group, as a result.[26] Discovering interpersonal affinities, and in them the raw material for a group identity, is just such a challenge. Diverse agency representatives to the Vegetation Management Consortium (East Bay hills fire prevention case) came to recognize that "We are all . . . [reading] from the same basic book, just maybe different chapters—'resource management'—and vegetation management is just a sub-piece of this . . . we all care about the land . . . that is a shared value, public use of the land," according to Tony Acosta of the Oakland Parks and Recreation Department. Acosta

26. Diehl and Stroebe (1996); Hogg (1992).

continued, "When we started meeting, we found that we were a lot more alike than we had thought. [We all worked in bureaucracies, and] there is only one type of bureaucratic behavior. We all have nonexpert political boards and constituents to keep happy while we are providing our core responsibilities. . . . We are all customer-service oriented. . . . [And] you have to be able to deal with single individuals with passionate points of view."

COLLOCATION. From the point of view of service users and clients dealing with multiple agencies or service providers, agency collocation is an opportunity to reduce costs in travel time and money. Collocation might also make life easier for the providers and improve the quality of service. Many collocated field workers enthused that it also creates a medium for communication and trust building among the agencies' staff. More precisely, though, it is a potential medium, because the use of it is not automatic. One observer said of the several agency staff who had collocated welfare-to-work services at a community college facility: "They were all practically on the same hallway. But their doors were closed. And they might as well have been at opposite ends of the city for all they talked to each other."

Of course, whether collocation qualifies as a smart practice in any particular situation depends on whether its advantages outweigh the financial costs of moving and the less tangible costs of disrupting and reconstituting organizational routines.

TRAINING. Although some ICC participants and observers consider training a smart practice in my sense of producing a lot of value on the cheap by exploiting some latent opportunity, I turned up many dissenters. A great deal depends on the nature of the objectives, on how training is done, and on the effectiveness of low-cost alternatives such as allowing teams to learn informally on the job.

At the operational level, cross-agency training takes advantage of what appears to be the underused capacity in a worker from agency A to perform tasks hitherto done only by workers in agency B. Training A in this case is almost the equivalent of acquiring a new worker for agency B—for example, joint training for firefighters from both Berkeley and Oakland expanding each department's capacity for handling very large fires. The value of such an investment clearly depends on how often the A staff will actually perform those tasks. I have already mentioned this possible limitation in describing the multimedia environmental enforcement symposia in chapter 3.

Another sort of technical training involves activities that neither agency A nor agency B had previously undertaken (much) but that they might jointly undertake in the future—for example, assisting families by means of the "family unity" model. In this sort of training, the intention is not merely to provide the tools that will make collaboration effective but to encourage collaboration by providing a new and—the trainers hope—inspiring tool. Several day-long interagency trainings in the conceptual underpinnings of managing resources to preserve biodiversity, organized by the Bureau of Land Management and by the California Biodiversity Council, fit this model.[27] In this case the value of training may depend greatly on whether it can indeed provide the inspiration the trainers desire.

This model can also be applied as an organizational development tool *within* an organization, say to educate staff across hierarchical levels. The Delaware Department of Services for Children, Youth, and their Families trained frontline workers in a holistic, family-systems-oriented approach to help families and then continued the training with these workers functioning as agents of change and management as the targets of change.[28] In the Linn–Benton JOBS district, AFS and Employment Department staff outstationed at the community college held "A Day in the Life" trainings for their co-workers and managers back in the home offices to encourage them to refer individuals to their program. They even invited observers from outside the district to show off their program. In addition to the organization-wide and the wider political benefits, said one of the enthusiastic organizers, "it was great for our own team-building."

Because the hoped-for effects are intangible—inspiration about new ideas, team building—documentation of effectiveness is rare, and the willingness of government to support such efforts is often slight. The standard protraining view is expressed by Ed Cole, who had managed the integration of two agencies in Tennessee into a single Environment and Conservation Department. When I interviewed him in 1996, he was helping to create the new Children's Department. He claimed that the biggest mistake in the integration process had been the failure to prepare the managers psychologically and cognitively:

27. Thomas (1997a, pp. 256–57).
28. Cohen and Ooms (1993, p. v).

We needed help thinking in functional terms . . . we had people that agreed with the vision, people that were excited by the vision, and those very same people fought this organization. Somewhere there I think we could have minimized conflict. But you get into the meeting with your managers and you're trying to say, "How are we going to consolidate organizations?" or "How do we do this better?" And the capability to deal with those kinds of questions is just not there.

He also expressed the widespread view that government is usually short-sighted about investing in training:

A new organization comes into new being, what's the first thing the governor says? "No net new positions, and no additional expenses. We don't bring new organizations into being to raise new expenses and add new people. It's the other way around. I expect to see probably position reductions and I certainly expect to see dollars go down. We're going to be more efficient." So, immediately, the tools to make this happen are denied us. . . . It's just my experience in two of these, one complete and one in the middle of it.

Training might also be a cost-effective means to improve the personal (and interpersonal) skills that interagency team members typically use in managing their work and themselves.[29] The commercial marketplace offers an unending variety of trainers who give workshops of varying duration and intensity in such "process" matters, and many managers I interviewed had participated in them and sent their employees to participate. Suffice it to say that although most such workshops were judged worthwhile, my informants warned that many such offerings proved disappointing. There was particular skepticism about "feel-good, get-to-know-you" retreats and the like. The manager of the Contra Costa County service integration program conjectured that staff demand—and not just upper-management reasoning—should drive the schedule and content of trainings, and that training would therefore

29. See, for instance, Ancona and Caldwell (1992) on the importance of diversity in cross-functional teams, but the difficulties of making them work well. Training may be a partial solution (pp. 162–63).

be best conceived as an intermittent stream of relatively focused prob-lem-solving workshops over the long period of ICC development.

Katherine Armstrong, who was a popular and reputedly effective trainer of integrated services staff in Contra Costa and elsewhere, sug-gests the difficulty of knowing what really works in training: "I did a lot of the training for the teams when we first started. I really thought I was profoundly effective. And after three meetings with the teams in operation, I realized that nothing I said was heard, recognized, or in any way thought to be relevant. It was as if nothing I'd said had had any effect. So I had to give that up, just because I saw so profoundly the lack of appreciation—there was not even a repeating back to me of the words. It was as if they were not even said. . . . Nevertheless, I was eval-uated as being very entertaining and inspiring!"[30]

Turnover undoes training. Formal training is vulnerable to orga-nizational turnover, as is the sort of training that simply comes from on-the-job experience. Turnover is probably a worse problem for ICCs than in other organizations for simple arithmetic reasons. An organizational role—thinking of the ICC as an organization, that is—played by a team of two persons has twice as great a chance, on aver-age, of losing one of its key elements as does a role played by just one person. A representative of the Denver business community active in the welfare-to-work effort said, "The biggest problem that job devel-opers are having now is the transient population within the business community. It seems like you just get something working and the person you are coordinating with moves on. It is part of . . . the buy-outs that are occurring. The professional staff move in and out of the company so quickly. . . . The next person comes in and they're going to throw out the project because it wasn't theirs . . . and then you have to wait till they go and the next person comes in and then you can start all over." This was echoed by an administrator at the Community College of Denver: "We had this incredible victory, the

30. The private sector research on dealing with teams in trouble is relevant. Katzenbach and Smith (1993, p. 152) make the point well: "In fact, teams can make no greater mistake than to try to solve problems without relating them to performance. Broken interpersonal dynamics, for example, often trouble stuck teams. Clearly, it is a mistake to ignore such issues altogether. But it is also a mistake to try to get people to 'work together better' as an end in itself. Instead, the parties involved must identify specific actions they can take together that will require them to 'get along' in order to advance performance. Otherwise, the values associated with teamwork or getting along just will not stick for very long."

people that own [X]. Fifteen percent of the staff in their regional office here were graduates of [Community College of Denver]. But then the person I was working with moved on and a new person came. The relationship totally changed. They stopped hiring our people altogether. It didn't make sense because 90 percent of the people we had placed there were still there after three years. So they were performing well. But it was just a personality thing. She just didn't want to work with our people. They gave lip service to the relationship, but they were not doing it."

EXPLOITING NATURAL LABOR MARKET DYNAMICS. The bright side of turnover is that it is sometimes a partial solution, in the long run, to the skill, knowledge, and experience deficits that training tries to address in the short run. Personnel movement from one agency to another or within an agency from one functional role to another disperses relevant skills throughout the whole cluster of collaborating agencies.

The Marin County CYSC, which defined as part of its mission the development of a collaborative learning capacity within the whole spectrum of agencies to which it was connected, intended to rotate agency people through its own staff roles to seed collaborative skills and attitudes throughout the agencies. It also undertook to help these agencies develop more collaborative practices in parts of the agencies altogether unconnected with CYSC functions.

In the human services, professional social workers and allied professions (for instance, nonmedical mental health counselors, youth guidance counselors) appear unusually mobile. A social worker might work one year for a county social services agency, the following year for the probation department, and two years later for a private nonprofit agency specializing in drug abuse—and all three might be part of a community-focused collaborative. One such individual, attached to a School-Based Youth Services program in New Jersey, observed that her profession's mobility was so much at variance with what she took to be the immobility of local educators (this in a rural area too) that the resulting clash of worldviews was one of the biggest barriers to effective cooperation between the two bureaucracies.

Another common path for natural migration was one that kept individuals in their same subject field—for example, solid waste management—but took them across jurisdictional lines—for example, from one local government to another or from a state agency to a counterpart local agency.[31] In his valuable study of collaboration among several local and regional public transit systems in the San Francisco Bay area, Donald Chisholm found that interagency personnel mobility performed useful coordinating functions. The movers imported expertise and knowledge of practices and conditions in their former agency homes, and they left behind a cadre of people who could be called on informally should the need for coordination between their new and their old agency homes arise.[32]

If there are programmatic and process-related skills in making ICCs run well, and if these grow with experience—and I believe both premises are true—then the reservoir of individuals with such skills will increase over time, and labor market dynamics will slowly disperse these skills throughout the ICC. Levin and Furman, in their study of community-based youth employment programs in the late 1970s, found a strong presence of urban entrepreneurs who had begun their careers in the antipoverty organizations of a decade earlier and whose culture included suspicion of organizational boundaries.[33] In the human services area, many of the ICC entrepreneurs of the late 1980s and early 1990s also had community organization backgrounds—for example, Arthur Bolton in CISFAN, the engines behind the welfare-to-work collaborative in Denver (DFO),[34] and the reformers within the Oregon Department of Human Resources aiming to overhaul services to children and families. One of the latter said, "I told [my administrative chief] it is the community organizers who can do this. If people don't have the background, then make sure they get advice and consultation about how to do it from people that do."

The difference in the 1980s and 1990s, however, was that the street-level organizers of twenty and thirty years earlier had become the top administrators. No longer did they need to disguise from their agency supervisors that they were meeting with "outsiders" in the community on their lunch hour. The lunch meetings would be in their own offices, and they were the supervisors and deputy directors and directors.

---

31. I believe it was a lot less common, however, to find individuals crossing agency lines when this meant giving up the advantages of agency-specific or subject-matter-specific knowledge—for example, a specialist from the state Water Board moving over to the Waste Management Board.

32. Chisholm (1989, pp. 122–23).

33. Levin and Furman (1985).

34. East (1993).

Accountability and Quality

Even the most integrated, well-functioning, and well-performing teams need supervision, if for no reason other than accountability norms requiring it. However, the flattening of hierarchy and the loosening of overhead and control restraints, especially budget and expenditure controls, raise concerns about traditional methods of accountability for effective and economical performance.

Although traditional methods do provide symbolic reassurance, it is not clear that they are very functional as genuine tools of accountability anyway as opposed to being mere methods of protectionism. Indeed, the whole thrust of the move to reinvent government is that these traditional methods have degraded performance and increased costs. In any case, various aspects of ICC structure and functioning furnish novel opportunities to add new methods of accountability to the existing portfolio, especially if we think of *accountability* as a complement to the effort to improve quality and not merely as substitute for it or as a necessary drag on it.[35] With regard to agency workers themselves, we consider here three variants of a candidate smart practice that might be called accountability as a form of organizational learning: peer accountability, a clearer focus on results, and the greater involvement of consumers or clients or customers in the administrative process.

Peer Accountability

More than customers, clients, and hierarchical superiors, peers know how much effort, care, and creativity they put into their jobs. Although the praise and criticism of peers may not in all cases be as consequential as that from superiors or from customers or clients, it may often be better informed in cases in which the productive task is technical and its actual results hard to assess—for example, many emotional and some physical therapeutic interventions, some natural resource management practices, most education strategies. It is not surprising, therefore, that many of these activities are undertaken by professionals—that is, people who are morally obliged to monitor themselves, allow themselves to be monitored by their peers, and in turn monitor their peers. Fortunately, for many of the policy areas in which ICC development has the highest payoff, professionals are well represented among front-

35. Bardach and Lesser (1996).

line staff and hence among interagency teams. This means that the norms of peer accountability are understood and are at least accorded lip service. Furthermore, to the extent that the role expectations and constraints within one's own bureaucracy often interfere with professionally indicated conduct, the interagency setting, which weakens the hold of one's own agency, may free people to act in what they would consider a moral fashion.[36]

Professionalism aside, peer relationships in teams are also a source of quality motivation, although the research bearing on this proposition has been restricted to the private sector and to within-firm settings.[37] Exactly how, and whether, peer relationships work to motivate effort and quality in public sector interagency team settings—when they work at all—is well beyond the scope of this book. I have seen no published research on the topic, and my own observations have been limited. I offer some conjectures, however.

First, collaborative peers do seem to be a significant influence on individuals' efforts to do quality work. This influence operates independently of influences from the opportunity to work on job-enriched tasks, from conscience, and from supervisors.

Second, in certain situations the peer group often appears (to my surprise) to have a powerful psychological reality as a group and not simply as a collection of individuals. Not only did the participants talk about one another as a "team" but as a "family," a "network." The family metaphor was evident, however, only in collocation settings in which staff were working with families or individuals with salient family responsibilities or needs (in other words, welfare recipients). For such staff the family is a metaphor that comes easily to mind and perhaps structures not only their thoughts but their feelings.

The network metaphor was (weakly) in evidence among self-conscious change agents creating the Denver Family Opportunity program and pushing for more integrated and holistic service approaches in the Oregon Department of Human Resources. What was more important than the network metaphor per se, however, was the expressed willingness on the part of the participants to think about themselves as a diffuse cadre of potential allies who, though not necessarily in frequent contact, knew who had what skills and connections and could be trusted

---

36. O'Toole (1985).
37. Katzenbach and Smith (1993). See also earlier discussion of peer pressure on p. 127.

to be of help when opportunities or crises arose. Peer accountability in network relationships was exercised more through the control of reputation than through direct emotional rewards.

Third, the interagency peer group was not just an environment, it was—or had the potential to be—a medium of expression. Doing good work was not only a way to get approval *from* the group, it was a way to further develop the very identity of the group and, therefore, the identity of one's self as a member of the group. Probably the strength of this potential varies directly with the degree of interdependence of the group's members. Collocation probably increases the potential. So does joint operational responsibility, as in the case of the Medford implementing network, which in fact had a formal title, the Operations Group. So does a sense of being a spearhead in a process of organizational or systems change.

Fourth, in face-to-face groups, accountability works mainly through praising good behavior and withholding praise in cases of dereliction or failures. I believe that, unless they are part of a strategy to force a peer out of the peer circle altogether—as happened in many quarters in the Tennessee Children's Plan case[38]—overt expressions of criticism are rare. I was surprised by this. Assuming it is factually correct, I believe the explanation lies in something more than a human reluctance to disturb a social equilibrium or to make one's self vulnerable to subsequent reprisal. It is genuinely difficult to know whether one's peers from other agencies are responsible for their sub-par performance or whether the circumstances of their agency and its environment may be to blame.

The failure of peers to make use of constructive criticism seems to me unfortunate, whatever the causes. Feedback is lost that might be useful for self-correction. The creative potential of one or more outside observers is lost, people who might have good ideas about possible remedies. It is especially important to find a way to feed information back to higher level individuals in the partner agencies about an agency's problems that impair the ICC's, though not directly the team's, performance. It should not be difficult to develop teachable techniques to improve the practice of peer accountability in interagency team settings. There may even be a profitable opportunity for commercial consultants.

38. See pp. 72–75.

Clearer Focus on Results

Common sense, as well as every management researcher, says that the closer you can get to measuring results you care about rather than some proxy for them—typically inputs or process activities—the more likely you are to elicit the desired performance. Osborne and Gaebler, for instance, devote the better part of their chapter on "Results-Oriented Government" to the value of measuring results, paying for measured results, and budgeting for measured results.[39] When New York State shifted from its old-fashioned personnel lines and expenditure-item contracting with The Door to the new format in its master contract, the state and The Door stipulated their mutual expectations about the following results:

> After a year's instruction, forty-five non-English-speaking youth will have learned to read, write and speak English, as evidenced by changes in pre- and post-test scores and the New York City Place Test.
>
> Seventy youth will have secured employment through The Door.
>
> Sixty-five youth enrolled in drug treatment will have stopped or significantly curtailed their drug use. A random sampling of twenty-five case records will be reviewed to corroborate this outcome.
>
> Fifty youth will have temporarily stabilized their living situation by completing a referral to an emergency shelter or by using emergency food packages.

My interest at this point, however, is not mainly in the question of whether measuring results motivates better performance; it is on how the process can facilitate interorganizational collaboration. For instance, can the results measurements contemplated here, which originate in part in the desire to make programming more flexible, meet the accountability demands of the contracting agency and of the legislative overseers who in turn hold it accountable? The answer can only be that we cannot be sure. In New York, the relevant agencies were betting on the affirmative. However, we could imagine critics of the process raising several questions—for example, about why their own favorite measures were

---

39. Osborne and Gaebler (1992).

not chosen,[40]—and about how the numerical targets are set. If the targets are set too low, even an ineffective and inefficient agency could meet them, and if they are set too high even the best agency could look like a failure. Another question has to do with ensuring that the contractor will not produce the results by means that undermine the intentions of the contracting agency—for example, in The Door's case by "creaming" from a less troubled or less hard-to-serve population. The designers of the master contract might have felt obliged to have designed more stringent targeting controls if The Door had not already been well known to state funders as an unusually effective and dedicated agency that clearly focused its services on the urban minority poor. But can state agency spokespersons convince those who do not know The Door that the agency deserves this level of trust?

Eventually, I believe, it will be discovered that results measurement is not by itself a solution to a great many accountability problems, including those that ICCs experience. But results measurement need not, and should not, be deployed by itself. It should be thought of as another tool to help structure an ongoing dialog about performance between the control agency or the funders and the program entity.[41] The language of numbers will help the participants converse more intelligently about matters of capacity and intensity of effort. The language of results will help the participants focus on the underlying rationale for programs and expenditures. The amalgam of numbers-talk and results-talk will help focus on concrete actions and their supposed causal connection with concrete results. There will, of course, be limits to how much of the important realities can be captured by this improved language of discourse. But we will not know what they are until we have tried harder and longer.

Consumer Involvement

All service processes, from an ATM machine dispensing cash to a public mental health physician dispensing antidepressant medication, depend on some sort of cooperation by the service recipient, whom for convenience I call here "the consumer." Consumers can even be

40. Lynn (1997, p. 99).
41. DiIulio (1992).

thought of as coproducers, working jointly with the person or system whose explicit role is to provide service.[42] At the very least, they have to furnish the service provider with accurate and reliable indications of their identity and their presence. Sometimes the service provider depends on them for information about symptoms—"Does the engine rattle at low speeds as well as high?" The better the consumer does her share of the work, the better the service provider can do his share, and the better off the consumer will be as a result.[43]

Conversely, the less well the service provider understands the needs and desires of the consumer *without* consumer involvement, the more value consumer involvement can add to the result. Middle-class white architects, for instance, designing a community multiservice center for an inner-city location may miss entirely the desire of mothers in the community to have play rooms for their children protected from the street and from the drive-by shootings that might take place there.

In the case of government "people-changing" programs targeted at low-income and ethnic minority individuals or "high-risk" populations in general—welfare-to-work programs, say, or family preservation programs—consumer participation can be an important element in the change process. It creates opportunities for the consumers to practice the skills and habits of self-help. The "family unity" model is a perfect example. Also, as the "family unity" advocates point out, involving the families as consumers is simply more respectful.

In people-changing programs with poor or minority clienteles, involvement of the consumers themselves can also serve as an accountability tool—a "reality check," some might say—vis-à-vis the professional and bureaucratic staff, some of whom may be out of touch with their clients' perspectives, needs, and strengths. In principle, such an accountability tool should be applicable to ICCs as well to single agencies. The professionals and bureaucrats managing a youth

42. Moore (1996, pp. 117–18).

43. Consumer participation can also reduce costs to the service provider, which in turn may get passed back to the consumer—for example, when one pumps one's own gas rather than having a station attendant do it. Even in government this occurs. Assessing one's own federal tax liability (an unwelcome "service," to be sure, but still a type of service) rather than having the IRS do it surely holds down the costs of tax administration and ultimately holds down the revenue needs of the government. Individuals who wish to buy their way out of this collective decision for low-cost tax administration have access to an array of private tax preparers.

services collaborative in Oakland, for instance, kept organizing planning meetings of provider and advocacy groups during school hours until some youthful potential consumers bluntly explained that this practice was strong presumptive evidence of the collaborative's incompetence to plan wisely without more youth involvement.

How best to blend the consumer voice with the voices of professionals and bureaucrats is not always easy. The large and multidisciplinary gatherings of professionals that participated in CYSC parallel case reviews could have had their sometimes heated discussions constrained by the presence of the clients. And even were the discussions to have been milder and more consensual, the presence of so many high-status professionals could have been, and sometimes was, intimidating to clients. One of the advantages of the "family unity" model is that it has a clear role for the consumer. However, as the current CYSC executive director explained, it may not always have enough of a role for the professional. At least, though, involving the consumer gives the provider agencies in an ICC yet one more common point of reference to keep their communications on the same wavelength.

The most radical approach to involving consumers in the service delivery process would be to give them the power to be their own purchasing agents. For certain kinds of services—say those involved in employment and training programs—why not let consumers have vouchers or some other type of cash equivalent to make use of one or more service offerings by one or more providers? In addition to the advantages of putting more power in the hands of the population whose interests need better protection, self-management along these lines can contribute to dignity and personal growth. Consumers could package the services in a way that suited them, just as middle-class individuals would do in a less directly subsidized marketplace, thereby functioning both as quality managers and as service integrators. "A voucher," according to one advocacy group, "would offer recipients quick access to placement and support agencies such as America Works in New York; the Goodwill Job Connection in Sarasota, Florida; state-run job placement programs; temporary subsidized private sector work experience or on-the-job training; microenterprise training programs; and other employment-based services."[44] An experiment with a "smart

44. Hogan (1996, p. 10).

card" in one state of Mexico "has had remarkable success," according to an article in *The Economist*.[45] Like a bank debit card, the smart card permitted families to access eighteen different subsidy programs administered by a variety of competitive providers. Those who were favored by the card users got to claim reimbursements from the state government. The card undercut bureaucratic discretion over who got what and permitted consumers an unprecedented degree of discretion with regard to what food to buy and where to buy it.

The design of such a program would have to take account of the vulnerability of some proportion of the potential consumers to the false or misleading advertising of some of the providers of service. Private vocational training schools have sometimes enrolled students who brought with them federal subsidies but have provided ineffective training or training for nonexistent jobs and have left the students with the burden of loans for tuition in excess of the portion covered by the subsidies. Because integrating different services might not always be so easy, vouchers might be available for consumers to choose personal assistants to help them do so.

Money and Quality

Agencies often refer cases for service or for regulatory management to some partner agency in the ICC production network better able to offer it. The referral partners may have superior expertise, more appropriate jurisdiction, unique access to categorical funds, or less constrained capacity, to note only the most common reasons. A well-functioning interagency production network would be a way for agencies making such referrals to have some assurance that the recipients of the referral would act in a high-quality manner—that is, first accepting the referral and then managing the case effectively and efficiently. How can such a network be organized?

One possibility is that the more linkages among the participating agencies, the better. A study of mental health networks throughout the communities of Albuquerque, New Mexico; Akron, Ohio; Providence, Rhode Island; and Tucson, Arizona; found a weak relationship between the sheer proportion of bilateral linkages within the provider community

45. *The Economist*, May 11, 1996, p. 38.

and the quality of clinical outcomes. One might question the causal interpretation, however. The best clinical outcomes were in Providence, which rated high on the quantity of linkages but which was also the network in which purchasing power was largely centralized in a powerful mental health agency. This agency may have been able to leverage the revenue and legitimacy concerns of its network of smaller providers.[46] I am inclined to think that the financial incentives permeating the network relationships were more important than their density.

In any event, it is the manipulation of financial incentives that I explore in this section. I shall discuss two ways this occurs: through the design of payment schemes and through the threat of withholding (or sometimes the promise of offering) patronage. Because each of these topics is quite broad, I will restrict my discussion to the highlights and focus on those practices that have to do with interagency collaboration rather than with the design of financial incentives more broadly. Only the simplest of them, paying for successful performance in the same way that one pays one's lawyer a contingent fee for a successful suit, looks like a smart practice. The conditions that make such a simple arrangement work are not common; however, variants designed for other conditions have many weaknesses as well as strengths, and even the best designs can be derailed if they do not manage to get a host of details right.

Payment Schemes

In the private sector the quality of provider services is motivated through a combination of competitive market pressures (often mediated by reputation effects), warranty promises, contract enforceability, and professional ethics. When reliable information about quality is relatively low cost, when switching providers is easy, when the transaction costs of enforcing warranties and contracts are either low or can be pushed back onto the providers, and when the profession is a strong one with clear norms and an effective enforcement capability, the system works quite well for quality-conscious consumers. Because some or

46. Provan and Milward (1994, 1995). Provan and Milward implied that strong fiscal controls were the central feature of the integration mechanism in Providence. This seems likely. However, it is possible that these fiscal controls operated relatively indirectly, setting up the possibility of control through softer measures than the threat of removing clientele—for example, what I later call *education*. See also Grusky and others (1986).

all of these conditions are often not met where the services of the sort needed by interagency collaboratives are concerned, securing quality is more difficult.

The archetypal contingent-payment scheme designed to induce quality was the Riverside GAIN program's contract with adult schools that paid them for each grade level improvement of each GAIN participant referred to them. The payments were relatively generous, at least in the early years, and the GAIN participants seemed to do fairly well (although without adequately matched comparison or control groups it is hard to know for sure). Hence all parties were happy. Payments to job training providers under the Job Training Partnership Act are a well-known specimen of performance contracting, although with much more complex stipulations about what sort of performance would entitle the provider to what level of payment.

In Maryland the governor and legislature created a scheme to reward localities for bringing back children from out-of-state placement and for preventing out-of-home placements even within the state. The localities would receive 75 percent of the cost savings to spend on prevention programs. The state agencies were to be rewarded as well, being allowed to spend the other 25 percent on new prevention programs. I heard no complaints about the financial-incentives aspect of these payment arrangements, although the localities have complained about the adequacy of the new revenue base as a foundation for serious programming.

Payment schemes are also used to induce cost savings. Before the era of reforms by David Manning in Tennessee (see chapter 3), the child-serving agencies were often contracting with residential care facilities for the right to use facility capacity rather than paying for capacity actually used. For various reasons the agencies often bought what appeared to outside observers to be an excess of capacity. The Manning-era reforms included a change to per diem payments, paying the providers only for beds and days actually used. This scheme shifts risk and uncertainty onto the providers and at least raises the questions of what is a fair and efficient distribution of risk and uncertainty between the state and the industry, many of whose firms depend largely or exclusively on state agency referrals. Program managers on both sides of the relationship, as well as political overseers, certainly have a right to worry about whether too much or too little money is likely to be paid out.

The probability of paying out too much or too little is also affected by the choice of a baseline against which to assess performance. We have already seen this problem in the discussion of New York's master contract with The Door.

Policy planners usually try to design against undesirable incentive effects. The new Tennessee scheme requires a design addition that discourages or prohibits facility owners from holding on to their residents past the time that is, by some reasonable standard, clinically indicated. Many existing arrangements also have undesirable incentive effects—for example, county mental health clinics "dumping" their hard-to-treat and expensive cases into the state mental hospital, and childrens' services providers turning their clients into "medical" cases to have federal medicaid pick up most of the tab. I made note previously in the discussion of The Door master contract of the possibility that the performance standards would provide an incentive for creaming.

Often both dumping and creaming stem from more fundamental design flaws in the fiscal incentives that agencies face. Dumping usually can be curtailed if the referring agency is obliged to pay a portion of the cost of the service on which the client is being dumped—for example, by charging the local mental health clinic for state hospital treatment for patients it refers there, perhaps over and above some allocation of state hospital patient days that can be used at no charge. A more sophisticated approach is to give the referring entity a portion of the savings that accrue from reductions in dumping along with permission (and perhaps a requirement) to invest the savings in some array of community-based prevention services. This has been done with good effect in regard to mental patients, who have been kept out of state hospitals, and to children, who have been treated at home rather than having them placed in foster care or in residential treatment. The logic of the approach is long familiar from the practices of health maintenance organizations (HMOs), which substitute outpatient and preventive treatment for expensive inpatient service.

Getting such a system to work correctly depends on numerous details and on managerial ingenuity.[47] High incentive payments to referring agencies to avoid expensive placements may lead to suboptimal utilization of the services associated with those placements unless professional norms are permitted to operate as an effective counterweight. If the incentive payments come in the form of a lump sum to a county for, let us say preventing foster care placements, the size of the

47. Brach (1995); Kramer and Grossman (1987, p. 52).

block grant should increase if, by reason of in-migration or an increase in child abuse because of crack cocaine, the at-risk population increases. But it is usually hard to know if the at-risk population truly increased or if the county agencies simply have not been doing their job very well. If, at the agency level, the incentive payments are attached to named, particular individuals, as is the practice with capitation plans (for example, in HMOs or managed care plans), they create an incentive for agencies to cream the best risks. It is also hard to get the capitation payments right if the sorts of preventive services that are the most cost-effective do not have a payoff until five or ten years down the road, or if the population is so mobile that a locality's investment in prevention simply moves, in necessitous conjunction with the person in whom it was made, to some other locality.

Designing the system details to prevent creaming is not easier. For agencies or case workers in the employment and training field, the fraction of successful placements is often the indicator of merit. This can be manipulated by inflating the numerator with placements that would likely have occurred anyway (for example, the temporarily laid off who return to work with their former employer or individuals who are motivated by financial distress to take almost any job that comes along and do so very quickly) or by deflating the denominator by defining the caseload as only those who have passed some sort of enrollment threshold. More important, this threshold can be set to eliminate, sometimes indirectly, the least motivated and hardest-to-place individuals, the ones that consume lots of staff time and energy. Of course, there are partial solutions to these and other such problems. But none is perfect or comes without administrative costs of its own.

The Uses of Competition

In a competitive market, the referring agency can favor providers who are believed to provide good service and shun those who do not. Both practices would push providers as a group to supply higher quality services. Because the nature of the pressure—and the problems with applying it—is similar (though not identical) for both practices, I will discuss only the practice of discouraging and eliminating providers of unacceptably low quality.

A paradigmatic example of what is involved comes from Detroit (circa 1992), where a JOBS case manager said of one of the "job clubs" (a

five-week job preparation and job search workshop) run by another
public organization that the JOBS program paid for its services:

> I only deal with the good job clubs. I do not deal with the job clubs
> where the job clubs teacher has no good outcomes. I dealt with
> one job club that's very close to this office and I could not get
> progress reports or transportation logs. I would even go there and
> sit there and they still didn't get this to me regularly. And none of
> my clients got jobs. I don't deal with that job club anymore. They
> cannot pay me to deal with that job club. Because my [other] job
> clubs get results. They are dedicated. Plus, it makes them look
> good in their job and they appreciate my sending them clients and
> I appreciate them getting my clients jobs.

Leveraging the power of competition is not easy, however. First,
there may be some incompatibility between the deference due the interests of an individual client who, let us say, finds it geographically convenient or philosophically satisfying to use the services of job club
provider X and the interests of the client population as a whole, which
might be better served by dumping X and relying on Y. If there are
enough clients who want X, then the referring agency may be stuck
with X. In the case of Detroit job clubs the availability of alternative
providers within an acceptable geographical area made it feasible to
take a hard line about the offending job club provider. This might have
been much less feasible in a rural or suburban area.

Second, because the offending job club provider in this case was a
public bureaucracy, it was not as sensitive to the removal of its clientele
and the reduction of its revenues as a profit-seeking or a nonprofit
provider might have been. Third, some providers occupy a politically
protected niche. Consider the hypothetical case of Family Friends, a
venerable child mental health counseling agency whose socially prominent board members have connections on the county board of supervisors. Even though professionals in the field regard Family Friends as
expensive, only marginally effective, and reactionary in their approach
to treatment methods, the social services director might be given to
understand that Family Friends must continue to receive a decent number of referrals.

Fourth, there has to be competition. As Kramer and Grossman
pointed out, in some geographic areas, the degree of provider special-

ization virtually guarantees that many providers in the social services area will be effective monopolies.[48] Moreover, providers find ways to divide turf and responsibilities to create and then protect each others' monopolies. Grubb and McDonnell studied the local systems of vocational education and job training in eight communities and found "little evidence of overt competition, and minimal service overlap." "Competition is considered undesirable by virtually all program administrators because of the disharmony and uncertainty it generates."[49] In many communities the providers create what could be referred to either as a rational division of labor or as a scheme for turf protection, depending on one's preconceptions about the mix of underlying purposes.

All these difficulties are seen through the eyes of the contracting agency. From the point of view of the contractor, the threat of exit may represent not a proconsumer use of leverage but an attempt to pressure the contractor to conform to inappropriate or undesired methods and objectives. The Denver Family Opportunity program (DFO) put up with what, in the eyes of some of its leaders, was inadequate performance on the part of one of its nonprofit contractors, a community-based organization specializing in service to a minority community, for more than one budget cycle before declining to renew its contract. The DFO "tried and tried to educate them," according to one observer, but without success. But the DFO was not universally well-regarded in the Congressional Budget Office contractor community: too bureaucratic, not sufficiently results oriented, not sufficiently attuned to the special needs of certain ethnic groups, too willing to throw its weight around acquired by virtue of its monopoly on day care funds, or so it was alleged. Some believed that the "education" would have been better directed from the CBOs to the DFO rather than vice versa.

Education

Perhaps the DFO and the CBOs should have been involved in an educational process, independent of who in the end did a better job of educating whom.[50] But how is such mutual education to occur? Given

48. Kramer and Grossman (1987).
49. Grubb and McDonnell (1996, p. 256).
50. Dehoog (1990) called this mutually educational relationship a cooperative contracting model. She claimed to find it preferable to competitive contracting or arm's-length negotiations, but noted its potential to breed complacency and cronyism.

that the government agency and the contractor must interact over contract-related financial and performance issues, an opportunity exists to make these interactions into an educational medium as well. The network literature cited in chapter 2 suggests that the opportunity for mutuality based on expectations of a relatively enduring relationship exists. It appears, however, that this opportunity is not exploited often.

PROBLEMS. The barriers are surely formidable. Grounds for mutual hostility and suspicion are abundant. The government often pays late, requires excessive and costly paperwork, fails to take account of start-up difficulties, and demands detailed input accountability rather than the sort of broad output (or outcome) accountability that would give contractors desirable flexibility. On the other side, some contractors are ineffective, wasteful, sloppy in their accounting practices, given to financial abuse, and moderately dishonest about how high a priority they assign in practice to contractually defined objectives.

The same sorts of problems plague interagency relationships between levels of government. Grant payments are late, meaningless planning documents and progress reports must be submitted, recipient governments live under the threat of audit exceptions. It hardly matters, then, *who* deals with government agencies if they are in the role of funds recipient or for what reason they are receiving the funds. The procurement, budgeting, auditing, and disbursement procedures make any such relationships difficult.

An even worse source of impairment is the defect-finding mission, and therefore attitude, of audit staff sent by the funding agency to oversee the contractor. Susan R. Bernstein's interviews with eighteen nonprofit social service agencies in New York City in 1987 make it clear that the relationship between government funder and contract provider is one long struggle over the minutiae of waste, fraud, and abuse.[51] There is rarely a pretense of a constructive dialogue. Nor is there often a possibility for such dialogue inasmuch as the auditing staff often lack the knowledge or the concern to engage in such a dialogue. Moreover, their own agencies are often in turmoil so that no dialogue would be heard beyond the few individuals who had actually engaged in it.[52]

51. Bernstein (1991).
52. Some auditor–contractor relationships also carry a burden of the past. One informant explained to me that the New York State Office of Alcohol and Substance Abuse Services, up until some fifteen years earlier, had run "an expensive network of treatment

SMART PRACTICES. Rescuing the contract oversight process as an educational medium probably depends on finding ways to broaden the focus beyond cost and expenditure controls and the prevention of waste, fraud, and abuse to encompass performance as well. Although there are many ways to do this, the novel accountability issues raised by ICCs may present a powerful new opportunity.

Consider, for instance, the periodic oversight visits that the New York state funding agencies paid to The Door as part of the master contract evaluation process. The participants in the process gave it high marks all around. Comments by The Door's director were particularly interesting. Because under the master contract system the state auditors and evaluators arrived for a once-a-year week-long site visit, the director would assemble his divisional managers for comprehensive evaluations of their own, a collective activity they had never undertaken before and that they all valued for the unusual degree of candor and critical thinking that it stimulated. Moreover, the education in teamwork could be reciprocal and continual:

> If the state people can work as a team, then we can certainly work as a team. And vice versa. If they are seeing us—these people who are professionals in their own right and sometimes competing professionally—find a way in our own program to remove these competing viewpoints and work together comprehensively, then maybe they can learn from us. So there was a lot of sharing of professional ideas and methodologies. It helped the state people rethink some of their requirements and programs.

It may have helped, too, that the state people, working within the new master contract framework, were able to see the big picture of the state's overall fiscal relationship to the contractor. One staff member from the Council on Children and Families said, "With a master contract you'd be able to see whether the head of the contract provider was drawing more than 100% of his salary" by charging it redundantly to different contracting agencies. In addition, it would be possible to

---

facilities which was closed down. There are some people, including the commissioner, who used to run one of those facilities, and I think maybe there's an overhang there, that 'We used to do this, and they took it away from us, and now they have these [contractor] guys do it.' I don't know but there's certainly a sense . . . that 'We've got to watch them.'"

remove potentially troublesome financial glitches such as more than one agency requiring that its dollars be used as the funds of last resort. Hence the dialogue between overseers and contractor could shuttle back and forth between more rational thinking about performance, of special interest to the contractor, and more rational thinking about financial control, of special interest to the government overseers.

Whether an effective relationship of mutual sharing and education is possible depends to an important degree on the larger political climate. Under pressure from the Oregon attorney general's office, Adult and Family Services was obliged to start a competitive bidding process to choose the prime contractor in each of its fifteen service districts statewide instead of simply renegotiating the contract with the lead agency then in place. To many participants this flew in the face of the partnership philosophy that AFS had been trying to promote for several years. The competitive process, in the end, produced no change whatever in the set of prime contractors.[53] Because public opinion, and hence legislative opinion, often cares less about quality performance than about the prevention of abuse and sloth, government procurement and contracting practices often favor competition even when the result is to degrade performance or increase overall costs.[54] (Computer procurement in the federal government is the best documented example).

Of course, a defender of the seemingly tough-minded competition-at-all-costs approach could well say that "accountability" is what the government-contractor relationship ought to produce, not professional "partnership." This position can be defended by reference to history, tradition, and the frequent demands of legislative and executive branch overseers that taxpayer dollars be protected. Within limits this is an acceptable defense. But it still leaves open what the "protection" of these dollars might entail. In many cases it might well mean cutting back the investment on fault finding and blame avoidance and spending the money saved on improving the quality of service delivery.

The truth is that the tools of fiscal accountability are a poor means of trying to induce quality performance by government agencies. Legislators often seize on them because they are much more easily available

---

53. In the one case in which a rival won, the agency backed out before taking up its responsibilities, which reverted to the incumbent.
54. Kelman (1990).

than other means, because their power of the purse is sanctified by the U.S. Constitution and its counterparts in the states, and because their control over the purse is a weapon in occasional policy struggles with the executive branch. But there is no reason for disinterested observers to accept the limited legislative version of accountability as the only or the best version. Nor, given the possibility of developing peer accountability, results-focused accountability, and consumer-driven accountability, as discussed in this chapter, is there necessarily a need to do so.

Summary

An ICC's tasks are typically to manage cases of one kind or another. To function well, the ICC must be designed to give line staff teams and the implementing network an unusual degree of flexibility, more than is common in public sector settings. It must also be creative at motivating high-quality effort and fostering mutual intelligibility and trust among agency-professionals from different agencies. Interagency financial relations also must be considered part of the overall operating system.

The chapter identifies several smart practices for implementing an effective operating system for the ICC and many more that, because they might run high political risks or would expend funds on uncertain ventures (such as certain kinds of process skills training), are not so obviously "smart" in the sense of the definition introduced in chapter 2. The most promising candidates for status as smart practices I take to be these:

—At the line worker and implementing network levels, flexibility and efforts to produce high-quality results can both be pursued by means of self-managing teams and job enrichment.

—Human relations approaches to improving teamwork can take advantage of natural propensities toward reciprocity. Consensus-building techniques can structure conflict to clarify points of agreement and disagreement.

—Accountability need not be sacrificed provided one understands that the currently enshrined systems of close fiscal oversight do not actually produce much accountability for performance or economy. Indeed, certain practices that I call accountability as a form of organizational learning could actually improve accountability: peer accountability, focusing on results, and consumer involvement.

—Up to a point interagency financial relations can be structured to provide incentives for desired performance. But after that point, constructive dialogue, on a foundation of trust, is required.[55]

Implementing these smart practices requires substantial time, talent, and commitment. It would not be surprising if people regarded the price of these and other resources as too high. Then again, they might consider that the alternatives might imply a high cost as well, in the form of an opportunity lost to advance the public interest and, in some cases, their own bureaucratic and career interests as well.

55. Thompson (1993).

5

How an Interagency Collaborative Acquires Resources

The potential for interagency collaborative capacity is much more prevalent than its actualization. Hence the cases I examined for this book are unusual. For at least a brief period of time, they existed.

What prevents ICC capacity from even getting off the ground, in most cases, is the unwillingness of potential partners to contribute resources. The first half of this chapter explores the variety of motivations to withhold or block the contribution of resources. The second half considers the opposite set of motivations: why potential partners might indeed be willing to contribute, and how smart practices might augment this willingness.

Looking through variance-analysis lenses, one might say: add up all the forces (motivations) pushing for collaboration, subtract the sum of the forces (including constraints) resisting collaboration, and predict that, other things being equal, the greater the positive sum (or the smaller the negative sum), the greater the likelihood of reaching some threshold of effective ICC capacity. Craftsmanship theory would add to this an important amendment: when estimating the magnitudes of the various forces, adjust appropriately for the enhancing effects of smart practices on the positive side and their diminishing effects on the negative side. It would also add: be aware that the forces of both sorts are varied and subtle, admitting the possibilities of much creativity and plausible rhetoric in some actors' efforts to bargain with, manipulate, and persuade potential allies and enemies.

The resources of greatest consequence, and on which I shall focus, are these:

Turf. By "turf" I mean the domain of problems, opportunities, and actions over which an agency exercises legitimate authority. Sometimes "turf" is literally land, as in the case of timber land controlled by the U.S. Forest Service. Sometimes it is a potential client population, such as everyone diagnosed with tuberculosis in some geographical area, or a communitywide function, such as public school education. Sometimes it is the behavior of other public agencies, such as the expenditure practices of municipal agencies which, for the comptroller's office that oversees these, counts as turf.

Autonomy. I mean this in the sense of freedom to make decisions and take actions without prior agreement by partners or the need to furnish excuses to them after the fact.[1]

Money. Money might come from an agency's budget. Or it might come as "new money" granted by a foundation or by the legislature or raised as a result of successful commercial activity.

People. By this I mean the quantity and quality of manpower needed to make the ICC function at an acceptable level, taking account of its stage of development. I include here all the intangible resources that people can contribute to ICC development, such as enthusiasm, intelligence, technical expertise, creativity, time, and commitment.

Political standing. Typically, this is accorded an ICC by the political community in which it functions, in particular by the official and unofficial leaders of the community.

Information. By this I mean all kinds of information, including whatever is relevant to the management of particular cases (such as clients, firms, or geographical areas), interpretation of aggregate trends or patterns, and gossip or "intelligence" about political developments, among others.

The Variety of Protectionist Purposes

In the preceding chapter I observed that protectionism played a role in the evolution of important policymaking and policy-implementing institutions. Protectionism breeds unwillingness to contribute re-

---

1. James Q. Wilson (1989, pp. 181–85) more than almost any theorist of bureaucracy postulates autonomy as the primary bureaucratic goal. He regards turf protectionism as merely an expression of the desire for autonomy. In my treatment it is that but much more as well.

sources to an ICC as well.[2] Consistent with the discussion of purpose in chapter 2, I distinguish three types of protectionist purpose: careerist, bureaucratic, and value-oriented.

The varieties of protectionist purposes are often fused. For instance, people sometimes protect bureaucratic turf because they wish to protect the agency's mission, which they value because of the public interest, because it serves their careerist purposes, and because turf protectionism is implied by their bureaucratic roles. One of these purposes may have preceded the others, to be sure, but after a time they will all have reciprocally reinforced one another to the point that subtle distinctions about primacy become irrelevant.

Even in cases in which the underlying distinctions remain—perhaps because the variety of purposes prescribe conflicting courses of action— it may be useless for an observer to try to penetrate the underlying reality. Because careerist and bureaucratic purposes are often disapproved, individuals do not admit to outsiders, such as academic researchers, that they are present. They do not necessarily admit them to themselves, or even understand them. Bureaucratic purposes such as budget or turf protection are often rationalized as inevitable imperatives of political life, which indeed they are. Rationalization of careerist purposes in terms of bureaucratic imperatives or value commitments is also common.

Self-understanding is further complicated by the fact that such purposes are often subtle and are mediated by estimates of empirical contingencies. Consider, for instance, the mixture of assessments and purposes evident in the inner ruminations of Johnson, a division chief in a large environmental regulatory agency:

If our agency picks up this new collaborative task in accord with the wishes of Thompson, the governor's aide, this could bolster

2. How prevalent are problems caused by protectionism? My own interviews suggest they are very prevalent. So does Sandford F. Borins's analysis of 217 semifinalists in the Ford Foundation/Kennedy School of Government Innovations Awards program, which identified 512 instances of obstacles to innovation as reported by the applicants. Borins (1998, p. 67). Ninety-two of these he coded as "bureaucratic," which I take to be, in his usage, a virtual synonym for "rigid" or "protectionist." This slightly exceeded "inadequate resources" as the main source of identified obstacles (p. 89). Borins does not explicitly say whether the bureaucratic obstacles were disproportionately concentrated in the 61 percent of his cases in which holism, and therefore interagency relationships, was at issue, but this can be inferred from his examples (pp. 67–68).

the status in our agency of Roberts, Thompson's long-time professional associate, whose philosophical views are antagonistic to my own. Although I favor the stated aims of this particular collaborative venture, I doubt that the design details, insofar as I can understand what they really are, give it good odds of actually producing worthwhile results. Whether a newly inflated Roberts would treat my unit's budget and that of my professional allies within the agency fairly would depend on how visible his actions would be outside the agency and on how much he feels restrained by his own sense of fairness—the nature and depth of which is presently unknown. It also depends on what policy situations turn up in the next few years that would tempt him to try to alter the status quo dramatically in favor of his professional ideologies. My own career prospects would probably not suffer—and they might even be enhanced were I to be seen by my allies as an effective counterweight to Roberts.

If Johnson decides to oppose Thompson's wishes, to what degree is she motivated by value, bureaucratic, or careerist aspirations? And what exactly is the character of any of these? What if we observe that Johnson decides to go along with Thompson's wishes? If the decision turned on a slightly different calculation of the empirical contingencies, the mixture of purposes could well be the same as if she had decided to oppose them, and yet the outside observer could easily be misled about the underlying nature of Johnson's purposes and about the inferred strength of the various forces acting on Johnson.

In chapter 7 we shall see how the difficulty of inferring the nature and strength of purposes bedevils potential partners' calculations of one another's trustworthiness. They also bedevil any observer's interpretations, including my own, of why and how organizations are reluctant to contribute to collaborative efforts.

I offer no personal judgment of approval or disapproval of purposes, nor of the mere fact of organizations' reluctance to contribute to ICC development, whatever the purposes. I might be readier to have a personal judgment, and to recommend it to readers, were I confident I could disentangle multiple purposes and unmask rationalizations. But even in that case, there would be little point in doing so because I have much less interest in judging people and the forces that surround them than in understanding them and helping readers to do the same.

Value-Creating Purposes

Value-creating purposes come in a variety of forms. What they have in common is the perception that protecting one or another aspect of one's institution or agency maintains or creates public value.

MISSION-RELATED RISK-AVERSIVENESS. One of the most powerful motives—and rationalizations—for protectionism is fear that an important public mission for which one's agency is uniquely responsible will suffer if collaboration goes too far. This motive fuses normative commitment to protect the weak, obligation to one's agency-professional role, fear of blame by superiors and overseers, risk-aversiveness with respect to existing assets,[3] and a realistic theory about the uncertainties inherent in a political environment. In Maryland a veteran employee of the Department of Juvenile Services explained how, in the view of many in the agency, their unique mission had evolved and how it might be threatened:

> Historically, the kids who are known to our department are kids who have been excluded from other service delivery systems. [They've been involved] with child welfare, certainly the schools, occasionally mental health, and have not had successful outcomes in any of those systems, and eventually they wind up with us. We've had to create the whole service delivery system in sort of a parallel format. We have mental health programs for delinquent kids, we have alternative schools for delinquent kids.
>
> Constituency battles play out between the agencies. One of the things I frequently say in meetings is that I need to represent what is in the best interests of the kids and the families that we are responsible to serve. . . . I'm not aware of any citizen organization that is aligned to protect the interests of juvenile delinquents. I mean we just don't have them. So we are that.
>
> I'm always concerned as to whether or not, if we put all of our money into one big pot, will the delinquent population receive its fair share? History, twenty-some years in this business, has said to me that this is the last population that will get served. Every year more and more kids are excluded from the juvenile jurisdiction and put into the adult jurisdiction. The same thing would happen

3. Dawes (1988, p. 40).

with services. I think they'd be triaged out of the service delivery system as . . . not worthy of the effort. The other populations in the child services area, the mental health population, the child welfare population, seem to be more palatable to the service providers at the service delivery systems, they are victims and not victimizers.

So we push hard for making sure that . . . these kids are not excluded from the service delivery system. There's a theory that if the service delivery system is more unified, and more collaborative . . . we can be more cost efficient. . . . But as long as we're competing for services, then there's a risk that they could be pulled away.

It is no accident that agencies' missions are narrowly defined and relatively inflexible. In some cases legislatures created them this way in order to deal with a particular problem—for example, the regulation of toxic substances. In cases in which their original mandate was broader and more flexible, a program structure nevertheless evolved that over time matched organizational subunits to defined budget categories and sometimes to well-defined sets of activities. These did not always add up to a real mission but at least served as a day-to-day proxy for one.

The logic of accountability monitoring reinforces such a result. The logic goes even further: If this is your agency's mission, then it is no other agency's mission; and if you don't perform it, no one else will. And because this mission is important to the society, you had better attend to it and not allow collaborative programming to threaten your capacity to carry out your unique social responsibilities. As an attorney for the Department of Toxic Substances said, "Never mind water. Our mission is to enforce the Toxics Act, period."

COMPETING MEANS SERVING THE SAME PUBLIC PURPOSES. ICC development is an opportunity cost charged against the value-creating agency-improvement budget, analogous to Margolis's personal altruism budget that I referred to in chapter 2. This seems to me one of the most important, but least recognized, reasons for the relative absence of ICC capacity in the world of public administration. Even in cases in which interagency collaboration would directly support the agency's existing mission, its other noncollaborative activities, presumably, would do so too. Collaborative activities must compete with these. According to a veteran field enforcement agent for Toxic Substances:

> One of the things that is very tough is that you have assignments, and your assignments take your time. You wouldn't have those assignments to do if they weren't your workload. You start trying to cooperate with other people, and come up with a collaborative effort—that's generally going to take more time. And when you can do it yourself, it takes only so much time; but when you have to involve this person and that person, and they are from other agencies, and you can't just walk down the hall and talk to them, it takes a lot more time. . . . When you have to go out and talk to Mary at the [Waste Board] and John at the Air Board and Paul over at the Water Board, you have just quadrupled the time you're spending on that project.

As I pointed out in chapter 1, interagency collaboration is a type of administrative reform, similar to contracting out, empowering line-level employees, and so on. This similarity has important implications for how much priority reform-minded executives and senior managers accord ICC construction. If it is part of a broad-gauge reform strategy, it might have a relatively high priority, depending on how reformers see its causal interconnectedness with other reform elements. In the more likely case of piecemeal reform, interagency collaboration competes for managerial attention and employees' limited store of willingness to tolerate change that imposes private cost. As one former senior manager in the New York City Department of Human Resources said to me, "We had so many things to take care of in-house, I would have been very skeptical about spending anybody's time across town meeting with other agencies."

LIABILITIES OF THE NEW. The noncollaborative way of serving the public interest carries the blessings of history and its own line items. According to a Cal/EPA official,

> Many times, Bill [Carter] had to bargain or plead to get the Water Board or an Air District to participate [in a task force or strike force] . We had to put out a sales pitch every time. It wasn't that it came naturally. As much as we did multimedia inspections or

required folks to work together, cooperatively, we had to fight that same battle over and over again. . . . "We can't afford to do it at this time . . . we're not budgeted for this type of activity." Sometimes it's cash out-of-pocket. One of the Water Board guys says, "We don't have a financial code that we can put down for participation in strike forces, so we can't go."

CORE MISSION AND PERIPHERAL ACTIVITIES. "My fire is not your fire," one official at Cal/EPA said. The Waste Board approached the facilities it regulated with more of a consultative spirit than did, say, the Water Board. It was unwilling to jeopardize its painstakingly built relationships with the members of its regulated community in order to engage in joint compliance efforts with Water. It had its own statutes and regulations to enforce, its own environmental mission, and its own methods. These had to be its priorities. If joint efforts with other agencies could be accommodated, fine; if not, they would be undertaken only under duress.

The less related the peripheral (ICC) activities are to the core, the harder it will be to pry resources loose for them. During the period the Vegetation Management Consortium was preparing its plan, the University of California, one of the important partners, was so strapped for funds that it allowed more than 10 percent of its senior faculty to be induced into early retirement by very handsome financial benefits and slightly cut the salaries of existing faculty. Partly as a result, its contributions to the vegetation management function were less than $50,000 annually.[4]

CONFLICTING PROFESSIONAL AND SOCIAL VALUES. Sometimes the fit between potential partners is thrown off not just by competition between their priorities for scarce resources but by a tension between fundamental purposes or values. A consortium of drug abuse treatment programs in San Francisco in the mid 1970s successfully created a simplified tracking system that permitted the participating agencies to improve their follow-up procedures. It ran into trouble, however, when the relatively "establishment" mental health center attempted to consolidate all intake and diagnosis in a central unit before referring clients to the variety of clinics, halfway houses, and other treatment facilities. The

4. Kuiper (1997, p. 11).

African American halfway houses in the Fillmore district and the counter-cultural halfway houses in Haight-Ashbury insisted on retaining their right to select suitable clients and to treat them in what they took to be culturally appropriate ways. They also disliked the treatment methods in the methadone clinic and refused to send clients there.[5]

POLITICAL IMPERATIVES. An even more compelling basis for conflict is the obligation of constituency representation. Ours is a pluralist political system that is intended to give minorities the power to hold out against threatening majorities or other minorities. Bargaining is intended to be at least as important as persuasion, conflict as functional as collaboration. Government agencies are more or less intended to represent certain social interests and to withhold cooperation from one another if their leaders believe that doing so accords with the desires of the interests they represent. Hence when a state environmental agency and a state road-building agency nearly come to blows over the route of a proposed new freeway, this might be more an expression of underlying political conflict than of interagency conflict.

In regulatory programs the intergovernmental relationship often involves the exercise by "lower" levels of government of authority delegated by a "higher" level—for instance, regional air quality boards in California enforcing state and federal regulations as well as their own. The delegation occurs for technical reasons—for example, to bring local knowledge into the implementation process or to exploit economies of scale. However, it inevitably implies, as I said in chapter 1, political consequences about what sort of spin or coloration will be put on the enforcement process, especially the question of whether the local authorities should be given any formal latitude. The reason is that conflicting political constituencies have differential access to different governmental jurisdictions. Environmental interests, for instance, historically have had better access to the federal government and the EPA than they have had to most state governments, whereas regulated businesses on average have had better local and state than federal access. Interagency tensions across jurisdictional boundaries, therefore, will tend to mirror political tensions.

Differential interest group access also explains certain tensions in the financial management of many service delivery programs. Interests

5. Gans and Horton (1975, p. 223).

with relatively greater power at the higher level of government want to ensure that grant funds originating at that level reach the favored beneficiaries and service provider constituencies at the local level. One method of doing so is to specify in detail, with regard to some line-item set of funds, who shall receive what kinds of services from what sorts of providers. The auditing apparatus of every relevant level of government can then be brought into play to enforce these restrictions. This is the main reason that liberals and Democrats are often skeptical about giving social service block grants to the states.

MAGNITUDE MAKES A DIFFERENCE. It is arguably a smart practice to set value-creating collaborative goals high enough to attract attention and commitment. When legislators and editorialists rail about the need for more "coordination" or the desirability of achieving economies by eliminating "duplication," it is not surprising that not much happens. Such goals rarely enhance any bureaucrat's career or speak to his or her needs to protect or enhance the bureaucracy. Nor do they speak to the aspirations of the value-creating constituency within the bureaucracy, whose energies are indispensable for any sort of collaborative effort.

But pressures to perform differently or to perform to a higher standard touch more responsive chords, as in the case of the East Bay fire. In many cases such pressure may even be appreciated by bureaucrats looking for an excuse to put performance pressures of their own on subordinates or peers. Such pressures could work in two different ways. Increasing bureaucratic fear of punishment is one pathway. As discussed in chapter 3, the welfare caseload reduction rate in Oregon achieved unprecedented levels following a legislative threat of budget cuts and further staff layoffs. Another pathway works through goal setting. At the individual level, performance rises to meet challenging goals even when no reward or punishment is associated with success or failure. Challenging goals are especially motivating (so long as they are not unrealistic or fanatical).[6] Furthermore, as I have already suggested, because the high costs of achieving some minimum level of collaborative capacity appear to justify only relatively ambitious collaborative efforts, political pressures that set ambitious performance goals nicely reinforce managers' preferences.

6. Locke, Latham, and Erez (1988).

As an instrument both of threat and of setting challenging goals, quantitative measures of performance outcomes probably have a more powerful effect than goals expressed less concretely.[7] Furthermore, properly conceived outcome measures can be part of a larger managerial strategy for developing interagency collaborative capacity. Consider the goals for reducing teenage pregnancy enshrined in the Oregon benchmarks program, a statewide program originally intended to propel the state toward 259 numerically defined social goals over two decades. Like most of the benchmarks, the pregnancy reduction goals are ambitious: Decrease the birthrate per 1,000 females ages 10 to 17 from 11.6 in 1992, to 5.4 in 1995, to 4.0 in 2000, and hold it there till 2010.[8] Commissioner Beverly Stein, the elected chief executive of Multnomah County (Portland and environs) and a former legislator who promoted both the benchmarks concept and the development of human services collaboratives, calls these "a magnet for collaboration":

> When you see the level of achievement that's expected, it's obvious that no one sector could do it. The County runs the Health Department here. But we can't achieve the benchmark on teen pregnancy ourselves. Even though we run school clinics and do a variety of things, unless we involve the churches and the nonprofit agencies, and schools, we wouldn't be able to achieve it.[9]

Careerist Purposes

In Max Weber's classical theory of bureaucracy, bureaucracy is a neutral instrument of policy. To some extent, of course, this is an accurate assessment. But it is also an instrument that serves individuals' very personal aspirations for security, income, prestige, power, and the

---

7. Latham and Lee (1986).

8. Oregon Progress Board, *Oregon Benchmarks: Standards for Measuring Statewide Progress and Government Performance*, Salem, Ore., 1992. In 1997 the Oregon legislature trimmed the number of benchmarks to 92 and "streamlined" the priority benchmarks from 39 to 22. Oregon Progress Board News, January 1998, p. 3.

9. See discussion on pp. 147–48. Performance measures, even when faithfully constructed, are not necessarily used to good effect. One program evaluation specialist in Multnomah County complained that the county's measurements never entered into decision processes of any importance. However, I do not know how reliable this observation is. Fletcher (1997).

opportunity to do meaningful work. Interagency collaboration can threaten all these aspirations.

Whether such threats can themselves lead to successful efforts to prevent an agency from contributing to collaborative activity is a different matter. If the threatened parties are at the top of the agency, they may well have the power to block collaboration. If they are at the middle and lower levels, delay and distortion may be more likely than real blockage.

JOB AND INCOME SECURITY. Collaboration can threaten job security by eliminating redundancies, leaving n-minus-x people doing a certain amount of work where n had done it before. Also, by reengineering it can remove the need for whole functions to be performed:

—San Diego County air quality inspectors working for the Environmental Health Department regularly visit gas stations to monitor emissions. It would hardly have added to their burden to test the accuracy of the pump readings at the same time. But this would have shrunk the workload of the county weights and measures inspectors. Although officials in the county recognized the potential savings, after some initial discussions the concept was quietly dropped.

—A close observer of the Coordinated Youth Services Council opined that, although the council was "a middle manager's dream," the heads of the participating public agencies were keeping their distance. Their situation, he said, was that of people who have built nice, comfortable houses and then one day discovered that the neighborhood was changing and "there isn't room any more for all those nice houses."

—The master contract simplified the reporting and application requirements of The Door so much that the highly paid controller position was downgraded, the controller left the organization, and several other overhead jobs were eliminated. As it happened, The Door was in poor financial straits and was being forced to downsize one way or another. As a nonprofit contractor used to living on the financial edge, looking for economies even at the expense of staff jobs was not unknown to them. For the public agencies that funded and regulated The Door, such layoffs would have been another matter. A middle manager for one of them described the situation:

Everyone is for staff protection. Nobody wants to see loss of staff. If you tell me that you're going to eliminate my job function, my first reaction has to be, "What about my own security, what about my job, what am I going to do? What does this mean? Will I have a job?"

Governmental agencies become very, very protective about that. That's why they need the widget reports: I've got to have those reports, it's part of my job function. And that's a big part of government. . . . I see that self-protectiveness all around. People don't want to do something that is going to ostensibly reduce their workload. If I have ten staff under me and I'm complaining that I am overworked, and you're telling me that you're going to reduce my staff requirements by 50 percent, what I'm going to think is, "Hey, that means that my staff will be expendable. That means they're going to lay off my staff. And then I'm expendable." And it goes on down the line.

Finally, when collaboration comes mixed with a heavy dose of prevention philosophy, as it usually does in the human services, it threatens to shrink the workload of agencies that depend on prevention's absence, or its lack of success, for their steady supply of clients. One veteran youth services manager said, "District attorneys and public defenders worry about too much success in preventing juvenile incarcerations. There might be too little work in their offices." In at least one state I visited, private providers of group home services for youths removed from abusive or threatening home situations have opposed "excessive" reliance on family-preservation-oriented systems reform and probation. A reputedly very idealistic residential treatment center provider who was also a staunch supporter of the Coordinated Youth Servics Council said,

> For all of us, there is self-interest that gets in the way, and I am not excluding myself. . . . I run residential treatment centers . . . and one of the [CYSC] agendas is to not place kids in residential treatment centers. So, while I also see the value of prevention and early intervention and getting kids out of residential treatment centers as soon as they can possibly get out of them, I also have a vested interest in wanting to continue to run what I do—and because I think [residence in a treatment center] is valuable for some kids and maybe the only way to grab hold of a kid for a period of time and refocus them so that they can be put back out

in the community. So you have these times when your stomach gets tight and when you realize that you may be helping to put yourself out of business.

STATUS. Any sort of reorganization implies change in the status trappings of individuals affected by it. Although there is always a mix of winners and losers following such a reorganization, the before-the-fact distribution of hopes and fears is probably weighted rather heavily toward fear. In addition, it is simply a lot easier to predict the variety of ways in which existing status arrangements can be shattered than it is to predict the new arrangements on which individuals will be able to capitalize. Because ICC development is experienced as a mild version of reorganization, there is likely to be more resistance than enthusiasm. A manager involved in Maryland's Systems Reform Initiative said, "Everyone seems to agree on the principles of the SRI. However, when it comes to the operationalization, departments may have different ways of approaching issues. . . . Sometimes people act cooperatively, but in reality they sabotage the work because they feel very threatened. In essence, we are asking staff to reinvent a system. That is not what they were hired to do and they do not know how they will fit into a new system."

ICC development can also pose status threats specific to certain professions. Higher-status professionals, such as physicians, may dislike the egalitarian connotations of working with lower-status professionals such as nurses and social workers in an ICC. Conversely, the lower-status professionals may wish to avoid exposure to the hierarchical claims of their higher-status partners. This would be especially likely in settings in which professions such as nursing and social work have successfully established organizational structures of their own, with decision hierarchies based on principles of professional autonomy and self-monitoring.[10] When the Marin County director of Health and Human Services mooted his plan to create a Children's Division with mental health therapists, social workers, and public health nurses blended into a more generic category, "there was this incredible furor . . . that professional disciplines were being devalued, that 'I am a Public Health worker, not a social worker.' . . . 'I'm better than somebody else because I'm one of these' . . . that runs up and down this system."

10. Iles and Auluck (1990).

STRESSFUL, TIME-CONSUMING, LABORIOUS WORK. As we saw in chapter 4, designing and running an effective ICC is not easy. The system has many moving parts, and they are hard to align and to keep aligned. George Bernard Shaw is said to have remarked that the trouble with socialism was that it required too many Wednesday nights, and the same is true of ICC development. It is a process laden with meetings, negotiations, memorandums, reports, diplomacy, and ever more meetings, not just across the partner agencies and the various professions associated with them but across hierarchical levels within any single agency. Furthermore, because community members are often involved, some of the meetings take place in the evenings and on weekends. In communities such as Oakland, where "collaboratives are all the rage," said one staff person for a youth agency, "it is terribly difficult getting the agencies to collaborate, and then you've got to go another level and get the collaboratives to collaborate. There are a dozen people in the city who do nothing but go to meetings."

FEAR OF FUTILITY. Like any innovation, interagency collaboration runs the risk of failure, embarrassment, criticism, and perhaps damage to one's career. "Failure" has a particular meaning in the case of ICC—namely, that many people, including oneself, put in a lot of time and effort, create expectations of change for themselves and for outsiders, and then have the whole venture stall, decline, and disintegrate. Why take the risk—nay, for many veteran bureaucrats who have seen enthusiasms wax and wane, why accept the virtual certainty—of experiencing such futility?

One problem with such an outlook is that once it becomes pervasive it is also a self-fulfilling prophecy. As with many collective action problems, if the parties convince themselves that the prospects of joint action are poor, the prospects *become* poor. I will discuss this dynamic in more detail, and some smart practices to deal with it, in chapter 8.

Bureaucratic Purposes

ICC development raises the unpleasant prospect of competition for an agency's resources of budget, turf, and autonomy, both from the partner agencies and from the emerging ICC itself. It also makes managers worry about becoming entangled with partner agencies whose incompetence or indifference might cause criticism and blame to fall on themselves.

MONEY. The contributions of public agencies to collaborative ventures take the form of personnel (dispatched to work in interagency teams, usually), facilities, information, or equipment but almost never money, which could in some subsequent budgetary cycle become permanently dislodged from the budget of the contributing agency. This is largely because such resources are so constrained to begin with. Council on Children and Families staff working on The Door master contract said, "The agency people view it as 'our money' and 'What do we give up?' and 'What do we get?'" Legislative and finance department overseers do not approve of agencies having access to flexible funds, however desirable that might sometimes be from the point of view of improving agency effectiveness and efficiency.

Even when such funds are available, agencies do not like to give their ICC partners any more claims over them than they absolutely must. This implies not just withholding the money, which is easy enough, but also withholding information about the existence of potentially useable funds or about the degree of flexibility with which they might be used for ICC-related purposes. Many an informant has told me, in effect, "Relations were good until it came to money." As one participant in Coordinated Youth Services Council case reviews said, "You ought to see what happens when we begin to discuss who will pick up the costs for a client. Everybody's antennae shake." At the council level, one informant said, "What we have now [mid-1997] are people very reluctant to push. We have public sector very reluctant to tell the agencies what they really think about them as partners in the planning. We have private agencies afraid to push the public sector: 'Come on. You're not dealing with this. You're not playing with us.'"

A particularly dramatic case of budgetary sensitivity is evident in the East Bay vegetation management plan. The two-volume plan covers almost everything from the physics of ignition and flame spread to the desired treatment of each five-acre polygon in the East Bay hills. Even the tasks to be performed by each agency or jurisdiction are delineated in some detail. What is missing is how much money they would each have to budget to get the job done.

TURF. Turf is probably the most fundamental of all elements of bureaucratic infrastructure. It is even more important than budget because turf can be used to justify budgetary claims, whereas budgets cannot be used to justify turf claims. Its boundaries are guarded with proportionate zeal. It is a reasonable hypothesis that the more agencies find themselves competing for the same resource niche, be it funding or problem domain or clientele group, the more they will distrust each others' motivations, fear each others' enhanced visibility, hide information about their own resource caches, and thus experience more difficulty in collaborating. Some of the most notorious examples of noncollaborative, even life-threatening, conduct come from the military services.[11] Conversely, one is not surprised to find that a Minnesota recycling program that had county mental health clients employed sorting batteries for a local environmental agency was not very hard to set up.[12] The environmental agency simply responded to one of the routine advertisements placed by mental health in the county newsletter about their clients' availability for employment. There was hardly even any negotiating over the amount of reimbursement to be paid to the mental health agency. Most of the reimbursement paid went to the clients, though a little was retained for overhead by the mental health agency.

As with budget, the potential competitors for an agency's turf are both the ICC itself and the partner agencies. Consider, for instance, a welfare-to-work program. The job development and placement functions can be performed by a variety of agencies. The Job Training Partnership Act agencies and the state employment departments can and do perform them. Although it is more of a stretch for them, community colleges and welfare agencies sometimes do the same. So do some job training contractors. Ownership of the job development and placement turf can be up for grabs.[13]

Agencies can try to protect their turf by fashioning distinctive competencies. After surviving merger and abolition threats from the governor's office, the conservation education unit of the California Integrated Waste Management Board and its counterpart in the Department of Conservation found a way to stay separate. The former concentrates on

---

11. See Hadley (1986, esp. pp. 3–22) on the failure of the hostage rescue mission in Iran in 1980.

12. This was a Ford Foundation and Kennedy School of Government at Harvard Innovation awards semifinalist.

13. The zeal to control this turf may be lessened by the fact that welfare recipients make for very unappealing clients for some of these agencies.

schools and general recycling, the latter on beverage containers and on households and businesses. However, one price the public may have paid for their politically induced specialization was the reluctance of these agencies to explore opportunities to create value by joint action— for instance, the joint sponsorship of publicity events. The Federal Emergency Management Agency and the California Office of Emergency Services both give grants to disaster victims and communities, and both have some role in disaster preparedness.[14] It is probably more difficult for them to differentiate themselves from one another than it is for the conservation education agencies to do so. Close observers say that the two agencies' relationship, beneath the surface of cordiality, is as noncollaborative as they can both manage.

AUTONOMY. Even when there is no danger of losing turf, agency managers may eschew collaboration in order to protect their decision-making autonomy. In 1983 three state and three federal agencies in California and the private nonprofit Nature Conservancy agreed to an interagency effort to identify significant natural areas and recommend management alternatives. The group, made up entirely of ecologists, assembled to work on the project, almost immediately became moribund, and was not resuscitated for three years. The cause of death, said one of the ecologists who helped to bring it back to life, was that someone from the California Department of Fish and Game "came in and said 'thou shalt do it this way,' and everybody said 'bye!'"[15]

Not all forms of collaboration threaten autonomy equally. Having to hold hearings, receive testimony, and listen to advice is not as troubling as having to prepare an analysis such as an environmental impact statement and respond in writing to other agencies' criticisms. Entering into a contractor relationship with another agency, and receiving funds

14. For a critical report on the Office of Emergency Services, see California State Auditor (1996, especially chap. 2).

15. Thomas (1997a, pp. 128–29). A study (Gans and Horton, 1975, p. 84) of thirty service integration projects in the early 1970s reported, "The most detrimental attitude was the desire of service providers to retain agency prerogatives with respect to control of service delivery. . . . It appeared often in super-agencies in which the integrator was attempting to consolidate established, traditional state or local government departments with their own clientele, federal grants, and degree of influence." However, Gans and Horton do not conjecture why service providers had this attitude—whether because of concerns about turf, autonomy, budget, mission, and so on. On alliances in the health sector, see Zuckerman, Kaluzny, and Ricketts (1995).

thereby, does not threaten autonomy if, after a souring of the relationship, it is easy to downsize or to find an alternative source of funds. In fact, the more varied the sources of funding, the less dependent an agency is on any one of them.

Agencies will therefore attempt not just to eschew autonomy-threatening relationships but to recast necessary relationships in their least threatening form. This may sometimes undermine ICC capacity to take effective action. In 1982 the commission constituted to review the 1980 East Bay Hills fire argued without success for a joint powers authority with taxing power. Some of the same players chose not to try the same arguments in 1992 and opted for the voluntary Vegetation Management Consortium instead. This concession to the spirit of localism, as well as to the complexity and duration of the process that would have been required to form a joint powers authority, may have been unavoidable. Most participants at the time also thought it would be inferior to a more informal arrangement in terms of effectiveness.

That autonomy is threatened by collaboration implies that agencies that are confident of their autonomy are more likely to collaborate than those that are not. Charles Bruner, a former Iowa legislator who led a movement to integrate funding streams for children's services, has written, "Healthy and secure agencies usually find it easier to collaborate than those in less favorable circumstances. Agencies mired in budgetary or other crises, lacking leadership, or subject to internal dissension are less likely to negotiate as equals with collaborative partners."[16]

Because many collaborative ventures start as pilot or demonstration projects with limited-term funding, agency managers may be reluctant to absorb such a project lest they create claims on funds for higher priority activities when the project funds run out. In addition, managers do not like the prospect of having to lay off people should they hold the line against reallocating funds to continue the "demonstration" project. A former Marin County health and human services director rejected a proffered foundation grant for these reasons, and critics accused him of having a "fear of funds."

ACCOUNTABILITY. Informants have rarely told me that they personally were concerned about turf or budgets, and they have only occasionally talked about autonomy. But they have frequently voiced

16. Bruner (1991, p. 19).

concerns about their agencies' accountability for certain kinds of performance that they have hesitated to entrust to their ICC partners. Conversely, they have attributed concerns about turf and budgets to their partners, concerns that these partners, they said or implied, were disguising as concerns about their accountability.

Consider a case of child sexual abuse followed by death that occurs while a family is under the nominal supervision of the Child Protective Services agency but in which the agency has delegated the management of this particular case to a public health nurse who works in the child's school and sees the child and her mother regularly. How likely is it that the Child Protective Services director will have to answer to legislators (and perhaps the press as well)? It takes only one legislator to make the life of the agency director miserable. The purposes that might inspire any one of dozens of legislators to go on the attack are numerous and varied, ranging from the desire to conduct responsible oversight to the wish to embarrass the executive branch controlled by the opposite political party.

In any case, the director should realistically fear that she will be held accountable in the event of trouble. Would not any director prefer to have direct control over the circumstances that might cause trouble rather than indirect control via a partner agency? The answer is not necessarily yes. Countervailing considerations might be that (1) Public Health might generally be better equipped to prevent such incidents than Child Protective Services, or (2) there might be such superior results from the partnership with Public Health across such a range of cases that a slightly increased risk of catastrophe was worth taking. One may suspect, however, that very few Child Protective Services directors would be able to view their personal risks, when faced with such a calculation, with the detachment required to opt for delegating the supervisory role to Public Health and the school system.

A much more pervasive anxiety than being criticized for ostensibly permitting a child's abuse and death is the anxiety that arises from the alleged mismanagement of public monies. The funding agencies that supported The Door were extremely reluctant to consolidate their oversight of The Door's expenditures with the oversight activities of other funding agencies lest. . . . Well, lest what, exactly? I asked many of the participants in the master contract and consolidated auditing reform what might happen. None would provide more than a vague scenario that "there could be trouble," and none would say that "trouble" was really very likely. But one could never tell. . . .

ETHNOCENTRISM. One might have thought that such concerns as were expressed in the previous section would be traceable to one or two historical incidents in the tribal bureaucratic memory in which perfectly honorable bureaucrats had been scapegoated by publicity-hungry legislators or something of this sort. I was unable to find any traces of such memories, however. This fact might signify that bureaucrats are the victims of irrational fears, or that they are selfishly self-protective even against relatively slight, but real, risks, or that the realistic basis for fear was large and properly understood but simply unknown it its details. Whatever the truth of the matter, it does sometimes make sense to think of agencies as being like tribes. Consider, for instance, the ethnocentric us-versus-them language that one frequently hears when people talk about relations between their agency and some partner agency. "We" are striving to carry out our mission, unite our diverse constituencies, muster our scarce resources for the common good, negotiate in good faith, and cooperate rationally in joint problem-solving. But "they" are unduly interested in protecting turf, hiding their real resources, pushing their policy agenda, and keeping control.

The ubiquity of ethnocentrism in human groups suggests that it would be present in this case, as in so many others.[17] The question is what it might explain that other perspectives—say, the dozen or so that I have already discussed in this chapter—could not explain more parsimoniously, meaning by that term in this context rationally and commonsensically rather than emotionally. The answer lies not just in the tendency to be unduly suspicious of involvements with agency outsiders but in the propensity to conform strongly to the customs and adhere to the beliefs that prevail in the agency.[18] These customs and beliefs sometimes include looking askance at the comparable practices that prevail among agency outsiders. In this situation, the ethnocentrism hypothesis predicts that antagonists collaborating with some other agency could effectively use insinuations of disloyalty to try to muzzle those who might be more favorable and to keep them from

17. LeVine and Campbell (1972).
18. On the possible ethnocentric roots of conformism and emotional solidarity, see Ostrom and Sedikides (1992); Ridley (1997); and Wilson (1978, pp. 162–64).

having even exploratory contacts with "outsiders." Whether they would actually do so, however, might depend on a number of other conditions, such as their opponents' skills in launching a counteroffensive. The ethnocentrism hypothesis would also predict an inappropriately high level of fear about the motives and power of agency outsiders. Based on my own year-long observations working in the Office of Policy Analysis in the U.S. Department of the Interior in 1974–75, bureaucratic ethnocentrism is far from trivial. However, I was not close enough to the cases I studied for this book to offer examples of the phenomenon with any confidence.

Countervailing Purposes

Mere reluctance to contribute resources to ICC development does not mean that an organization will not actually contribute. It very well might. Although the motives for protectionism are numerous, varied, and sometimes powerful, in many settings they are overmatched by countervailing purposes, the efficacy of which can sometimes be enhanced by certain smart practices.

The preeminent smart practice is simply to be aware of the great variety of countervailing purposes that are potentially in play and that may therefore be appealed to. As in the previous section, I consider countervailing purposes in three categories—value-creating, careerist, and bureaucratic—although in most real-life cases purposes are numerous, varied, and often mutually reinforcing.[19]

Value-Creating Purposes

Recollect the fundamental assumption, promoted in chapters 1 and 3, that, at least for the nineteen cases examined in this book, there exist genuine opportunities to create public value through interagency col-

19. Consider this advice, for instance, by the editor of a book about the value to adult education programs of cooperating with other institutions: "Cooperation is important because through cooperation the adult education agency can achieve vital ends that it cannot achieve easily in other ways." Beder (1984, p. 6). The ends mentioned include offsetting resource insecurity, increasing programmatic flexibility, and protecting autonomy. A study of how hospitals integrated primary care satellite facilities into their operations found that three mutually reinforcing and rather different strategies were used to persuade the medical staff to accommodate the change. First was to have a distinguished older physician take the lead. Second was to sell the idea that the specialists would bene-

laboration. Because it is so hard to disentangle or to know individuals' motives for action, I have not made a concerted effort to count the number of individuals who were motivated to a large extent by the desire to exploit these opportunities. My impression is that they are numerous. Less numerous, but still very evident, are the bureaucrats who are sufficiently stirred by these desires to want to have their agencies contribute agency resources to the collaborative efforts. Without wishing to be invidious by omitting any references, I would offer by way of example the many school principals who have facilitated the presence of Healthy Start and School-Based, the middle managers who started the Coordinated Youth Services Council, the executive cadres in Oregon's Department of Human Resources and Adult and Family Services, most of the agency managers involved in the Vegetation Management Consortium, the California state director of the Bureau of Land Management (with respect to the memorandum of understanding on biodiversity), and the Air Resources Board top management with respect to multimedia enforcement efforts. I include also the great many line workers whose time and energy are not just their own but also their agencies' resources and who are committed contributors to collaborative teams.

Probably more numerous, and very important, are value-creating bureaucrats who, although not offering agency resources, are sufficiently inclined to support an interagency effort that promises to increase public value that they will acquiesce if called on. The practitioner literature on collaboration in the human services areas emphasizes the immense importance of creating and disseminating "a vision," and it is for motivating this sort of audience, I suspect, that this prescription is most relevant.[20]

Arranging for value-creating reinvestment is a smart practice that can buy support for shifting resources toward an ICC. The state legislature's commitment to reinvest welfare savings in Oregon's JOBS programs almost certainly reinforced efforts among the agency partners at the district level and in Salem to make the collaborative effort produce substantial results. In the environmental enforcement area, California returns penalties collected from enforcement actions to the participating agencies. According to Gerald Johnston, these may cover

---

fit from increased referrals. Third was an ideological appeal that the change would benefit the poor. Shortell and Wickizer (1984).

20. See, for instance, Melaville and Blank (1993, pp. 5–18); Chynoweth and others (1992, pp. 45–46); Mattessich and Monsey (1992, pp. 28–29).

some 80 percent of the costs of the action, although the agencies may have to wait six to twelve months for the monies.

Advocates of preventive integrated services programming in regard to children and families usually argue that savings effected by reducing out-of-home placements could, and should, be reinvested in preventive programming. In Maryland, for instance, the state agencies in this domain have been promised 25 percent of the savings for this purpose, but I have little information about how effective this offer has been in motivating more collaborative effort. More important, Maryland created a new political constituency for reinvestment dollars, and indirectly for collaboration, at the local level, inasmuch as the other 75 percent of the savings came back to this level.

Organizational actors are sometimes on the lookout to promote their own particular conception of the public interest, and to do so by trying to influence the directions of their own agencies. A minority within their own agencies, support for the memorandum of understanding on biodiversity, and for other elements furthering this agenda, came from ecologists in California Fish and Game, the Bureau of Land Management, the Forest Service, and the California Department of Forestry and Fire Protection.[21] Interagency collaboration may be an especially favored technique for minority factions within potential partner agencies, because it gives them a legitimate way to engage in political coalition building external to their agencies.

Even if a minority viewpoint is limited to a few individuals in an agency, these can serve as strategic points of access for actors from outside the agency. When Lynn Dwyer was shuttling among regulatory agencies trying to line up umbrella permits for conservation projects in the Elkhorn Slough, a veteran in the Coastal Zone Commission who was well-connected and well-respected throughout the community of people concerned with the slough, Les Strnad, was able to steer her toward individuals in the agency who "understood their agency's mandate more widely or creatively."

For some actors it is the policy objective and not the agency at all that is the primary object of orientation. As I noted in chapter 3, interagency networks of like-minded political activists pushed the services integration agenda in Oregon and the Denver Family Opportunity community mobilization agenda in Denver. In the New York State master

21. Thomas (1997a, chap. 3).

contract case, the Council on Children and Families staff spearheading the effort worked to the degree they could through a network in the concerned agencies of management reformers. For Bill Carter at Cal/EPA the multimedia enforcement effort was probably as much about raising the prominence of enforcement as a regulatory tool—as opposed, say, to consultation, education, financial incentives, and so on—as it was about the multimedia focus. He was able to rely on enforcement-minded staff in all the state and local agencies he sought to bring into his orbit.

Careerist Purposes

Economists appreciate that the invisible hand of the competitive market can convert the private desire for personal gain into a socially desired mix of goods and services. Albeit with considerably less reliability, personal aspirations for career enhancement in bureaucratic and policy settings can sometimes lead to equally desirable results.

PERSONAL RENEWAL. Few people can be as enthusiastic about their agencies after five, ten, or twenty years as after five, ten, or twenty months. Most will still believe in their agency's mission, its general competence, and the good intentions of their fellow workers. However, most will also have noticed that its mission is often compromised by the necessity to limit political conflict, to serve personal agendas, and to bear a host of procedural and accountability burdens. Many of these individuals therefore will be attracted to the opportunity for personal renewal promised by interagency collaboration on a new programmatic or policy vision. As the state deputy director of School-Based remarked, "The secret of collaboration: When things get tough, just keep focusing on the children. That's what keeps people going." Citing Marilyn Ferguson and John Naisbitt, *The Aquarian Conspiracy*,[22] the deputy director talked about the many reservoirs of commitment and purpose to be found everywhere. "There is all this energy in little pockets" in the community and in agencies.

This is not to be confused with idealism. Far from it. This is realism, but of the special sort that holds the important reality not to be the bureaucracy and its imperatives but the deeper purposes for

22. Ferguson and Naisbitt (1987).

which the bureaucracy was created and continues to be funded by the public.

In more traditional settings getting involved with an ICC may be a way of breaking out of the confines of one's agency—perhaps in some agency settings the only way or the most accessible way to do so. One can feel that it is easier to work according to one's own philosophical or professional lights by being detailed to work with staff, and perhaps according to the routines, of some partner agency. This would be especially true if one's co-workers in the partner agency were professional or philosophical soul mates.

Working at an interagency boundary is also a smart practice for getting some creative sparks flying, which might strike a receptive opportunity. Writing about the private sector, Rosabeth Moss Kanter noted,

> Many of the best ideas are interdisciplinary or interfunctional in origin—as connoted by the root meaning of entrepreneurship as the development of "new combinations"—or they benefit from broader perspective and information from outside of the area primarily responsible for the innovation. . . . regardless of the origin of innovations, they inevitably send out ripples and reverberations to other organization units, whose behavior may be required to change in light of the needs of innovations, or whose cooperation is necessary if an innovation is to be fully developed or exploited. Or there may be the need to generate unexpected innovations in another domain in order to support the primary product, like the need to design a new motor to make the first Apple computer.[23]

The first two of these reasons apply to the public sector as well, although certainly to a lesser degree. Some twenty to twenty-five senior career bureaucrats from eleven federal departments, two independent agencies, and the White House met almost weekly for about two years, beginning in 1991, pursuant to a presidential mandate "to strengthen the delivery of support for rural development." They were called the National Rural Development Council. As a group, Beryl Radin reported, "they [found] meaning in the challenge of trying something in an environment where career bureaucrats are thought to be resistant to

---

23. Kanter (1988, p. 171).

change."[24] Radin's interviews about what the participants learned produced answers such as, "I got a sense of hope that government could operate well and that career officials could be positive and productive," "there is more creativity and professionalism in the federal bureaucracy than is usually perceived," and "this reinforced my belief that interagency initiatives are possible."

The opportunities for personal renewal are considerably expanded if ICC development occurs along with the kinds of job enrichment strategies described in chapter 4. The Oregon Adult and Family Services in the mid-1990s was becoming "a great place to work now, and people feel it," said Debra White, a member of its executive staff. The new tasks were personally inspiring, she said:

> As our functions began to change, and we saw this through the pilots, all of a sudden it wasn't just that our [Quality Control] rates are okay. Our function is now to figure out how to develop a system that can give people tools to move away from welfare. You just can't get there with a simple hierarchical structure, you just can't. Before we were "the welfare organization," and we owned welfare clients. Now I spend most of my time talking to community partners saying that welfare clients are just members of the community, and they are not so different from other members of the community.

Furthermore, the teamwork and collaboration were effective and satisfying:

> The new [workforce development] function forces you into both asking and telling. At all levels our people are dealing with their JTPA and Community College partners. So they are getting information about how those organizations work.
>
> Within the JOBS unit [in AFS headquarters] we say we're a team, [and that] means that it frankly doesn't matter if I or [my associate] gets called away at the last minute. The team can carry on and move forward without me. That is really different from what I've experienced before.

24. Radin (1996, p. 160).

Also, the constraints of hierarchy weakened, personal autonomy increased, and the spirit of collaboration crossed organizational levels:

> In every level, in order for people to do that kind of work, people have to be able to use their discretion, to figure out what makes sense in the context of what people really need. You can bet that every conflict the managers are experiencing the staff are having them too. The tips can go from staff upwards, or from managers downwards, about how the other organization is behaving. . . . I can't go into any meeting and make a proposal without everybody making objections and offering comments. There is no handing down orders!

An additional attraction of working collaboratively outside one's own organization is that it is not the same dull bureaucratic routine. The tasks involved are moderately complex. This implies a relatively greater number of stimulus sources and a heightened sense of arousal. These are satisfying work conditions.[25] Indeed, in some settings—and Oregon may be one—the excitement of the challenge may even extend to "reinventing" the entire system of governmental administration, of which ICC's creation is only one part.

OFFERING SECURITY. If the object of a collaborative effort is to increase programmatic performance rather than to reduce costs, it might make sense to promise that job security will not be compromised by the ICC. When it emerged that school guidance counselors, fearing their jobs would be threatened, were resisting School-Based, state officials promised that no one would lose his or her job as a result of the program.[26] When Contra Costa County was beginning to explore some integrated services–community development possibilities, the county administrator made peace with the skeptical county employee unions by promising to cut their caseloads in the integrated service teams by 50 percent.

An obvious and continuing work overload in the agency may be an even more persuasive guarantee of job security. Multimedia enforcement generally presented no layoff threats, I was told, because there

25. Campbell (1988).
26. Exactly how much political weight such promises have is a question that deserves research.

was such a large overhang of regulatory tasks that apparent redundancies, were there to be any, would easily be soaked up. At the 1995 multimedia enforcement symposium an attorney with long experience on the San Diego task force observed that there were no turf struggles over which agency should take the lead on a case because there was such a large workload the greater risk was in having too few volunteers, not too many.

CAREER OPPORTUNITIES ON THE COLLABORATION TRACK. ICC development occasionally offers some new career opportunities. At the line-staff, supervisorial, and middle-management levels, demand increases for people who have the personal skills for collaborative work and who can be trusted to work with the degree of autonomy that is often required (see chapter 4). Sometimes the demand is expressed in new positions. In School-Based, for instance, every one of the local sites required a director. Many of these came from among the bureaucrats working in one of the potential partner agencies. In other cases it is simply that people take on new functions that gives them more visibility, more of an opportunity to show off their talents.

Because the individuals who will profit from such career opportunities rarely know who they are during the crucial political gestation phases of a project, little help should be expected from this quarter in the earliest developmental efforts. However, once an ICC is up and running, these individuals can be counted on to try to protect it and to advocate for more resources from the partner agencies and from other sources too.

Bureaucratic Purposes

Agency professionals' struggles to protect and enhance bureaucratic turf and budgets might or might not advance ICC construction. Having seen above how they might not do so, we turn now to how they might.

ENHANCING AGENCY REVENUES. One of the nation's best-known advocates of integrated children, youth, and family services, Sid Gardner, is often quoted as saying, "Nothing coordinates like cash." The $6 million a year in new funds that New Jersey put behind School-Based bought a lot of local-level interagency collaboration. One of the main beneficiaries of the Denver Family Opportunities program has been the Community College of Denver, which found in JOBS clients a major new clientele group and with them a source of subsidized tuition payments and justification for budgetary subventions. It has been a main supporter of the DFO. The president of the college has also been the chair of the DFO steering committee. In Maryland the Systems Reform Initiative office made efforts, similar to those in New York, to have a single master contract with children's services providers. The initiative director proudly testified to a state senate hearing in early 1994 that this and related efforts at simplification had created 215 new private sector jobs, that Maryland was no longer shunned by service providers, that 100 interested providers had come to an orientation meeting the week before with state officials who were seeking to encourage them to offer their services in the state.

In Marin County the Probation Department was suddenly able to claim federal reimbursement (under Title IV-A of the Social Security Act) when it began to participate in the Coordinated Youth Services Council collaborative along with more traditionally reimbursable agencies such as Social Services. It received some $750,000 a year, which offset county general funding cuts of the previous year. It was also a lubricant for the collaborative process in general. A participant reported, "People began to talk about, well, how do you get this funding, and what's that, and pretty soon people start to have a more collegial kind of environment about the funding streams and realize in fact that maybe there's a way we could help you out. And we'll go back this way and you guys get this kind of money; and we'll take our eight percent— it's good for us, it's good for you."[27]

There are limits to what cash can buy, however. It cannot necessarily buy loyalty, enthusiasm, or commitment to the mission of the donor agency once the money stops. A study by Bruce Jacobs of social service agencies in the late 1960s, during the War on Poverty, found that many of these agencies, which traditionally served non-poor constituencies, moved somewhat toward offering more services and employment opportunities to the poor. The movement was relatively small, and many factors contributed, such as the occurrence of a riot in a city, but heading the list was grant money given by the local Community Action

27. Another informant had a different perspective, however. She said that Probation refused to contribute more to the collaborative despite the federal funds windfall and resented the fact.

Agency.[28] It was anticipated, though, that when the grants stopped, the old priorities would reassert themselves. "Without the [Community Action Agency's] grant, the program wouldn't last six months," one agency director in Jacobs's study said. Half of 287 social service agency directors in the study said that their programming would revert to the old pattern once War on Poverty money stopped.

One solution to the problem, though perhaps one of limited applicability, is to promise that the money will not stop. The originators of School-Based proclaimed in as many forums as possible, "This is for real; it is permanent. It is not a pilot or a demonstration. Look at the $6 million."

NEW TURF. If collaboratives often threaten existing turf, and are for that reason denied existing resources, they sometimes create new turf and for that reason attract what one might think of as bureaucratic venture capital. An unusually motivated bureaucratic empire builder might envision that any ICC likely to emerge from some particular venture she had begun would be likely to fall under her agency's, and perhaps her own, aegis. After all, if all the possible losses in money, power, status, and the like that I detailed previously could be *gained* by other program agencies and their managers, rather than simply dissipated, a helpful political constituency might form around such expectations.

Because it is bad form for agencies or their managers to be—or be seen to be or be thought to be—creating new turf or enhancing existing turf, no one is prepared to announce this as a strategy pursued by their agency or themselves. I was surprised to discover the characterization of ICC development as a form of turf creation was rare even in circles in which one might have expected it simply as an expression of tribal mistrust. However, I either heard directly or learned indirectly of turf grabbing being attributed to

—the Systems Reform Initiative in Maryland;

—the Department of Finance and Administration in Tennessee, its director David Manning, and also the state Health Department,

—the Adult and Family Services in Oregon and its director Steve Minnick;

—Arthur Bolton and the Center for Integrated Services for Families and Neighborhoods in Del Paso Heights with regard to the Prescott Project;

28. Jacobs (1981, p. 97).

—the Denver Department of Social Services with regard to Denver Family Opportunity;

—the Council on Children and Families in New York State;

—the Coordinated Youth Services Council in Marin County.

I do not appraise these attributions of turf grabbing independently; I merely report them. In a more general sense, though, it is a mistake to view turf grabbing as necessarily negative. It is like the pursuit of profit or the passion for honor. Although such motives may be selfish, they may, and often do, have beneficial social consequences. Turf creation and enhancement, to be sure, are more suspect than the other instances because the social system of which they are a part—governmental bureaucracy—is not, unlike markets that allocate profit or public opinion that allocates honor, well-designed to convert private interest into public benefit. Nevertheless, because there is probably too little interagency collaboration rather than too much, more initiative from would-be turf creators would probably do more good than harm.

Unfortunately, the suspicion of turf creators on the part of potential partner agencies inhibits this potentially useful dynamic. I shall argue in chapter 6 that this failing leaves an opening for what I will call facilitative leaders—for example, community foundations, low-level and low-profile staff working for nonthreatening agencies, and outside consultants.

ENVIRONMENTAL DEMANDS. Because the world is constantly changing. Because it does, no one can choose simply between the benefits of ICC development and its risks and costs. The bureaucratic costs of standing pat must be considered as well. The perception that "somehow, things are getting worse" often underlie efforts toward ICC development.[29] They underlay efforts in all the cases I studied for this book except multimedia enforcement, military base reuse, and antitobacco education. Social problems were getting worse: family disintegration, social disorder, human suffering, welfare dependency, habitat destruction, fire hazards. So were the institutional problems of government bureaucracies charged with coping: caseloads increasing, taxpayer-imposed fiscal constraints worsening, politicians getting more demanding, courts effectively rewriting agency procedures, public resentment of bureaucracy increasing. If in the face of such negative trends "something had to be done," interagency collaboration, because it is relatively

29. Chynoweth and others (1992, p. 44).

inexpensive and is symbolically as well as substantively "rational," is qualified as a very good something. Even agencies that would prefer not to contribute to whatever ICC is at hand often feel obliged to make at least a token contribution.

There are also sometimes demands from legislatures, governors, and the media for more programmatic performance or for more budget savings than can plausibly be accomplished without better collaboration— for example, with regard to East Bay fire prevention. There may also be pressure for interagency collaboration simply for symbolic purposes. Because program managers and agency heads usually wish to give at least the appearance of cooperation, especially if the stimulus is an explicit legislative or executive branch mandate, they convene interagency working groups and issue statements of collaborative intent. They are often lifeless affairs, with some participants simply going through the motions and others containing their frustration at the waste of time or the apparent futility of their efforts.

In addition to the real balance of risks shifting away from business as usual to trying some interagency collaboration, the psychology of risk taking pushes the same way. One of the more intriguing findings of cognitive behavior studies in psychology is that, when it comes to possible losses, people will tend to prefer to gamble on having to bear a large loss to paying out an actuarially equivalent sum to prevent it for certain.[30] A 20 percent chance of a $10,000 loss, for instance, is generally preferred to a $2,000 investment in seismic reinforcement that would prevent the loss for certain. Hence when all options look bad, the relatively large gambles entailed by an ICC may look less bad.

Furthermore, the perception of "crisis" may further exacerbate this tendency.[31] One reason is that, if an agency is badly failing in its current mission, the opportunity costs of trying something drastically different may be very low.[32] Debra White said the large-scale change came a lot more easily to the Adult and Family Services than to other agencies in

30. Dawes (1988, pp. 40–41).

31. Depending on one's definition, the perception of crisis may have been implicated in five cases in my set of nineteen ICCs: the spotted owl decision behind the memorandum of understanding on biodiversity, the foster care budget increases in Tennessee and Maryland, the legislative threat to fire department autonomy in the East Bay fire prevention case, and a toxic spill in 1989 that prompted interagency work on emergency response in the California multimedia enforcement case.

32. Brock and Cormick said the same about the willingness of organizations and groups to negotiate their way out of conflict over regulations.

Table 5-1. *Environmental Demands Help*

Environmental demands	ICC success level[a]		
	High	*Medium*	*Low*
High	Base cleanup New Jersey School-Based Youth Services Oregon Integrated Services Oregon Welfare Fire prevention Maryland Systems Reform Initiative New York contract administration	Memorandum of understanding on biodiversity Antitobacco education Del Paso Heights Tennessee Children's Plan Healthy Start	Base redevelopment
Medium and low	Elkhorn Slough Multimedia environmental enforcement	Riverside GAIN Denver Family Opportunity	Prescott Project Marin County Coordinated Youth Services Council

a. See chapter 3.

Oregon State government that have also been groping toward more collaborative work and flattening the hierarchy: "We had the advantage that everybody hates the welfare system, the taxpayers, the clients, ordinary citizens. . . . Other organizations are not rejecting their past as much. It was a lot easier for everyone in this organization to get the idea that our function was going to change. Other organizations are not looking for dramatic transformations, just a little tweaking."

Table 5-1 assesses the level of environmental demands for interagency collaborations for each of the nineteen ICCs described in chapter 3. Seven out of thirteen cases with high environmental demands are rated high success, compared to only two out of six cases with low or medium demands. Again, despite the small number of cases and the very rough assessment procedures, the table overall suggests that environmental demands do indeed have some effect.

It is possible to take advantage of environmental demands to induce or accelerate organizational change and improvement. It may even be advisable to create them if they do not already exist, "embracing rather than shunning accountability," in the words of Mark Moore.[33] One of Moore's prime examples is a new police commissioner reorienting the department toward proactive community policing by making highly visible public commitments to do this. The commissioner, Lee Brown in Houston in the 1980s, thereby increased his ability to challenge his own organization. Brown then won the support of a few managers who, betting on his success, undertook innovations consonant with his vision. Those who managed these innovations "experience[d] the organization as one that challenge[d] them to undertake new tasks and that [had] different purposes than those previously served." As they succeeded, they acquired new skills and found themselves converted to the new purposes and methods.[34]

The embrace-accountability strategy, smart practice though it is under some conditions, is not so clearly adaptable to the ICC context. An ICC cannot obviously embrace accountability, because it is not usually an entity that can be held accountable by an external constituency. Leaders of the partner agencies could in theory do this if they could define the exact ways in which they want to embrace the new accountability. But this is at best a slow and complex process (like the drafting of the New York master contract) and not the sort of bold stroke that is needed to outflank if not undermine the bureaucratic ethos.

Summary

I count fifteen to twenty reasons why agencies and people who work for them would be reluctant to contribute resources to an interagency collaborative and another eleven to fifteen reasons why they might overcome their reluctance or, indeed, contribute with enthusiasm. In the final analysis, though, how do these pros and cons stack up?

Obviously a simple count of "reasons" to give or withhold organizational resources proves nothing. The number of relevant players in any situation in which an ICC might conceivably take root is large. So is the number of relevant causal conditions or stimuli. Clearly one must understand the strength, not just the number, of the tugs of inertia and the

---

33. Moore (1996, p. 274). I take this to be an expression of the psychologist's prescription that it is often more motivating to constructive action to frame a crisis or threat as an opportunity. The threat frame may paralyze action or divert it into destructive channels (Weiss, 1996, pp. 134–35).

34. Moore (1996, pp. 267, 274, 283).

countervailing tugs of opportunity. Moreover, if ICC advocates are aware of the great variety of possible motivations to contribute personal and organizational resources to the cause—a decidedly smart practice—they may be able to frame arguments and create situations that enhance these.

If my original assumption is correct—that collaborative opportunities lie in wait in much greater number than people consider acting on them—then I think it is reasonable to infer that the additive force of all those inertial tugs is quite substantial. Once an ICC achieves some threshold level of momentum, though, the situation changes. The opportunities that my procollaboration theories of motivation depend on are not even perceptible until a few people begin to articulate them and then to trumpet them. Once that happens, the ICC is susceptible to a new dynamic. Inertial tugs to remain at rest, one might say, are countered by inertial tugs to remain in motion. The trajectory of the ICC becomes much more hopeful.

It also becomes much more dependent on ICC steering processes, the culture or ethos of the ICC, the dynamics of ICC development, and the presence or absence of strategic management skills—all to be discussed in the next three chapters.

6

How an Interagency Collaborative Steers a Course

If an ICC is similar to an organization, then like other effective organizations an ICC needs to be able to articulate its vision, define its mission, and choose its concrete goals. In tribute to Osborne and Gaebler's nice metaphorical distinction in *Reinventing Government* between "steering"—or goal and policysetting—and "rowing"—or implementing policy—we may call this overall process steering a course.[1] This chapter is about designing the mechanism for steering well.

The design challenge is complicated by the fact that steering a course is not just a technical process: It is a political process as well. Values, ideologies, constituencies, turf, power, and ego are all in play. Moreover, it is a political process with two levels. One involves setting direction. The other involves a struggle over the nature of the structure and the process for setting direction; it is in effect a constitutional struggle. The design challenge is complicated even further by the fact that those who steer are also, often, those who row. If they do not like the results of the steering process, they can nullify them by rowing weakly or out of sync with the other rowers.

Steering Well

Steering includes formal, overt, and self-conscious activities such as an executive board adopting a mission statement, rejecting a proposed budget, or deciding in principle to commit resources to sex education

1. Osborne and Gaebler (1992, chap. 1).

outreach activities in some neighborhood. It also includes many less obvious, less formal activities, such as an ongoing dialogue about mission and goals that is audible in the ICC environment. In some cases the "dialogue" is tacit and takes the form of someone from a partner agency simply doing something that signals to the other partners that a particular goal is now being legitimated or undermined—and perhaps some other partner agency entering objections and another rallying in support. Thus actions, nonactions, debates, and decisions are all potentially part of the steering process, and they can take place at all organizational levels, although the ones at higher levels typically are more consequential. This broad conception of the steering process is necessary to permit us to consider a broad range of design alternatives.

Steering well has three different dimensions. First, the quality of the chosen destination is important. In particular, how closely does the chosen course head toward "the public interest," however we define that term? Second, the course should be intelligently chosen. Steering toward the public interest is not just a matter of pointing in the right direction and relaxing. Energy and intelligence are required to make mid-course corrections, to recognize novel opportunities as they appear on the horizon, and to feed ideas back into the process for other participants to take account of. Third, there are process and the values associated with a "good" process.

Each of these three dimensions has, in addition to a technical component, an irreducible value component. My own values, therefore, will be evident in the discussion that follows.

The Public Interest

What is "the public interest"? It depends on whom you ask. Managers of each of the separate partner organizations in the ICC will have their own view of the most worthwhile destination for the ICC. It would be surprising if this view did not also have a bias toward construing a public interest that contained a large component identified with the mission of his or her agency. It might also be somewhat biased toward preserving the status quo. Therefore, any one individual's conception of the public interest can never be taken as more than a partial answer.

Elected officials who generally oversee the performance and spending of the ICC partners also cannot be counted on to give more than partial answers. The electoral system ensures this. Most elected officials

represent geographical districts rather than a whole polity. All are elec-
table by simple majorities or pluralities; these are decision rules that
leave either small or large minorities without much effective leverage.
Even were the election procedures to empower all voters equally, lack of
information on voters' parts about the actual conduct of their representatives would limit their effective leverage.

Elected officials do carry a vague mandate to somehow "rise above"
their electoral constituencies and represent the polity as a whole. They
can also claim a mandate, and therefore a right, to act on their own best
understanding of the public interest, even if this sometimes means
ignoring voters' preferences. But elected officials' claims actually to be
doing so need not always be taken seriously. Like the rest of us, elected
officials often permit some gap between their claims and their true
intentions, and between their true intentions and the conduct that actually emerges.

Where, then, are we to turn for a conception of a "public interest"
against which we can measure the worth of alternative ICC steering
processes? First, I propose to start with the rough and ready utilitarian
calculus that economists, policy analysts, and many ordinary citizens
apply to government agencies in general. On the positive side, how
much do its customers value its services? Are there many such customers? Is the ICC reaching the full set of potential customers? On the
negative side, what are the direct financial costs? Besides these, are there
nonfinancial opportunity costs (for example, regulatory delays)? And
how burdensome are the various "hassles" of dealing with the ICC?

Second, how much do citizens in general value what the ICC does?
This question is important because customers are not the only people
with legitimate standing to evaluate the ICC's performance.[2] ICCs in a
regulatory line of work, for instance, affect individuals who may never
have direct contact with any of the partner agencies but who indirectly
experience benefits and costs that these agencies' policies and their
administrative activities impose.

Third, because the costs and benefits created by many agencies may
not be understood by almost anyone besides a small circle of policymakers and policy analysts, we may ask how the more technically
gifted and disinterested members of this small circle estimate such costs
and benefits. A proper benefit–cost estimation of the ICC's destination

2. For a useful elaboration of this point see Moore (1996, pp. 36–38).

will almost always take into account the values imputed by customers and citizens. Hence this third, philosophically utilitarian approach to assessing the public interest in my view comes closer to providing a "good" answer than the others.[3] Mark Moore, as I read him, adds a further, and I believe appropriate, test of a good answer: Those who believe in it ought at some point to be able to persuade citizens and elected representatives to continue to endorse it once it becomes clear what it is.[4]

Steering Intelligently

Steering well means not only choosing a proper destination (that is, close to the public interest) but an intelligent course to get there. Intelligence of this sort grows out of accumulated knowledge and incoming information. If the partners are intelligent in the way they handle this knowledge and information, they share it among one another to a fair degree and find a way to create what Innes, Gruber, and their colleagues call *intellectual capital*.[5] By this they mean "agreed on facts, shared problem definitions, and mutual understandings [that] not only [provide] a common basis for discussion and [move] the players toward agreement on policy issues, but [allow] them to use this shared information to coordinate many of their actions."[6] Collaborators cannot always choose partners who share intellectual capital, but I would count it as a smart practice for them to create it as they go along.

SHARED DEFINITIONS OF PROBLEMS AND OPPORTUNITIES. One form of intellectual capital is well-documented technical information about conditions that are at least arguably definable as problems or opportunities. In the cases studied by Innes, Gruber, and others, for instance, participants in the San Diego Regional Growth Management Strategy carried out statistical projections of growth and infrastructure

3. Provided they are also part of the explicit or implicit policy mandate, we should also take account of substantive (and often contested) values that are not so easily captured by a utilitarian calculus, values such as religious freedom, justice, respect for others, concern for poor and oppressed individuals.

4. Moore (1996, p. 53).

5. Innes and others (1994, pp. ix–x).

6. Innes and others (1994, pp. ix–x).

needs.[7] In the San Francisco Bay management project, the key players "moved away from adversarial science, which had been encouraged by the use of litigation as a conflict resolution strategy, to consensual science," for which the key step was agreeing on the facts that the experts deemed relevant.[8] The East Bay Vegetation Management Consortium, over a two-year period, produced a two-volume *Fire Hazard Mitigation Program and Fuel Management Plan for the East Bay Hills* that became a standard reference document for all the players thereafter.[9]

In welfare-to-work programs, understanding grows over time among the diverse collaborators about where the intersection lies of client aspirations, public expectations, and agency philosophy. For instance, mutual understanding ideally would increase between welfare staff and community college staff about such matters as how to focus on course content and class scheduling that the welfare participants need and want and that the welfare agency may need bureaucratically to meet certain prescribed programming standards.

PROBING. Another form of intellectual capital is knowledge of the relevant local political landscape. The significant details are surprisingly minute. They are the situations and personalities that could enable an actor to know what will work to build a functioning operating system, to pry resources loose from skeptical agency heads, to build momentum, to create political protection, and so on. Such knowledge comes from probing, from careful asking and observing. It also comes from trial and error. Of necessity, the trial and error part of the process is slow and filled with mistakes and misperceptions. The implementing network around the New York State Council on Children and Families wasted weeks or months of working with fiscal experts to design the state's master contract with The Door, because when the program experts were finally brought into the process, they explained that the envisioned contracts would completely undermine program managers. It took some two years for the Prescott organizers to put on a highly appreciated health fair in the neighborhood.

Learning also occurs through success. As Karl Weick wrote in his famous 1984 presidential address to the American Psychological

7. Innes and others (1994, p. 49).
8. Innes and others (1994, p. 50).
9. Amphion Environmental Inc. (1995).

Association, published in the *American Psychologist* as "Small Wins: Redefining the Scale of Social Problems," a successful venture provides confidence, information, "stirs up the setting," and makes the next project possible. People and organizations learn about themselves, their capabilities, and their environments.[10] It was only after their relative success with a welfare-to-work collaborative that the Colorado Trust moved to form a collaborative to deal with teenage pregnancy, a much harder problem.[11]

STRATEGIC IDEAS. Detailed information and technical understanding, however abundant, do not by themselves lead to a workable strategic conception of how to steer better. An interpretive lens is necessary, a lens that provides focus and enables insight. Such a lens is typically a verbal formula or slogan such as "multimedia enforcement" or "preventing wildfires in the buffer zone" or "services integration" or "doing everything in our power to promote [welfare client] self-sufficiency" or "keeping families together and safe." Such verbal symbols suggestively link an idea about objectives and an idea about means, however roughly and indistinctly. That is why I call them *strategic ideas*.

My concept of a strategic idea is similar to the concept of *vision* that practitioners talk and write about ("Partners establish common ground . . . share information about each other and the needs of families and children in their community . . . create a shared vision of what a better service delivery system would look like. . . .").[12] I use *strategic idea*, however, because it is more general than *vision*. *Vision* has rhetorical overtones that may be meaningful for children's services but are inappropriate in the context of, say, criminal environmental prosecutions.

In some cases the strategic idea is weak at first, barely coherent. It gains definition over time, as top managers and others in the organization act, reflect on action, try out first one set of words and phrases, then another. Eventually something emerges that the organization sticks with. Robert D. Behn calls this process "groping along" and exemplifies it with the experiments in slogan making by the Massachusetts Department of Public Welfare when it was inventing ET Choices, its

---

10. Weick (1984).
11. East (1993, p. 67); Weatherley and others (1987, p. 87).
12. Melaville and Blank (1993, p. 20).

welfare-to-work program of the mid-1980s. They finally came up with "route out of poverty."[13]

In other cases, the strategic idea is so strong that when combined with situational realities and resource constraints it leaves relatively little room for a council or a board to do much steering at all. In the case of Healthy Start, among sixty-six sites funded in 1992 and 1993, it made relatively little difference what choices the collaboratives asserted during the planning phase: All the sites delivered a similar mix of services. The most extreme difference among sites was 6 percent more health and mental health services in cases in which these goals were part of the plan than where they were not.[14]

THE ENVIRONMENT TEACHES. It is a mistake to think of the people involved in steering as the only active element in the learning process. The ICC environment is also an active teacher. More precisely, people in the environment praise, complain, suggest, criticize, act, and react; and so it is the people in the environment who are the active teachers. Their "teaching" is not necessarily didactic. Sometimes it is just a matter of stirring up thoughts and accidentally activating an idea that had been unconsciously taking shape in someone's mind. Of course, the "teaching" is more effective if it meets someone who is prepared and open-minded. When Gerald Johnston took over as multimedia enforcement champion at Cal/EPA, his two big strategic ideas were a statewide SWAT team and local environmental enforcement task forces in only the populous counties in the state. These dissolved into two quite different ideas linked in one big strategic idea of task forces in every region or county able to draw on the entire reservoir of resources available to the Cal/EPA. The shift occurred almost unconsciously. A county district attorney who was an old friend and colleague of Johnston's asked for some help setting up a task force in a rural region. Then a U.S. attorney in another part of the state asked for similar assistance. The SWAT idea then faded into the background, and the idea of committing to total statewide coverage by task forces took its place. It would prove to be

13. Behn (1991, p. 133). In an earlier publication, Behn analyzed the groping along of Ira Jackson in his first few years as head of the Massachusetts Department of Revenue. Out of this groping came Jackson's characterization of his own strategy: "Honest, firm, and fair revenue collection" (Behn, 1988, p. 644). (See discussion in chap. 2.)

14. Wagner, Newman, and Golan (1996, p. 3-6).

politically popular, require little in the way of new resources, and be almost immediately implementable.

Process Values

Process values also should count for something—inclusiveness, representativeness, accessibility, fairness, openness, and integrity, for example. In practice these often boil down to a prescription to try to build a broad consensus behind the goals of the ICC.

The practical difficulties of following this prescription are substantial, however. The fragmentation of political and bureaucratic power in our pluralistic system is such that authority alone is rarely able to cause agencies to line up and salute. The same pluralistic political system that causes agencies' task activities to be so fragmented as to make collaboration potentially valuable also stands in the way of allowing the collaboration to take place. To the extent that the pluralist political system can be overcome, therefore, it is largely by behavioral adaptations by actors in the system, in this case by means of reaching out to one another across the fissures within the system.

Just how complete and deep does consensus need to be? At a simple level more is better. Consensus building is a "nice" thing to do. It reflects egalitarianism, inclusiveness, and, in certain policy contexts, a desire to help the weak. Fully 98 percent of the Healthy Start sites "agreed" that decisions were made by consensus, and 30 percent "strongly agreed."[15] I do not doubt that the widespread existence of consensus decisionmaking reflects an equally widespread belief that it is the right thing to do.

Furthermore, what broad and deep currents of public opinion hold to be normative, democratic politics must deem to be prudent. Neglecting to bring into the founding consensus an important community group representing African American interests delayed the startup of the CYSC for at least six months while repair work was done. The executive director of a community development collaborative in rural Oregon built largely on a foundation supplied by the local schools, and the state social services agency was careful to involve the school board

15. Wagner and others (1994b, p. 2-19). Leadership also tended, over time, to gravitate toward a shared mode and toward a leader chosen by the collaborative itself, as opposed to being selected by tradition or in response to regulations (Golan and others, 1996, p. 4-9).

members in her work even though she assumed they might prove hostile: "We like to have them where we can watch them."[16]

Who exactly is to be brought into the consensus-building process? "Inclusion of all key stakeholders is important," according to Innes and colleagues.[17] But who or what is a stakeholder? There are certain objective stakeholders: any agency that engages in tasks that might usefully be incorporated into the repertoire of the ICC, and any agency whose budget, turf, or employees might be affected by the actions of the ICC. Citizens who receive benefits or services, or who are subject to regulation by the ICC or its components, would also count as stakeholders. So would those for whom the ICC in any of its manifestations might create symbolic or political stakes—for example, the Oakland City Council member who would not tolerate a community development ICC taking root in a poor district in her neighborhood without her blessing. In the last analysis, therefore, stakeholders are probably people who decide to think of themselves as stakeholders.

CONTRARY ARGUMENTS. Yet there are normative and prudential arguments against such broad inclusiveness. On the exclusively normative plane, the more open-ended and inclusive the consensus-building process is, the more leverage it typically gives to those stakeholders who would protect a mediocre status quo.[18] These are bound to be more numerous and more determined than those who favor change. Apparently in part to avoid this problem, a consensus-building process in Oregon, led by the state Commission on Children and Families, did little to bring the state Children's Services Division into the final consensus.

Open-endedness and inclusiveness also increase pressure to buy off stakeholders who may not have much to contribute to the ICC but whose consent needs to be bought somehow, perhaps with a small contract to provide service or an implicit promise to permit the hiring of someone's nephew.

16. Technical problems in managing large numbers of participants are constantly being addressed. In the early days of negotiated rule making, Susskind reported that groups as large as twenty-five were successfully managed using two or three skilled facilitators (Susskind, Babitt, and Segal, 1993, p. 155).

17. Innes and others (1994, p. xii).

18. It also gives a handhold to interests that would rip off the system. Probably in part to avoid this problem School-Based was happy to avoid the Newark Board of Education in favor of the Essex County Vocational School system. (Newark is located in Essex County.)

Finally, the more protracted the goal-setting process and the less ambitious the goals the ICC appears ready to choose, the less motivated are stakeholders to want to contribute resources to it; as we saw in chapter 5, without some compelling vision of the future, there is often no reason *not* to protect the status quo.

A strategic choice needs to be made about whether to try to co-opt possible adversaries by bringing them into the consensus-forming process or to protect the process from disruption and delay by excluding them. Bureau of Land Management California director Ed Hastey, in organizing the Executive Council on Biological Diversity, made a conscious decision to exclude the regulatory agencies such as the regional office of the EPA, the state Water Resources Control Board, and the national Marine Fishery Service. "The regulatory agencies don't look at things in the same light as land management agencies . . . they're so focused on regulations and what's black and white. The only way this thing is gonna work is [if] people . . . give a little bit."[19] The celebrated effort in the mid-1980s to forge a national coal policy acceptable to environmentalists and coal companies succeeded with these players. It subsequently foundered, however, when excluded or marginalized interests—truckers, railroaders, miners, members of Congress, the Office of Surface Mining, and other agency officials—pointedly ignored or opposed the proposed policy.[20]

Regulatory ICCs run a special risk. Although they might intend to bring in the regulated parties as a way to legitimize whatever consensus might be achieved and perhaps even to improve on its substance, the "co-opted" might become the "co-opters." An agency ecologist close to the Biodiversity Executive Council noted that when the counties eventually joined

The hammering we'd get from . . . legislative offices almost just stopped. At earlier meetings, the legislators, and friends of loggers, and the wives of loggers, or somebody was *always* there, and really just being disruptive. Now . . . it may be that they realize

19. Thomas (1997a, p. 172). Hastey was also inclined to limit the scope of the council to terrestrial habitats and ignore the aquatic. For resource management purposes, BLM domain is nearly all terrestrial.

20. Gray and Hay (1986).

there's no threat to their way of life. . . . It may be that in that case [the Council] is a dud. If something isn't causing friction politically, then maybe it isn't doing anything.[21]

The norms of inclusiveness and consensus imply discussion, indeed many hours of discussion with many tens or hundreds or thousands of people. Activists involved in ICC development commonly lament that the process is endless and wearisome. Moreover, if one were to take seriously the progressive-sounding and oft-recommended idea that "buy-in" from all stakeholders is also needed for organizational change, including "buy-in" from lower-level organizational staff, then the amount of consensus building required is truly amazing. A standard design challenge, therefore, is how to reconcile the norms of inclusiveness and consensus with the value of keeping the steering process manageable—another process value sometimes not sufficiently appreciated.

Some help is to be found in the fact that not every stakeholder needs to acquiesce in the consensus with great enthusiasm, or even agree on every issue. Grudging and silent toleration will do in some cases, provided these reluctant stakeholders are not too numerous or in a position to effectively sabotage the ICC. In other cases, the only agreement needed on something that affects the ICC in its entirety might be between two organizational actors dealing with a relatively minor issue. Minor stakeholders, who would not have much to contribute to the ICC in any case, can easily be allowed to withdraw entirely, as happened in the case of the New York master contract. The state Department of Labor could not accept the new arrangements and pulled out its funding.

Moreover, the majority of stakeholders might be prepared to accept a set of goals, operating relationships, and resource commitments that a small and active minority will be able to construct, if they are given the right to review and try to amend the work of the minority at some timely point along the way. The minority can be said, following the eighteenth-century political philosopher Edmund Burke, to supply "virtual representation" to the majority. In the ICC case this clearly happens within organizations, when the numerous stakeholders at

21. Thomas (1997a, p. 235).

middle and lower levels allow top management to represent them, and, conversely, when top management allows the middle and lower levels, implicitly, to act on their behalf.[22]

Finally, a norm of sufficient consensus would permit effective consensus to be considerably less than complete. The lower the level of sufficiency in both an absolute and a relative sense, the greater the manageability and dispatch in getting productive work to move ahead.[23] How much counts as sufficient, however, differs according to the type of steering structure in question. I shall return to this issue later.

Smart Practices in the Design of Steering Processes

In this section I discuss three smart practices that bear on the design and management of steering processes: substituting "management" for "governance"; letting form follow function; and legitimating a leadership role.

Substituting "Management" for "Governance"

As I pointed out in chapter 3, community organizing advocates and theorists have worried a great deal about issues of who was to control the steering structure for whatever ICC was to be created. The same is true of the many policy intellectuals concerned with promoting an inte-

---

22. Mizrahi and Rosenthal (1993, pp. 27–29) provide a useful summary of methods used by community organizers to resolve some of the tensions between inclusiveness, equality, effectiveness, and expeditiousness. Some of them apply to ICCs more generally: What a group loses in voting rights can be given back, in part, with respect to power to set the agenda and vice versa; the group can use honorary, technical, and advisory membership rights in addition to membership status with more comprehensive rights; the group can permit or encourage parallel groups or caucuses of outsiders.

23. The effectiveness of such a process finds support in an interesting simulation study in the theoretical literature. Fritz W. Scharpf and Mathias Mohr have conducted a fascinating exercise simulating social decisionmaking under conditions rather similar to those that would confront a typical set of agency representatives attempting to construct a service collaborative. They concluded that the general good is best served by a decision-making process that (1) permits a core coalition possibly much smaller than the whole set of provider agencies to take the lead in designing the operating system for the collaborative but (2) has this coalition in effect buy the consent of the provider agencies not included in the coalition. The logic is that a relatively small core group can hold down the transaction costs of figuring out what sort of collaboration would make good sense, but that their temptations to self-interested exploitation of the situation are curbed by the necessity to gain consent from the outer ring (Scharpf and Mohr, 1994).

grated services agenda for children and families.[24] The standard mix of senior executives and bureaucrats would not do, the argument has gone, because these actors were too much in thrall to the status quo and perhaps to the historical habits of institutions and professions. In addition, because customers, clients, and consumers are heterogeneous—at least as heterogeneous as the partner agencies themselves—they might have different priorities regarding what the collaborative ought to be doing. The greater the heterogeneity, the more important the procedures for appointing representatives and for making decisions become. This is especially so when the stakes are high—that is, when the scope of the collaborative is turning out to be broad and its ambition large. This was the case with the model cities demonstration agencies and community action agencies of the mid- and late 1960s.[25]

This line of thinking is generally on target, except for one important assumption: *Governing* is not the only way to do *steering*, and for many purposes it is surely not the best way. *Governing* is too serious a business. Its basic organizing principles are dignified by the adjective "constitutional," and setting up and running a constitutional order can entail high costs in time and energy. Time spent debating who is entitled to how many seats on what sort of a board that will have exactly what sort of powers is time that might otherwise have been spent on raising resources, improving the operating subsystem, or doing productive work at the line level.[26] This expenditure has to be justified by reference to significantly better steering (or something else, like more political protection from outside critics) in the long run. Clearly, not everyone believes it so. The residents of the Del Paso Heights community, offered several versions of a community governance model over the years, never accepted any of them. "There was no upsurge of community support," according

24. The Pew Foundation, when it was funding demonstration projects aiming at ambitious system reform, commissioned a study that ended up surveying an astonishing variety of conceivable structural forms. See Reveal (1991).

25. Brager and Specht (1973, pp. 52–53).

26. "The experience of community interventions suggests that much of [the] attention to building an organizational structure (e.g., designation of committees, task forces, roles and responsibilities) is ephemeral or even counterproductive. Too many coalitions spend significant amounts of their resources initiating and revising organizational charts rather than focusing on purposes and program activities to accomplish them. This tendency can be exacerbated in coalitions with professional staff who have experience in organizations because they tend to emulate traditional organizational structures." (Phillips and Springer, 1997, p. 5).

to an evaluation report to the Sacramento county executive in July 1995.[27] I heard persuasive objections also from a children's services advocate in Marin County about the highly prescriptive local governance structure required by SB 997,[28] a law that permitted limited decategorization of funds for serving children and families; something like CYSC was a "leaner and more graceful" way to accomplish the same thing, one observer said. Arthur Bolton claimed, in an interview in mid-1997, that his ideas about the desirability and practicability of the ideal governance structures for the CISFAN projects were wrong-headed, "entirely too mechanistic."

If *good governance* suggests a steering process perhaps too encumbered by its own apparatus, might *good management* be better? For most purposes it is. It suggests the importance of steering intelligently, an evaluative stance that looks critically at investment in its own overhead functions, a bias in favor of consensus building rather than majority-rule decisionmaking. In its contemporary manifestations of reinvention, reengineering, and TQM—concerned, as these are, with customer service, quality, excellence, and continuous improvement—it even addresses some of the concerns that the rhetoric of steering by governance raises, namely, improving bureaucratic responsiveness and accountability and respecting the rights of consumers. During the 1960s, before it occurred to anyone to try to reform public agencies from within, the only evident strategy for making a local ICC function better was to turn it over to a nonbureaucratic set of rulers. An alternative strategy today is to turn it over to collaboratively minded elements within the governing bureaucracies.

This was clearly the approach of the fire prevention ICC in the East Bay hills. The partner agencies rejected a joint powers authority partly out of a desire to protect the agencies' autonomy and partly on technical grounds pertaining to the diversity of legal entities (cities, counties, independent districts, the University of California) and the complexity of spelling out the exact jurisdiction of a joint powers authority over as broad a domain as fire fighting and fire suppression. The Hills Emergency Forum was a workable substitute as a discussion and policysetting group, whereas the operational work, and everything but the budgetary power, was devolved to the middle-level professionals and managers in the Vegetation Management Consortium.

27. Minnicucci Associates (1995, p. 35).
28. California Welfare and Institutions Code, sec. 18986.

In multibranch ICCs the managerial strategy requires a two-pronged approach: Constitute ICCs locally that are steered by collaboratively minded bureaucrats and see to it that the state or other central bureaucrats who oversee or support these local ICCs are themselves of a collaborative bent. How does one choose the local sites? One approach is to move site by site or district by district on the basis of local voluntarism, as has been done in Healthy Start, School-Based, Oregon Integrated Services, CISFAN's community organization projects, The Door, watershed-based biodiversity protection (Elkhorn Slough), and multimedia enforcement under Gerald Johnston. Voluntarism of this sort is something of a smart practice for a number of reasons. If some sort of resource, such as state-level managerial attention, is in limited supply, it allows the most motivated communities or site-based leaders to access this resource first. Voluntarism is also a filter: It is a way of identifying and giving low priority to the sites that are *less* likely to have what it takes to make the ICC succeed. This saves resources and protects the momentum that comes from being able to demonstrate early successes in what promises to be a long developmental period (see chapter 8).

This strategy is vulnerable to mistakes in the selection process. The CISFAN leadership proved to be mistaken in selecting the Prescott neighborhood. The local motivation may simply have been absent. Another vulnerability concerns the adequacy of support from the central organizations, which I discussed in chapter 4.

The other main approach to choosing local sites is to promote reform on an organization-wide or statewide basis all at once—for example, the Tennessee Children's Plan, the memorandum of understanding on biodiversity, Maryland Systems Reform Initiative, the Riverside Department of Social Services GAIN program, the Oregon Adult and Family Services, and the California Anti-Tobacco Education Program. This is manageable in small organizations such as the Riverside Department of Social Services. It is much harder on a large scale, and I return to this topic in chapter 8.

CONSUMER REPRESENTATION. As we saw in chapter 4, formally involving consumers in the service delivery process was one way of trying to offset the bias of professionals and bureaucrats to think too abstractly, too narrowly, and too unimaginatively about the real needs and desires of the individuals they are serving. The same applies to steering the ICC as a whole and to introducing a force for change in what can be an even larger strategy of bureaucratic reform. The odds of steering in a public interest direction improve if consumers are brought into the process.

In the human services area, it is not uncommon for collaboratives to install consumer representatives on their advisory boards or even their policymaking bodies. After all, the agency managers who are progressive enough to wish to consider collaborative strategies are also "progressive" enough to take steps to counter the professional and bureaucratic bias of themselves and their fellow service providers.[29] If they are not in fact that progressive, they nevertheless are unwilling to acknowledge this to their colleagues who are pushing for consumer representation. Although a study of the forty Healthy Start sites funded in 1992 found only 19 percent included parents on the collaborative membership lists, 45 percent reported parents participating in at least some of the collaborative's decisionmaking. Half reported that parents were members of working groups that aided the collaborative. In a third of the collaboratives, parents were hired as staff members.[30]

The general prescription for consumer representation in the councils of the powerful does not apply in all cases. Provider representatives sometimes need to be able to air their dirty linen with minimal embarrassment and without fear of punishment by external critics. They also need to be able to talk about sensitive matters such as their relationships with legislators or finance department analysts without worrying that their strategies and tactics will be disclosed. Presumably, however, any steering structure, no matter how concerned to provide a cloak of privacy, can create a consumer advisory panel or some other such structure.

Getting the consumer representatives to play an effective role is another problem, however. As the irate youth representatives to Oakland's collaboratives (see chapter 4) pointed out, meetings are often held during the work day (or in the case of Oakland, the school day), when it is convenient for the service providers but not for the consumers. The consumers cannot easily conceptualize the operational system that an ICC will embody, its resource requirements, or the political constraints. They are certainly unfamiliar with the language of public administration and the jargon of the service professionals (and sometimes even their mother tongues). In some cases they can simply func-

29. In Healthy Start, collaboratives that reached out to parents also tended to reach out more to other programs in the community (Golan and others, 1996, p. 4-14).

30. Golan and others (1996, pp. 4-14, 4-15).

tion as problem identifiers, critics, and general gadflies, and they will be of genuine value to the system in doing so. However, it may be hard for the consumer representatives to see how much value they actually create in the process. It is not uncommon for their participation to drop off substantially after some initial period of enthusiasm.

It is possible to compensate for these problems in some degree by trying to design a more accommodative meeting schedule, paying consumer representatives a per diem sum for attendance or a fee for pre-meeting preparation, and providing training in the substance of the programs and in the skills of group work. In the Vaughan Street School in Los Angeles, where the parents constitute 50 percent of the board that runs both the Healthy Start program and some aspects of the regular educational curriculum, the parents thought it essential to begin by getting trained in just such group skills. In the forty Healthy Start sites begun in 1992, 77 percent said they routinely provided interpreters at or after meetings; 63 percent provided child care at meetings or other events; 62 percent encouraged parents to voice their ideas about the school or the program; 47 percent held meetings after working hours; 28 percent educated staff about parents' perspectives; and 23 percent arranged for training.[31]

SPECIAL PROBLEMS OF REGULATION. In the case of environmental and other types of regulation, interagency collaboratives might logically look to the parties they regulate as one type of customer whose advice could usefully be sought. Insofar as the regulated enterprises wish to cooperate with the spirit of the regulatory regime, the regulatory agencies and the enterprises can indeed be thought of as exchanging services with one another; and the enterprises are indeed like customers of the agencies. Because agency–enterprise relationships can sometimes be adversarial, however, bringing the regulated parties into the circle of stakeholders is either undesirable or must be handled with great care.

Proposing to do so is also likely to cause disputes among officials of the regulatory agencies. At the 1995 Environmental Enforcement Symposium, some agency attorneys and staff from district attorneys offices strongly objected to the presence in the audience of individuals representing the regulated community. "We are giving away our trade

31. Golan and others (1996, p. 4-16).

secrets, our strategies, our vulnerabilities. How can we say publicly that budgetary problems make us want to avoid criminal prosecution?" Their position was overruled, however, by the organizers, who argued that they were revealing nothing business did not know already. Jim Morgester, compliance division chief of the Air Resources Board and one of the principal organizers, argued further that the more clearly industry understood what was expected of them, the better able they would be to comply. "What's the point of playing 'hide the ball' with industry? So they won't know what to do?" Attendance at such an intensive regulatory training activity would also increase environmental consciousness: "In some of our trainings, we have had 60 percent from industry, and some of those guys become real zealots. Not the environmental engineers, but the blue-collar guys with their hands on the valves."

Letting Form Follow Function

How an ICC should structure its steering process ought to be contingent, among other things, on exactly what functions the structure has to perform. These will differ depending on how much latent consensus exists among the collaborating partners as to ICC direction, how heterogeneous the partners are with respect to budget and political strength, how concerned they are to prevent slacking in general or in some of their members in particular, how able they are to communicate with one another, and how much they are willing to invest in discussion about where to go as opposed to just getting on with the work. We may distinguish four generically different steering structures, each of them adapted to emphasize a different function: a council, a board, a forum, and an implementing network.

The choice among structural forms should be determined by first figuring out which of the functions deserves primacy. If that form is chosen, then presumably it can be somewhat adapted to fulfill some of the secondary functions. However, this secondary level of analysis is beyond the scope of this book.

ALLOCATING BY A COUNCIL. Assume that the ICC controls some funds or personnel more or less autonomously. These resources make it worthwhile to jockey for position in steering the ICC. A formal system of representation, along with rules of procedure and rules for decisionmaking—a governance structure, in short—will often make the jockeying more orderly. It might even make it more fair. I call a governance structure with these objectives a *council*.

Of course, council members might prefer to operate more by informal consensus than by formal voting; but what is distinctive about the generic council is the opportunity it affords for participants to fall back on the formal procedures should they wish, or need, to do so. A generic council in addition to its governance powers also exercises certain managerial powers—for example, reviewing ICC performance and suggesting improvements.

Some instances of councils in my nineteen cases include the CYSC; the Healthy Start collaboratives in California; the governing body of the Mutual Assistance Network in Del Paso Heights; the joint powers agencies that Arthur Bolton contemplated for the Prescott Project and Del Paso Heights but never attained; and a very elaborate scheme for a state-level Commission on Children and Families proposed by a task force that worked throughout 1996 to redesign the basic constitution of systems reform in Maryland.

The more powerful the council, the more carefully its internal governance system must be designed. In light of the substantial proposed powers for Maryland's state-level commission, the task force proposed a complement of seventeen members who were to provide balanced representation between the public and the private sectors, business and nonprofit providers, state and local governments, and advocacy and community groups. In particular, the task force asserted, "Representatives of LMBs [local management boards that were to oversee the contracting process with local service providers] and local government, through participation on the Commission, will help to assure that local concerns are addressed."[32]

INDUCING AND MANAGING RESOURCE CONTRIBUTIONS BY A BOARD. An ICC that does not control significant financial or personnel resources independently of what its partner agencies choose to contribute or to withhold presents a different sort of steering problem. Its steering structure, like that of a council, evaluates ICC performance and recommends changes; but its role in resource management is not so

32. Maryland Governor's Task Force on Children, Youth, and Families Systems Reform, "Recommendations to Governor," 1996.

much to allocate resources as it is to induce partners, and wary out-siders as well, to maintain or increase their levels of contribution and to informally negotiate the terms on which they will do so. I call such a generic structure a *board*. One might even call it an advisory board except that in many cases its members will see themselves as either deserving or having more influence than that implies. Some members, however, seek only symbolic status and are not interested in even offer-ing advice.

The Denver Family Opportunity Council is perhaps the archetype of a board, although it did control some modest funds and internal staff posi-tions. It was a medium to rally community resources to the JOBS pro-gram, to support and sometimes criticize the Department of Social Services and other agencies, and to undertake studies of policy and pro-grammatic needs. Other examples of the board type of steering structure are the Neighborhood Services Agency advisory board and the board of the Mutual Assistance Network in Del Paso Heights. These had overlap-ping memberships, further underlining the centrality of their functions in integrating and managing a total resource pool for the community.

EDUCATING AND PERSUADING BY A FORUM. A *forum* supports a steering process so light in its touch that it hardly seems like steering at all. It brings together representatives of parties separated by a signifi-cant power differential but who nevertheless—or perhaps for that very reason—have an interest in mutual education and persuasion. Breadth and diversity of participation generally help.[33]

Regulatory agency representatives, for instance, can meet in a forum setting with representatives of businesses they regulate. A forum can also include representatives of advocacy groups, technical experts, and elected officials. In my set of cases, for instance, the enforcement sym-posium in cross-media training included representatives of industries that were going to be the object of enforcement. A wide array of inter-ests participated in the Federal Facilities Environmental Restoration Dialogue Committee and the Defense Environmental Remediation Task Force.[34] The Biodiversity Council is another example. In San Diego forum-type functions were performed in an unusual setting that brought together staff from the Air Pollution Control District and rep-

33. On the virtues of cosmopolitanism in the process of private sector innovation, see Delbecq and Mills (1985).
34. For further details, see chapter 3.

resentatives of the regulated community organized in the Industrial Environmental Association (IEA). The IEA actually was supplying technical management assistance to the district staff, more or less along the lines of total quality management. The IEA reasoning was that a more efficient and intelligent Air Pollution Control District would mean shorter permitting times, less friction, and, for any given level of abatement, less costly solutions.

ADJUSTING GOAL AND ASPIRATION LEVEL WITH AN IMPLEMENTING NETWORK. It is one thing for the partners in an ICC to agree in the abstract on mission, goals, and objectives, and another to discover what is possible and desirable operationally. A great deal of steering takes place at this operational level. Following my usage in chapter 1, I call the entity that does this an *implementing network*. Compared to council, board, and forum, it is quite amorphous. Because it is relatively focused on technical tasks, it brings in experts or other knowledgeable persons as needed. But because it also adjusts ICC goals and aspirations from time to time, particularly in regard to the reach and scale of the emerging ICC, it may need to reach out to more authoritative figures to have them bless adjustments. It may have a self-conscious corporate existence, such as the Medford Operations Group, or it may be diffuse. The network may be small and have an identifiable communications center, such as the network that revolved around Council on Children and Families staff in the New York master contract case, or that which centered on the five or six middle managers who met in the 1986–88 period to plan what became the Coordinated Youth Services Council in Marin County.

An ICC may be steered by more than one type of process or structure. The Vegetation Management Consortium—an implementing network—steered the East Bay fire prevention ICC, but so did its nominal parent body, the Hills Emergency Forum. Because an ICC, like any organization, has separate components, each of these may also be steered separately—for example, the special fire assessment districts that functioned as councils controlling, or at least influencing, both financial resources and policy direction.

Any actual steering structure or process, if it is working well, performs primarily the function for which it has been designed. But it can also be seen as a resource that to some degree is in play, available for other ICC-related functions if it can be somewhat controlled, reshaped, redirected. The DFO council (in my terms primarily a board) was also a forum to discuss issues of broad policy philosophy and the originator and therefore legitimator of task forces that in effect became implementing groups. In the DFO case this sort of multifunctionalism was desired and valued by most of the parties, but this need not be the case in general.

"SUFFICIENT CONSENSUS" IN EACH TYPE OF STRUCTURE. How much should be invested in broadening the consensus in each structure?

A council specializes in being able to fall back on formal theories of representation and the use of formal voting rules for resolving conflict. The very fact that a council exists signals that the underlying interests are probably too much in tension to produce perfect consensus. Unfortunately, the underlying tensions combined with the almost certain design shortcomings of the formal machinery—no design, I believe, can be free of at least some shortcomings—may produce unwise decisions, decisions not in the public interest. Consensus-forming processes should be thought of as ways to compensate for the imperfections of the formal process.[35] If the actors themselves can see consensus-building in this light, they will probably have a better shot at using it for this purpose. More important, if planners recognize the potential for *compensatory* consensus building at the stage when they are designing the council's institutional machinery, they may be able to design a simpler institution to begin with.

In a board the main concern is not alienating important resource contributors. Hence the meaning of sufficient consensus in this context is the level that permits resources to be maintained at a minimally workable level or higher. Call the sufficient consensus in this context, therefore, a *workable* consensus. During at least one phase of its existence, the DFO built its workable consensus out of the more human-capital-oriented community partners and allowed the more employment-oriented partners to feel slightly alienated.

In one sense, a forum does not need to produce much of a consensus at all. Mutual education can be successful even if consensus-

35. Jennings and Krane (1994, p. 347) wrote, in the same spirit, "Whether the coordination mechanisms include formal contracts, nonfinancial agreements, or detailed plans is less important than building a treaty-like consensus about the functional division of responsibilities among the various agencies, as well as consensus on the areas of joint action."

building persuasion is a failure. The actors holding the trump cards can proceed to play their trumps no matter what. The only question for such a favorably situated player is whether the losers will be so angry that they will refuse to acquiesce in the game's continuing by the current rules and will find a way to make their anger effective. From that actor's point of view, a sufficient consensus would be an acquiescent consensus. The question for observers, however, is whether the public interest has been well served. Although in particular cases one can look at the details of the winner's policy solution to decide the answer, we need a general test, a procedural test that will serve as a proxy for case-by-case substantive judgments aggregated over many situations. First, has the party with greater power made a good faith effort to improve on his or her own conception of how to serve the public interest by trying to understand the other parties' arguments and point of view? Second, has the effort now reached a point of negative returns, such that further time invested in efforts at understanding would not be justified by the likely improvements in decisions that might follow? If so, then the resulting impasse is a good thing, and whatever consensus has been reached up to that point is, in my view, sufficient and legitimate. That consensus includes the points agreed on and an agreement to disagree about the rest. I call this a *contested consensus*.

For example, representatives of the Defense Department and all the environmental policy stakeholders in the base reuse arena worked hard to reach a consensus on future land use policy, but without much success. All agreed that DOD should clean up the environmental waste to some level that was economically rational given the applicable law and that was consistent with the land use intentions of the local reuse authorities for the parcels in question.[36] They disagreed on whether the DOD should pay for cleanup to the higher level should the landowner in the future decide to use the parcels for purposes requiring cleanup to a higher standard. The split was fairly clean: The DOD representatives said no and the rest said yes. Many months later the DOD promulgated the exact policy it had failed to sell to the stakeholders. I have read reports of the work of the forum that brought the DOD together with its

---

36. One might have argued that the applicable laws set irrationally costly cleanup standards to begin with, but none of the parties was contesting this point.

critics and consider that the contested consensus reached in the end met my tests of legitimacy.[37]

On the redevelopment side, a contested consensus would have been an improvement over the lack of any attempt at consensus formation or creation of a forum in which the process could take place. The military base redevelopment ICC had a good strategic idea, which was arguably in the public interest: Return base land to economic use as soon as possible. It had a good instrumentality as well: the Economic Development Conveyance. But a few of the partners—especially the staff of the House Government Reform and Oversight Committee—had an interest in maximizing revenues to the federal government. Together with some elements in the military service departments, they were able to deflect the goal of expeditious redevelopment. A forum in which this coalition would have had to defend its ideas and actions might not have altered the outcomes, but it would have improved the odds of doing so. Moreover, it would almost certainly have forestalled the astonishingly aggressive criticism from community representatives in public venues, the ceaseless pressure from the White House, and the innumerable ad hoc interventions by members of Congress representing the affected communities.

As a steering mechanism the implementation network is probably, in most ICCs, more consequential than the other three. As I hope chapter 4 made clear, the operating subsystem of an ICC is a very subtle piece of human engineering, liable to break down in many ways that policy planners, advocates, top agency executives, and others at a far remove are unable to see, anticipate, or identify. Often, the technical issues must be resolved by implementation network participants with technical understanding. Because their solutions may often be challenged on value grounds in some other steering context (a board, for instance), it is important that the technical aspects stand up to scrutiny and that they be backed by a technical consensus.

Among my cases I know of three examples of an implementation network that, whether self-consciously or not, was setting an ambitious

37. That does not mean that the DOD policy is more in the public interest than alternatives favored by its critics. I happen to think that, in its general thrust if not its details, it is. The DOD and military services components, as they are called, which have responsibility for environmental management, have generally (in the past four years, at least) been reasonably good forum partners, open to discussion and reason and willing to bring environmental advocates and regulatory agencies into the steering process.

course for its ICC and was concerned about its legitimacy and standing: the Medford Operations Group, the small implementation network crafting the master contract with The Door, and the Vegetation Management Consortium. In all three cases the participants aspired to, and largely achieved, a very high level of technical proficiency in their work and came to virtually complete consensus on technical issues. Otherwise, their work, and perhaps they themselves, would have been unacceptably vulnerable.

Legitimating Leadership

Councils, boards, forums, and implementation networks are structures for steering. Leadership is a more personal way of steering. Leadership can go well beyond the steering function. It is, depending on circumstances, a means for diagnosing and implementing improvements in the operating subsystem of the ICC, for inducing resource contributions, for nurturing an ethos of interpersonal trust and organizational pragmatism, for executing a long-range developmental strategy, and for diffusing expectations that one's own personal or agency efforts will be matched by efforts from potential partners.

My definition of leadership is purely functional. It is a set of focus-giving or unity-enhancing behaviors that would help some collectivity, in this case an ICC, accomplish useful work.[38] This definition implies nothing about whether, in some particular ICC setting, leadership behaviors will actually be performed. Nor does it imply who, if anyone, will perform such behaviors, nor what action style—say, domineering or facilitative and low-key—the leader might employ. It does not even imply that leadership behaviors would best be performed by a single individual thought of as the leader. They might sometimes be better performed by a duo or by a threesome. For most military bases with environmental cleanup work going on, the local rehabilitation advisory board has one cochair from the civilian community and one cochair from the base. In San Diego County several task forces representing business and environmental agency managers work with cochairs, and knowledgeable informants there reported that this method worked successfully. In Del Paso Heights, two leadership groups interlocked, one

38. Heifetz (1994).

focused on the Neighborhood Services Agency and the other on the Mutual Assistance Network.

IMPORTANCE OF LEADERSHIP. A single strong leader in the Pentagon might have been able to organize the proper forums for the services and the local reuse authorities to work collaboratively on base redevelopment processes. The same is true for the state agency contribution to the California Anti-Tobacco Education Program: Local leaders often complained that their collaborative efforts were impeded by poor modeling at the state level and by the state leaders' failure to supply the flexibility that the locals needed. It is conceivable that, had the East Bay fire ICC produced more of a singular, high-profile leader capable of addressing public opinion, that leader would have organized the public education campaign needed to keep the Oakland and Berkeley assessment districts going.

Judy Chynoweth, director of the Foundation Consortium for School-Linked Services, has said that bad leadership is the single most important cause of failure in that policy domain.[39] If good leadership is not absolutely essential for helping an ICC to thrive, it surely helps.[40] This is shown by the data in table 6-1. As I have remarked, the classification tools are impressionistic and imprecise, but the results are suggestive nevertheless.

The main effects observed for the leadership variable are especially impressive, despite the small numbers.[41] Of eleven cases of highly effective leadership, eight rate as high success and another three as medium, compared to none of the three cases with low leadership. I omitted in table 6-1 three cases in which leadership quality fluctuated substantially over the course of the ICC development process. If we consider these cases as well, the leadership effect appears stronger still. In the CYSC case, we can define three periods in the history of the council when it had different types and qualities of leadership. From

39. Chynoweth made this remark at a conference on interagency collaboration with regard to children and families sponsored by the Sierra Health Foundation held in Sacramento, December 3, 1993.

40. Michael Porter argues that a key solution to the problems of inducing collaboration among business units in a large firm, which are in most respects similar to those of ICC development, can be solved by constituting a working group that represents the various units and putting a leader-like figure in charge—an "executive" who should possess excellent managerial skills (Porter, 1985, chap. 11).

41. This is consistent with other reports in the literature (Kagan, 1993; Yessian, 1994).

Table 6-1. *Leadership Helps*

Effective leadership	ICC success level[a]		
	High	*Medium*	*Low*
High	New York contract administration Multimedia environmental enforcement Base cleanup New Jersey School-Based Youth Services Elkhorn Slough Oregon Integrated Services Oregon welfare Maryland Systems Reform Initiative	Healthy Start Riverside GAIN Memorandum of understanding on biodiversity	
Medium	Fire prevention	Denver Family Opportunity	
Low		Antitobacco education	Base redevelopment Prescott Project

a. See chapter 3.

the mid-1980s, when the collaborative vision began to emerge until they hired their first executive director, leadership was in the hands of a core group. Given the tasks at hand, this core group was reasonably effective, and the collaborative moved along, albeit slowly. The first executive director was a powerhouse—a visionary leader with facilitative skills as well as the political skills to manage the dynamics of the developmental process. In most respects the CYSC flourished under her leadership, although problems of staff burnout were accumulating and neither she nor others in the organization quite recognized the limitations of their case management model. It also appears that her eagerness for CYSC to become the coordinator of all Marin County Healthy Start programs may have left the organization overburdened. All these problems surfaced once she had left, and her successor was not able to take effective action. The board too, according to some informants, was ill equipped to deal with the problems or to give adequate guidance to the new executive director. The history of the CYSC, therefore, adds support for the hypothesis that effective leadership makes a big difference.

The same is true for the Tennessee Children's Plan, in which case Manning's effective leadership was critically important in launching the effort and his failures of leadership were equally important in causing the problems of the postlaunching period. In the Del Paso Heights case it was a collapse of leadership at the county level that left the Neighborhood Services Agency fumbling for resources and direction and the rise of leadership from the community level that brought it to a relatively high level of collaborative capacity.

FACILITATIVE AND ADVOCACY STYLES. Because the agency stakeholders are normally so sensitive about their resource contributions and their political vulnerabilities, traditional "heroic" or positional top-down leadership behaviors in an ICC are often suspect. Stakeholders often prefer leadership of a kinder, gentler sort, sometimes called *servant* or *facilitative* leadership.[42] Chrislip and Larson have argued that such leadership should work from four principles: Bring people to the table and help them work constructively, create a "credible, open process in which participants have confidence, stimulate broad-based involvement," and "sustain hope and participation" against the inevitable frustrations.[43] A good facilitative leader is someone with appropriate self-awareness about the nature of the role and a natural gift for diplomacy. It is often someone with a broad-gauge, general background or cross-disciplinary training and experience.[44] It is reasonable to assume, furthermore, that ICC leadership efforts would be helped, as are many managerial efforts, by having a relatively positive personal disposition[45] and, as is the case for intrafirm champions of technical innovation, by a personality that welcomes risk-taking and desires achievement.[46]

More important, it is also in many cases someone with the right institutional position in the loose community of potential partners,

42. Svara and others (1994).
43. Chrislip and Larson (1994, pp. 139–40).
44. Melaville and Blank (1991, p. 25). In their successor handbook, published two years later, the discussion of leadership had been downgraded. It occupied only a paragraph and recommended that "Partners need to work collegially . . . for genuinely shared leadership" (Melaville and Blank, 1993, pp. 30–31).
45. Staw and Barsade (1993).
46. Grover (1993); Howell and Higgins (1990, p. 333).

someone who will be perceived as neutral, someone "with no ax to grind." Even a person of middling diplomatic gifts might succeed if he or she comes from the right institutional base.[47] When welfare-to-work collaboratives were first taking shape in Oregon in the early 1990s among the welfare agency, the community colleges, and the Job Training Partnership Act agency, none of these agencies was permitted to manage the interagency contracting process. Instead, a seemingly neutral agency, the state Office of Economic Development, was given the role. The Council on Children and Families was designed explicitly to play a neutral and coordinating role in New York State. In the state rural development councils "leadership came from representatives from the private sector or other groups that were not viewed as traditional rural actors."[48]

Foundation representatives often perform leadership functions in local collaboratives involving families and children—for example, the Marin Community Foundation for the CYSC, the Annie E. Casey Foundation in Maryland and other states that initiated collaboratives; the Zellerbach, Stewart, and other foundations in the CISFAN efforts, the Peninsula Community Foundation in San Mateo County (California). The Elkhorn Slough Foundation plays a similar role among local, state, federal, public, and private parties involved in the Slough conservation effort in California. The Nature Conservancy did the same in the case of arranging an environmentally protective growth management in the Coachella Valley in California.[49] The Piton Foundation and the Colorado Trust played organizing roles in the launching of the Denver Family Opportunity Council.

The facilitative style is largely a consensus-building style. It is not appropriate for situations in which one cannot count on consensus to emerge and in which there is a high probability of at least some losers,

47. Innes and others (1994, p. 223). An interesting parallel can be drawn between the multidimensional leadership role in an ICC and the multidimensional facilitative role played by Occupational Safety and Health inspectors in unionized manufacturing plants. Conceptualizing the inspection situation as a multistage game between employer and employees, OSHA's involvement can help reduce bargaining costs involved in finding a mutually agreeable level of investment, reduce the employer's temptation to deviate from the cooperative equilibrium, and provide reliable information to employees about the employer's true level of investment. See Scholz and Gray (1997).

48. Radin and others (1996, p. 221).

49. It helped that they were putting up a substantial percentage of the money to acquire the land.

perhaps even some sore losers. I call the main alternative to the facilitative style an *advocacy* style. It approaches consensus building in a rallying spirit and carries it as far as it can reasonably do so. At some point, though, it is ready to allow holdouts to go their own way. The advocacy-style leader stops short of attacking or demonizing opponents or noncooperative resisters but legitimizes disengaging from further efforts to bring them into the consensus.[50] In my own cases, leaders more or less in the advocacy style were Arthur Bolton in the CISFAN projects; Bill Carter at the Cal/EPA; Daniel Mountjoy, Les Strnad, and Lynn Dwyer in the Elkhorn Slough; Lawrence Townsend at Riverside GAIN; David Manning in Tennessee; Steven Minnich and Sandy Hoback at the Oregon Adult and Family Services; and Ed Hastey with regard to the memorandum of understanding on biodiversity.

Even advocacy leaders must respect the partners' demands for their neutrality. If the facilitative leader does this by subordinating him- or herself equally to the views and interests of the several partners, the advocacy leader does it by subordinating these evenhandedly to her own vision, which she in turn tries to legitimate among the partners by at least affecting to believe that they share it with her and with each other. All the would-be advocacy leaders in my cases employed this strategy, and all but Manning succeeded with it. Manning failed because he paid little or no attention to the details of execution, turning them over to subordinates who were not in a position to carry off such leadership.[51]

RECRUITMENT CHALLENGE. As helpful, perhaps even as essential, as good leadership is, it is not always forthcoming. The conventional one-liner explanation of collaboration failure points to excessive turf-consciousness on the part of agency-protecting bureaucrats. But in many cases this may not be as penetrating as an explanation that points to underdeveloped leadership recruitment processes. In the conceptual language of craftsmanship theory, although turf protectiveness is inevitably a defect of the raw materials available to the process of cre-

---

50. In the literature on public and private sector innovation, this role is often termed the *champion*. Borins (1998) used the term *local hero*, though he may have intended this term to cover what I term *facilitative leadership* as well.

51. Manning's policy appears to be succeeding in Tennessee despite his own shortcomings as an advocacy leader. He was a revolutionary more than a reformer, and the success of revolution proceeds along different lines.

ating an ICC, skilled, craftsmanlike leadership is often able, when it is forthcoming, to compensate even for such defective materials. But what prevents such leadership from coming forth?

Were the market for ICC leadership a normal economic market, the supply would be there. But both the supply and the demand side of the market have problems. On the supply side, people have to be willing to step forward and assume the burdens of leadership. What is required to motivate them is an opportunity of the sort catalogued in chapter 5—that is, the sort that motivates agency resource contributions in general: a chance to serve the public interest, champion some innovation or other pet idea, take on a task that promises self-renewal, gain career-enhancing visibility. Although there is no shortage of individuals willing to perform some sort of leadership of this type, doing it in the inter-agency context may be less attractive than doing it in connection with some intra-agency project. Just how much of a barrier this is on the supply side I cannot say, because one should ideally study a sample of potential collaboratives that never got off the ground to see how many failed for lack of a motivated leadership and just what caused the lack of motivation in those cases.

The demand side of this market is complicated by the requirement that any of the partners—that is, any ICC "insider"—who steps forward to be a leader ipso facto appears not to be neutral. But in many cases there simply may not be neutral outsiders available to take on the job. Hence, between supply-side and demand-side constraints, the pool of potential leaders might be close to dry. How can the pool be refreshed?

Although the image of neutrality is enhanced by coming from outside, it is also possible for a leader to come from inside—for example, Mountjoy and Strnad, Minnich and Hoback, Hastey, Sherri Goodman in the DOD, and Lenny Siegel within the environmental advocacy community. Being accepted in an ICC leadership role requires, most critically, an ability to elicit trust from the several partners, and many interviewees told me that these individuals had this ability. This trustworthiness requirement holds whether the leader comes from inside or outside and acts mostly as a neutral facilitator or as an advocate. Although a full discussion of trust is reserved for chapter 7, suffice it to say that it is the mistrust that springs from process-related problems that looms largest in the minds of the partners. For instance, in the facilitative role—and even the advocate will play a facilitative role to some extent—the leader must be able to protect the parties from being exploited by others using information obtained in the course of ICC planning or operations. His or her qualities of discretion must therefore be rated highly. Moreover, because ICC development is so difficult and so vulnerable to failure, the partners must trust in the capacity of the leader to hold the doubters in line, keep participants' energies flowing, and generally function as a competent entrepreneur.

Is it possible for facilitative leadership to be transformed, in appropriate situations, into advocacy leadership? Perhaps. A facilitative leader has a hard and perhaps menial job, especially if it includes chores such as arranging meeting times and places and fielding complaints from the various partners about how the process is or is not working. One reward for accepting such tasks, and for fulfilling them creditably, is that others in the group accord small increments of trust, discretion over procedural issues, and eventually latitude in regard to issues of greater substance. These increments may accumulate over time into permission, a weak mandate, to define ICC goals or possibly even a "vision." Eventually this new leader could begin to represent the group to outsiders, and thereby earn more credit internally. The process could continue until a full-fledged advocacy leader had emerged, acknowledged as such by both insiders and outsiders. Although I did not observe this process in its entirety in the cases I studied, it seems to me that in the New York State contract administration case Lepler and Rosenkranz were on such a trajectory, which was interrupted only by the defeat of Governor Cuomo.

Summary

Compared to most other public sector organizations of significant scope and size, an ICC gets its sense of direction in a diffuse, collectivized way. Elected officials and the partners' top managers are involved, of course, but so are middle-management implementing networks, line workers, consumers, and assorted others. The steering processes are multiple, sometimes overlapping, and often complex. They perform various functions and take on various forms: a representative council, a board dominated by the service providers, a forum in which partners with unequal power attempt to reach principled consensus, and an amorphous implementing network of individuals interacting around a constellation of assorted values, interests, and emerging operating requirements. One smart practice is to make sure that the chosen steering structure is appropriate to the primary functions that it must play.

The search for consensus dominates all ICC steering processes. Because complete consensus is always either impossible or very time-consuming, another smart practice is to limit the search for consensus to what is sufficient for its particular purposes. Again, out of consideration for the costliness of elaborate governance procedures, a related smart practice is to trade in *governance*, to the extent possible, for quality-oriented *management* processes.

Leadership is a big help, whether it is of the facilitative or the advocacy type. Despite equalitarian norms, and a normal suspiciousness of those who would rise above the crowd, ICC partners should find a way to legitimate leadership. However, it may be hard to find people willing to take on the leadership role who would also do it well and would be sufficiently trusted by the partners.

7

The Culture of Joint Problem Solving

L
ike other organizations, an ICC has a culture, and this culture can either enhance or degrade organizational effectiveness. In this chapter I analyze those aspects of the culture that bear on
the partners' capacity for joint problem solving. First I consider how
joint problem solving is affected by the culture of bureaucracy. I then
turn to the negotiating process, a common context for joint problem
solving. Finally I look at trust.

Pragmatism and the Culture of Bureaucracy

Almost nothing about the bureaucratic ethos makes it hospitable to
interagency collaboration. The collaborative ethos values equality,
adaptability, discretion, and results; the bureaucratic ethos venerates
hierarchy, stability, obedience, and procedures. Making the transition
from an existing way of doing agency business to a new and more collaborative way requires actors to withdraw at least temporarily from
the bureaucratic ethos. They must spurn something they may have at
least respected if not cherished. They must be willing to discard it if
necessary or, if possible, break it up into components, some of which
might warrant being salvaged and recycled. They must adopt the stance
that purpose should dictate structure rather than allow structure to dictate purpose. They must think about bureaucracy pragmatically.[1]

---

1. Indirect evidence that hierarchy decreases trust and therefore cooperation comes
from LaPorta and others (1997). They examined survey results from 1,000 randomly

Embracing Change?

Many experienced bureaucrats are unable to step outside the bureaucratic ethos even to undertake smaller changes than most collaborative work would entail. While interviewing in Medford, Oregon, in 1995 I met the district Jobs Council director, Janet Diamond, who had worked in the Massachusetts Department of Public Welfare in the mid-1980s as part of a break-the-mold top management team creating the nation's first major welfare-to-work program (ET Choices). She spoke of "people who become lifers in bureaucracies" as valuing "safety . . . doing the same thing over and over again," avoiding risk. But the risk, she said, was more psychological than real. The risks were not being fired or losing status but "in maybe trying something different and not knowing the answers . . . trying to do something and being wrong. Some people . . . think that being wrong is the worst thing in the world."

Diamond had wanted to organize focus groups with some welfare recipients, pay them for participating, and then exempt the payments from being counted against the state's limit of $30 for casual income. Long-time employees "said to me, 'Well, but you can't do that,' and I said, 'Well, why not?' and they said, 'It's against the rules.' I said, 'Excuse me, who wrote the rules? Who are the ones that wrote the rules? You wrote the rule. Let's write a new rule. It's just a piece of paper!' And I ripped open a policy manual, and tore out pages, and threw them around . . . People were aghast. [I said] 'It's just paper, it's not sacred.'"

Diamond had come to Oregon in 1995 and discovered a statewide culture, in the welfare-to-work area at least, that she found "wonderful. They know no bounds. They're totally empowered to do whatever it is that needs to be done. Their system of problem-solving means that the program runs itself. . . . I had an idea, when I first came, and I talked about it, and told it to the staff, and they went 'Hmm' and they

---

selected people in each of forty countries in the early 1980s and again in the early 1990s. Trust appeared correlated with performance of large-scale institutions in these countries. Countries dominated by hierarchical religions tended to have lower levels of trust at the individual level. A study of thirty firms engaged in downsizing (Cameron, Freeman, and Mishra, 1993), which usually threatens bigger and more stressful changes than interagency collaboration, found that success was correlated with employee involvement, an "advanced" version of a quality culture, and having a systematic and planned strategy.

developed a plan for implementing it and then they went off and implemented it. Just like that. I didn't have to cajole, I didn't have to bribe. I didn't have to threaten."[2]

Even in pragmatic, benchmarks-driven Oregon, modest bureaucratic changes can seem very trying to those who carry them out. A group of ten managers from different agencies created a task force to enable human services clients to establish their eligibility for any of a range of services with one intake process. They announced their project to the world in a newsletter that began, "Dared to think the impossible. . . . Brought together the widest range of human service agencies that exist in Clackamas County. . . . Put the issues on the table. . . ." It continued, "Who dared?" and listed the honor roll of agencies participating and then went on to praise "the enthusiasm and commitment . . . along with the wide array of extremely talented and experienced players." This committed group of talented enthusiasts was not out in the field attempting some really impossible feats such as organizing community development activities in the Prescott neighborhood of West Oakland; they were simply altering a bureaucratic information system.

In any case, the two Oregon ICCs did stand out among the nineteen cases I studied. I rated eight collaboration sites with regard to their general disposition to treat bureaucracy pragmatically. Because this assessment on my part was extremely impressionistic, I omitted eleven ICCs about which I had either mixed or inadequate impressions. Oregon and Denver were the only sites I felt confident in rating high in this regard. As table 7-1 shows, they had only slightly more success overall than the six sites I rated low on pragmatism.

However, table 7-1 taken by itself may be misleading. My field experience in both Oregon and Denver, and particularly in Oregon, convinced me that the culture of pragmatism is a very powerful influence indeed. I believe that, in the absence of strong inhibiting conditions, it acts nearly as a sufficient, though not a necessary, condition for relative success. Among other reasons, it also increases the rewards, and reduces the risks, to potential leaders. Furthermore, the two cases of high success in table 7-1 that occurred despite a low culture of pragmatism can be attributed in large part to the compensatory effects of

2. A district manager based in Salem said that the culture of collaboration among employment and training agencies was such that "it would be alien to not collaborate." He quoted a caseworker's remark to him, "I'm hard to supervise but I'm easy to lead."

Table 7-1. *A Culture of Pragmatism Probably Helps*

Culture of pragmatism	ICC success level[a]		
	High	*Medium*	*Low*
High	Oregon Integrated Services Oregon welfare	Denver Family Opportunity	
Low	Mulitmedia environ-mental enforcement New York contract administration	Antitobacco education	Base redevelopment Prescott Project

a. See chapter 3.

unusually strong leadership (see the discussion of the leaders in these cases in chapter 6).

Co-opting the Traditionalists

In these two cases the nature of the compensation is especially interesting, because a highly pragmatic leadership was able to ally itself to the more traditionalist bureaucracy by helping the members of the bureaucracy to succeed in quite familiar terms. In the multimedia enforcement case, both Carter and Johnston were able to counterpose to the bureaucratic ethos the professional ethos of a good prosecuting attorney's office. They said, in effect, "We legal and investigative professionals need the discretion and the resources to pursue the outlaw element. Our flexibility and pragmatism makes it possible for the more routinized part of the regulatory system to function all the better." Lepler and Rosenkranz in the New York case used as their political base the Council on Children and Families and ties with the governor's office. The message already was, "We are friendly outsiders to the bureaucratic system." The difficulty was making the "friendly" part of the message credible. They did this mostly through persistence and good cheer, and by always making it plain that they were making the effort to see the world through the eyes of their more bureaucratically minded partners. They also used the advice and the brokerage services of the state government's internal office of management consulting, the Office of Regulatory and Management Assistance.

Robert Behn's study of how the Massachusetts ET (welfare-to-work) program managed to get at least part way to the goal describes the co-optation strategy in a different context. The ET leadership generated resources for use by local offices and education and training contractors, and the central office disseminated ideas about effective practice to managers and case workers around the state. As disseminators they used the innovators themselves, which added credibility to the message and boosted morale. "Supporting the field—that's what the job of the central office is all about," according to the director of the department.[3]

A perhaps critical component of the co-optation strategy is a method for overcoming anxiety about change. Behn quoted Janet Diamond on the necessity to build long-term trust throughout the agency, though he did not say how to accomplish this.[4]

Ronald Heifetz is a public management theorist whose training in psychiatry has led him to conceptualize a therapeutic holding environment for individuals undergoing the stress of organizational change. This is a "relationship in which one party has the power to hold the attention of another party and facilitate adaptive work."[5] In a managerial setting the relationship is between organizational members and a leadership that uses the resources of both formal and informal authority. The strategic principles of leadership in managing this relationship are identifying the adaptive challenge; keeping "the level of distress within a tolerable range for doing adaptive work"; focusing attention on "ripening issues and not on stress-reducing distractions"; "giv[ing] the work back to the people, but at a rate they can stand"; and protecting the voices of "leadership without authority"—that is, those people who "raise hard questions and generate distress—people who point to the internal contradictions" of the system.[6]

What might this imply when the nature of the adaptive challenge is to think pragmatically about the institutions and practices of bureaucracy themselves? What might keep the level of distress within a tolerable range? One possibility is to help bureaucrats to hold on to the forms of bureaucracy while encouraging them to be creative with its substance. Consider the self-defined mandate of the Oregon task force

3. Behn (1991, pp. 122–24).
4. Behn (1991, p. 122).
5. Heifetz (1994, pp. 104–05).
6. Heifetz (1994, p. 128).

working on a single procedure for verifying eligibility. It was something like, "Sophisticated, dedicated, talented bureaucrats! Use your talents and creativity and bureaucratic expertise to replace a dysfunctional, cumbersome, inhumane system with a simpler, better design of your own! All you need do is protect the partner agencies' missions, target services very precisely, and rigorously impose some form of accountability for results or some reasonable proxy for results." The mandate is not to give up being a bureaucrat or to scuttle the bureaucratic ethos but to use the craft skills of the veteran bureaucrat, and the bureaucrat's sense of responsibility to the values of order and accountability, to make the institutions of bureaucracy work better.

These craft skills are in fact widely distributed and a source of pride to those who have honed them. As Tony Acosta of the Vegetation Management Consortium said, he and his fellow managers from diverse agencies were pleased and gratified to discover that they shared "bureaucrat" as a common identity. (See the fire prevention case in chapter 4.) Such pride constitutes a potential resource for those who would reform bureaucracy. It would be a smart practice to take advantage of it.

Another smart practice is to find a way to protect the actors with craft skills and a lively sense of value-creating possibilities from those in their own organizations who are more bureaucratically oriented. Although it is hard to generalize, usually this means keeping line workers, and in some cases top managers, out of the way of change-resisting middle managers. In some cases, however, it means the opposite: protecting change-tolerant middle managers from their more turf-conscious senior managers. Why might some middle managers be less turf-conscious, in at least some contexts, than higher executives?

First, for civil servants at least, the higher executives tend to benefit personally from their agencies' budgetary and turf positions more than do the middle managers. The higher executives' careers are more dependent on the size, responsibilities, and budgets of their agencies. Second, relatively young middle managers will have somewhat less to lose by switching to jobs working in other agencies or even leaving government altogether.[7] Third, the very concept of middle manager is

---

7. What has been said so far of some middle managers being less turf conscious than agency executives could also be said of professionals. It appears, for instance, that in federal resource management agencies such as the Bureau of Land Management, the Forest Service, and the Fish and Wildlife Service, individuals sharing similar professional

almost defined by expertise in coordination functions. Hence for some middle managers their particular kind of turf interests may actually be advanced by the new scope for coordination activities presented by an ICC.

This last point, however, suggests the more common conflicting possibility too: A well-functioning ICC might eliminate some of the coordinating jobs that were necessary prior to the ICC. Or, only slightly less threatening, it might eliminate the need for the human capital of certain middle managers, capital that takes the form of knowledge about how to resolve certain organization-specific or program-specific administrative complexities. That is, although middle managers might be less sensitive to agency turf than their seniors, they might be extremely protective of the turf pertaining to their own intra-agency unit or function. In the light of these distinctions to be made within the overall category of middle managers, selecting which ones to work on ICC development would be an especially sensitive task.[8]

Negotiating

Whether at the topmost level of the ICC, where collectively steering a course is the central concern, or at the middle-management levels, where the operations of the partner agencies are often coordinated, or at the line level, where interpersonal teamwork usually counts the most, collaboration is a matter of exhortation, explication, persuasion, give and take. To collaborate is to negotiate.

The social science literature on private sector negotiations is comparatively well-developed, and much of it, though not all, translates well from the private sector to the public and not-for-profit sectors. As with partners to a private negotiation, the differences in taste or production capability among ICC partners are an opportunity for creating new value through exchange. But the degree to which any party P benefits will depend further on (1) all the parties' jointly structuring an exchange that extracts the greatest possible value from their different

---

identities and attitudes form bridges for cooperation and potential ICC development (Thomas, 1997a). Line-level professionals from education and from public health agencies have also been the key players in many local school districts in California that are attempting to implement antitobacco programs (Balbach, 1994).

8. Craig Thomas, in a personal communication, hypothesizes that middle managers with aspirations to upward mobility in their agencies will be particularly turf conscious.

situations, and (2) P's ability to appropriate a larger share of the new value. These two different sources of benefit are often called *value creating* and *value claiming*.[9] A common problem in negotiations is that the parties focus so hard on value claiming that they undermine their ability to work cooperatively on value creating. Much of the social scientific research on negotiations in the past twenty years has been devoted to the problem of how to create more joint problem solving and hence more value for the parties independently of who gets to claim it.

Triple Concern

One strong finding is that negotiations in the private sector in which the participants show joint concern—a concern for satisfying both their own interests and the interests of their partners—produce more joint problem solving and joint value than negotiations in which the concerns are dominantly either selfish or selfless.[10] This is also true of ICC negotiations.

In the private sector, the joint concern is a dual concern. It does not take account of third parties, parties not at the negotiating table. Third parties must hope, if they are aware of the situation, that they are protected by the liability law, government regulation, or some other social mechanism. In the ICC case, because the parties are governmental or nonprofit agencies that represent some aspect of the public interest, they may believe that they adequately represent all relevant third parties and that dual concern will therefore suffice. They may be mistaken, however.

First, some of the parties may be more zealously watchful of their bureaucratic interests than they are of the third parties they are supposed to represent. Second, "third parties" is a very large set; and even if the agencies effectively represent those for whom they are responsible, some subset may remain underrepresented by any agency at the negotiating table. (Taxpayers are one common omission. Consumers, customers, and clients are others.) Third, even if all third parties are represented in some sense by their own agency, it may be that the full range of the parties' interests is not adequately represented—for example, troubled families whose interests in privacy or in minimizing needless bureaucratic contact are underappreciated by service agencies.

9. Lax and Sebenius (1986, pp. 29–45).
10. Pruitt and Carnevale (1993, pp. 109–12).

A partial offset is to include in the negotiations representatives of those parties whose interests are least likely to be spoken for. Another possible offset lies in the fact that the interaction among the parties during the negotiation process can produce creative ideas about how to serve the public interest that none of the agencies would have thought of independently. How to structure a dialogue that produces this result is an open question. In some cases the dialogue might be entirely courteous and Socratic. In others an element of adversarial challenge could be helpful. As I pointed out in chapter 4, collaborative efforts create a venue for peer monitoring and criticism as well as support. In any case, simply making the effort to jointly articulate a common vision could be helpful. Howard Raiffa, the doyen of contemporary researchers into the dynamics of negotiations processes, wrote,

> When parties contemplate the merits of starting negotiations, it is only natural to ruminate about the issues that divide them and the possible compromises that will have to be made to get an agreement. Little thought goes into contemplating visions about what the future could bring if only the dispute that confronts them can be surmounted. It's my impression, and I admit it is very subjective and biased by my notion that "negotiations" are good, that if the long-run future were appropriately factored into the analysis, the efficient boundary [in other words, the range of conceivable mutually beneficial settlements] would be further extended northeasterly [in other words, the region on a graph where such settlements are conventionally mapped]. I think the Greek and Turkish Cypriots, the Arabs and Israelis, and other pairs would do well to plan actively together what true peace might bring to their region in the long run. They should share visions.[11]

Making the Needed Effort

ICC negotiations often demand a lot of effort—and creative effort at that. They involve complex role playing in order to present one's own case persuasively and to try to get into the minds of the other partici-

11. Raiffa (1995, p. 140).

pants.[12] Those involved have to speak—and listen—in their capacities as individuals, representatives of bureaucratic or political organizations, and would-be interpreters of the public interest to the extent that it is understood to be at all distinct from their constituencies' interests. The negotiations literature more or less assumes that creative effort will be forthcoming. Perhaps this is because the literature talks primarily about private sector rather than public sector phenomena—for example, deal making among business people, and property and custody settlements among divorcing spouses. For such situations watching out for one's own concern guarantees quite a lot of effort. But the public sector is different. The prospect of personal benefit, usually financial, can motivate efforts to make private negotiations succeed, whereas public sector parties, being bureaucrats in the main, will work hard to achieve success only under limited conditions—for example, if they care deeply about producing public value or are fearful of political repercussions for failing to reach agreement.[13]

When it comes to doing joint problem solving, *some* public sector bureaucrats have a distinct advantage over their private sector counterparts. They are supposed to be producing value for the public and not just for themselves or for their agencies or for some specialized constituency. They are supposed to be serving the community, helping the weak, protecting the environment, and so on—all values that might transcend the values of any particular agency and that would be conducive to collaborative work. There may even be a specialized vocabulary and culture related to these higher order values. Peter Haas, for instance, attributed the "success" (relative to skeptics' expectations, that is) of negotiations to protect the Mediterranean from pollution to the fact that the negotiators formed an "epistemic community" that intellectually grasped the nature of the ecological threat and were committed to the ecological values at stake.[14] Craig Thomas sees the same process at work in regard to agencies protecting biodiversity.[15]

---

12. Innes and Booher (1996).

13. In the latter case, as we saw in chapter 5, any agreement reached might represent nothing more than the most bureaucratically convenient outcome with not much yield in terms of public value.

14. Haas (1990).

15. Thomas (1997a).

Available Normative Frameworks

Visions are easy to share. Costs are harder. Many of my academic colleagues, when initially trying to explain why interagency collaboration occurs so infrequently, reach for a collective action model with a free rider outcome: When everyone desires some outcome that can be produced only by cooperation, if everyone also tries to let the other guy pay for it, there will be no production at all. This is the model first given prominence outside economics by Mancur Olson.[16] In this case, however, despite illuminating some aspects of the process, the model blurs important realities.

First, the classic model presumes that the parties are unable to coordinate their actions. But in the ICC case coordination is possible. Elected officials and their appointees can coordinate the public sector partners in a top-down fashion if they choose to do so, and the parties themselves can sit at a table to negotiate.

Second, the actors are not entirely self-interested, or at least they may not be. The public and nonprofit agencies officially are supposed to—and despite bureaucratic and careerist interference often do in fact—tend to some value-creating purpose. It is true that the actors will normally try to avoid the costs of collective action to the extent possible, free-rider style. They will attempt to shift the costs onto others as much as they can and put up as little as they can get away with. But such efforts are not necessarily self-interested in the sense assumed by the Olson model. Protecting one's agency's budget may be motivated by public interest considerations. Moreover, such efforts to shift costs will be resisted by the other partners.

Cost-shifting efforts are typically accompanied by appeals to a principled framework based on equity and justice. The collective action problem that can lead to suboptimal outcomes is not cost avoidance per se but the collectively generated friction and delay that accompanies maneuvering over which framework to apply and how to apply it. But frameworks are not created from scratch. Negotiators work from preexisting models. This has the advantage of making at least some language of discourse available, but the disadvantage of importing into the discourse, along with the constructive symbols and understandings, all the irritants and confusions. In my set of specimens I observe five frameworks in common use.

16. Olson (1965).

—Affordability. The agencies that can most readily afford to bear a larger burden should do so. For the public sector agencies this usually means having a large budget. Rightly or wrongly, observers assume that the larger an agency's budget, the easier it is to find pockets of discretion over personnel or expenditures that can be converted into a willingness to contribute resources to the ICC. The negotiating friction in this case has to do with how much discretion an agency really has over exactly what level of resources, and how much of its total discretion, it needs to reserve for use in connection with other needs or priorities.

Affordability issues are part of nearly every negotiation over the distribution of burdens. However, they have special features that vary with the exact relationship among the partners. The issues are cleanest in the case of agencies that are both subject to the same political authorities and funded by the same tax base—for example, youth services and social services in the state of Maryland, adult family services and the employment department in Oregon.

—Mutualism based on shared professional identity or common conceptions of the public interest. Suppose that the agencies are from different levels of government and only minimally overlap in the tax bases on which they draw. If the level of resource commitments is low enough to be handled easily within the level of discretion of the wealthier agency, the negotiators could invoke a normative framework based on professionalism or a common philosophical view of the public interest. For instance, the ecologists sprinkled throughout the various agencies involved in the biodiversity memorandum of understanding were very clearly a collaboration-seeking force within the ICC. Gerald Johnston, leader of the Cal/EPA multimedia enforcement effort, saw no problem in offering limited Cal/EPA funds and technical assistance to the local district attorneys' task forces that could not afford environmental enforcement efforts on their own. I suspect that the mutualism framework is strengthened if there is also a history of grant-maker/grant-recipient relations between the agencies in question.[17]

—Fiscal federalism. If the level of resource commitments at issue is relatively high, it may trigger use of a normative framework based on intergovernmental fiscal relations across a broad front. In Maryland, for instance, the normative issues concerning partner contributions

---

17. Mutualism applies even more powerfully to agencies within the same governmental structure and financed by the same tax base.

and prerogatives to systems reform were covered by the larger ongoing debate over state–local relationships. Because this debate in Maryland was relatively frictional, the systems reform community might have been better off had this particular normative framework not been so available.

—Nonprofit versus public sector comparative advantage. Osborne and Gaebler hold that the nonprofit sector is better able than the public sector at reaching out to diverse populations, acting with compassion and commitment, treating problems holistically, and inspiring trust. The public sector is supposedly better than the nonprofit sector at acting with stability over time, handling issues outside of a central mission (such as affirmative action), and acting with immunity to favoritism.[18] How well Osborne and Gaebler have actually grasped the intersectoral comparative advantages is debatable. The point, though, is that whatever they are, these advantages exist and help to establish a normative framework for discussing the parties' respective contributions to an ICC. Foundations, for instance, that put some money into collaboratives for children and family services can set limits based on their desire to supplement and not supplant public expenditures, to use their funds to leverage public (and private for-profit) contributions, to provide the glue money to create a service package out of mainly categorical funds, and to stimulate worthwhile and replicable innovations.[19]

It is not surprising that the issues of affordability and comparative advantage often look quite different to a nonprofit service delivery organization and a public sector partner. In the social services domain, often the nonprofits see themselves as small and struggling and their public sector partner as an 800-pound gorilla. They see themselves as creative, nonbureaucratic, low-cost, and effective, and their public-sector partner as essentially clueless. The public sector agencies, on the other hand, may see some of their nonprofit partners as amateurish, fiscally unaccountable, unstable, and so on.[20]

—Private sector commercial relations. The military services and the local reuse authorities (LRAs), for instance, are engaged in deal making surrounding property ownership and management, and they expect one another's behavior to conform in some respects to the norms that

---

18. Osborne and Gaebler (1992, p. 347).
19. On glue money, see Gardner (1989).
20. Bernstein (1991); Kramer and Grossman (1987); Smith and Lipsky (1993).

prevail in such deal making in the private sector. Neither side lives up to the expectations in many cases, the LRAs mixing business with local politics and the services being invested in highly bureaucratic procedures and ways of thinking. Relations are also complicated by the fact that official national policy is to regard the LRAs as business partners that deserve to be treated with exceptional forbearance, and it is unclear just how much is appropriate in particular situations.

Structural and Dynamic Aspects of the Negotiation Process

An interesting generalization about successful private sector negotiations is that they often move from an early period of contentiousness to a "hurting stalemate" to a period of joint concern and constructive problem solving.[21] In the contentiousness period, demands are high, concern for one's own interests is high and concern for the other parties' is relatively lower, and the parties explore to see how much they can extract from each other without having to give a great deal. The usual answer is that not much can be extracted in this way. A stalemate ensues during which they are obliged to contemplate how much better off they would be with an agreement than without one, and they then shift into a more cooperative mode.

Is there a way to skip the contentiousness stage and get right to the constructive problem solving? If the function of the contentiousness period is primarily to bring information into the open about the needs, interests, and desires of the negotiating parties, one can certainly think of other means to do this. The key question is whether the parties will regard information that has not been elicited by threat and torture as a reliable basis for action. Given the prevalence of strikes and of eleventh-hour settlements in the private sector, one may infer that the answer is often no. In the ICC context, however, where public agencies (and sometimes nonprofits) are the negotiating partners, much of the needed information is already public. This is another of the (few) advantages that ICC negotiations have over private sector negotiations.

If there are stages in ICC negotiations analogous to the contentiousness–stalemate–constructiveness dynamic in private sector negotiations, they are probably these:

21. Ancona, Friedman, and Kolb (1991); Pruitt and Carnevale (1993, pp. 113–14).

—Stage 1. The parties convince one another that a latent opportunity exists to create public value through some sort of collaboration. The opportunity looks sufficiently large to justify exploring the efforts and risks to develop the required collaborative capacity.

—Stage 2. The parties convince one another that the collective efforts and risks are probably manageable.

—Stage 3. Problem solving proceeds that works out the more detailed ICC goals, steering processes, operating system design, and the sources of the required resource contributions.

This hypothetical sequence is part of a larger developmental dynamic that I will explore in detail in chapter 8.

In both private sector and ICC negotiations there could be a fourth phase if the parties were very creative. Ancona and colleagues observed that negotiation groups involved in integrative—that is, value creating—bargaining often tend to settle prematurely on inferior solutions simply in order to get agreement.[22] One remedy for this is to work under a group consensus to reopen negotiations after agreement has been reached. I would conjecture that the problem of premature closure is more consequential for ICC parties than for the private sector because the "own interest" component of bargaining will not motivate renewed effort as strongly, and that therefore it would be even more advisable to have a rule for reopening negotiations to improve on the first agreement.[23]

Mediators

Students of private sector negotiations consider the assistance of neutral third parties, or mediators, a smart practice. A study of 400 mediated and unmediated cases in Maine's busiest small claims court found that 81 percent of the mediated cases resulted in full compliance by defendants compared to 48 percent of the unmediated cases.[24] Mediators can

—present a party's proposal to his or her negotiating partner to minimize the well-documented dynamic of reactive devaluation, that is, the tendency to diminish the apparent value or attractiveness of a particular proposal or concession simply because it has come from an adversary.

22. Ancona, Friedman, and Kolb (1991).
23. Raiffa (1982).
24. McEwen and Maiman (1989).

—"induce parties to reveal information about their underlying inter-ests, needs, priorities, and aspirations that they would not disclose to their adversary." Armed with such information, mediators can then help to craft more win–win options.

—"foster a problem-solving atmosphere" and in particular focus the parties on achieving enlightened self-interest rather than the chimera of equity or fairness.

—offset principal–agent problems, such as when a middle manager acts to prevent a settlement that would be good for the firm but would be harmful to the manager's personal career.

—"serve as educator and relationship builder." Humanizing the negotiators in their own eyes encourages constructive settlements; and mediators can invent many large and small ways to do this. In addition, they can educate the parties about the many documented pathologies in the negotiations process, such as reactive devaluation, and thus serve to inoculate against them.[25]

All these potential functions of the mediator in the private sector are also relevant to the ICC case. The problem is how to find people who are able and willing to perform them—and who are trusted by the parties.

Let us first take up willingness and ability. Mediators who serve private parties are normally paid for their services. Payment makes for willingness. It also recruits people of ability, both to the case at hand and to the mediation industry overall. But in the public sector, agencies that hired a mediator in order to facilitate negotiations among them-selves would be criticized as spending money on frills. It might be said that first they created unnecessary and dysfunctional turf barriers that made them unwilling to negotiate and then they compounded their offenses by throwing money into a remedy that they could have and should have devised on their own.

It is often leaders that play the mediator role. By definition, leaders are in some sense insiders in the process and therefore do not fit the model of a typical mediator. But facilitative leaders do not fit the model of traditional leaders either. To see how facilitative leadership and mediation can be conjoined in the same person, consider the dynamics that create facilitative leadership. Mediating was simply another of those functions, like doing staff work, mobilizing resources,

25. Ross (1995, p. 28); Mnookin and Ross (1995, pp. 22–23).

and participating constructively in the steering process, that made people willing to think of someone as a legitimate source of leader-like ideas, suggestions, and conduct. In fact, in the ICC case the mediation function is almost entirely subsumed by the facilitation function.

But not entirely subsumed. In the context of the advocacy, rather than the facilitative, style of leadership, the mediation functions of the leader are played in an entirely different way. The facilitative leader earns trust by appearing weak, nonthreatening. He or she specializes in actions and ideas that are value creating for the parties rather than value distributing. Value distribution would immediately endanger the facilitative leader's legitimacy. The advocacy leader is also a value creator, but has the potential to earn trust—not just lose it—by getting involved in value distribution as well. Bill Carter, multimedia enforcement champion at the Cal/EPA, was able to mediate disputes among the agencies by being superior to the fray, not simply outside it. He was able to gain and hold the legitimacy of a neutral player partly by virtue of his high political standing with the agency head but also because he was perceived as being equitable and trying to allocate the burdens of participation according to the neutral and legitimate principle of what would best serve the cause of multimedia enforcement. All things considered, then, it is not so much neutrality as impartiality that is really essential to mediator legitimacy.

A modest amount of research also shows the compatibility under some conditions of the role of advocate and the role of mediator. Carnevale found that disputants who had expected a mediator to be biased against them before negotiation but who then saw the mediator act in an evenhanded and unbiased manner gave that mediator the highest marks.[26] In the McEwen and Maiman study of Maine small claims courts, much of what happened during the mediation process involved a discussion of general moral and interpersonal obligations as well as legal obligations. Many mediators, despite an initial promise not to judge the case, "were not reluctant to tell the parties what they thought of some of their claims and counterclaims."[27]

In this regard the process may have moved toward the mode of doing mediation in nonindustrial societies, in which mediators "are generally known by the disputants and often have high community status and con-

26. Carnevale (1992, p. 387).
27. McEwen and Maiman (1989, p. 61).

siderable power." They often bring to the mediation considerable knowledge of the events in the dispute and the character of the disputants and are often "quite directive, advocating settlements that accord with notions of justice commonly accepted in their societies."[28] In chapter 5, I characterized a strand of agency turf consciousness as ethnocentrism. I would note here that if the tribal groupings can engage as a mediator some wise or powerful elder whom they can all respect, they can then use his or her knowledge and legitimacy to their collective advantage.

Delegates and Their Agencies

Interagency negotiations are carried on by agency delegates who must in some sense represent the interests, perspectives, and values of their agencies. That most agencies are heterogeneous in some degree complicates the representation function.[29] Even when the agency is relatively homogeneous, however, the unique interests, perspectives, and values inherent in the delegate role add their own complications.

Delegates tend to be cautious. They generally do not wish to exceed their authority or to be accused or suspected of doing so. Nor do they wish to have their commitments repudiated by their constituencies.[30]

---

28. Merry (1989, p. 85).

29. The complications may be overwhelming when the agencies are themselves composed of loosely coupled entities—for example, universities and public school systems (Keating and Clark, 1988; Schlechty and Whitford, 1988; Williams, 1988).

30. A staffer at the Medford Jobs Council who had been "caught cooperating," as he put it, with other welfare-to-work partner agencies on the simple problem of designing a reporting format, was obliged by his superiors to send a memo to his negotiating partners saying, "I am not the JOBS team leader. I had assumed that function on a temporary basis only. [X] . . . is the JOBS team leader." And whatever the actual degree of risk they are running, middle managers' uncertainties may exaggerate it. See Bardach (1993, chap. 3).

The Versar report on the variable oversight approach to military base environmental cleanup describes the many risks that individuals and organizations feel they are taking by working more collaboratively:

The Federal facility is taking the risk that the regulators will not second guess decisions, and the new players (and behind the scenes experts) will not require at a later date that work that had been completed based on agreements reached be redone. The regulators may perceive themselves as potentially undermining their enforcement responsibility and taking a risk as to whether the Federal facility will carry out its agreements. Finally, community participants in the process may be concerned as to whether they are adequately reflecting the interests of the public, and whether other public participants in the process may chastise them for being so involved in the process that they have been 'co-opted' and inadequately reflected the concerns of public groups." (Versar, 1995, p. 7-2)

Hence they often have to check back for approved reactions to the other parties' proposals or counterproposals. All this takes time, creates opportunities for genuine misunderstanding, and raises the possibility that the delegate and the agency are using the checking-back process for manipulative purposes.

The research literature amply documents that delegates also tend to be less forthcoming than their constituencies; and the more accountable they are, the more contentious their negotiating styles. A number of factors related to accountability have also been shown to decrease a delegate's readiness to be forthcoming: relatively low standing within the constituency, being distrusted by the constituency, and being under surveillance by other negotiating team members or other audiences (although, if the constituents favor conciliation, surveillance pushes the team toward conciliation).[31]

In the interagency context the delegate not only represents the agency to the ICC but represents the ICC to the agency. The ICC, after all, has its own evolving needs and interests. From the constituent agency it needs resources, flexibility, and constructive ideas. The delegate is a communications channel that works in both directions. Because the delegate has occasionally to ask for something from his or her organization on behalf of the ICC, suspiciousness of the delegate increases on the home front, thereby increasing his or her inflexibility vis-à-vis his ICC negotiating partners.[32] At the same time, the delegate's increased inflexibility elicits reciprocal inflexibility from the other delegates, all of whom are subject to their own role conflicts with their own constituencies. Agreement becomes harder to reach, delegates experience considerable stress, and such agreements as are reached may be suboptimal.[33]

In the interagency context, it is probably fair to say that the heart of the problem is the mutual uncertainty about preferences and loyalties that links the delegate and the superior to whom the delegate is immediately accountable. The superior has her own superiors to worry about, moreover, and her supervisor has hers. Each level of the hierarchy introduces further uncertainty. Hence the more hierarchical the agency, the greater the uncertainty. The uncertainties are amplified in

31. Pruitt and Carnevale (1993, pp. 56–58).
32. Pruitt and Carnevale (1993, p. 156).
33. Pruitt and Carnevale (1993, p. 157).

bureaucracies with many levels but with unclear or overlapping responsibilities among the many offices at one level or between levels. Most delegate behavior in such bureaucracies is destined to be extremely cautious, slow, and rigid. In their negotiations with the LRAs, the military services have generally fallen into this pattern. Any meeting of LRA representatives will produce dozens of horror stories about the difficulty of getting a straight answer, a creative answer, or a timely answer from the service with which they have been dealing. A possible pattern of exceptions to the general rule occurs when the service delegate is a particularly aggressive individual, perhaps nearing retirement and relishing his prospective freedom, who has fallen into the delegate role and exploited the uncertainties in his military department to take on an entrepreneurial, almost buccaneering, style.

If mutual uncertainty between delegate and the home agency hierarchy is the source of problems, are there smart practices that can reduce this uncertainty? Although I am unaware of any so obviously cost-beneficial that they would surely qualify, I will mention a few less clear-cut possibilities. First, agencies that have gone some way toward flattening hierarchies, establishing good communication channels between levels, and empowering their lower level staff have already solved some of the problem. In any case, clarifying the delegate's mandate should help both the delegate and the superior. This can be done by specifying the general objectives and giving explicit freedom to craft a detailed solution. This approach was said to have worked for some agencies in negotiations over the Systems Reform Initiative in Maryland.[34] In Oregon the effective mandate to interagency work teams had come down from the highest executive level in the state in the form of the state's basic JOBS charter, a document called "Local Planning Guide: Jobs for Oregon's Future."[35] More important, perhaps, this document was backed by an evolving understanding among top administrators all across the state and across many different agencies that collaboration was indeed expected to occur. Another possible solution is to have the topmost layers of the partner agencies take over the negotiations themselves at some point. Moreover, if all the parties know that this is the script, the delegates in the early phases might feel

34. Informants in Maryland credited an organizational development consulting group in Philadelphia, the Center for Applied Research, with the basic idea.
35. Adult and Family Services Division, Oregon Department of Human Resources, March 1990.

freer to be creative, secure in the knowledge that their bosses would be able to remedy problems.

Developing Trust

Another approach to the problems that arise among negotiating partners is to improve the ties of trust between the partners, so that when any of them run into trouble with their respective agencies the others will know how to make allowances. This means (1) assessing the trustworthiness of individuals and the institutions they represent, (2) persuading others of one's own trustworthiness, (3) learning how to trust, and (4) taking collective measures to develop trust.

Trust Defined

But what exactly is "trust"? The social science literature aiming to conceptualize trust is extensive but, for my purposes, not entirely adequate.[36] My own conceptualization is this: Trust is confidence that the trustworthiness of another party is adequate to justify remaining in a condition of vulnerability. I shall briefly discuss the key terms.

VULNERABILITY. I would first draw attention to the nature of the situation in which trust operates, a situation of vulnerability, uncertainty, personal risk, and the power of others over oneself. There is little point in talking about trust in situations in which one has taken or could take nearly costless precautionary measures against harm—for example, dispatching low-level delegates to ICC negotiations whose very circumscribed and contingent promises could be repudiated by senior managers later with no loss of agency credibility. Moreover, vulnerability is low, and hence irrelevant, if there is in effect no risk of damage—for example, in a commercial setting in which, although a trusting handshake substitutes for a formal contract, nonperformance by the parties can be deterred by the prospect of denying the offender repeat business or inflicting social ostracism or pronouncing a supposedly effective curse on their children to the tenth generation.[37] I hasten to add, however, that because there are usually real costs to an offended party invok-

36. For a survey, see Thomas (1998).
37. Williamson (1993).

ing punishment and some possibility of coming out less than 100 percent whole after compensation has been furnished, there may indeed be an acceptance of vulnerability that ought to be called "trust."

CONFIDENCE.   Trust has an emotional component. More precisely, it has two. The first is the fear that comes from feeling vulnerable. The second is the confidence that is necessary to offset the fear.

Note that my definition does not stipulate confidence *in* another party but confidence *about* the trustworthiness of another party. That is, Smith may have confidence *about* Jones's trustworthiness because Smith believes Jones to be a person of exalted integrity or because Smith simply believes *in* Jones and his disposition to act in accord with his job description. It does not rule out the possibility that confidence-about is rooted in a more personalized confidence-in, but it does not necessarily require it.[38]

ADEQUATE TO JUSTIFY.   Justification is a rational process involving a comparison between fear and confidence. The comparison has two components. The first has to do with the level or amount of confidence: the greater the fear, the greater the confidence level needed to offset it. The second has to do with the qualitative nature of the confidence. The fear is not simply an undifferentiated lump of anxiety but a bundle of concerns about particular vulnerabilities and particular sorts of untrustworthiness; it has a certain shape. The nature of the offsetting confidence, therefore, to some degree corresponds to this shape.[39] If Smith worries that Jones will not intercede actively with his boss Brown on behalf of the ICC because Jones might be somewhat cowardly, the offsetting confidence has the shape, "I will trust Jones to be brave enough at least to speak to Brown, even if not as forcefully as we might wish."[40]

38. Thus it is more general than the definition used in one of the better social psychological papers on trust in work relationships: "a state involving confident positive expectations about another's motives with respect to oneself in situations entailing risk." The definition is that of S. D. Boon and J. G. Holmes, quoted in Lewicki and Bunker (1995, p. 117).

39. In a paper examining the relationship between public trust in governmental institutions and the particular hazards those institutions are set up to manage, Thomas (1998) is sensitive to this matter of shape.

40. The social psychological literature has missed the dual emotional component of trust, overlooking the fear and, as a result, also missing the differentiated and measured nature of the confidence that trust entails. See, for instance, the papers in the volume edited by Roderick M. Kramer and Tom R. Tyler, two prominent psychologists in this area (Kramer and Tyler, 1995).

TRUSTWORTHINESS. Besides one's own vulnerability to being harmed, rational assessment must be directed at the degree and kind of the other party's possible untrustworthiness or, conversely, trustworthiness.

What is the nature of the trustworthiness that a negotiating partner would be concerned about? Assume Smith is a mid-level manager, representing her agency in a multilateral negotiating and problem-solving forum. Assume that she herself is committed both to the furtherance of the ICC and to the protection of the mission and bureaucratic interests of her own agency. What would represent ideal trustworthiness in a negotiating partner from Smith's point of view? She would want the partner to be about as committed to the ICC and as concerned about the mission and interests of her agency as she herself is. She would also want the partner to be competent at tasks involving joint problem solving (including representing the ICC to the partner's agency) and candid in bringing information about the agency's strengths, weaknesses, and attitudes toward the emerging ICC back to the rest of the participants in the forum.

To these dimensions of trustworthiness that pertain to the ordinary participant in negotiations we must add a few more that pertain to participants who aspire to be mediators. As we saw, impartiality is needed for legitimacy. Creativity and persuasiveness also help in that a good mediator is also one who can craft value-creating enhancements to the present solution set and discreetly promote them to the several parties.

Assessing Trustworthiness

Suppose Jones and Smith are both participants in a middle-management interagency implementing network. The participants allocate and schedule resources to various ICC tasks. Inevitably, they have to commit their agencies' resources and flexibility, and in doing so they are in effect their agencies' delegates. The odds of their performing their required tasks well will be greatly improved if:

—they can reveal to one another the true extent of their agencies' resources that might responsibly be committed to the ICC;

—they can be honest with one another about the true level of performance capabilities within their respective agencies;

—each feels they can trust the other's agency to take his or her own agency's needs and interests into account when political, fiscal, or other sorts of difficulties arise;

—each can rely on the personal integrity, effort, and talent of the other. Thus mutual trust will make it a lot easier for them to accomplish their joint managerial tasks. Mutual trust begins with each party's appraising the trustworthiness of the other. What sort of data might Smith, for example, use to appraise Jones's trustworthiness?

REPUTATIONAL INFORMATION. Some Joneses will have reputations that precede them: Jones is "a bureaucratic empire-builder" or "a very smart politician" or "a fighter for good causes" or "an extreme environmentalist." Although prior reputation may sometimes be a passable predictor of behavior in the current context, I would guess that it is more likely to be misleading than helpful. It has been subject to pro-Jones distortion by Jones and his friends, and to anti-Jones distortion by his enemies. It is also likely to have been distorted by what psychologists call *attribution bias*, with all those who have contributed to Jones's reputation over the years attributing more to Jones-the-person and less to Jones-the-actor-in-a-situation than was warranted. Reputations are also subject to oversimplification effects, altering the grays in Jones's character or competency to blacks and whites.

CATEGORICAL KNOWLEDGE. This is made up of rough generalizations about the various classes with which Jones is identified—for example, Jones's agency, profession, age cohort, prior professional attachments, and ethnic identity. A social worker once explained to me about the incoming director of his state mental health agency that all he knew about him was that he had held a high position in the public health service—but that was plenty.

Like all stereotypes, such categorical knowledge usually has some validity as a first approximation. But in matters as subtle as ICC negotiations, first approximations are too crude to be useful. True information about differences between "average" individuals belonging to different categories masks equally true information about the great heterogeneity that is usually found within the categories. Furthermore, the very fact that Jones is to be found in an interagency forum to discuss ICC development probably reflects something unusual about him. If he occupies a role in his own agency that routinely brings him into contact with the world outside the organization, he might be more open-minded than average. He might be more politically astute—even, perhaps, more devious. He might also be in relatively low standing in his own organization and have been sent to what his boss regards as bureaucratic purgatory. In any event, Smith would almost certainly make a grave error were she to use categorical information to form more than a first impression.

PRIOR PERSONAL EXPERIENCE. An evaluation of the planning process in the California Healthy Start program found that trust appeared to grow simply as a result of experience working together. In addition, a strong correlation showed up between the planners' ability to work collaboratively on Healthy Start and their prior history of working together collaboratively.[41] Many negotiators in the ICC context have encountered one another in some previous professional setting. This is especially true in small towns and rural areas where, relative to large urban areas, there are few agencies operating in any domain and many of the staff have been in place for a long time. Even in urban areas, though, this sort of interpersonal network often exists. As Levin and Furman have pointed out in their study of several cities' youth employment programs in the 1970s, a cadre of professional antipoverty workers had taken root in the mid- and late 1960s and, some ten to fifteen years later, were available to staff the social programs of that era. They were also distributed throughout public sector and community-based organizations and so were able to forge good working relationships in many cases.[42]

A preexisting reservoir of such relationships is a part of what is often called *social capital*.[43] This is a creative capacity that inheres in a community rather than in a single individual or organization.[44] Examples are a common language, an effective system of self-governance, a wide-

41. Wagner (1994, pp. 2-13, 2-17).
42. Levin and Furman (1985).
43. Putnam (1993).
44. Like other concepts we have encountered in this book, *social capital* is a potentiality (see chapter 2). We might say, for instance, that a community with much social capital hosts a high number of potential interpersonal networks, any one of which could be activated to work on developing an ICC. The exact network that did in fact emerge might, in its ex post facto particularity, seem surprising. But the fact of some such network emerging might have been perfectly predictable. See chapter 9.

spread readiness to trust one another, an informal network to disseminate and channel communications,[45] and reliable knowledge about who
can be trusted to perform what kinds of tasks with unusual competency.
The utility of social capital in exploiting collaborative potential has been
documented by Innes, Gruber, and their colleagues, who studied fifteen
cases of consensus building among diverse interests around issues of
community growth and redevelopment.[46] They observed that months
and years of conversations among the representatives created reservoirs
of mutual familiarity and approachability. They quote one federal participant in a multiparty, multiyear project to formulate plans to preserve
and otherwise manage the San Francisco Bay, which has been threatened by pollution and fill:

> One major result of the process is I now have networks into 40 dif-
> ferent groups representing different values and points of view. If
> they have frustrations they can call me. I get called a lot. I call
> them a lot too. I am on the phone with the Sierra Club almost
> every day. I try to find out what they are doing and to see what I
> can do to help that is consistent with (our agency's) objectives.[47]

In many communities social capital is surprisingly absent.
Anonymity prevails even among physical and organizational neigh-
bors. An early and steadfast supporter of Marin County Coordinated
Youth Services Council reported,

> We had Probation and County Schools [Office of Education] and
> Health and Human Services together for a policy meeting. The
> directors were there, the Superintendent of the Schools, and their
> immediate subordinates. Many of these people worked in the
> same building in the county for twenty years and they were just
> meeting each other. They were shaking hands, introducing each
> other, saying "Hi, nice to meet you." And I realized that not only
> had people not collaborated, they hadn't even met. That's a kind

45. Jennings (1994); Jennings and Krane (1994).
46. Innes and others (1994). The literature also recognizes "calculus-based trust" or
"deterrence-based trust" (Lewicki and Bunker, 1995, pp. 118–21). As I said, however, I do
not define confidence in the other party based on rational presumption of the party's fear
of noncompliance as trust at all.
47. Innes and others (1994, p. 48).

of beginning to saying, "It [collaboration] could happen," because [just with the meeting] you build some trust.

No prior acquaintance could be a benefit, to be sure, if the alternative is to get past a history of discouraging experiences. When that history exists, Smith must consider why it is not necessarily a source of valid information about Jones's current trustworthiness. The pressures on Jones may have been different in past situations than they are in the present one. Unless Smith is very good at distinguishing what was personal and enduring in Jones's earlier behavior from what was merely situational, as a result of the attribution bias mentioned earlier she is likely to err in the direction of underestimating Jones's current trustworthiness. Furthermore, Jones's persona may actually have changed in some way. Aging and progress in his career may have made him less idealistic or, alternatively, more secure as a risk taker. The more varied Smith's prior experiences with Jones have been, and the more contextual information available to Smith to help her interpret Jones's behavior, the more valid her current understanding of Jones's trustworthiness is likely to be. Smith could greatly improve the validity of her database were she able to canvass her friends and colleagues for useable information about their prior personal experiences with Jones.

CURRENT EXPERIENCE. A highly reputed Oregon manager in the area of children and family services, with much experience in ICC development, put it succinctly: "I watch to see how they conduct themselves in the course of our working together. That's what counts. Do they come to meetings prepared, or do they show up with lame excuses?" Besides showing up prepared, I heard in the course of my interviews about many other points of conduct presumably bearing on one or another aspect of trustworthiness: Did Jones seem to be running risks in his agency to bring unpopular ideas about interagency collaboration to the attention of his superior and peers? Did Jones put in long hours, travel through rush-hour traffic, or traverse great distances to attend ICC meetings? Did Jones contribute creative ideas to problem-solving discussions? Did Jones self-consciously approach the limits of bureaucratic propriety in conveying information about personality conflicts in his own agency or about weaknesses in its top management? Did Jones allow himself to take pleasure in ICC-related tasks and form rewarding personal attachments with other participants? When Jones permitted

himself the use of rhetoric betokening commitment to ICC development, was it possible for Smith and others to discern the indications of
personal trustworthiness, of "character," in Jones's facial expressions,
tone of voice, body language? In concluding this chapter, I shall discuss
steps to help create this sort of experientially based trust.

THE BIGGER PICTURE. An important source of data bearing on
Smith's assessment problem is the overall political and organizational
environment in which Jones and Smith are both operating. If Smith
observes that the political powers are putting pressures on the director
of Jones's agency to collaborate with Smith's agency, or that Smith's
boss is angling for a job in a foundation that supports the idea of interagency collaboration, Smith can infer that Jones will be more reliably
committed to ICC development than he might otherwise be. Data about
such bigger pictures demand a high level of interpretation and inference making to squeeze out a supposition about Jones's day-to-day conduct as a negotiator and problem solver.

One critical aspect of the big picture is the prospect that the negotiating partners might, or might not, find themselves working together in
the longer run. Belief in a long-term future could make it easier for the
parties to reach agreement by encouraging concessions and a constructive state of mind in the expectation of eventual reciprocity. On the
other hand, prospects of a long-run relationship might have the opposite effect, raising the stakes of creating disadvantageous precedents,
status relationships, or expectations for further institutional change.

When it comes to creating the bigger picture, and to helping participants make sense of it, leadership counts. A realistic understanding of
the big picture does not come easily in the sometimes Byzantine world
of interagency political relations. It is usually top agency leaders who
have the best grasp of such matters and who should therefore work to
inform the troops. But what if the troops are bureaucratic veterans who
no more trust their own leaders than they do the minions from ostensibly collaborating agencies? A close observer describes how the director
and deputy director of the Oregon Adult and Family Services agency
handled this sort of problem in their welfare-to-work collaborative:

Steve [the director] and Sandy [the deputy] really provided the
leadership here. What Steve was saying to the internal managers
was what he was saying to the outside partners—and this was a

powerful message. For instance, suppose he is telling the internal staff about how we really need to get the community colleges to move to a year-round calendar, and how those folks have to be pushing on them to do this [because they are resistant], and then he is in a meeting with . . . the Commissioner of the Community Colleges, and the managers would hear him say, "Well we're just so pleased about how well the Community Colleges are working with us," there is a disconnect. But again and again, we all saw how they told the same story all around.

SIMPLIFYING THE ASSESSMENT PROBLEM. Fortunately for Smith, it is not necessary to assess Jones's trustworthiness in any absolute sense. As in any organization, it is only with respect to some particular array of ICC-related tasks that Jones's professional trustworthiness need be gauged. Can Jones be trusted to bring back useful information from his agency about their budgetary incentives? Can Jones be trusted to represent the emerging ICC point of view in legislative hearings next month? Will he make a real effort to sell the ICC to suspicious advocacy groups outside government?

How Can the Joneses Persuade the Smiths?

Whereas Smith has a stake in correctly assessing Jones's trustworthiness as a partner, if Jones is in fact reliable he has a stake in seeing to it that Smith makes the correct judgment. He also has a stake in making Smith's assessment job easier for her. How is this to be done?

First, Jones can assume that Smith makes some use of categorical and reputational information about himself and, if Smith and he have a history of previous professional relationships, about this source of information as well. If he can guess how Smith perceives him on this basis, he can attempt to provide positive references—though being careful to avoid sounding like a name-dropper. If he needs to modify such perceptions, he can try discussing them explicitly: "You may have heard that a few years ago I opposed exactly the sort of collaboration we are now discussing; but in fact I was not opposed in principle, I was only opposed to some of the details concerning funding." Or, as Felicia Marcus has done (see chapter 4), "I am from the EPA, but I am now being reasonable."

Second, Jones can produce the sort of conduct mentioned previously that he knows Smith to be looking for, such as coming to meetings well prepared, enduring long travel times, bringing back sensitive information, doing his bit to help the group over the inevitable periods of frustration and bickering.[48] The most convincing sorts of signals for Jones to send about his trustworthiness would be the costly or slightly risky sort that Smith would take to be senseless from Jones's point of view, and therefore Jones must really be as reliable as he seeks to indicate.

Third, Jones can create emotional and political hostages to secure his commitments. He can nurture personal attachments to his colleagues in the working group and to the symbols of their collective efforts, attachments that will imply genuine pain should others in the group come to believe he has failed them or played them false. The greater the presumed pain of a violation, the greater the degree of warranted trust in Jones.

Occasionally "Jones" and "Smith" are not single individuals but institutions or groups. The same principles apply, though. Art Bolton described how grass-roots organizers in Del Paso Heights sought to evoke trust from Sacramento county bureaucrats, who would normally be suspicious of such organizers:

> We've developed a different approach in Del Paso. We know that many of the things we want really can't be given to us by the county agencies. When we sit down with agencies, our approach is that we feel sorry for the agencies. They have an enormous burden, and they have not done well. So, we go to the agencies with the attitude: "How can we help you achieve your objectives in this neighborhood?" They do need our help. They find this refreshing! Now, if they are willing to contract with us, we can employ neighborhood people, and the agencies can look good. The block grandparent program is $100,000 now, and we contract with the county agencies. These are all people who have successfully raised their own children. They are having a big impact on recidivism in child abuse. They receive over 100 hours of training before they go out in the field. We are making the county look good! Our attitude is: These agency people are not bad people, they are just working with ineffective systems.

48. Katzenbach and Smith (1993, pp. 150–51).

Beyond the Merely Cognitive

From where does Jones's pain come following a suspected violation? And from where does the anger come that Smith would feel for Jones were she to believe he had betrayed her confidence in him? In the discussion to this point I have focused only on the cognitive aspect of trust, on the nature of the evidence that an ICC partner looks for in others to assess whether confidence is justified. But like the fear that it mirrors, confidence has an emotional component. The exact nature of this emotional component is puzzling, however.

The social psychology literature distinguishes between knowledge-based and identification-based trust, and it seems to be the latter that carries the emotional freight in a trust relationship. Lewicki and Bunker distinguish the two types as follows:

> Knowledge-based trust occurs when one has enough information about others to understand them and accurately predict their likely behavior. . . . It develops over time, largely as a function of the parties having a history of interaction that allows them to develop a generalized expectancy that the other's behavior is predictable and that he or she will act trustworthily.
>
> [Identification-based trust] is based on identification with the other's desires and intentions. . . . Trust exists because the parties effectively understand and appreciate the other's wants; this mutual understanding is developed to the point that each can effectively act for the other. . . . People may in fact empathize strongly with the other and incorporate parts of his or her psyche into their own "identity" (needs, preferences, thoughts, and behavior patterns) as a collective identity develops. A suitable metaphor for identification-based trust may be a musical one, such as "harmonizing."[49]

I do not think, however, that believing the other party shares one's own "desires and intentions" is really central to the emotional component of confidence in that party's trustworthiness, at least not in relations among professional bureaucrats involved in building ICC capacity. Delegates from partner agencies are *expected* to hold incompatible desires

49. Lewicki and Bunker (1995, pp. 119, 121, 122, 123).

and intentions to some degree. This does not necessarily preclude a high level of mutual confidence, even a very personal sort of confidence based on something such as identification. What is missing from the conception of the other party about whom knowledge is acquired or from whom identification is expected is a moral dimension involving traits of character such as uprightness, honesty, integrity, and sincerity.

In my interviews, informants often told me something like, "Collaboration is relationship-based. It is based on people. I'll trust Jones because I know him. We have an ongoing relationship. It goes way back. I couldn't manage the same sort of collaborative work with Brown." Clearly the trust relationship with Jones thus described is rich and complex. If it includes knowledge of character it certainly includes a lot more as well. But character is part of it. Moreover, the dimensions of character are almost certainly themselves rich and complex.

One such dimension is participation in an agency–professional culture in which role obligations entail a fairly high degree of trustworthiness in their dealings with one another. Still another dimension of character, and probably the most important, is character as a partner in an ongoing relationship built on a shared commitment to reciprocity and mutual aid. Such a relationship is personal without necessarily being familiar and involves concern that does not necessarily have anything to do with empathy. The aspect of character relevant to such a partnership is honor in keeping one's commitments, however tacit they may be. Finally, there is an element of individual or private character that in some cases underlies both professional morality and reciprocity-based morality. This is integrity. A person of integrity would experience guilt if she violated her commitment to reciprocity or her role responsibilities as a professional.

Learning How to Trust

Interagency collaboration, the joke goes, is an unnatural act committed by non-consenting adults. Learning how to do it takes time and a willingness to make the effort—even a willingness to understand that a problem exists for which time and effort are required. "It took a long time for people to stop saying, 'Now that we're collaborating, they'll finally do what we tell them to do,'" said one of the architects of Oregon's highly collaborative JOBS program.

"We didn't know how to collaborate, but we didn't know that we didn't know," said Donna Stark, the former director of Maryland's integrated services Systems Reform Initiative. As a result, according to Walt Wirsching, who represented juvenile services in Maryland, they did not take enough time in the early stages to establish trust among the major players and were for many months thereafter building on a weak foundation. Not knowing how to share information was the most fundamental problem:

> When we first started it was, "OK here we are, let's go." People started asking us for information. Our tendency was to withhold . . . information on dollars, numbers of services, types of services we were providing, where we were providing them. Those kinds of things. We were very skeptical. It probably could have been gotten in some other way but we weren't willing to just give it up. We were wondering what people were up to, what was going to happen.
>
> The advice I'd want to give is pay attention to the relationship. You start this stuff, you get the relationship started right, and then you'll progress.

Smart Practices for Developing Trust

One candidate smart practice for developing trust is to hire professional help. Wirsching's reference to Marty Blank is indicative of the growing importance of professional organizational development consultants and trainers in the ICC development process. This industry has come to serve as at least a partial solution to Stark's problem of "not knowing that you don't know," for it is prepared to legitimate not knowing and to make the acquisition of knowledge and skills a much easier task than it otherwise would be. Although there is great quality variation in the industry, as a whole it is almost certainly a useful contributor to the steering capacity of many ICCs. However, most collaboratives do not have the budget or the time, inclination, or expertise to hire professional help. What might they do?

In a decently managed world we would be more likely to trust people who really are trustworthy than those who really are not. Delegates to interagency settings ought to be genuinely concerned about making the ICC work well, and they ought to be genuinely reliable—trustworthy—in their dealings with their counterparts from other agencies. In this case other delegates could trust them, and negotiations would proceed more smoothly. What is the likelihood that the delegate selection process disproportionately favors such individuals?

Consider a planning group drawn from some implementing network. If the participants have voluntarily joined the group—perhaps because they are high enough in their organizations to be able to have moved on their own authority—they will probably be motivated as well to approach the group's deliberations in a constructive spirit. If the participants have been sent to represent their agencies, however, there is no special reason to count on this, even leaving aside whether top agency management wishes them to do so. The main, almost universal, procedure is to send someone whose bureaucratic position supposedly enables him or her to speak with technical and administrative understanding of the issues. But occupancy of a seemingly appropriate position is no guarantee that the occupant has such understanding and even less that he or she will put forth constructive effort.

Selecting a representative deserves more thought and creativity than this—provided, that is, that the manager making the selection actually wants the ICC to succeed. Finding a way to pick someone who will be constructive, in personal as well as in technical terms, is of some significance. The methods might range from taking unobtrusive soundings to asking overtly for volunteers who will swear loyalty to the ICC concept. A difficulty with any method, unfortunately, is the potential breach of bureaucratic etiquette that is involved in not selecting—or selecting only as part of an agency team—the seemingly appropriate bureaucratic position occupant. Moreover, the bureaucrat whose goodwill is at issue is, by definition, well-positioned to obstruct further ICC development at a later point in time.

As for planning groups that have already been constituted, it might make sense for the participants to create early opportunities to take readings of one another's trustworthiness or lack thereof and to create joint experiences that feed into reciprocity-based commitment. In labor–management negotiations, for example, these functions are accomplished as a by-product of standard rituals such as staying up all night in marathon bargaining sessions, going out for beer together, and occasionally "cussing like a normal guy."[50] In San Mateo County, the chair of the public–private task force designing a family-preservation-oriented children's plan once began a meeting with the members passing around photos of themselves as children, and once fed them lunch of peanut butter and jelly sandwiches with the crust cut off.[51] In San Diego, in the course of inventing what became the New Beginnings school-linked services program, hundreds of individuals participated in a lengthy needs assessment of children and families and a resource inventory of what schools might contribute to meeting these needs.[52]

This, of course, is a much vaster undertaking than most planning groups would require. But I have found that most interagency planning groups in fact make no special effort at all to develop a culture of mutual trust. I suspect this can be traced to a lack of understanding of the usefulness of doing so, and perhaps also to a lack of imagination about how it might be done.[53] In chapter 4, I discussed a number of issues regarding the design of training programs for line worker teams and implementation network participants. The same analysis applies in this instance.

Finally, leadership has an important role to play, this time in promoting norms of trustworthiness and trustingness. Negotiations over the Tennessee Children's Plan in 1991 spiraled downward into mutual suspicion and apathy because the prime mover and visionary, the governor's director of Finance and Administration, David Manning, abandoned the process and turned it over to someone who did not have the confidence of the parties that she would be able to rein in the less trustworthy participants among the agency negotiators. This contrasted with the situation in Oregon, where many people gave credit to the top management of Adult and Family Services for trying, with reported success, to create a culture of trust. Not only did the top managers disseminate realistic and consistent information to a wide variety of players across hierarchical and organizational boundaries, but they also made a point of indicating how important honesty had to be in the new

50. Friedman (1992, p. 152).
51. The chair was Audrey Seymour. She said these gimmicks were a great success.
52. Jehl and Kirst (1992, p. 101).
53. It might also be a result of an underestimate of how drawn out ICC development processes can be. See chapter 8.

order of things. One observer said, "They modeled how you put realities on the table."

In the case of base environmental cleanup, many observers credit Sherri Goodman, the deputy undersecretary of defense for environmental security, and her staff for their philosophical commitment to establishing better partnerships with all the stakeholders, from citizens groups to the EPA, to the states' attorneys general, to the military services themselves. Goodman had a strong reputation as a highly intelligent and effective executive. She had professional experience working in many different organizational settings. Before coming to the defense position in early 1993, she had been an attorney in a major Boston law firm, working mainly on environmental litigation but also in commercial disputes and in construction arbitration. For three years before that she had been a staff member working for Senator Sam Nunn, chair of the Armed Services Committee.[54] One of her main institutional assets was the centralization of planning and budgeting functions for the environmental cleanup effort in the DOD rather than in the military services. This gave her an independent base from which to create a communications network across diverse institutional and ideological stakeholders.

Her counterpart in the world of environmental advocates outside government was Lenny Siegel. Siegel had been a student movement organizer at Stanford during the late 1960s and early 1970s and, having taken up permanent residence in Silicon Valley, subsequently became a self-taught expert and activist concerning the social, economic, labor, and military implications of high technology. He participated on the Technical Review Committee overseeing the environmental cleanup of Moffett Field and subsequently organized the Military Toxics Project. He served on the Federal Facilities Environmental Restoration Dialogue Committee organized by the EPA and lobbied effectively for the creation of restoration advisory boards at each military cleanup site, boards that furnish a means for citizen participation in the process. He also set up an Internet-based newsgroup linking the portion of the environmental activist community focused on federal facilities. Siegel was widely respected in the activist community and in the Pentagon as well.

54. I would also like to think that her master's degree in public policy from the Kennedy School of Government at Harvard improved her management abilities.

He was an important communications channel in what was in effect a national forum, as defined in chapter 6.

Summary

The cutting edge of interagency collaboration is interpersonal collaboration. If interagency collaboration is supposed to create new value, that value will almost certainly be bigger and better if the people involved can work together easily and constructively. One barrier to doing so is the bureaucratic culture. It is at its core hostile to the required spirit of pragmatism. A possible smart practice is to use the culture of bureaucracy to cure its own problems: Have interagency teams of experienced bureaucrats exercise their bureaucratic craft skills to design a simpler, less bureaucratic approach to accomplishing the same ends as some existing but too cumbersome system.

Interpersonal collaboration is to a large extent a process of negotiation within a matrix of interpersonal trust, some of it originating in social capital. As the literature on private sector negotiation suggests, mediation helps. So does an experience-based approach to cultivating trust among the negotiators. ICC negotiations may be somewhat more difficult than private sector negotiations because the parties tend not to be as highly motivated to succeed and the layers of intra-agency hierarchy tend to reduce negotiator flexibility. Leadership can do much, however, to promote the needed spirit of pragmatism and to create a secure environment for agency delegates to work collaboratively with one another.

8

Developmental Dynamics

Interorganizational collaborative capacity is born quietly and without ceremony. It might first show up as a gripe session about common programmatic issues among managers from different agencies working in the same problem domain or as some informal information sharing among line staff from different agencies dealing with the same polluting firms or the same distressed families. Such births are commonplace. Once in being, though, will a nascent ICC survive and eventually thrive? How large will it grow? How close will the ICC come to achieving its full potential? What smart practices can be employed to improve the prospects for a full and productive life?

The answers to these questions are given in part by the presence or absence of conditions, opportunities, and smart practices discussed in the preceding four chapters. In this chapter I look to the dynamics of ICC development to supply more of the answers.

Although the analysis in the preceding four chapters was mainly static, there were some hints at dynamic analysis that bear repeating. The ideal ICC contains an evaluation mechanism that collects feedback on program performance and improves the ICC's operating subsystem and its administrative machinery over time. Also, the shared language of interagency work is enriched over time among frontline workers and participants in the implementing network. The steering capacity improves as intellectual capital accumulates, ICC participants learn skills relevant to steering collaboratively, and some sort of leadership capacity emerges. Trust grows as ICC participants share in joint problem solving and make some effort to get to know one another's virtues and limitations.

As to the gathering of sufficient resources, I observed at the conclusion of chapter 5 that the inertia keeping managers and other actors from even trying to exploit collaborative opportunities was substantial, but that once an ICC achieves some threshold level of success the situation changes. It becomes susceptible to a new dynamic.

This dynamic is complicated and involves the development of a high-quality operational capacity as well as the gathering of resources. This chapter explores two major, linked subprocesses in this dynamic: platforming and momentum building. The first primarily has to do with operational capacity; the second, with resources. They are connected in a complementary way. Momentum building depends in part on people's perceptions of how much ICC construction is actually taking place, what the emerging collaborative capacity will probably look like, what interests will be well- or ill-served by it, and so on. Conversely, the capacity-building process involved in platforming depends on the emergence of real consensus on goals and the flow of real administrative and operational resources, realities that depend in part on the momentum process.

The platforming and the momentum-building processes, which are linked, constitute the development process. For the purposes of exposition I treat them separately first and then bring them together in the concluding section on the pace of the development process and its vulnerability to disruption.

The challenge confronting ICC leaders and other activists is to sequence the steps or moves in both subprocesses to extract a bonus in political momentum and in quality and extensiveness of operational capacity from proceeding "in the right order." This means taking steps in some optimal sequence, rather than taking steps all at once, at random, or in some sequence that has genuinely destructive effects.

The two subprocesses are often complementary but may sometimes be in tension with each other in that a given sequence might be optimal for the momentum-building process but harmful to the platforming process, and vice versa. David Manning's *blitzkrieg* approach to setting up the Tennessee Children's Plan, for instance, was valuable for breaking down turf barriers but also undermined the potential partners' ability to craft an effective operating system. In the case of the Marin County Coordinated Youth Services Council, careful attention in the early days to assembling resources, designing an operating system, and creating a consensual steering process left political relations with minority constituencies to drift for too long a time.[1]

Platforming

In building a physical structure, there are some steps that, when fully or partially completed, serve as a platform from which to take some subsequent step—to return to the building metaphor, for example, finishing the framing so that it is then available for applying the plasterboard. Each step has a dual value: It is a contribution to the completed structure, and it is also a contribution to the unfolding building process. Just how efficient a contribution it is in this latter sense will depend on the sequence in which all the steps occur. Some sequences constitute richer opportunities for rapid and cost-effective progress than others. A sequence of steps that aims to create and then exploit such a chain of opportunities I call *efficient platforming*.

What makes efficient platforming possible? On the one hand, it can be a product of rational, pragmatic design. Craftsmen, looking for time- and money-saving ways to build, may figure out how to do it, and eventually the knowledge becomes virtually codified as good practice, or in our terms smart practice. On the other hand, the laws of social nature also dictate the sequence.[2] In general, it is not natural to lay the

1. Research on the innovation process in industry, which is somewhat analogous to the ICC development process in that it is trying to create something new and find a home for it within the organization, comes to the same conclusion about the simultaneous complementarity and tension among subprocesses. Angle and Van de Ven (1989) have tried to conceptualize the process as the conjunction of three differentiable paths: activities governed by historical institutional rules that follow a simple sequence of stages (initiation, development, implementation, termination); activities sequenced according to various technical logics with multiple divergent paths that eventually converge into an overall cumulative sequence; and activities governed by an emergent process logic of a generally political nature (pp. 672 ff.). Although each of these three subprocesses has its own internal logic, "confusion arises when these logics interact" and cause "proliferating complexity" (p. 673). My conception of the ICC development process has only two subprocesses, compared to their three, because in the ICC case the institutional and the technical processes are largely the same thing, and together are to be distinguished from the political process.

In principle, a smart practice would be to sequence the steps in the overall ICC development process in such a way as to take advantage of the potential complementarities between the two processes and to minimize the disruptions. Such an analysis is outside the scope of this book, however.

2. Abbott (1990, pp. 376–79).

foundation after doing the framing or to do the framing after the plasterboard. Nor is it natural—moving from the physical to the symbolic world—to have the information about where the baseboards go before knowing exactly where the floors and walls meet.

It would be useful to have a purely naturalistic model of an efficient platforming sequence, one that excluded effects attributable to smart practice. We would then be able to identify opportunities for smart practice to improve the sequencing. Also, we would be able to work at understanding the natural, underlying, sequencing processes without having our vision obscured by craftsmanlike interventions. Unfortunately, the nature of platforming does not permit this neat separation. Sequencing is always determined to some degree by actors' insight into the natural sequence of causes and effects and by actors' foresight about troubles or opportunities that lie ahead under different contingencies, which include their own interventions. It is hard to separate conceptually the kind of foresight that should count as merely natural and that which should count as smart practice. Furthermore, even with a conceptual scheme in hand, it is hard for the observer to distinguish the two empirically, because the critical empirical objects lie buried in actors' minds.[3]

My own approach to disentangling naturalistic development and smart-practice-induced development begins by relegating to the category of smart practice almost all sequence orderings intended to affect the political aspects of the process. To the extent possible, I restrict my naturalistic model to technical matters such as defining the problem to be solved, articulating a vision, and thinking about operational issues. I then use as the basis for my understanding of good, though natural, practice in technical matters the five-stage model proposed by Atelia I. Melaville and Martin J. Blank in *Together We Can* that, although written for practitioners in the children and families area, also has more general applicability.[4] That practitioners in fact found the model useful in at

3. Lawrence B. Mohr astutely observed some fifteen years ago that *variance explanations* and *process explanations* were quite different in style and intention (Mohr, 1982) and argued that process explanations had been generally ignored in organizational studies. Unfortunately, very little has been done since then to deepen our understanding of how to create and test process theory. Mohr's own effort in that book dealt with a very particular kind of process, quite unlike the developmental process analyzed in this discussion.

4. Melaville and Blank (1993). I also drew inspiration from a case study of a government-sponsored interfirm and interindustry collaborative for research and development purposes reported by Hausler, Hohn, and Lutz (1993). In 1984 seventy-six participants

least a good practice sense is attested by Walt Wirsching, who represented Juvenile Services to the Systems Reform Initiative project in Maryland. Considering the process in retrospect, he said,

Do you know Marty Blank? Marty does this handout of this sort of taxonomy in development of reform . . . that was very helpful for me in understanding what happened to us in going about reform. . . . Some of the beginning is the trust building and the like. We didn't start there. We started in the middle, and what we tend to do [now] is go back to the beginning a whole lot to make sure that we're all on the same page, that we understand each other's motives, that we trust one another in what we're doing, that we're willing to share information with one another.

The Melaville and Blank model proposes a construction process in five stages: "Getting together, building trust, developing a strategic plan, taking action, going to scale," and twenty-four milestones distributed across these five stages that detail the stages even further.[5] My model differs in some ways: (1) At the substantive level, it is more self-conscious about the problems of resource acquisition and the desirability of leadership; (2) at the conceptual level, it translates *stages* into *capacities*; and (3) it is more explicit about some developments that occur

---

interested in creating markets for adhesion technology were convened by two research institutes acting for the West German Federal Ministry for Research and Technology. My reading of the case study suggests this developmental process in this case. Firms from the demand and the supply sides of the market came together to establish a forum for deciding whether an opportunity for value creation existed. They then created a process for narrowing the participation to a core of players who had the combination of technical capacity and financial interest to carry the project farther. At the same time they found a solution to the problem of creating a facilitative internal leadership and also produced a credible picture of their relative vulnerabilities vis-à-vis one another—in this case relatively equal and relatively low. Once they were able to find reassurance in this picture, they were able to do further work of a technical nature and to develop a capacity for the delegates to this working group to do successful internal marketing back to their own organizations. (In this particular case, there did not appear to be much negotiation over the distribution of costs, which were borne 45 percent by the government, with the rest borne by the participants.) I was struck by the importance in this process of the step in which parties developed a common picture of their mutual vulnerabilities. Although it was a relatively sharply defined step in the R&D collaborative, I observed something like it in most successful ICC processes, though in less dramatic relief. I therefore included it in my model.

5. Melaville and Blank (1993, p. 21).

Figure 8-1. *Each New Capacity Is a Platform for the Next*

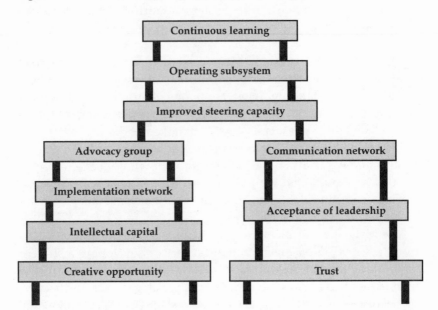

contemporaneously. In my model, a capacity is to some degree valuable in its own right, and it is also valuable as a platform from which to build the next level of capacity. My model of the efficient sequence of capacities is displayed graphically in figure 8-1. The model is to be "read" from the bottom upward. The significance of the two separate pillars for the structure is that construction proceeds relatively independently for each pillar until the platform labeled "Improved steering capacity" is reached, at which point the construction becomes more integrated. I have kept the model simple by omitting relatively weak connecting links between the two pillars and by neglecting the reinforcing processes that undoubtedly originate in some upper-level capacities and have effects on some lower-level capacities.

Even though the sequence, when read, could mistakenly imply a plodding sort of activity, stretching over months and even years, it could just as easily take place in a few days. In cases in which an advocacy leader such as Bill Carter is on the scene, someone who has used all the capacities between *creative opportunity* and *advocacy group* in his own persona, the process may literally begin with *trust* or *leadership*.

Because the platforming model described by figure 8-1 is about a theoretically efficient sequence, it is normative rather then descriptive. However, the model also happens to be an approximately realistic description of processes that in fact occurred, in my set of cases, in regard to the Coordinated Youth Services Council 1986–94, Denver Family Opportunity, East Bay fire prevention, Oregon welfare-to-work, New York State contract administration, and the Elkhorn Slough. In some of these cases, the relatively early emergence of a leader did in fact expedite some of the steps. This process may have taken place in other sites connected with my cases, but I do not know enough details to be sure.

I do not wish to make too strong a claim that my particular model of the steps in an efficient platforming sequence is correct, whether descriptively or prescriptively. Although the platforming sequence diagramed in Figure 8-1 is almost certainly more effective and efficient than a random sequence, it is not necessarily the best for all circumstances, and is certainly not the only plausible sequence that would be effective and efficient. Other researchers will surely have other ideas, as will practitioners.

I do, however, wish to claim an advantage for my approach of defining a number of incremental ICC capacities and leaving it for empirical and explanatory analysis to determine (1) whether they can be sequenced in more or less efficient ways, (2) if so, what those efficient ways might be, and (3) how much the attractions of efficiency influence actual developmental sequences. I believe my approach compares favorably with the practice of many scholars who, when writing about developmental processes, divide them into so-called phases and then assign these phases labels that conflate description and explanation. For instance, one paper on the development of buyer–seller relationships posits that relationships "evolve through five general phases identified as (1) awareness, (2) exploration, (3) expansion, (4) commitment, and (5) dissolution. . . . Each phase represents a major transition in how parties regard one another."[6] Gray wrote of three sequential phases in interorganizational collaboration: problem setting, direction setting, and structuring.[7] Clearly these labels are not meant to be descriptive only; they also imply that, for instance, problem setting somehow facilitates or "causes" direction setting and, less directly, structuring. But

6. Dwyer, Schurr, and Oh (1987, p. 15).
7. Gray (1985, pp. 916–17).

Gray does not explain the reasoning behind the implied causal claim or state the implied counterfactual against which the postulated sequence is supposed to hold causal supremacy. This is generally a problem for all analyses postulating phases, though in some cases the causal analysis is more explicit and believable—for example, the research of Van de Ven and his colleagues.[8]

My own analysis of the logic behind the platforming sequences in figure 8-1 asserts a rather weak causal claim, because it is only against the counterfactual of random sequencing. I leave it to future research to postulate plausible rival platforming sequences to which the sequences in the figure should be compared.

Momentum

Compared with the platforming process, the momentum process is less structured. There are many ways to enhance momentum, none obviously more plausible in a general sense than another, and all quite dependent on opportunities and constraints peculiar to the relevant policy domain and the local environment. All take advantage of the fact that any sort of success represents an opportunity to create even more success in a self-expanding cycle of effects.

—Enthusiasm effects. Perceiving an opportunity for interagency collaboration that will create public value and will advance personal career interest or bureaucratic interest, a small network of advocates comes into being. Their enthusiasm grows by drawing energy from the network, infects still others with enthusiasm, heightens expectations, and elicits resources. A smart practice is to increase and channel this enthusiasm. As Melaville and Blank cautioned, actors should not wait to convene a planning and visioning group "until everyone is at the table. The enthusiasm of a wisely selected and enthusiastic core group can cool while others are being brought in. Do not waste time!"[9]

—Bandwagon effects. One of the reasons that organizations and individuals are willing to contribute resources to an ICC is to stake a claim on access to the ICC's general resource pool and to its steering processes. Hence the more an ICC looks like it will succeed, the more resources it will attract. As with the strengths of a legislatively oriented

8. Van de Ven and Walker (1984); Van de Ven and others (1989); Van de Ven (1993).
9. Melaville and Blank (1993, p. 33).

coalition, the more individuals, organizations, and assorted powerful role occupants give verbal and practical support to the ICC, the more likely that neutral parties will run into others who express favorable attitudes about it. Furthermore, the increasing prevalence of supporters is itself taken as a signal of presumptive success.

—Consensus effects. The more people who certify an ICC as a good and valuable endeavor, the more likely still others are to certify it. Moreover, as with bandwagon effects, the more widespread the consensus, the easier it is for neutral or uninformed individuals to run into, and be influenced by, individuals who are part of the consensus.

—Trust effects. If consensus is about the emerging ICC itself, trust is about the people involved in building it—as individuals and also as the aggregate of trustworthy and trusting individuals who make up the network of ICC supporters, or their community, or however they choose to define themselves. As we saw in chapter 7, interpersonal trust grows with experience and spreads in part by means of reputation and self-advertisement. This means that an expanding circle of trust creates the communications capacity and the social capital to expand still further.

Like platforming, momentum can be a product of either craftsmanlike smart practice or of underlying laws of social nature. As in the case of platforming, it would be useful to have a model of a natural momentum process, one that did not include smart practice. I do not, however, have an even approximate idea about how to conceptualize in this case where nature ends and smart practice begins. I deal with this perplexity by setting my sights low. I will try only to analyze smart practice and will simply ignore all the other analytical challenges. As I have done throughout the book in discussing smart practices, I will adduce real-life examples. Unfortunately, the very nature of certain momentum-enhancing smart practices makes this treacherous. These are the ones in which the actor makes smart calculations about the future and, based on them, makes smart moves in the present to affect the future. In such cases it is difficult to know just what foresight-based calculations actors are making. Asking them might not prove helpful. Even the actor—perhaps especially the actor—has a hard time knowing much about his or her decision process. Moreover, even if one could know the truth in a particular case, to conclude that a momentum-enhancing (or momentum-maintaining) practice was "smart" would require the observer to make an independent assessment of the situation, appraise the smartness of the actual practice and of the possible alternatives to it independently, and then offer an appraisal of the practice. I have found this to be next to impossible.

Consider, for instance, the fact that Ed Hastey was reluctant to invite the EPA to join the original ten-member Biodiversity Executive Council in 1991. Regulators had the wrong outlook, he thought; they might not work well with the traditional resource management agencies. Was Hastey's decision not to include the EPA an example of the smart practice of protecting a consensus one is in the process of building from possibly irretrievable disruption? Was it a mistaken, slightly paranoid fear of the unfamiliar? Was it an equally mistaken misperception of a traditional political antagonist based on stereotypes? Or none of the above?

An alternative to mind reading is assessing the outcome. Did the apparent momentum-enhancing strategy work? One problem with this approach is that chance and circumstance may play an unusually large role in outcomes that occur only over the course of time. A deeper problem is that one does not know very well how to specify the counterfactual. In 1994 the EPA did join the council, part of a wave of new members that had reached thirty-five by the end of the year. No harm was done by their participation. It brought experience and expertise in the protection of biodiversity in aquatic habitats, an area in which terrestrially focused agencies such as the Bureau of Land Management were not much interested. It appears, after the fact, that the council was deprived of a political and technical resource longer than it need have been. Hence Hastey's practice may not have been so "smart." On the other hand, by 1994 the council had become well-established—the consensus of that earlier period had been adequately protected. It is impossible to know whether in 1991 EPA's participation might have destroyed the consensus and stopped the momentum.

My own solution to the problem of adducing real examples is to choose ones that appear so solid that the possibility of underlying purposive intelligence, and hence the intention of smart practice, was clearly high—whether the actuality matched the possibility or not.

Getting off the Ground

Before there are any calculations about momentum to be made, the ICC has to get off the ground. It has to make it past the opportunity stage in the platforming process. As I argued in chapter 1, only a minority of potential ICCs actually do so. Inertia bars the way. Inertia is partly a product of skepticism. One kind of skepticism holds that there is really very little latent potential to improve policy or program outcomes through interagency collaboration. Another holds that even if there is such potential, the barriers erected by turf protectiveness, budget constraints, disagreements over appropriate goals, mutual mistrust, and the like are simply too high to overcome. Thus the initial exploratory efforts to establish feasibility do not take place.

A smart practice is to make use of a crisis or other such attention grabbing and generally perceived circumstance—for example, an apparent hemorrhaging of the foster care budget, a train wreck that dumps toxic wastes into a nearby river (one major stimulant for Cal/EPA multimedia and interagency collaborative work, which took place in 1989), passage of a new law (the 1988 Family Support Act that stimulated welfare-to-work collaboratives), the spotted owl decision (for the memorandum of understanding on biodiversity), the sudden availability of new antitobacco education funds.

Momentum Rewards Performance

Somewhere near the core of every initial coalition of ICC developers is a good government constituency, people who care about improving the government's ability to deliver value for money or who can be induced to care about it. They can become valuable political allies if they can be persuaded that programmatic success is likely and can agree on the definition of "success."

LOW-HANGING FRUIT. ICC leaders attempt to offer indications of its benefits to this good government constituency as quickly as possible by "plucking the low-hanging fruit."[10] The earliest published evaluation of Healthy Start played up improved access to services on the part of previously underserved populations.[11] Programs with some sort of family preservation objective, such as the Systems Reform Initiative and the Marin County Coordinated Youth Services Council, focused on declining out-of-home placements and the attendant avoided costs to the state and county. One of the top priorities for Bill Carter's multimedia environmental enforcement campaign was a visible assault on

10. Innes and others (1994); Weick (1984).
11. Wagner and others (1994).

seemingly egregious misconduct by the Unocal refinery in San Luis Obispo, California. New York State administrative reform, stimulated by the Council on Children and Families in managing contract service providers, began with The Door, where the prospects for success could hardly have been better. In Albany, Oregon, the JOBS collaborative on the community college campus began with offering classes for dislocated timber industry workers, for whom successful teaching and placement was almost ensured, and then moved on to welfare recipients, a much harder group.[12]

PUBLIC RELATIONS. Whatever the performance improvements, and however well or poorly documented, they need to be publicized and celebrated.[13] Most of the cheerleading techniques for doing this are obvious and need no special discussion. One that is not so obvious, however, involves word of mouth communication of ICC success back to staff in the contributing agencies. The director of the Pinelands School-Based Youth Services program in New Jersey gave a glimpse into the process:

Kids come down for their scheduled appointment [with a representative of the probation department located in the School-Based offices.] She sits in here, and the kids come to her. They know when their appointments are. She can also refer them to family therapists from where she sits. She can also get them health care, and jobs. What a nice package—but I don't pay for it. Probation is helping me out by doing it, but they *want* to do it. Because it works. It's that kind of thing that makes it grow. I had a call this morning [from a public employment service agency] talking about school-based employment. So these things kind of start to build onto it. So it works for all agencies that are interested.

Compared to achieving good statistical results on performance, this process is faster and more persuasive. But it also depends on what might

12. In Maine the first major interagency collaborative activity of the Rural Development Council was well-defined and popular. It was to gain regulatory relief from wetlands controls for the state cranberry industry, an important contributor to the state economy (Radin and others, 1996, pp. 191–93).

13. An exception to this occurs if publicity is likely to provoke too much unwanted attention from opponents who would otherwise ignore the ICC process.

be weak links in the chain of communications. These links can be strengthened by encouraging satisfied consumers as well as fellow line staff from the various agencies to talk up the program and by arranging for occasional open houses to which other agencies are invited. They can also be strengthened by rotating a large number of partner agency staff through the ICC for training. This happened serendipitously in the case of the CYSC. Probation assigned its officers geographically and could not assign one as its permanent CYSC in-kind contribution. Public Health also had reasons for not initially assigning a nurse to CYSC. Instead, said one of the veteran observers of CYSC's development:

> They had all of their staff run through the CYSC case review process, so every probation officer in the county came to one CYSC case review meeting or another. That was true of many of the school districts as well, where principals and teachers came to case reviews. It was true of Public Health nurses [too]. . . . It actually became a training process for them where they got—oh, well, this is kind of neat—"We're all here making a decision together and I can get a hold of all of these colleagues who I've tried to get on the phone fourteen different times." So in that sense Probation and Public Health became very invested in the value of the project whereas with Social Services and Mental Health, they did in fact locate a full-time or part-time staff on site and those people were identified by their peers as getting a cushier deal—"They got a lower case load, they're a pet"—So there was resentment on the part of the other workers; they were less able to collaborate and to work with the project and there was much less cross-training . . . in those agencies.

MILESTONES. Getting some actual performance results is not the only way to demonstrate forward momentum. Planning and implementing activities that have no direct performance effects themselves can also serve as the raw material for such demonstrations. In a planned, orderly, momentum-signaling sequence of ICC activities, there is sometimes a long-range plan with a schedule of milestones to be reached. Reaching such milestones would be natural occasions for sending out the word of collective self-congratulation and the reaffirmation of resolve to press ahead. *Together We Can* lists twenty-four, beginning with "Decide to act" through "Build community constituency," and passing through points such as "Define target outcomes" and "Adapt and expand prototype."[14] These are grouped into the five stages I indicated. After successfully achieving each stage, Melaville and Blank recommended, "Reflect and celebrate."

Only a minority of buildup processes move forward with such advance planning. Most improvise their moves as the process unfolds. But a process of improvisation, surprisingly, also has its milestones, which are achieved by means of rewriting history to suit the needs of the present. When Bill Carter was welcoming attendees at the Cal/EPA 1994 Enforcement Symposium in Cross-Media Training, he backdated the first milestone of interagency collaboration to 1989, in the aftermath of a massive spill of toxic chemicals from a derailed train into the American River near Dunsmuir. The response by state and local environmental agencies had been slow and confused. Eventually a network of relevant agencies worked out emergency response plans, which subsequently proved effective, and this network became Carter's first milestone.

Such after-the-fact placement of milestones may require a little imagination. The 1994 symposium was jokingly hailed in the organizer's welcoming speech as "the first annual. . . ."[15] Such a quip is, of course, an expression of hopefulness, a call to action, and a source of chuckles. It signals, "You can make a difference and, what's more, you are not alone." Moreover, quipping about the present as though it were an omen about the future serves a critical cognitive function. It is a shorthand way of making sense out of what a heterogeneous community is collectively doing. It is a way for the group to develop self-consciousness about its ability to act meaningfully in a disorderly world.[16]

---

14. Melaville and Blank (1993, p. 21).

15. In fact, since that first annual symposium, the symposium has been held annually.

16. The orienting effect of seeing one's actions as part of an unfolding development is so powerful that Karl Weick (1979) advised managers to describe the hypothetical future as though it were already part of an unfolding past. He called this *retrospective sense-making* (pp. 195–97) and "thinking in the future perfect tense"—that is, describing "what will have happened": "Somehow the things I'm doing right now are more readily understood as working on/in the future perfect tense. There is less of a question about whether my current efforts are sensible. Instead I have the feeling that . . . [these efforts are] contributing to the future perfect discussion because it's taken for granted that that's what's being produced. . . . the simple future tense is a difficult tense to work with because any possible outcome might occur. Future *perfect* thinking, on the other hand, can make speculation more manageable by focusing on single events. If an event is projected and thought of as already accomplished it can be more easily analyzed" (pp. 198–99, emphasis in original).

Choosing the Right Targets

Plucking the low-hanging fruit—that is, selecting problems that permit relatively rapid and relatively demonstrable progress—is a nearly universal strategy. The same type of momentum-enhancing opportunity is available when selecting three other kinds of targets: political constituencies, operational tasks, and program sites.

POLITICAL CONSTITUENCIES. Like every other public organization, a mature ICC has its political constituencies; and an ICC in its nascent phase has it potential constituencies. The momentum strategy suggests mobilizing the more favorable constituencies early in the process and deferring approaches to more skeptical and less favorable constituencies. As would-be catalyst of the Prescott ICC, Art Bolton began his constituency-creating activities by first soliciting support from foundations and the legislature, where he was well-connected. Line and mid-level staff in the relevant service provider organizations he put off until most of the other contacts had been made and commitments collected. In the interval between these two points he and his associates attempted to mobilize interest among Prescott community leaders and some potential allies in Oakland city government and Alameda county government. Bolton's strategy was clearly influenced by his years in the legislative staff, where this sort of sequencing was simply the natural way of building a coalition behind a legislative proposal.[17]

We can also think of potential constituencies within operating organizations—for example, top management, middle management, and line staff. The collaborative potential at any of these levels is likely to differ. Although all three levels must ultimately be integrated into the workings of an emerging ICC if the ICC is to function well, the order in which their cooperation is secured is not too important to the long-run functioning of the operation. A choice about sequence can therefore be made on political grounds, which implies that the level with the highest collaborative potential should be activated earliest. This will often be the line staff and middle managers, the individuals most aware of, and motivated by, the opportunities for creating value through interagency collaboration. Borins's analysis of Ford/KSG Innovations data found that 48 percent of the innovation champions were middle managers and line

17. For more on the logic of sequencing in legislative coalition building, see Bardach (1972).

workers, whereas only 18 percent were politicians and 23 percent were agency heads.[18] A range conservationist with the Soil Conservation Service and a veteran of the Coordinated Resource Management and Planning process said,

> Often . . . cooperation is greater at the local level, with local [staff] who begin to buy into the community and begin to get a sense of how to manage their particular resource or agency mandate within either their county, their town, their forest, or whatever local unit they have. I think the local people were striving for a way to get people to cooperate even when the powers-that-be in Sacramento, Portland, or San Francisco were loathe to do so. . . .[19]

Other things may not be quite equal, because the line and middle-management levels can be frightened of collaboration if they fear that top management will disapprove. This argues for securing the blessings of top management before looking to lower levels. Of course, the blessings of top management do not by themselves ensure subsequent cooperation at the lower levels. Top management wishing lower levels to embrace the cooperative enterprise will often have to mount a deliberate campaign of persuasion, co-optation, and occasional strong-arm tactics.

OPERATIONAL TASKS. It may be that certain kinds of operational tasks are much better suited than are others to supplying the material for an early string of small wins in a long campaign. Bill Carter at Cal/EPA thought that the right sequence for collaborative tasks, going from easiest to hardest, was criminal enforcement, civil enforcement, site mitigation, and permitting. (To add to his list based on my own observations, collaborative regulation-writing might fall between site mitigation and permitting.) That this sequence would hold true for circumstances beyond those at Cal/EPA in the early 1990s seems likely to me.

18. See also pp. 128–29. Any generalization about the relative propensities of different organizational levels to innovate, however, must take account of the fact that there are vastly more line workers and middle managers in the world than there are elected officials and agency heads. Hence innovation champions are a much smaller proportion of line workers and middle managers than they are of agency heads and elected officials.
19. Thomas (1997a, p. 122).

But I doubt that one can make many strong generalizations about the more promising targets among operational tasks. To take only a single further example, consider information pooling. Creating shared databases was the most tangible activity to result from the memorandum of understanding on biodiversity. A common database is extremely important as a tool for rational planning and resource management and seems to threaten no turf. Yet it is technically difficult to work out, requires many procedural changes in the partner agencies, and opens up the possibility that agency outsiders will be able to second-guess one's decisions.

Human service agencies aiming to share data on their common clients often run into problems over confidentiality. Although there are many genuine barriers in this context, some are more imaginary than real; and agency representatives sometimes suspect that their ICC partners are disguising a reluctance to cooperate behind phony legal and ethical prohibitions. One informant said, "You know, people tiptoe around these information-sharing issues, and take forever working them out—but if you go into the waiting room [of our multiservice center] you hear them telling one another all about their troubles in embarrassing detail." Fortunately, the administrative rationale to share client data does not need to arise until the technical and political groundwork for collaborating on many other functions has already been completed.

From the point of view of the leadership of an ICC, it would be extremely convenient if there were in fact no strong generalizations about which operational tasks offered the most or the least promising prospects as targets. This would leave the leadership much more latitude to proceed according to whichever political constituency, site, or problem seemed most promising. It would mean that essentially political considerations could prevail without endangering the technical rationality that might be inherent in putting one operational task in front of, or behind, another.

PROGRAM SITES. In a program with multiple sites, it is a smart practice to attack the most promising sites earliest—for example, those who volunteer (see chapter 6). Skeptics might ask, to be sure, whether the initial successes are real rather than merely apparent, comparisons with tightly defined control groups or situations nearly always being absent. Skeptics can also ask whether initial successes, if real, are also a harbinger of a future equally as bright as they might suggest, given the unrepresentative nature of the earliest sites, which are often demonstration sites or have volunteered to be pioneers. A fair comeback in some cases would be that, although later experiences would likely prove less successful, even lesser degrees of success might merit the effort.

COMMUNITIES IN A FEDERAL SYSTEM. A special case of site selection involves the choice of local communities or of administrative units within a federal system in which money and technical assistance flow from a political and administrative center—for example, a state to support locally based organizations or communities building their own collaborative capacity. (In some cases, it is regulation more than money and technical assistance that dominates the outward flow.) Such systems present special problems and opportunities for ICC capacity builders. On the one hand, we can see that each local community within the federal system is host to developmental processes internal to itself. On the other hand, actors in the center of the federal system may be concerned about the capacity of the federal system as a whole to produce collaborative results in each of the local communities. The capacity of the federal system to do this on a large scale must therefore be viewed as a particular element in the capacity-building process within each local community. If, for instance, a fight breaks out between a local school board and the nonprofit board running New Jersey's School-Based Youth Services in a community, representatives of the state are available to local leaders as trouble shooters, mediators, and club-wielders.

Conversely, the abilities and dispositions of local actors, whatever they may be, are, from the center's point of view, raw material for its own ICC-building activities. The question is how best to make use of them. There are many techniques. In the case of School-Based Youth Services, subsidies and technical assistance were the preferred means. In the case of local landfill regulation in California, the state Integrated Waste Management Board "encouraged" local landfill inspectors to cooperate with local water quality regulators by inviting them along on site visits and reporting suspected water quality violations to them if they were not present. Outside funders, that make grant funds available to local communities for collaborative work, both public sector agencies and nonprofit foundations, often require that the grant applications be cosigned by all the potential partners.

Are there better and worse ways for the central actors to promote collaborative capacity building by agencies at the local level? Undoubtedly there are. Money clearly helps in some ways. It can attract attention and usually helps to overcome at least short-term and modestly sized fears that an agency's priorities will be completely sacrificed to some other party's agenda. In some cases it can also buy the kind of staff support that I have argued is necessary. But money, when doled out sparingly and in pilot-sized quantities, may simply signal tokenism, a "pilot" that will, like most pilots, never go to scale no matter what the result.[20] Fortunately, money may not always be necessary. The Oregon State Department of Human Resources Initiative to encourage localities to sponsor innovative programs for children's services promised negligible amounts of money but large amounts of encouragement, the services of "barrier busters" within the Department of Human Resources, and a generous dose of enthusiasm and publicity.

How about centrally prescribed mandates for the representatives of various agencies and other interests to meet and consult and act in some sort of coordinated fashion? We have seen in the previous chapter how critical in the capacity-building process are the subjective aspects of capacity: trust, confidence, enthusiasm, learning, and honest communications. These hardly seem amenable to prescription from outsiders. Indeed, they seem like they might very well be casualties of perceived heavy-handed intervention from outsiders. Yet this is not bound to be so. Although coercion cannot make unwilling minds work in harmony, the path toward a harmony of minds sometimes leads through the physical proximity of bodies. If the bodies can be forced into one meeting after another frequently enough, the minds might decide to make the best of them. The Oregon state government approach to building welfare-to-work capacity at the local level was essentially to mandate it. Supplemented by a great deal of drum beating, training, cheerleading, and advice giving from the Adult Family Services headquarters in Salem, it worked.

The point is to avoid dogma. In a decentralized bureaucratic system implementing a process with any degree of subtlety to it, the central actor is at a disadvantage. Money, mandates, permission, cheerleading, technical assistance—they are all weak tools. The central actors get to

20. Linden (1994, p. 245). The pros and cons of pilots in seeding change in large business organizations are nicely explored in Kanter, Stein, and Jick (1992, p. 514).

place their bets on what will best catalyze the locals to do what the central actors wish them to do. Their choices are, and of course must be, influenced not only by what might conceivably work for the problem at hand but by the political and budgetary limitations on their capacity— and willingness in the light of possible personal risks—to fund, threaten, regulate, train, advise, or cajole.

The tool in which they have the greatest comparative advantage, advice, is probably also, thanks to its low price tag, one of the most cost-effective. The staff in the center—and the barrier busters in Oregon's Department of Human Resources are an excellent specimen—are in a good position to collect, interpret, and disseminate information about what is happening in the varied localities within the federal system. They are probably well-equipped to disseminate smart practices among localities and can furnish compelling examples through one or another medium. They can also pass along warnings about the vulnerabilities of these smart practices that they will have noticed. If funds are available, they can arrange for practitioners from the various localities to visit high-performing sites and for representatives of those sites to take their show on the road as well.

Finally, the staff in the center learn what changes need to be made in the subsystems run by the center itself to facilitate further capacity building at the local level. When the barriers erected centrally cause some threshold level of problems identified locally, it is time for a change. In the Oregon Department of Human Resources, managers expected that it would take about thirty local projects to generate the needed information. And certainly as important as the payoff in technical, problem-diagnosing information are the payoffs in potential momentum and in political support. A veteran of the barrier busters process remarked, "We have enough projects in enough places so that it makes it in the DHR interest to make the system change. . . . We are not undergoing an upheaval for the sake of one place [which could be handled through making exceptions]. . . . If you have enough exceptions out there, then [large-scale change] is worth the effort." This is one of the ways in which Karl Weick's strategy of "small wins" can add up over time to significant changes in a large system.[21]

---

21. Weick (1984).

A BIAS FOR ACTION. If it takes a long time, pursuing the best targets is probably not as important as just hitting something, advertising it as a successful hit, and not letting up on the rate of fire. As long as each hit is at least somewhat helpful, there is progress in the right general direction, and the commotion energizes even more firing. This is what Peters and Waterman called a "bias for action."[22]

I asked Jim Morgester, the reputedly shrewd veteran staff director of the California Air Resources Board, what targets Gerald Johnston, Bill Carter's successor after a year's delay, ought to choose first as an object of multimedia enforcement. "It doesn't matter," he replied, "so long as he just goes for something and shows that he can get the big egos who are the [separate bureau] compliance chiefs to go along. It takes charisma, personality, leadership, and Johnston has to show he can do it."

Ideally a strategy predicated on a bias for action ought to be linked to a capacity for learning from mistakes, which are sure to occur. Indeed, they are sure to occur even in a more deliberate and planful process. I mentioned previously the waste of time by the fiscal people designing The Door master contract. Some agencies that had promised resources to the Coordinated Youth Services Council failed to deliver when the time came. A social services director in Denver promised a minimum number of contracts to certain community-based organizations that proved impossible to deliver, and an embarrassed deputy was then obliged to go to the organizations and apologize for reneging. In Del Paso Heights, a poorly performing supervisor needed to be replaced after causing chaos. When an ad to recruit a new MediCal worker went out and no one responded, "The word got out that we were so disorganized nobody wanted to go work there." I could provide many more such examples.

Like any good organization, an ICC should be able to profit from trials that end in failure as well as success.[23] The collapse of the CYSC parallel case review process enabled it to discover and embrace what I

22. Peters and Waterman (1982, pp. 119–55). One of the current state leaders in erecting a Department of Children's Services in Tennessee recommended reading Tom Peters's *Thriving on Chaos* (1987), and one of the managers in the Contra Costa County Service Integration Teams program recommended Margaret Wheatley (1992).

23. This is more easily said than done, however. Even when the raw facts are clear, making a realistic causal interpretation is difficult. Usually, multiple interpretations are possible, and psychological and political biases confuse efforts to choose among them. Imperfections of organizational learning, write Levinthal and March (1993), "suggest a certain conservatism in expectations."

take to be the superior "family unity" model. The failure of the 1982 version of the East Bay hills fire prevention ICC taught lessons to those who planned the 1991 to 1992 version. The collapse of the Center for Integrated Services to Families and Neighborhoods project in the Prescott neighborhood set the stage for a more promising effort based around Healthy Start but eliminating reliance on the Prescott school.

Avoiding Blocks

So far I have been talking about strategies for building positive momentum. It is occasionally even more important to avoid events that might cripple the ICC when it is young and especially vulnerable. As shown in chapter 6, within the groups that oversee or control steering processes, consensual norms tend to be very powerful. This gives great bargaining power to any group willing to threaten a veto—or indefinite delay, which can amount to the same thing—unless its terms are met. In contemporary policymaking, the most common situations in which these conditions occur are probably interjurisdictional negotiations over joint environmental regulation and land-use planning. In such cases, most of the parties might plausibly reckon that unilateral action on their part is worse than joint action on almost any terms consensually agreed to, and that some sort of consensus is indeed possible. Yet the path to negotiating any particular consensus must traverse territory in which the actions of veto groups wrongly convince the participants that an eventual consensus is impossible.

What strategies are available to protect the entire group of participants on such a journey? One possibility is a partial consensus that will function as a political counterforce bearing on the holdouts. This was apparently Ed Hastey's strategy in keeping the EPA out of the Biodiversity Council until the council was on more solid footing. Another strategy is to touch base with potentially hostile groups, keeping lines of communication open, and waiting to see what price has to be paid for their cooperation or at least acquiescence. Hastey used this strategy on the county supervisors in counties in which private interests were likely to oppose the emerging biodiversity thrust. This is generally the strategy used on public sector employee constituencies and their unions. Sometimes it ends up in substantial promises and concessions to these constituencies (for example, the school counselors in School-Based) and sometimes not (for example, Oregon welfare-to-work). A third strategy is to hide behind the fig leaf of pilots and demonstrations. As one of the key backers of the effort to streamline contract administration in New York State said, "If the funding agencies had not treated this [experiment with The Door] as 'merely a pilot,' they never would have gone along."[24] Finally, there is the radical option apparently chosen by David Manning in Tennessee: Use raw power and authority to create a new situation that will force the reluctant collaborators to craft a workable operating system. This may often be a smart practice, taking advantage of people's latent resourcefulness and sense of responsibility. However, from the Tennessee experience it is obvious that, at a minimum, it has to be accompanied by skillful and energetic efforts to create an ICC culture of mutual trust and joint problem solving.

Vulnerability to Setbacks

One might suppose that if success feeds on itself in a positive way, failures and setbacks might have a corresponding negative effect. And there are plenty of failures and setbacks with which to deal. I mentioned earlier the waste of time by the fiscal people designing The Door master contract. Many nonprofit organizations that had promised resources to the CYSC failed to deliver. As mentioned above, chaos ensued when a poorly performing supervisor had to be replaced in Del Paso Heights.

That such experiences would represent a genuine loss of momentum is likely. I suspect that in many cases the effect would be small, though, because even optimists must expect setbacks—the pessimists would discount ICC prospects altogether, as might many a realist—and would impute little significance to their occurrence beyond signaling a possible need to regroup and rethink. And if the failure happened long enough ago, or with a substantially different set of actors, it can be represented as the sort of thing "we can't let happen again." This was the rallying cry in 1991–92, when the emerging East Bay fire prevention ICC harkened back to the failed collaborative efforts, well known to many of them, following the 1923 and 1980 East Bay hills fires.

24. One of the drawbacks of starting with a single pilot is that it does not provide the comparative information about the contextual influences on outcomes that would be obtained were there to be pilots in several or many sites. Robert D. Behn, personal communication.

Moreover, the nature of a *loss* or *setback* or *failure* in an endeavor as complex as building an ICC is so ambiguous that it can almost always be redefined as an event that merely stretches the timetable a little. Did the newly elected city council representative denounce the Prescott Project as an intrusion in the affairs of "her" district without her review, permission, and blessing? Well, then, this was unfortunate but surely she was still uninformed and her support could be secured in due course. And it was.

If setbacks and failures can be discounted and interpreted away by those who wish to protect momentum, we must ask why celebrating milestones and other such attainments should fuel optimism and reinforce effort. For one thing, various psychological mechanisms known as dissonance reduction cause people to perceive selectively what they wish to perceive and to screen out, distort, and reinterpret what they do not wish to perceive.[25] Social and political mechanisms are also at work. Because like gravitates to like, people's small-scale social environments are dominated by others who share their own attitudes and aspirations. If the pro-ICC coalition has any sort of leadership, the leadership will often arrange meetings and other events in which the participants will come together to reinforce their mutual impressions of positive momentum. On the other hand, it is quite unusual for opponents of ICC development to assemble in this way or to be mobilized by a concerted leadership. The exceptions have to do with union or professional opposition to ICC development that is fairly easy to organize when the union members or the professionals hold periodic meetings anyway and are concentrated in an agency "at risk of collaboration."

In any case, disappointments and failures are an inevitable companion to all creative activity, particularly the sort that relies on groping along and trial-and-error learning. The alternative is trying to preserve the status quo. But, as I argued in chapter 1, this is not a good idea. Even when trial-and-error learning produces failures, it is important to keep the costs of failure in perspective. Regarding the CYSC's failure with parallel case review, for instance, it harmed mostly the overworked staff who carried it out and who tried to sell it to the regular agencies. No clients were harmed. Furthermore, more planning would not have obviated the failure or reduced its costs.

25. Cooper (1996).

How the Development Process Can Be Disrupted

So far in this chapter I have discussed how good or lucky sequencing, perhaps augmented by various smart practices, can help ICC development. Now I turn to conditions that disrupt development: the hazards attendant on the slow pace of development, mistakes made in the natural course of trial-and-error learning, vulnerabilities that naturally emerge as a consequence of ICC growth and success; turnover of key players. Some smart practices may be available to offset these.

Slow Pace of Development

Building ICC capacity seems awfully slow. From the viewpoint of the ordinary citizen, and especially one who has a personal stake in the output of the ICC, the pace of governmental self-improvement is snail-like. Even veteran bureaucrats have unrealistic expectations about how long it takes. In the New York State master contract case, Lepler and Rosenkranz said that the governor's chief staff person overseeing their work was expecting them to get it done in six months, when it took about three times that long, and another player in the governor's office accused them of "dragging their feet." Spending a long time in planning and discussing may be hard to justify if there is a faster way that is only slightly less efficient in a technical sense.

How long does it take to complete building ICC capacity up to some satisfactory level of performance?[26] It depends on how deep the foundations are to be laid, how complex is the structure to be erected, how forthcoming are the resources that are required, how numerous and varied are the negotiations needed to manage the whole process, and what level of quality is demanded. Ignoring the many possible qualifications and empirical variations that are possible, however, we can offer rough estimates as follows.

---

26. In the abstract, I would define "satisfactory" to be the level at which the benefits from operations begin to exceed the incremental operating costs. Some public programs never produce nominally intended benefits that exceed their costs but are nevertheless regarded by legislators and the public as satisfactory because they symbolize community or good intentions. For the present purposes I include the symbolic, though nominally unintended, benefits as real benefits. Answering the "how long" question in any concrete case depends on defining a reasonable beginning point, which is difficult conceptually and empirically.

Changes in operating procedures take about three to twenty-four months, with the intervening time taken up by intraagency discussion (for example, the case of the New York State master contract, Oregon integrated services, Cal/EPA multimedia enforcement, and School-Based).[27] The rate of change is limited in these cases by the rate at which negotiations can be completed. Also, however expeditious or slow the negotiations, there is usually some extra delay attributable to system catch-up—that is, waiting for budget cycles and personnel clearance backlogs. Changes that require the construction of complex infrastructure, such as shared information systems, personnel management systems, or systems of governance may take three to five years (for example, the CYSC, the Center for Integrated Services to Families and Neighborhoods projects, the Oregon information systems projects). Changes that require policy-level coordination among different levels of government can proceed relatively quickly if only regulatory policy is at stake, but they will take longer, perhaps five to ten years, if they provoke politically well-entrenched opponents, involve new fiscal relationships, pose the risk of cost shifting, or alter the targeting of resources funds away from favored beneficiary or provider groups (for example, managing publicly owned resources for the benefit of biodiversity,[28] systems reform in Maryland and in Tennessee).[29]

COSTS AND RISKS OF A SLOW PACE. A very slow development process can fall victim to general turbulence in the political environment. "Several planets lined up together" is how many ICC participants

27. William Morrill, of the National Center for Services Integration and Mathematica, said, "People should expect to spend 6 to 18 months planning services integration strategies" (Melaville and Blank, 1993, p. 47).

28. The biggest obstacles to implementing the memorandum of understanding on biodiversity was not internal to agencies but private interests that depended on making use of Bureau of Land Management and Forest Service lands.

29. The state rural development councils started up at the end of 1990, and Radin and others said that in mid-1994 (or possibly later), "To date, networking activity has not had substantial impact on council [members'] own agencies in most of the states. . . . the current chair [in Oregon, a relatively successful state] said that while the council has had a positive impact on members and their agencies the longer-term impact has yet to be realized. The council creates dialogue and improves communication, he said, but 'singular events don't change how organizations function. The lack of communication among federal agencies is a long-term problem'" (Radin and others, 1996, p. 167).

And yet they say in excusing lack of immediate effect on jobs and income, "Councils are too new to expect much. . . . Overall, the costs of the effort were outweighed by the benefits gleaned from it" (pp. 224–25).

describe the fortunate combination of circumstances that permits ICC development to jump ahead. But circumstances eventually come out of alignment. In Colorado, a children and family services ICC started in the early 1990s was obliged to survive fiscal constriction caused by a tax limitation amendment passed by the voters in 1992, a 20 percent cut in education funding after a ballot measure to protect the funding failed that same year, and an antigay ballot initiative in 1993 provoked a recall movement against the governor whose support had been critical to the ICC. In Maryland the Systems Reform Initiative had begun life with great expectations in an era of fiscal surplus and then had to survive fiscal retrenchment that affected its ability to put up state funds to match a $7.5 million grant from the Annie E. Casey Foundation.[30] The political readiness to turn over many more services to private nonprofit providers also suffered when the Department of Juvenile Services' closely watched initiative to privatize one of its training schools quickly ran into serious trouble.

Political turbulence tied to the election cycle is probably the most predictable and the most disruptive sort of turbulence. The Center for Integrated Services to Families and Neighborhoods effort in Oakland, California, had been gathering momentum for well over a year and had been picking up local political support at a rapid clip when a newly elected city council member representing an area in which the CISFAN site was located decided to take umbrage that she had allegedly never been consulted about the project. Her threats to block further city cooperation never materialized because the CISFAN leadership eventually managed to appease her. But she probably could have sabotaged the whole effort had she become determined to do so. In New York State, the drive by the Council on Children and Families to streamline the contracting process and rationalize relations with local provider agencies was largely ended as a project of state government when Democrat Mario Cuomo lost the governorship to Republican George Pataki. The key figures in the process left state service and set up their own consulting group to carry on the process, but without the clout of gubernatorial support.

30. The Annie E. Casey Foundation wrote of its experience with its ambitious New Futures program, "Circumstances change. A charismatic, politically skillful leader may move on to another job; the inauguration of a new mayor can send an initiative 'back to the drawing board' in terms of the readiness and commitment of city hall . . . the initially strong relationship among key players become much less solid" (Annie E. Casey Foundation, 1995, p. 13).

One can also point to some instances in which political change has made it possible to advance ICC development at a rate previously not experienced. The election of Pete Wilson as California governor in 1990 opened a window of opportunity for the theorists and would-be managers of interagency collaboration in the children's services field. Though facing a crisis in state government finance, the Wilson administration nevertheless chose to spend "new money" on the Healthy Start program of school-linked health and social services. However, the political–fiscal cycle is not symmetrical in its treatment of ICC development. Positive events would probably not counterbalance negative events even were they to outnumber them by a modest margin, which, given secular ideological shifts favoring collaboration as a form of reinvention, I suspect is occurring. Positive events help to initiate or speed ICC development, but negative events not only slow or halt construction of the ICC edifice but threaten to destroy it entirely. In the absence of mitigation strategies, the efforts that might have gone into more incremental reforms, producing small but real benefits, are simply wasted.

Normal personnel turnover in high places is another important source of turbulence. If turnover hits a key leadership position in any organization, trouble is likely, and this is true of an ICC as well. Bill Carter's departure from Cal/EPA essentially stalled multimedia enforcement for a year until a permanent replacement took over. Also, as I mentioned in chapter 4 in connection with line-level staff, turnover is a bigger problem in ICCs than in most government organizations simply because an n-person team that really does depend on n people has n ways in which it can lose a key individual to turnover. An agency head in Sacramento County who had supported the Del Paso Heights Neighborhood Services Agency left and was replaced by someone who appeared distinctly unenthusiastic and could not cooperate on a personal level with the heads of important partner agencies. Donna Stark, who headed the Maryland Systems Reform Initiative effort in the early 1990s, listed high turnover as the first of seven challenges the initiative had faced: "With turnover there is a need of constant redefinition and recommitment to the vision underlying the reform initiatives by leaders, as well as a reassessment of state/local and intra/interagency issues."

Another source of disturbance in the development of an ICC is the emergence of a political agenda that competes for the attention and resources of the same people and institutions that are building the ICC. In one bioregion covered by the memorandum of understanding on biodiversity, the process of developing policy in accord with the memorandum was barely off the ground when President Clinton announced a Northwest Economic Adjustment Initiative funneling $1.2 billion into Oregon, Washington, and Oregon. Competition for funds in the Klamath, Oregon, area set off nasty intergroup and interpersonal rivalries that affected the ICC developing around the memorandum.[31] Another source of trouble, which can be either minor or major depending on the context, is lack of competency or alleged corruptibility in official positions of leadership. This is said to have occurred in Maryland in the Office for Children, Youth, and Families in the 1995–96 period. The convening of the lieutenant governor's task force was in part a response to this. However, the ability of the broad systems reform community in Maryland to rally shows that the ICC had a solid momentum.

SMART MITIGATION PRACTICES. One candidate smart practice is to get an early start. ICC builders can begin their work as early as possible in the political cycle. The Wilson administration began a full-court press for Healthy Start as soon as Wilson took office. A second is to build a broad and, it is hoped, bipartisan consensus behind the ICC that persists in the face of electoral changes. The base redevelopment ICC was naturally blessed with broad popular approval and with strong bipartisan support in Congress, in state legislatures, in the governors' mansions, and in the White House under Bush and then Clinton. The first serious political trauma that it had to survive was caused by the budget-cutting enthusiasts in the Republican-dominated 104th Congress, who initially threatened to cut environmental cleanup budgets for closing bases. However, these budgets have largely been protected by a bipartisan coalition, even while environmental cleanup has been cut back somewhat at facilities that were not in the process of being transferred for civilian reuse. In Oregon, the results-oriented strategy represented by benchmarking—a strategy so central to more broadly gauged government reinvention efforts—could not have survived without broad and deep support from both parties and both political branches of government.

31. Thomas (1997a, pp. 316, 339–45).

A related mitigation strategy is building a constituency that is not only broad but is strategically located in the political structure. Maryland's Systems Reform Initiative had allies in every county that was receiving state funds from a special account marked, in effect, "savings from out-of-home placements the state has avoided." The New Jersey School-Based Youth Services program saw to it that some state monies for the program were flowing into all twenty-one counties. School-Based also created a council of representatives from the collaborating agencies reporting to the governor so that it would have a forum to speak for the program when the governorship changed hands.

Another smart practice is to take advantage of any opportunities to modularize the development process.[32] Each module could be built within a time frame that fits comfortably into the political–fiscal cycle, and each such module could provide at least some value to the public even were the entire process halted after it had been put in place. In New York the reformers in the Governor's Council on Children and Families employed a strategy of pursuing first one site and then several at a time, so that when their gubernatorial protection ended, and they themselves left the government, some achievements were already in place.[33] Special protective features, such as multiyear appropriations, can also be put in place. One of the main functions of foundation support for human services collaboratives is to guarantee at least modest survivability in the face of the political–fiscal cycle. The foundations can give multiyear funding and provide some nonpartisan political legitimacy as well.

The turnover problem can be mitigated by not allowing the ICC to become dependent on relationships or leaders that cannot be easily replaced. Melaville and Blank recommended shared leadership mostly on egalitarian grounds,[34] but sharing also reduces the vulnerability of leadership turnover. Roberta Knowlton, one of the two top state managers of School-Based, spoke not just of multiple leaders but of multiple sources of leadership: "There are seven sources of leadership in School-Based, so that you can lose some and still not have catastrophe!" They are, she said, the lead agency and the way it manages things; the school

32. Simon (1969, pp. 90–92).

33. Although this strategy was chosen more for its value in building momentum (see earlier discussion) than in protecting a series of modules, it performed this latter function also.

34. Melaville and Blank (1993, pp. 30–31).

itself; the management capacity of the director of the program; the staff hired to work for the director (which ideally should be ethnically and linguistically appropriate); the community advisory board, the parent advisory board; and an evaluator. "There is a lot of instability in local programs. It's a matter of chance which of these seven factors are up or down at any time."

Finally, the development process can be accelerated to attain a higher level of resistance to disruption in a shorter period of time. The principal means of doing this is by smart practices to accelerate momentum, discussed previously. The problem is how to accelerate momentum without excessively shortening the lead time needed to accomplish certain steps in a presumably desirable platforming sequence.

This problem is difficult and a full analysis beyond the scope of this book. One fairly certain smart practice, however, is to eliminate needlessly complex or ambitious steps. I argued in chapter 6, for instance, that the elaborate design of governance structures was often unnecessary, provided management processes could be invented to compensate adequately. The same could be said of the production of plans or planning documents. Art Bolton, for instance, speaking in the context of grass-roots community development, asserted that needs assessments, priority-setting exercises, and planning all threaten to stall action, and "then, after a while they take on a life of their own." The agenda of community activities in Del Paso Heights, he said, should really be

> not the outcome of a plan [but] the outcome of a natural process. . . . I've learned that the planning activities that we normally engage in are really counter-productive . . . all that business of doing a survey to ask about priorities. . . . In so doing people have made themselves useless to everybody in the community who doesn't care about those [particular] things! . . . [What is important, he said, is action. It is especially important for outsiders to a community, who start with the burden of suspicion.] You have to show you care and you can actually get something accomplished that people in the community care about. Once you do that, you can begin to find other things to do, and then people will begin to come to you with ideas, and then it begins to snowball.[35]

35. Bolton went so far as to criticize "too much planning" as a "stupid mistake." Why did he and his colleagues make this mistake? His legislative experience. "In the legisla-

I would point out that creating a plan does not appear in figure 8-1. Sometimes, to be sure, a planning or needs-assessment *process* can spin off useful results even if the written *product* is not itself of particular value.[36] I suspect the functional equivalent in process-related benefits—improving intellectual capital, building trust, and creating the communications capacity that can turn into an implementation network—can often be produced with less trouble and greater genuine benefit by simple discussions. It may be desirable to memorialize the results of such discussions in a written document, perhaps a memorandum of understanding, but in any event something short and operational.

The more complex and multidimensional a collaborative undertaking, the less the sort of comprehensive rational planning that is supposed to prevent error is able to do. By implication, the less damage is likely to be done by a strategy of accelerating momentum. In Maryland, for instance, the Systems Reform Initiative had to deal simultaneously with interagency relations at the state level and at the local level, state–local relations, relations with the foster care facilities industry both in state and out of state, a shift to preventative programming, and relations between the regular child-serving agencies and a new bureaucratic entity close to the governor's office championing systems reform. The level of dissatisfaction about state–local relations evident in the 1996 task force report seems par for such a difficult course. It is hard to imagine how more efforts devoted to planning or platforming would have produced any better results. The reformers, in my estimation, got the two key strategies right: devolve to the local level, and reinvest as much as possible of the savings from out-of-home placement. The rest of the system was mostly devoted to keeping these two strategies in place; and if the process was messy, that was to be expected.

Emerging Vulnerabilities

A rapidly growing small business is vulnerable to predictable problems such as a dearth of managerial time relative to the number of new

---

ture, there is a bill, and a law, and a program and an agency. Linear thinking. All these good folks thinking they are doing good things. So you create a special program to do this, and then another little one to do that, and then there is all this machinery that is in the way, and then it gets self-serving."

36. See Jehl and Kirst (1992, pp. 100–01).

issues demanding attention, insufficient capitalization, alienation stemming from depersonalization, a shortage of feedback as a result of inadequate information-gathering systems, a confusion of hitherto clear goals and objectives, a top leadership still caught up in the romance of pursuing some original vision, a challenge to the original leadership by lieutenants sensing the founders' growing weakness.[37] Like small businesses, ICCs have their growing pains as well. Being overwhelmed by new infrastructure maintenance requirements is one that, when successful, they may share with small business. One informant, associated with the Coordinated Youth Services Council and many other children and family service agencies, said,

> Once you have an entity, an organization, personnel . . . you have to keep those plates spinning. You have to evaluate your executive director . . . formulate your budget, monitor your budget . . . do all the things any other entity does to keep the wheels turning. And if nobody is really steering the damn thing, you're going to go where the car wants to go, not where you want to go. . . . It's hard . . . when you're driving and trying to fix the tire at the same time. It's pretty hard to keep an eye on the road.

In other respects, though, the problems of successful ICCs are not much like those of their private sector counterparts. ICC founders must take insufficient resources (capitalization) as a condition of existence; goals and objectives start diffuse and get better focused over time rather than the reverse; leaders are catalytic rather than dominating. One might almost say that ICCs come into being at exactly the point in the life cycle as when a small private sector business faces its first life-threatening surprises.

The literature on aging public sector agencies that describes what happens as they grow from nothing into permanent institutions tells us that most lose idealism, become dominated by manuals and procedures, shrink from actions that might bring on political troubles, and suffer from pockets of employee incompetence and indifference. Some become captured by a dominant interest group, profession, or ideology. Do these afflictions lie in wait for an ICC?

37. See in general Kimberly and Quinn (1984), especially the chapters by Tichy, Lodahl, Walton, and Quinn and Anderson.

It is useful to remember that an ICC is more like a virtual organization than a real one. It exists in people's minds and in a set of reciprocal expectations and operating routines. Its temporariness, its fragility, its lack of real authority, budgets, or stable turf—these are part of its essence; and this essence immunizes it to some degree against the usual afflictions. Nevertheless, it is not completely immune. It may have some full-time staff assigned to it, and these are at some risk of behaving like turf-protecting bureaucrats.[38] Although it is not likely to become excessively rule bound and inflexible, once people's careers begin to depend on its long-run access to funding and stable turf, it is likely to start investing in organizational enhancement at the expense of activities more in the public interest. This reallocation may be relatively minor at first—and will be indistinguishable from the kind of organizational maintenance activities needed for simple survival—but it will grow with increasing scale. Indeed, those in the ICC may also fear the bureaucratization dynamic. Some of the board members of the CYSC were concerned that they were becoming "just another agency," and there was even some talk about how the CYSC should go out of business before this process had run its course completely. Nevertheless, I do not think that in most cases the ICC is at risk of bureaucratization, mostly because managers from the participating agencies work to deny it the assured turf and budgets that a stable bureaucracy requires.

RESOURCE-RELATED VULNERABILITIES. A visibly successful collaborative attracts resources. It in effect becomes a resource, and a not very well protected one at that. Community action and model city ICCs during the 1960s and 1970s were often vulnerable to old-fashioned corruption and abuse, which is bound to occur whenever new money and underdeveloped accountability systems are set in motion. Legitimacy can also be a sought-after resource. As the CYSC, before 1994, came to be respected for its performance, its administrative capacity, and its symbolic status as a seemingly successful collaborative effort, the Marin Community Foundation began to urge it to serve as a clearinghouse for youth services proposals from county agencies. Although the CYSC board was interested in helping to coordinate fund-raising and programming in one way or another, it was not eager to risk alienating its own constituents by acting as a gatekeeper between them and any

38. See the discussion of new turf in chapter 5.

source of possible funding. The CYSC board was also continually trying to sidestep requests from various therapists in private practice to affiliate with the CYSC, the several applicants desiring a seal of approval and possible access to informal or contract-based referrals.

In some sense the whole community in which an ICC functions is a resource that sometimes attracts unwholesome interest. A human services provider community that has the capacity to launch one or two or three collaboratives does not necessarily have the capacity to launch a hundred. Yet the capacity to launch a few collaboratives attracts funders without any obvious limit. Oakland, for instance, a struggling and minority-dominated city with a progressively minded city government, has attracted a great deal of foundation and government attention. One veteran observer estimated that it had, in 1996, at least thirty to forty efforts to build human services collaboratives running simultaneously. But "there are only, say, a hundred people involved in all of these, and they just keep running from meeting to meeting." The sort of collaboration funders like to see among service providers is not something, it seems, that they feel obliged to create among themselves.

The much more common problem in the long run is not a surfeit of support but a dearth. The foundations supply resources—money, expertise, neutrality, legitimacy—that are often of great value to ICCs in their early struggles. But because the boards and the directors of many foundations see their mission as stimulating innovation and experimentation, the apparent success of a collaborative venture funded by these sources can be almost as much a repellent to funding as apparent failure. The Colorado Trust funded the organizational efforts of the dozens of agencies that came to constitute the Denver Family Opportunities program network and after about five years backed away, leaving at least some of the participants feeling (perhaps unjustly) miffed or worse. "They just seemed to get bored," commented one participant.

Whether the Colorado Trust was or was not too hasty in pulling back from the DFO program network, the grumbling is indicative of an underlying problem. That there will be some divergence of interests between the foundation funders of an ICC and the ICC participants is highly probable. Foundations typically contribute seed money, and the practitioners simply must anticipate the need to find replacement funds or do without. Nevertheless, the dynamics of momentum building virtually guarantee that ICC expansion in the period when seed money or demonstration funding is available will not be completely supportable when permanent replacement funding is required.[39]

STEERING TRAPS. The need to settle on a set of goals and objectives that can command more or less consensual support and that entail producing some momentum-building small wins may set the ICC on a course that looks good in the short run but is suboptimal for the long run. Once set, however, such a course may become a trap.

The CYSC, successful as it probably was with the population of extremely troubled children and families on which it has focused, has had trouble mounting preventive services for less critical subpopulations, despite its original intentions to do so. In this regard, it has suffered from the same resource constraints that restrict preventive services in more established agencies. The Denver Family Opportunities ICC, some would argue, got stuck with only a vague sense of direction, or none at all, because it initially adopted the human-capital-plus-child-care philosophy and avoided a commitment to numerical goals or work-placement goals.

Another steering trap that might materialize with time and success is the reality or appearance of cliquishness. The core group of five or six who created the ICC that eventually grew into the CYSC had become "clubby" during the course of their work together, said one participant. Nearly all the core were middle-aged or older white men. For political reasons, if for no other, it would have been helpful had they widened their circle.

Summary

How much of its seeming potential is a nascent ICC likely to achieve? Previous chapters have explored the likelihood that different components of the ICC could be created or otherwise secured. Another important—in many cases even critical—set of influences comes from the developmental dynamics that unfold when the entire assemblage begins to be brought together and the ICC begins to operate on a small scale or within a limited scope but then expands in a relatively efficient way.

---

39. Healthy Start programs in California, for instance, have had mixed success in finding resources to sustain their efforts at their previous scale. See chapter 3.

The evolution of the ICC can follow a logic of efficient developmental sequencing—in fact, two such. The first, which I call *platforming*, is a sequence of developmental steps such that each one not only represents an achievement in its own right but creates a potential for more efficiently moving to the next one. The second, which I call *momentum building*, takes advantage of the fact that any success represents some kind of opportunity to create yet a further success. A bandwagon process is the simplest example, but the momentum process applies also to the emergence of trust, consensus, enthusiasm, and, most important, to the propensity of potential partners to contribute their resources to the collective effort.

On the negative side, as the ICC grows, and as time passes, certain vulnerabilities also increase—for example, its attractiveness as an object of capture or influence, the dissipation of talent and expertise that saw the ICC through its early months or years, and the various disruptions that come from changes in the political and fiscal environment.

9

Craftsmanship Theory
Applied and Appreciated

By way of summarizing and concluding, I discuss below the three somewhat different, albeit related, aspects of the argument that has been presented in this book. I first deal with inter-agency collaboration in general, reviewing the analytical highlights of how ICCs are built and what makes for success and failure in the process. I then revisit the lead poisoning problem from chapter 1 and apply the lessons for practice that are suggested by my general analysis. Finally, I draw out the implications of "craftsmanship theory," or my version of it at any rate, for certain philosophical issues pertaining to social scientific understanding in general.

Building Interagency Collaborative Capacity

Although there are plenty of opportunities for public sector agencies to create value by working cooperatively with one another, not all of them are taken. Probably only a minority are perceived, and many fewer are acted on. Some of these opportunities have to do with achieving cost savings by eliminating redundancies and effecting economies of scale, but the more numerous, and certainly the more interesting, ones have to do with improving agency performance. In particular, they have to do with being able to conceptualize problems more holistically than each specialized agency is capable of doing alone and to mass resources necessary to solve them.

One reason that more value-creating collaborations do not occur is that the task of collaboration is very difficult. Working cooperatively is often much more complicated than it sounds. It involves reconciling worldviews and professional ideologies that cluster within agency boundaries but differ across them. Moreover, it is often difficult to align agencies' work efforts in the face of governmental administrative systems that presuppose deliberate nonalignment. Indeed, they favor specialization and separateness down to the smallest line item.

When thinking about the behavior called "working cooperatively," I prefer to characterize it as a much more demanding sort of creative activity. I call it creating interagency collaborative capacity, or ICC. Such a virtual organization—or network, to some theorists—may even have tangible resources such as personnel and money. When it is functioning properly, an ICC also has intangible resources such as the cooperative dispositions and mutual understanding of the individuals who are trying to work together on a common task.

Unlike most previous scholarly efforts to understand interagency collaboration, I am concerned with more than the quantitative indicators of working together. I am also concerned about the quality of the collaboration, using the term *quality* in the sense intended by the total quality management literature in all its many variations. There is an even more than ordinary quality bonus for an ICC making use of certain strategies associated with a *postbureaucratic organization*, in Michael Barzelay's terms, or a *reinvented* one, in the terms of David Osborne and Ted Gaebler: flexibility, teamwork, high involvement, empowerment, training.[1] Therefore, although the collaborative aspects of running an ICC are hard enough, on top of these we must add a new way of managing that is against the hierarchical grain. Fortunately, because many people are now concluding that this postbureaucratic and reinvented way of doing governmental business is good on its own merits, the additional creativity required in building ICC capacity may be more within reach today and in the future than it has been in the past.

Up-to-date management thinking is not all that is required for an ICC. Real resources, such as talented and purposive people and flexible funding, are needed as well. A major barrier to taking on the collaborative challenge is that these resources are always scarce, probably somewhat more so in government than in the private sector. Agencies do not want to give up control over these resources lest their own traditional missions be compromised. Moreover, if a manager wants to work on creating value, creating collaborative capacity may not appear as

1. See Barzelay (1992) and Osborne and Gaebler (1992).

promising a way to invest time and energy as fixing agency capacity to do its own internal, self-contained, tasks better.

Managers can be counted on to resist putting scarce agency resources into ICC building for more self-serving reasons too. Career stakes are tied up in agencies and hence in the protection of agency autonomy. It is sometimes personally inconvenient to do quality work, perhaps because it means staying late and putting in time to get a job done well or straining relations with one's co-workers. Sometimes added to these instrumental motivations is a motivation that is more emotionally colored and rooted in human nature: the desire to band together in "our tribe" to protect it against threats from "other tribes." This implies risking charges of disloyalty by fellow "tribe members" for even having enough contact with outsiders to find out whether collaboration is possible on terms that might actually be internally acceptable.

The principal potential counter to such inertial forces is the desire on some people's parts to do good in the world according to their own lights and to participate in the creative challenge of doing it in a nontraditional way. But this potential can only be activated if actors see enough movement coming from the partner agencies to create some threshold level of contributions to the ICC venture, both tangible and intangible, to offer a realistic hope of success. This implies a bandwagon process, with resource contributions from the several parties growing as a function of their own past growth (up to some limit, of course).

If the partners can create and legitimate a leadership role, the bandwagon potential is more likely to be realized. A leadership role is also helpful when it comes to setting goals and otherwise steering the ICC. Although most ICCs need and create some kind of formal steering structure, like an interagency working group or sometimes a new formal coordinating organization with a board of directors, steering in most cases is done to a large degree by consensus. Therefore, an additional useful leadership role is to facilitate the formation of consensus and, to the extent possible, to keep the ICC from overinvesting in elaborate formal steering structures when informal consensus building can reasonably substitute.

Finding and motivating talented individuals to do the leadership job is a big and important challenge. The challenge is often not met successfully, and it is more often not even noticed. One might say that in many of the cases when ICCs do not arise, it is not just because agencies do not wish to give up resources and protect turf but that leaders have not arisen to help organize the potential partners. Such a failure may be variously attributed to inadequate incentives, resources, or legitimacy. The legitimacy problem is especially interesting because it is in a sense easier to solve with smart practices—practices that exploit opportunities to create public value on the cheap—than are other causes of failure. Among other smart practices, supporting and enacting the role of facilitative leader rather than top-down or positional leader is a way to gain the benefits of leadership without violating widespread and deeply held equalitarian norms.

Distrust also stands in the way of legitimating a leadership role and sometimes of legitimating the entry of particular persons into a leadership role. More generally, distrust is a corrosive presence in the creative process that ICC partners are necessarily engaged in. Negotiating partners cannot solve problems of ICC construction unless they are willing to reveal information about the strengths, weaknesses, resources, and constraints of their agencies and to have this information believed. Distrust also surrounds the question of whether individuals (and agencies) are really working hard in the common enterprise or are faking it, and the question of whether they will take pains to protect another's interests when they might conceivably exploit the other. Fortunately, there are many ways in which trustworthiness can be established and trust created. Because some of them take a long time, it is desirable if people can draw on the social capital in a geographical, professional, or ideological community of preexisting trust relationships. As in other dimensions of ICC development, leadership in identifying and mobilizing such social capital also helps.

Time is an enemy of the ICC development process because over time many vulnerabilities arise. Normal personnel turnover destroys communications channels and valuable ICC institutional memory and removes people whose trustworthiness has already been tested. It also jeopardizes fiscal and political resources partners have been relying on. But the ICC development process is usually slow. It is in some respects, after all, an evolutionary process. To maintain the pace and reduce the risks of mistakes that require rework, it helps if the developmental process unfolds in a sequence of steps designed in such a way that each one serves not only to advance the ICC toward some ultimate operational goal but serves also to make it easier to reach the next step along the way—a sequence I call efficient *platforming*. Trying to save time by accomplishing all the steps at once, say, with different task forces laboring on each of them simultaneously, jeopardizes this process, though sometimes the risks of delay may make such a crash effort worthwhile in any case. Creative and forward-looking leadership in an ICC may sometimes be able to anticipate future problems and vulnerabilities and to take preemptive steps to protect against them.

Lead Poisoning Revisited

Such is the message of this book as delivered from an academic mountaintop. But I am hopeful that its message of collaborative opportunities to be perceived, challenges to be understood, and craftsmanlike smart practices to be implemented will reach practitioners, whether directly or indirectly. Because each of the substantive chapters has gone into some detail about these points with regard to the five main tasks of ICC construction—fashioning a high-quality operating system, acquiring resources, creating a steering process, developing a culture of trust and joint problem solving, and managing a strategically sequenced developmental process—I will not repeat them. The several chapter summaries cover the highlights. However, I wish to provide practitioners who may read this book, as well as social scientists, with more of a sense that the concepts make sense for practice as well as for social science. Therefore, I return to the problem that introduced this book: the dismal prospects for collaboration between a municipal health department intent on having landlords removing hazardous lead paint from apartment walls and a housing department unwilling to let its inspectors participate in enforcing an abatement ordinance.

I next present a program brief about a hypothetical state grant program to county public health departments that would enable them to contract with local housing agencies to enforce a state regulation mandating the removal or permanent covering of lead-based paint surfaces in apartments where small children reside. For the purposes of the illustration, one need not assume that the hypothetical program is without flaws. Indeed, I build in some design flaws—of a common sort—in order to ensure that our hypothetical interagency collaborators in program implementation have a rich set of problems to solve. I do, however, assume (unrealistically) that the recipients of the program brief, some twenty-two county public health directors, are themselves motivated to undertake the program and that they are ready to play the role of facilitative leader or advocacy leader described in previous chapters. Hence no encouragement to assume such a role, or explicit advice about how to play it, is offered.

Ignoring canons of realism, I have written the brief in nonbureaucratic prose and have alluded candidly to political and interbureaucratic concerns that would ordinarily not be put in writing. I indicate in brackets the categories of the ICC capacity-building process discussed in previous chapters that are most germane to particular sections of the brief. Consistent with my approach throughout the book, I have emphasized the opportunities to implement smart practices that, in the context of the program, might produce a high payoff for low cost or little risk. I have also emphasized the vulnerabilities that might beset the emerging ICC. Although I generally say little in the brief about what might be taken to be good management practice in general—that is, practice outside the specific context of managing interagency collaboration—I make an exception for management practices distinctly relevant to the type of postbureaucratic operating system that is relatively so advantageous for an ICC.

Program Brief #27
State Grants Available for Lead-Based
Paint Abatement

TO: County Public Health Directors
FROM: Pat Duvall, State Public Health Director
SUBJECT: Questions and Answers about AB 1220,
the "LP Rehab Program"

Background

Q. What are the main features of the program?
A. The governor is recommending that $10 million be made available over a five-year period. Legislative leaders have been noncommittal in public, but the small size of the program and its noncontroversial character suggest that the prospects for full funding over the period are good.

The acceptable long-term solutions to the problem of lead-based paint exposure are removal or permanent covering with a suitable material, referred to collectively as "LP Rehab." We in the State Department of Public Health encourage you to design a program to reduce exposure as quickly as possible, ideally by 20 percent in the next year and 100 percent in the next five years.

The funds are to be used for administration only. A separate zero-interest revolving loan fund of $1 million is available to help landlords finance the rehab. Civil penalties of up to $2,500 per unit can be imposed for noncompliance.

In most cities within our state, a local housing agency enforces housing codes concerning conditions of habitability. This housing agency, not the county Public Health Department, is to administer the program in the field under contract to the County Public Health Department.

[The Benefits of Collaboration, chapter 1]

Q. Why is Public Health not administering this itself?
A. I supported the idea of relying on the housing agency for several reasons. Housing already has an administrative system in place for getting entry into apartments and for regulating land-lords. It has a system of imposing fines and hearing appeals. Its field staff know many of the landlords already from their prior regulatory contacts. The field staff are also experts on estimating the costs of various repairs, and can advise landlords on where to buy inexpensive materials. If necessary, they are better equipped than Public Health to make emergency repairs themselves.

In some cases, the LP Rehab inspection might also double as a scheduled general housing code compliance inspection. Housing inspectors also may be able to gain additional leverage over recalcitrant landlords by linking LP Rehab compliance orders with orders pertaining to other housing code violations.

Results from a two-year pilot project in two counties support this conclusion. Madison County gave the job to public health sanitarians, and Jefferson County worked out a collaborative arrangement with the county housing code enforcement agency. We had 30 percent success in the first two years in Jefferson compared to 10 percent in Madison.

[Acquiring Resources, chapter 5]

Q. The housing agency has to worry about lack of heat for tenants in the winter and stopped up toilets all year round. Why should they not treat LP Rehab as just another bothersome thing to do? (They probably feel understaffed anyway, just as we do!)

A. We are *paying* them! Public Health will reimburse them for their direct costs and add 25 percent for indirect costs in the first year and 15 percent in subsequent years. This reimbursement rate for indirect costs in the first year is high enough so that the housing agency might even realize revenues in excess of costs. We have obtained a letter from the auditor general holding that the local housing agency would be permitted to retain these excess revenues, should they accrue.

Q. Is the zero-interest loan fund big enough to cover all the LP Rehab costs? And what is to be done if it is not?

A. Landlords and tenants are as much your "partners" in the LP Rehab program as is the housing agency. Just as the program tries to buy the cooperation of the housing agency, it is also trying to buy the cooperation of the landlords, but to a much lesser degree.

Tentatively, the State Department of Corporations, which administers the fund, has set guidelines as to the maximum ($500) and the minimum ($150) to be loaned. Our department has advised on this. If the average loan were $400, the fund could support only 2,500 loans until repayments began to replenish the fund.

We would like to target the funds to those landlords who would be unable to finance the LP Rehab without this help. Many of them will need the full $500. On the other hand, spreading the help much more broadly, and thinly, might be politically more popular.

Clearly, a rational priority-setting scheme is needed, one that will target relatively narrowly but has a rationale that is intelligible and politically defensible. An interagency task force is presently working on the design of such a scheme.

Q. Given that buying landlord cooperation may be chancy, is the threat of a $2,500 fine a good enough substitute?

A. It is a big club. In those cases when one actually wants to use it, and can afford the hassles of doing so, probably big enough. But overt threats of noncompliance penalties of this sort will often be counterproductive or much too hassle ridden. It is better to persuade, cajole, and assist the landlords to come up with creative solutions to their cost problems.

Q. Can we at least expect cooperation from our tenant partners?

A. During the rehab process, tenants will be inconvenienced. In major jobs, the inconvenience could last for weeks. Many tenants will recognize the value of LP Rehab for the well-being of their children. But some will not, and these may look for ways to delay the rehab work. Given today's tight rental markets, they may also—quite realistically—fear that the rehab costs will be passed along to them in rent increases when their current leases expire. Landlords might, either subtly or not so subtly, reinforce these fears in order to encourage tenants to make common cause with them against the inspectors. As with the landlords, the inspectors will need to coax and to be creative.

Q. Is the state Public Health Department also our partner in this?

A. Yes. We are in fact a very enthusiastic partner. We will also keep abreast of problems and best practices around the state to be able to provide technical assistance to counties that request it. We will also run interference with the State Department of Corporations on your behalf should that ever prove necessary. We have already established friendly contacts over there. We intend to see to it that the governor and the legislature are made aware of the program's successes.

[Creating the Operating System, chapter 4]

Q. This is a demanding job for the inspectors. Can they really do it?

A. Probably not by themselves. Local public health departments should make public health nurses available as potential consultants and occasional sidekicks in the field. A telephone call, or if necessary a visit, from a public health nurse who would explain the dangers of lead paint exposure to the parents of young children may do the trick in many cases. The housing inspector should also come prepared with educational pamphlets to distribute to landlords and to tenants.

Q. How big a staff commitment from Public Health would be entailed by this?

A. You could start with one person assigned full-time for, say, a three-month start-up period, and see what develops. But the real issue is not quantity, it is quality. The nurse assigned to this task should also have a role in training the LP Rehab inspectors in the health issues involved. The better the LP Rehab inspectors become at education and persuasion, the less dependent they will be on the backup consultation and sidekick services available from Public Health. If the LP Rehab inspectors understand that Public Health intends to cut these backup services to half-time or less in some three to six months, they may be more motivated to learn how to fend for themselves.

Of course, this Public Health trainer, educator, motivator, and backup person must be unusually committed to the program and a talented people person besides. He or she would in effect be a "member" of as many "teams" as there were LP Rehab inspectors in the field!

Q. And besides that, aren't we assuming unusual levels of motivation, competency, and trustworthy discretion among the LP Rehab inspectors?

A. By normal public sector standards, perhaps. But we should not set our sights only according to past experience. Furthermore, we can improve the level of motivation, and therefore performance, for this task by taking care in recruitment. Some, perhaps many, current Housing inspectors would welcome the challenge of this assignment and would like the idea of contributing to children's health. The Housing director just needs to figure out a way of finding them—or at least finding the right middle manager and supervisor(s) to take charge of the program and to do the recruitment. It would be your job as Public Health director to win the Housing director's cooperation in these quality matters. That probably means one or two face-to-face meetings initially and some periodic personal follow-ups in person or by phone.

Q. What sorts of skills should one look for in what you refer to as the right middle manager and supervisors?

A. If ever there were a program that required managers to get into the spirit of a high-involvement organization, this is it. Because the motivation and creativity of the line staff are the keys to making this program work, the people nominally "above" them should ideally see themselves primarily as facilitators and supporters, figuring out ways to be helpful to them. Of course, they also have to be able to work in a collegial way with the public health nurse who serves as consultant and sidekick to the field inspectors.

[Steering, chapter 6]

Q. What about numbers? Aren't we to have measurable performance objectives?

A. Yes. You and the Housing director should set what you think will be some challenging ones at the outset. But we should all recognize that the initial targets could be completely unrealistic in either direction. Revising them after the first few months of experience with the program would provide a good opportunity for the staff involved in this program, at all levels and from both organizations, to collectively rethink all our initial assumptions. It might not be a bad idea to invite representatives of landlords and of relevant community groups to participate somehow in this process as well.

Q. That might be a little scary for some people! Who knows what might come out?

A. Don't forget that you have the ultimate authority. You can cancel the program and cut off the flow of funds to the Housing agency after whatever initial period you and Housing will agree to in a contract. But the chances are that more good will come out of such a collective rethinking process than harm. You—both plural and singular—might discover that this cadre of LP Rehab inspectors and their Public Health sidekicks are able to piggy-back some new objectives onto the program at little cost. Screening for kids with lead poisoning, for instance, or health education regarding other housing sanitation issues like vermin control, or detecting and correcting housing problems that are of a more traditional sort.

More interesting still is the possibility that both Public Health and Housing could learn something about how to implement a high-involvement management philosophy more broadly through-out your agencies.

[Trust, chapter 7]

Q. What sort of contract with Housing would make sense?

A. It has to be clear about the overall program objectives, the amount of money at stake, the time period, the rough number of personnel to be allocated by Housing and by Public Health, and the joint commitment to review program performance and opera-tions at certain intervals. But it should not get into details that cannot and need not be foreseen, such as how many inspections might be done or how many closed cases should be expected in a certain time period.

Q. How should those important details be resolved?

A. By reasoned analysis and honest discussion as experience accumulates. You need to create an atmosphere of mutual trust in which such discussions can proceed not only at formally planned intervals but informally and continuously as the need arises. Personal contact and a series of successful, though undoubtedly small, instances of joint problem solving are in order.

Q. At what level of our organizations?

A. At all levels, but the critical communications channel is between your nurse liaison and the program manager in Housing. Success at that level should be flagged and reported to you and your counterpart in Housing, and also to the LP Rehab line staff. These latter are a very important audience, because we want them to feel free to go to individuals in both agencies for help, and also not to suppose that they might be able to play one supervisor off against the other.

[Developmental Processes, chapter 8]

Q. What are the first targets we should be aiming at?

A. This is an important question because, given the amount of money available to the program, there could be a delay of up to four or five years between the time we rehab the first units and the time we get around to the last. Good candidates for early targeting would be those apartments where the children have a history of treatment for lead poisoning. Not only would this be good public health practice, but the tenants in those cases would be more likely than most to accept the inconvenience of the rehab effort. Their enthusiasm would make good publicity material.

Targeting landlords that own many apartment units would have the advantage of extending the reach of the program relatively quickly. Also, these landlords probably have easier access to financing than smaller ones. Moreover, there would be less public sympathy for foot-dragging on their part if any were so inclined.

Q. In four or five years the program should have completed its task. It will need to be phased out. Are there steps we should take now in anticipation of that time?

A. Contracting out would be the normal way to handle something of relatively short duration. That might prove difficult in this case, however, as there aren't firms specializing in this sort of work. It might be possible to create one, of course. Another strategy would be to shift experienced personnel into this program but hire only temporary workers to cover the workload the shifted parties will have left behind. Beyond these ideas, every local Public Health and Housing department should consider this downstream problem in light of their own particular circumstances .

Q. How else might we get sandbagged at some later point in time?

A. Sooner or later you will run into real conflict with a tenant whose landlord is clever enough to make political capital out of the conflict. The program will be tarred in the media as a "Big Brother" operation. Make sure that when that happens you are ready to hit back in the media with a "horror story" about a rusty-hearted landlord whose greed leaves young children to bear the health risks. Be assured that the state Public Health Department will be prepared for such contingencies too. And during my tenure we will back you up as you see fit. We are no less your partners in this than your local Housing Department.

Q. If we keep revising the program as we learn from experience, might we not look, to outsiders, like drunks who can't walk a straight line?

A. Hostile outsiders—possibly a landlord group—might characterize you this way. Unfortunately, Public Health will not have to take as much of this heat as your partner the Housing agency. This means that Housing will have grounds for mistrusting the promises of Public Health to stand by them when trouble comes. It is therefore important to be seen to be standing by them on matters large and small from the earliest days of the program.

Q. How much danger is there that the program will be terminated after the next statewide election?

A. There is always a risk. This suggests some other reasons to chalk up some early successes with high-risk populations: If you wait, you might never get to them, and the early successes could also help build protection against premature termination.

The Craftsmanship Conceptual Framework

Pat Duvall, the state director of the public health agency and hypothetical author of this memo, is one of many craftsmen expected to play a role in creating this relatively complex ICC that cuts across not only agency lines but state–local and public–private lines. In this memo Duvall is trying to create enthusiasm and a climate of trust and joint problem solving. It may or may not work, but it is surely nothing but an early step in a long and uncertain developmental process in which Duvall would play only a small part. Although Duvall would be an excellent specimen of a craftsman, I have tried in this book to keep the focus on the larger craft process. Rather than focusing on the cognitive and judgmental capacities of the craftsman, I have been drawing attention to the functional requirements of the craft process and of the product that issues from it. Although the talents of the craftsman are not absent from my conceptual framework, they take up only a small space within it. I created this conceptual framework for several reasons, the most important of which were methodological or even philosophical. I conclude by stating or restating these, in the hopes that other researchers will be encouraged to use, and of course to improve on, the framework.

First, craftsmanship thinking integrates the purposiveness and creativity of some craftsmen with the rest of the craft process. Yes, the carpenter assembles building materials, fits them together, and gives them shape, but her actions are to a large extent guided by historically developed craft principles in combination with the available materials and site and the purposes chosen by the owner. Similarly, the skillful and creative public managers, who loom large in so many public management teaching cases and in the best practices research literature,[2] can now be understood to be to some extent a product of the latent opportunities in their environment and other such external circumstances.[3]

2. Good examples of this literature are Barzelay (1992), Moore (1996); Chase and Reveal (1983); Levin and Sanger (1994); Behn (1991).

3. The opportunity concept helps solve a certain public relations problem posed by purposiveness. Despite its common-sense familiarity and its intuitive appeal, *purpose*, the parent concept of purposiveness, is not an idea in good standing in the social sciences. It has about it too much of the odor of free will, and so threatens the determinism that, at least rhetorically, undergirds much or most empirical social science. The rhetoric of determinism is helped by settling the primary locus of causation in the actor's environment. Economics, for instance, fastens on environmental incentives, which evoke what appears to be purposive action by somehow engaging an actor's preexisting preferences. If agency leaders choose to collaborate with one another, it is perforce because they perceive incentives to do so—for example, budgetary incentives, or personal career incentives, or in unusual cases mission-related incentives. Political science thinks of *interests* more readily than *preferences* and motivates action by holding forth stakes that actors pursue in order to satisfy their interests. But *stakes* is a virtual synonym for *incentives*, and the spirit of

Second, craftsmanship thinking naturally accommodates purposive-ness—in other words, what I defined in chapter 1 as creativity combined with public spiritedness. Not all craftsmen are purposive, and those who are often need not be so at all times and in all respects. However, unlike most models in the public choice or political economy tradition, craftsmanship thinking at least allows for the possibility.

Third, craftsmanship thinking constrains creativity within a functionalist conception of action: "We need to find a way of moving people through this building that will be compatible with the demands of the workers for quiet and a sense of tranquility." One understands the craftsman's creativity not as some sort of free-form, uncaused *jeu d'esprit* but as a disciplined response to challenges structured to some degree by the functional requirements of some craft process or some intended craft product. Our attempts to understand the creativity of public managers should also be carried out along such lines.

Fourth, craftsmanship thinking supplies the creative actor with a stock of ready-made ideas about smart practices. The chances are that creative action, in the public management setting, represents the adaptation of some smart practice to the situation at hand using local materials. What counts as a smart practice is partly a matter of definition, of course, and partly a matter of empirical validation in a more general domain. And craftsmen differ greatly in terms of their repertoires of smart practice possibilities as well as their skill in adapting them to local circumstances.

Fifth, craftsmanship thinking easily recognizes the causal importance of synergistic interactions in the development of both process and product. A building stands up not because it has strong building materials or a good design or rests on stable ground but because all three conditions are present together. A creative public manager succeeds in an endeavor because the politics, the personalities, and the policy, to name just three craft components, are all aligned at once, and not because any single one of them is successfully brought into play by itself.

---

environmental determinism pervades interest-based analysis in political science as much as it does economics. Psychology, when it refers to *motivation* and *motives*, is often no better because these too tend to be slotted into deterministic explanations of behavior or conduct. Because I do not believe determinism is true or value its rhetoric, I do not jeopardize a doctrine of much value to myself by allowing purpose to enter a causal schema as a prime mover. But for those who wish, symbolically at least, not to admit purpose unless it can be linked theoretically to some cause of its own, opportunity can play just such a causal role.

Sixth, craftsmanship thinking takes note of the causal role of qualitative potentialities (and limits) in the world—for example, the flexibility (or inflexibility) of some building material, the circulation efficiencies (or inefficiencies) inherent in some generic design for a building with an interior courtyard. The categories of qualitative potentialities I developed in this book to understand ICC development—challenge, opportunity, capacity, and vulnerability—should be easily adaptable to many other cases in public management.

Seventh, craftsmanship thinking illuminates the unfamiliar causal role in management and related creative activities played by what many people call chance. Chance should be seen as part of a Darwinian process of combination, disruption, and recombination. The fluid and chance-dominated environment of managerial craftsmen can be a relatively rich source of potential craft materials, that is, new opportunities, new incentives, new actors, and new substantive ideas. From this flux most will be discarded, but some few will be taken up and tried, in some cases only in craftsmen's thought-experiments. To continue with examples in this same vein, one can see potential craft materials as an attractive field trying, so to speak, to engage the fluid attentions of potentially attractable craftsmen who are moving in an environment from which one or a few might step forth to experiment with the more suitable materials. Furthermore, this same environment is also a source of many potential hazards, one or two of which might one day combine with the latent vulnerabilities of an ICC or a smart practice and weaken or destroy it. In these Darwinian scenarios chance is an active and partially predictable causal agent. It is made predictable not only by the laws of statistics but by the processes that shape the comings and goings of attractive opportunities, attractable craftsmen, and dangerous hazards, together with the interactions among all these streams.[4]

To many practitioners, and not a few academics, however, chance is at work in a causal sense only when the improbable happens. As many of my informants were wont to say, "Pure chance! All the planets seem to have lined up at the same time." And social scientists say, "Pure chance! Political and fiscal conditions were favorable, and some unusu-

---

4. The imagery of interacting streams that create "policy agendas" is nicely developed in Kingdon (1984). Machiavelli deserves the original credit for the powerful metaphor of streams and rivers in political analysis for his comparison of *fortuna* and a river in *The Prince*.

ally creative managers were on the scene, and at least one of them was using interagency activity as a career move, and the state hadn't caught on yet to the fiscal irregularities that would eventually slow them down." What such interpretations overlook is that latent potentialities lie under the surface of the visible world, organizing genuinely improbable occurrences into larger processes that have a good deal more internal causal structure. Perhaps even more to the point, they also overestimate the significance of what actually happens as opposed to the equally real potential for many different but somewhat similar things to happen.[5]

Finally, I started on the path to explore craft-related metaphors because I was looking for a way to bring a more systematic analytic lens to bear on certain kinds of managerial phenomena. These had integrative, purposive, and creative dimensions. Concretely, they were the introduction of programmatic innovations, large- and small-scale organizational reinvention, and, in general, any kind of complex capacity-building activity. Such phenomena are as analytically elusive as they are significant for creating public value and advancing the public interest. If future research using the craftsmanship conceptual framework is tested in domains in which it is analytically most suited, it will also illuminate problems and solutions relevant to public managers doing their most important public work.

5. For an evolutionary biologist's complaint along the same lines, see Jacob (1982). Of course, trying to understand the nature of a potential that is real but not actualized is to place great demands on counterfactual analysis, which such analysis is not always capable of meeting. See Tetlock and Belkin (1996) for the more optimistic view and Jervis (1996) for the more pessimistic view. For a philosopher's conception of how the limits of the possible constrain design and thereby make the extremely improbable nearly inevitable, see Dennett (1995, pp. 128–35).

References

Abbott, Andrew. 1990. "A Primer on Sequence Methods." *Organization Science* 1 (4): 375–92.

Acosta, Sandra, and others. 1994. *Review of New York City's Licensing and Permitting Process for Manufacturers*. New School for Social Research, Graduate School of Management and Urban Policy.

Agranoff, Robert. 1991. "Human Services Integration: Past and Present Challenges." *Public Administration Review* 51 (6): 533–42.

Agranoff, Robert, and Michael McGuire. 1998. "Multinetwork Management: Collaboration and the Hollow State in Local Economic Policy." *Journal of Public Administration Research and Theory* 8 (1): 67–91.

Agranoff, Robert, and Alex N. Pattakos. 1989. "Management of Human Services in Local Governments: A National Survey." *State and Local Government Review* 21 (Spring): 74–83.

Alexander, Ernest R. 1995. *How Organizations Act Together: Interorganizational Coordination in Theory and Practice*. Luxembourg: Gordon and Breach.

Allio, Michael K. 1993. "3M's Sophisticated Formula for Teamwork." *Planning Review* (November–December): 19–21.

Alter, Christine, and Jerald Hage. 1993. *Organizations Working Together*. Newbury Park, Calif.: Sage.

Altshuler, Alan A. 1997. "Bureaucratic Innovation, Democratic Accountability, and Political Incentives." In *Innovation in American Government*, edited by Alan A. Altshuler and Robert D. Behn, 38–67. Brookings.

Altshuler, Alan A., and Marc D. Zegans. 1997. "Innovation and Public Management: Notes from the State House and City Hall." In *Innovation in American Government*, edited by Alan A. Altshuler and Robert D. Behn, 68–80. Brookings.

Amphion Environmental Inc. 1995. *Fire Hazard Mitigation Program and Fuel Management Plan for the East Bay Hills*. Oakland, Calif.: East Bay Hills Vegetation Management Consortium.

Ancona, Deborah G., and David E. Caldwell. 1992. "Cross-Functional Teams: Blessing or Curse for New Product Development." In *Transforming Organizations*, edited by Thomas A. Kochan and Michael Useem, 154–66. Oxford University Press.

Ancona, Deborah G., Raymond A. Friedman, and Deborah M. Kolb. 1991. "The Group and What Happens on the Way to 'Yes.'" *Negotiations Journal* (April): 155–73.

Angle, Harold L., and Andrew H. Van de Ven. 1989. "Suggestions for Managing the Innovation Journey." In *Research on the Management of Innovation: The Minnesota Studies*, edited by Andrew H. Van de Ven, Harold L. Angle, and Marshall Scott Poole, 663–97. New York: Ballinger.

Annie E. Casey Foundation. 1995. *The Path of Most Resistance: Reflections on Lessons Learned from New Futures*. Baltimore.

Appelbaum, Eileen, and Rosemary Batt. 1994. *The New American Workplace: Transforming Work Systems in the United States*. Ithaca, N.Y.: ILR Press.

Arnett, Marilyn S. 1993. "Coordinated Youth Services Council Transitional Evaluation Services Report." Mill Valley, Calif.

Balbach, Edith DeWitt. 1994. "Interagency Collaboration in the Delivery of the California Tobacco Education Program." Ph.D. dissertation, University of California, Berkeley.

Bardach, Eugene. 1972. *The Skill Factor in Politics: Repealing the Mental Commitment Laws in California*. University of California Press.

_____. 1993. *Improving the Productivity of JOBS Programs*. New York: Manpower Demonstration Research Corporation.

_____. 1996. *The Eight-Step Path of Policy Analysis (A Handbook for Practice)*. Berkeley: Berkeley Academic Press.

Bardach, Eugene, and Robert A. Kagan. 1982. *Going by the Book: The Problem of Regulatory Unreasonableness*. Temple University Press.

Bardach, Eugene, and Cara Lesser. 1996. "Accountability in Human Services Collaboratives—For What? and To Whom?" *Journal of Public Administration Research and Theory* 6 (2): 197–224.

Barley, Stephen R., John Freeman, and Ralph C. Hybels. 1992. "Strategic Alliances in Commercial Biotechnology." In *Networks and Organizations: Structure, Form, and Action*, edited by Nitin Nohria and Robert G. Eccles, 311–47. Harvard Business School Press.

Barnard, Chester I. 1938. *The Functions of the Executive*. Harvard University Press.

Barzelay, Michael. 1992. *Breaking through Bureaucracy: A New Vision for Managing in Government*. University of California Press.

Beder, Hal. 1984. "Interorganizational Cooperation: Why and How?" In *Realizing the Potential of Interorganizational Cooperation*, edited by Hal Beder, 3–22. San Francisco: Jossey-Bass.

Behn, Robert D. 1987. "The Massachusetts Department of Revenue." Durham, N.C.: Institute for Policy Sciences and Public Affairs.

_____. 1988. "Management by Groping Along." *Journal of Policy Analysis and Management* 7 (4): 643–63.

_____. 1991. *Leadership Counts: Lessons for Public Managers from the Massachusetts Welfare, Training, and Employment Program*. Harvard University Press.

Belden, Timothy, and others. 1994. "Policy Strategy to Reduce Erosion in the Elkhorn Slough Watershed." Graduate School of Public Policy, University of California, Berkeley.

Bernstein, Susan R. 1991. *Managing Contracted Services in the Nonprofit Sector: Administrative, Ethical, and Political Issues.* Temple University Press.

Best, Larry. 1992. "The School-Based Program as a Model of Services Integration." Paper prepared for Annual Research Conference of Association for Public Policy Analysis and Management.

Blakely, Craig H., and others. 1987. "The Fidelity-Adaptation Debate: Implications for the Implementation of Public Sector Social Programs." *American Journal of Community Psychology* 15 (3): 253–68.

Borins, Sandford. 1996. "The New Public Management Is Here to Stay." *Canadian Journal of Public Administration* 38 (1): 122–32.

_____. 1998. *Innovating with Integrity: How Local Heroes Are Transforming American Government.* Georgetown University Press.

Brach, Cindy. 1995. "Designing Mental Health Capitation Projects: Policy Decisions for Public Officials." Paper prepared for Annual Research Conference of the Association for Public Policy Analysis and Management.

Brager, George, and Harry Specht. 1973. *Community Organizing.* Columbia University Press.

Brett, Jeanne M. 1991. "Negotiating Group Decisions." *Negotiation Journal* (July 1991): 291–310.

Brock, Jonathan, and Gerald W. Cormick. 1989. "Can Negotiation Be Institutionalized or Mandated? Lessons from Public Policy and Regulatory Conflicts." In *Mediation Research: The Process and Effectiveness of Third-Party Intervention,* edited by Kenneth Kressel and Dean G. Pruitt, 138–65. San Francisco: Jossey-Bass.

Bruner, Charles. 1991. *Thinking Collaboratively: Ten Questions and Answers to Help Policy Makers Improve Children's Services.* Washington: Education and Human Services Consortium.

California State Auditor. 1996. *Office of Emergency Services Has Met Most of Its Emergency Management Responsibilities Despite Administrative Problems.* Sacramento: California State Auditor.

Cameron, Kim S., Sarah J. Freeman, and Aneil K. Mishra. 1993. "Downsizing and Redesigning Organizations." In *Organizational Change and Redesign: Ideas and Insights for Improving Performance,* edited by George P. Huber and William H. Glick, 19–63. Oxford University Press.

Campbell, Donald J. 1988. "Task Complexity: A Review and Analysis." *Academy of Management Review* 13 (1): 40–152.

Carnevale, Peter J. 1992. "The Usefulness of Mediation Theory." *Negotiation Journal* (October): 387–90.

Center for the Future of Children Staff. 1992. "Analysis." *Future of Children* 2 (1): 6–18.

Chase, Gordon, and Elizabeth Reveal. 1983. *How to Manage in the Public Sector.* Reading, Mass.: Addison-Wesley.

Chaskin, Robert J., and Harold A. Richman. 1992. "Concerns about School-Linked Services: Institutions-Based versus Community-Based Models." *Future of Children* 2 (1): 107–17.

Chisholm, Donald. 1989. *Coordination without Hierarchy: Informal Structures in Multiorganizational Systems.* University of California Press.

Chrislip, David D., and Carl E. Larson. 1994. *Collaborative Leadership: How Citizens and Civic Leaders Can Make a Difference.* San Francisco: Jossey-Bass.

Chynoweth, Judith K., and others. 1992. *Experiments in Systems Change: States Implement Family Policy.* Washington: Council of Governors' Policy Advisors.

Cohen, Elena, and Theodora Ooms. 1993. "Training and Technical Assistance to Support Family-Centered Integrated Services Reform." Washington: Family Impact Seminar.

Cohen, Steven, and William Eimicke. 1995. *The New Effective Public Manager.* San Francisco: Jossey-Bass.

Cooper, Joel. 1996. "Cognitive Dissonance Theory." In *The Blackwell Encyclopedia of Social Psychology,* edited by Anthony Manstead, S. R. and Miles Hewstone, 104–09. Cambridge, Mass.: Basil Blackwell.

Creech, Bill. 1994. *The Five Pillars of TQM: How to Make Total Quality Management Work for You.* Dutton.

Crowson, Robert L., and William Lowe Boyd. 1993. "Coordinated Services for Children: Designing Arks for Storms and Seas Unknown." *American Journal of Education* 101: 140–79.

Dawes, Robyn M. 1988. *Rational Choice in an Uncertain World.* Harcourt Brace Jovanovich.

Dehoog, Ruth Hoogland. 1990. "Competition, Negotiation, or Cooperation." *Administration and Society* 22 (3): 317–40.

Delbecq, Andre L., and Peter K. Mills. 1985. "Managerial Practices that Enhance Innovation." *Organizational Dynamics* (Summer): 24–34.

Denn, Morton M. 1986. *Process Modeling.* White Plains, N.Y.: Longman.

Dennett, Daniel C. 1995. *Darwin's Dangerous Idea: Evolution and the Meanings of Life.* Simon and Schuster

Diehl, Michael, and Wolfgang Stroebe. 1996. "Group Productivity." In *The Blackwell Encyclopedia of Social Psychology,* edited by Anthony S. R. Manstead and Miles Hewstone, 274–79. Cambridge, Mass.: Basil Blackwell.

DiIulio, John J., Jr. 1994. "The Promises of Performance Measurement," Working Paper 94-2. Brookings Institution, Center for Public Management.

Donahue, John D. 1989. *The Privatization Decision: Public Ends, Private Means.* Basic Books.

Dwyer, Robert F., Paul H. Schurr, and Sejo Oh. 1987. "Developing Buyer-Seller Relationships." *Journal of Marketing* 51: 11–27.

East, Jean F. 1993. "The Denver Family Opportunity Council: A Case Study." Colorado Trust.

Elmore, Richard F. 1986. "Graduate Education in Public Management: Working the Seams of Government." *Journal of Policy Analysis and Management* 6 (1): 69–83.

Federal Facilities Environmental Restoration Dialogue Committee. 1996. *Consensus Principles and Recommendations for Improving Federal Facilities Cleanup (Final Report)*. U.S. Environmental Protection Agency.

Ferguson, Marilyn, and John Naisbitt. 1987. *The Aquarian Conspiracy: Personal and Social Transformation in the 1980s*. St. Martin's.

Festinger, L., and J. M. Carlsmith. 1959. "Cognitive Consequences of Forced Compliance." *Journal of Abnormal and Social Psychology* 58: 203–10.

Fletcher, Susan. 1997. "Accountability for Results in County Government: Implementation Strategy for Adopting Outcome-Based Measurements in Contra Costa County." Master's thesis, University of California, Berkeley.

Fontaine, Peter J. 1993. "EPA's Multimedia Enforcement Strategy: The Struggle to Close the Environmental Compliance Circle." *Columbia Journal of Environmental Law* 18 (1): 31–102.

Friedman, Raymond A. 1992. "The Culture of Mediation: Private Understandings in the Context of Public Conflict." In *Hidden Conflict in Organizations: Uncovering Behind-the-Scenes Disputes*, edited by Deborah M. Kolb and Jean M. Bartunek, 143–64. Newbury Park, Calif.: Sage.

Galbraith, Jay R. 1973. *Designing Complex Organizations*. Reading, Mass.: Addison-Wesley.

_____. 1977. *Organization Design*. Reading, Mass.: Addison-Wesley.

Gans, Sheldon P., and Gerald T. Horton. 1975. *Integration of Human Services: The State and Municipal Levels*. New York: Praeger.

Gardner, Sidney. 1989. "Failure by Fragmentation." *California Tomorrow* 4 (4): 18–25.

Glaser, Barney, and Anselm Strauss. 1967. *The Discovery of Grounded Theory*. Chicago: Aldine.

Golan, Shari, and others. 1996. *From Principles to Action: Local Implementation of California's Healthy Start School-Linked Services Initiative*. Menlo Park, Calif.: SRI International.

Golden, Olivia. 1990. "Innovation in Public Sector Human Services Programs: The Implications of Innovation by 'Groping Along.'" *Journal of Policy Analysis and Management* 9 (2): 219–48.

Gray, Barbara. 1985. "Conditions Facilitating Interorganizational Collaboration." *Human Relations* 38 (10): 911–36.

_____. 1989. *Collaborating: Finding Common Ground for Multiparty Problems*. San Francisco: Jossey-Bass.

Gray, Barbara, and Tina M. Hay. 1986. "Political Limits to Interorganizational Consensus and Change." *Journal of Applied Behavioral Science* 22 (2): 95–112.

Gray, Barbara, and Donna J. Wood. 1991. "Collaborative Alliances: Moving from Practice to Theory." *Journal of Applied Behavioral Science* 27 (1): 3–22.

Gresov, Christopher, and Carroll Stephens. 1993. "The Context of Interunit Influence Attempts." *Administrative Science Quarterly* 38: 252–76.

Grover, Varun. 1993. "An Empirically Derived Model for the Adoption of Customer-Based Interorganizational Systems." *Decision Sciences* 24 (3): 603–40.

Grubb, W. Norton, and Lorraine M. McDonnell. 1996. "Combating Program Fragmentation: Local Systems of Vocational Education and Job Training." *Journal of Policy Analysis and Management* 15 (2): 252–70.

Grusky, Oscar, and others. 1986. "Models of Local Mental Health Delivery Systems." In *The Organization of Mental Health Services: Societal and Community Systems*, edited by Richard W. Scott and Bruce L. Black, 158–95. Beverly Hills, Calif.: Sage.

Gueron, Judith M. 1996. "A Research Context for Welfare Reform." *Journal of Policy Analysis and Management* 15 (4): 547–61.

Haas, Peter. 1990. *Saving the Mediterranean*. Columbia University Press.

Hackman, Richard J., and Ruth Wageman. 1995. "Total Quality Management: Empirical, Conceptual, and Practical Issues." *Administrative Science Quarterly* 40: 309–42.

Hadley, Arthur T. 1986. *The Straw Giant*. Random House.

Hausler, Jürgen, Hans-Willy Hohn, and Susanne Lutz. 1993. "The Architecture of an R&D Collaboration." In *Games in Hierarchies and Networks: Analytical and Empirical Approaches to the Study of Governance and Institutions*, edited by Fritz W. Scharpf, 211–49. Boulder, Colo.: Westview Press.

Heifetz, Ronald A. 1994. *Leadership without Easy Answers*. Harvard University Press.

Hjern, Benny, and David O. Porter. 1981. "Implementation Structures: A New Unit of Administrative Analysis." *Organizational Studies* 2 (3): 211–27.

Hogan, Lyn A. 1996. "Work First: A Progressive Strategy to Replace Welfare with a Competitive Employment System." Washington: Democratic Leadership Council.

Hogg, Michael A. 1992. *The Social Psychology of Group Cohesiveness: From Attraction to Social Identity*. New York University Press.

Horn, Murray J. 1995. *The Political Economy of Public Administration: Institutional Choice in the Public Sector*. Cambridge University Press.

Howell, Jane M., and Christopher A. Higgins. 1990. "Champions of Technological Innovation." *Administrative Science Quarterly* 35: 317–41.

Iles, Paul A., and Randhir Auluck. 1990. "From Organizational to Interorganizational Development in Nursing Practice: Improving the Effectiveness of Interdisciplinary Teamwork and Interagency Collaboration." *Journal of Advanced Nursing* 15: 50–58.

Innes, Judith E., and David E. Booher. 1996. "Consensus Building as Role-Playing and Bricolage: Toward a Theory of Collaborative Planning." Paper prepared for Meeting of Collegiate Schools of Planning and the Association of European Schools of Planning.

Innes, Judith, and others. 1994. *Coordinating Growth and Environmental Management through Consensus Building*. California Policy Seminar, University of California.

Jacob, François. 1982. *The Possible and the Actual*. University of Washington Press.

Jacobs, Bruce. 1981. *The Political Economy of Organizational Change: Urban Institutional Response to the War on Poverty*. New York: Academic Press.

Jehl, Jeanne, and Michael Kirst. 1992. "Getting Ready to Provide School-Linked Services: What Schools Must Do." *Future of Children* 2 (1): 95–106.

Jennings, Edward T., Jr. 1994. "Building Bridges in the Intergovernmental Arena: Coordinating Employment and Training Programs in the American States." *Public Administration Review* 54 (1): 52–60.

Jennings, Edward T., Jr., and Dale Krane. 1994. "Coordination and Welfare Reform: The Quest for the Philosopher's Stone." *Public Administration Review* 54 (4): 341–48.

Jervis, Robert. 1996. "Counterfactuals, Causation, and Complexity." In *Counterfactual Thought Experiments in World Politics: Logical, Methodological, and Psychological Perspectives*, edited by Philip E. Tetlock and Aaron Belkin, 309–16. Princeton University Press.

Kagan, Sharon L., and others. 1995. *Toward Systemic Reform Service Integration for Young Children and Their Families*. Falls Church, Va.: National Center for Service Integration.

Kagan, Sharon L., with Peter Neville. 1993. *Integrating Services for Children and Families: Understanding the Past to Shape the Future*. Yale University Press.

Kanter, Rosabeth Moss. 1988. "When a Thousand Flowers Bloom: Structural, Collective, and Social Conditions for Innovation in Organizations." *Research in Organizational Behavior* 10: 169–211.

Kanter, Rosabeth Moss, Barry A. Stein, and Todd D. Jick, eds. 1992. *The Challenge of Organizational Change: How Companies Experience It and Leaders Guide It*. Free Press.

Katzenbach, Jon R., and Douglas K. Smith. 1993. *The Wisdom of Teams*. HarperCollins.

Keating, Pamela J., and Richard W. Clark. 1988. "Accent on Leadership: The Puget Sound Educational Consortium." In *School-University Partnerships in Action*, edited by Kenneth A. Sirotnik and John I. Goodlad, 148–66. Teachers College, Columbia University.

Kelman, Steven. 1990. *Procurement and Public Management*. Washington: American Enterprise Institute.

———. 1992. "Adversary and Cooperationist Institutions for Conflict Resolution in Public Policymaking." *Journal of Policy Analysis and Management* 11 (2): 178–206.

Kimberly, John R., and Robert E. Quinn, eds. 1984. *Managing Organizational Transitions*. Homewood, Ill.: Richard D. Irwin.

King, Gary, Robert O. Keohane, and Sidney Verba. 1994. *Designing Social Inquiry: Scientific Inference in Qualitative Research*. Princeton University Press.

Kingdon, John W. 1984. *Agendas, Alternatives, and Public Policies*. Little, Brown.

Knoke, David. 1990. *Political Networks: The Structural Perspective*. Cambridge University Press.

Kramer, Ralph M., and Bart Grossman. 1987. "Contracting for Social Services: Process Management and Resource Dependencies." *Social Service Review* 61 (1): 32–55.

Kramer, Roderick M., and Tom R. Tyler, eds. 1995. *Trust in Organizations: Frontiers of Theory and Research*. Thousand Oaks, Calif.: Sage.

Kuiper, Jennifer. 1997. "The Vegetation Management Consortium: Keeping the Flame Alive." Term paper, Goldman School of Public Policy, University of California, Berkeley.

LaPorta, Rafael, and others. 1997. "Trust in Large Organizations." Working Paper R97-03. Kennedy School of Government, Harvard University.

Latham, Gary P., and Thomas W. Lee. 1986. "Goal Setting." In *Generalizing from Laboratory to Field Settings*, edited by Edwin A. Locke, 101–17. Lexington, Mass.: D.C. Heath.

Lawler, Edward E., III. 1992. *The Ultimate Advantage: Creating the High-Involvement Organization.* San Francisco: Jossey-Bass.

Lax, David A., and James K. Sebenius. 1986. *The Manager as Negotiator: Bargaining for Cooperation and Competitive Gain.* Free Press.

Levin, Martin A., and Barbara Furman. 1985. *The Political Hand: Policy Implementation and Youth Employment Programs.* New York: Pergamon.

Levin, Martin A., and Mary Bryna Sanger. 1994. *Making Government Work: How Entrepreneurial Executives Turn Bright Ideas into Real Results.* San Francisco: Jossey-Bass.

LeVine, Robert A., and Donald T. Campbell. 1972. *Ethnocentrism: Theories of Conflict, Ethnic Attitudes, and Group Behavior.* Wiley.

Levinthal, Daniel A., and James G. March. 1993. "The Myopia of Learning." *Strategic Management Journal* 14: 95–112.

Lewicki, Roy J., and Barbara Benedict Bunker. 1995. "Developing and Maintaining Trust in Work Relationships." In *Trust in Organizations: Frontiers of Research and Theory*, edited by Roderic M. Kramer and Tom R. Tyler, 114–39. Thousand Oaks, Calif.: Sage.

Light, Paul. 1994. "Creating Government That Encourages Innovation" In *New Paradigm for Government: Issues for the Changing Public Service*, edited by Patricia Ingraham and Barbara Romzek, 63–89. San Francisco: Jossey-Bass.

Linden, Russell. 1994. *Seamless Government: A Practical Guide to Re-Engineering in the Public Sector.* San Francisco: Jossey-Bass.

Locke, Edwin A., Gary P. Latham, and Miriam Erez. 1988. "The Determinant of Goal Commitment." *Academy of Management Review* 13 (1): 23–39.

Lundberg, Kirsten. 1991. "Integrating Family Services: Maryland." John F. Kennedy School of Government Case Program, Harvard University.

Lynn, Laurence E., Jr. 1980. *The State and Human Services: Organizational Change in a Political Context.* MIT Press.

_____. 1996. *Public Management as Art, Science, and Profession.* Chatham, N.J.: Chatham House.

_____. 1997. "Innovation and the Public Interest: Insights from the Private Sector." In *Innovation in American Government*, edited by Alan A. Altshuler and Robert D. Behn, 83–103. Brookings.

Maloy, Kathleen A. 1994. "The Tennessee Children's Plan: How Do We Get There From Here?" Vanderbilt Institute for Public Policy Studies.

Mandell, Myrna P. 1994. "Managing Interdependencies through Program Structures: A Revised Paradigm." *American Review of Public Administration* 24 (1): 99–121.

March, James G., and Herbert A. Simon. 1968. *Organizations*. Wiley.

Margolis, Howard. 1982. *Selfishness, Altruism, and Rationality*. University of Chicago Press.

Master, Warren. 1992. "Interagency Cooperation Yields Quality Results." *Public Manager* (Summer): 45–48.

Mattessich, Paul W., and Barbara R. Monsey. 1992. *Collaboration: What Makes It Work*. St. Paul, Minn.: Amherst H. Wilder Foundation.

McEwen, Craig A., and Richard J. Maiman. 1989. "Mediation in Small Claims Court: Consensual Processes and Outcomes." In *Mediation Research: The Process and Effectiveness of Third-Party Intervention*, edited by Kenneth Kresse and Dean G. Pruitt, 53–67. San Francisco: Jossey-Bass.

Melaville, Atelia I., and Martin J. Blank. 1991. *What It Takes: Structuring Interagency Partnerships to Connect Children and Families with Comprehensive Services*. Washington: Education and Human Services Consortium.

_____. 1993. *Together We Can: A Guide for Crafting a Profamily System of Education and Human Services*. Government Printing Office.

Meltsner, Arnold J., and Christopher Bellavita. 1983. *The Policy Organization*. Beverly Hills: Sage.

Merry, Sally Engle. 1989. "Mediation in Nonindustrial Societies." In *Mediation Research: The Process and Effectiveness of Third-Party Intervention*, edited by Kenneth Kresse and Dean G. Pruitt, 68–90. San Francisco: Jossey-Bass.

Minnicucci Associates. 1995. *Creating a Neighborhood-Based System: The Del Paso Heights Experience*. Sacramento.

Mizrahi, Terry, and Beth B. Rosenthal. 1993. "Managing Dynamic Tensions in Social Change Coalitions." In *Community Organization and Social Administration: Advances, Trends, and Emerging Principles*, edited by Terry Mizrahi and John Morrison. New York: Haworth Press.

Mnookin, Robert H., and Lee Ross. 1995. "Introduction." In *Barriers to Conflict Resolution*, edited by Kenneth J. Arrow and others, 2–24. Norton.

Moe, Terry M. 1989. "The Politics of Bureaucratic Structure." In *Can the Government Govern?*, edited by John E. Chubb and Paul E. Peterson, 267–329. Brookings.

Mohr, Lawrence B. 1982. *Explaining Organizational Behavior: The Limits and Possibilities of Theory and Research*. San Francisco: Jossey-Bass.

Mondadori, Fabrizio, and Adam Morton. 1979. "Modal Realism: The Poisoned Pawn." In *The Possible and the Actual: Readings in the Metaphysics of Modality*, edited by M. J. Loux, 235–52. Cornell University Press.

Moore, Mark H. 1996. *Creating Public Value: Strategic Management in Government*. Harvard University Press.

Moore, Mark H.; Malcolm Sparrow, and William Spelman. 1997. "Innovation in Policing: From Production Lines to Job Shops." In *Innovation in American Government*, edited by Alan A. Altshuler and Robert D. Behn, 274–98. Brookings.

Morgan, Douglas, and others. 1996. "What Middle Managers Do in Local Government: Stewardship of the Public Trust and the Limits of Reinventing Government." *Public Administration Review* 56 (4): 359–66.

Nohria, Nitin, and Robert G. Eccles. 1992. *Networks and Organizations: Structure, Form, and Action.* Harvard Business School Press.

O'Day, Jennifer, Margaret E. Goertz, and Robert E. Floden. 1995. "Building Capacity for Education Reform." CPRE Policy Brief RB-18. University of Pennsylvania, Consortium for Policy Research in Education.

Oliver, Christine. 1991. "Network Relations and Loss of Organizational Autonomy." *Human Relations* 44 (9): 943–61.

Olson, Mancur, Jr. 1965. *The Logic of Collective Action.* Harvard University Press.

Osborne, David, and Ted Gaebler. 1992. *Reinventing Government: How the Entrepreneurial Spirit Is Transforming the Public Sector.* Reading, Mass.: Addison-Wesley.

Ostrom, Thomas M., and Constantine Sedikides. 1992. "Out-Group Homogeneity Effects in Natural and Minimal Groups." *Psychological Bulletin* 112 (3): 536–52.

O'Toole, Laurence J. 1985. "Diffusion of Responsibility: An Interorganizational Analysis." In *Public Policy Implementation: Analytical Models and Institutional Design in Federal and Unitary States,* edited by Kenneth I. Hanf and A. J. Toonen, 210–25. Dordrecht: Martinus Nijhoff.

Overman, E. Sam, and Kathy J. Boyd. 1994. "Best Practice Research and Postbureaucratic Reform." *Journal of Public Administration Research and Theory* 4 (1): 67–83.

Peters, Tom. 1987. *Thriving on Chaos.* Knopf.

Peters, Thomas J., and Robert H. Waterman Jr. 1982. *In Search of Excellence.* Warner Books.

Pfeffer, Jeffrey, and Gerald R. Salancik. 1978. *The External Control of Organizations: A Resource Dependence Perspective.* Harper and Row.

Phillips, Joel, and J. Fred Springer. 1997. *Implementation of Community Interventions: Lessons Learned.* Folsom, Calif.: EMT Associates.

Porter, Michael E. 1985. *Competitive Advantage: Creating and Sustaining Superior Performance.* Free Press/Macmillan.

Powell, Walter W. 1990. "Neither Market nor Hierarchy: Network Forms of Organization." *Research in Organizational Behavior* 12: 295–336.

_____. 1996. "Inter-Organizational Collaboration in the Biotechnology Industry." *Journal of Institutional and Theoretical Economics* 152 (1): 197–215.

Powell, Walter W., and Peter Brantley. 1992. "Competitive Cooperation in Biotechnology: Learning through Networks." In *Networks and Organizations: Structure, Form, and Action,* edited by Nitin Nohria and Robert G. Eccles, 366–94. Harvard Business School Press.

Provan, Keith G., and H. Brinton Milward. 1991. "Institutional-Level Norms and Organizational Involvement in a Service-Implementation Network." *Journal of Public Administration Research and Theory* 1 (4): 391–417.

_____. 1994. "Integration of Community-Based Services for the Severely Mentally Ill and the Structure of Public Funding: A Comparison of Four Systems." *Journal of Health Politics, Policy and Law* 19 (4): 865–94.

_____. 1995. "A Preliminary Theory of Interorganizational Network Effectiveness: A Comparative Study of Four Community Mental Health Systems." *Administrative Science Quarterly* 40: 1–33.

Pruitt, Dean G., and Peter J. Carnevale. 1993. *Negotiation in Social Conflict*. Pacific Grove, Calif.: Brooks/Cole.

Putnam, Robert D. 1993. *Making Democracy Work: Civic Traditions in Modern Italy*. Princeton University Press.

Radin, Beryl A. 1996. "Managing across Boundaries." In *The State of Public Management*, edited by Donald F. Kettl and H. Brinton Milward, 145–67. Johns Hopkins University Press.

Radin, Beryl A., and others. 1996. *New Governance for Rural America: Creating Intergovernmental Partnerships*. University Press of Kansas.

Raiffa, Howard. 1982. *The Art and Science of Negotiation*. Harvard University Press.

———. 1995. "Analytical Barriers." In *Barriers to Conflict Resolution*, edited by Kenneth J. Arrow and others, 132–48. Norton.

Reveal, Elizabeth C. 1991. *Governance Options for "The Children's Initiative: Making Systems Work."* Philadelphia: Center for Assessment and Policy Development.

Riccio, James, Daniel Friedlander, and Stephen Freedman. 1994. *GAIN: Benefits, Costs, and Three-Year Impacts of a Welfare-to-Work Program*. New York: Manpower Demonstration Research.

Ridley, Matt. 1997. *The Origins of Virtue: Human Instincts and the Evolution of Cooperation*. New York: Viking.

Rogers, Sally E., William A. Anthon, and Karen S. Danley. 1989. "The Impact of Interagency Collaboration on System and Client Outcomes." *Rehabilitation Counseling Bulletin* 33 (2): 10–109.

Rosenthal, Burton. 1973. "Lead Poisoning (A) and (B)." Kennedy School of Government Case Program, Harvard University.

Rosenthal, Stephen R. 1982. *Managing Government Operations*. Glenview, Ill.: Scott, Foresman.

Ross, Lee. 1995. "Reactive Devaluation in Negotiation and Conflict Resolution." In *Barriers to Conflict Resolution*, edited by Kenneth J. Arrow and others, 26–42. Norton.

Savoie, Donald J. 1996. "Just Another Voice from the Pulpit." *Canadian Journal of Public Administration* 38 (1): 133–36.

Saxenian, Annalee. 1994. *Regional Advantage: Culture and Competition in Silicon Valley and Route 128*. Harvard University Press.

Scharpf, Fritz W., and Matthias Mohr. 1994. *Efficient Self-Coordination in Policy Networks: A Simulation Study*. Cologne: Max Planck Institut für Gesellschaftsforschung.

Schlechty, Phillip C., and Betty Lou Whitford. 1988. "Shared Problems and Shared Vision: Organic Collaboration." In *School-University Partnerships in Action*, edited by Kenneth A. Sirotnik and John I. Goodlad, 191–204. Teachers College, Columbia University.

Scholz, John T., and Wayne B. Gray. 1997. "Can Government Facilitate Cooperation? An Informational Model of OSHA." *American Journal of Political Science* 41 (3): 693–717.

Schuerman, John R., Tina L. Rzepnicki, and Julia H. Littell. 1994. *Putting Families First: An Experiment in Family Preservation*. New York: Aldine de Gruyter.

Scott, Esther, and Michael Barzelay. 1993. "Preventing Pollution in Massachusetts: The Blackstone Project." Kennedy School of Government, Harvard University.

Shortell, Stephen M., and Thomas M. Wickizer. 1984. "New Program Development: Issues in Managing Vertical Integration." In *Managing Organizational Transitions*, edited by John R. Kimberly and Robert E. Quinn, 134–68. Homewood, Ill.: Richard D. Irwin.

Simon, Herbert A. 1969. *The Sciences of the Artificial*. MIT Press.

Sims, David. 1986. "Interorganization: Some Problems of Multi-Organizational Teams." *Personnel Review* 15: 27–31.

Smith, Steven Rathgeb, and Michael Lipsky. 1993. *Nonprofits for Hire*. Harvard University Press.

Staw, Barry M., and Sigal G. Barsade. 1993. "Affect and Managerial Performance: A Test of the Sadder-but-Wiser vs. Happier-and-Smarter Hypotheses." *Administrative Science Quarterly* 38: 304–31.

Strauss, Anselm, and Juliet Corbin. 1990. *Basics of Qualitative Research: Grounded Theory Procedures and Techniques*. Newbury Park, Calif.: Sage.

Susskind, Lawrence E., Eileen F. Babitt, and Phyllis N. Segal. 1993. "When ADR Becomes the Law: A Review of Federal Practice." *Negotiations Journal* (January): 59–75.

Svara, James H., and others. 1994. *Facilitative Leadership in Local Government: Lessons from Successful Mayors and Chairpersons*. San Francisco: Jossey-Bass.

Tennessee Department of Finance and Administration. 1990. "Assessment of Children and Youth Committed to State Care May 1989." Nashville, Tenn.

Tetlock, Philip E., and Aaron Belkin. 1996. "Counterfactual Thought Experiments in World Politics: Logical, Methodological, and Psychological Perspectives." In *Counterfactual Thought Experiments in World Politics: Logical, Methodological, and Psychological Perspectives*, edited by Philip E. Tetlock and Aaron Belkin, 3–38. Princeton University Press.

Thomas, Craig W. 1993. "Reorganizing Public Organizations: Alternatives, Objectives, and Evidence." *Journal of Public Administration Research and Theory* 3 (4): 457–86.

_____. 1997a. "Bureaucratic Landscapes: Interagency Cooperation and the Preservation of Biodiversity." Ph.D. dissertation, University of California, Berkeley.

_____. 1997b. "Public Management as Interagency Cooperation: Testing Epistemic Community Theory at the Domestic Level." *Journal of Public Administration Research and Theory* 7 (2): 221–46.

_____. 1998. "Maintaining and Restoring Public Trust in Government Agencies and Their Employees." *Administration and Society* 30 (2): 166–93.

Thompson, Fred. 1993. "Matching Responsibilities with Tactics: Administrative Controls and Modern Government." *Public Administration Review* 53 (4): 303–18.

Tidrick, Steven G. 1992. "Fire Prevention as a Public Good." Undergraduate seminar paper, Harvard University.

Tyack, David. 1992. "Health and Social Services in Public Schools: Historical Perspectives." *Future of Children* 2 (1): 19–32.

Van de Ven, Andrew H. 1993. "Managing the Process of Organizational Innovation." In *Organizational Change and Redesign: Ideas and Insights for Improving Performance*, edited by George P. Huber and William H. Glick, 269–94. Oxford University Press.

Van de Ven, Andrew H., and Gordon Walker. 1984. "The Dynamics of Interorganizational Coordination." *Administrative Science Quarterly* 29: 598–621.

Van de Ven, and others. 1989. "Processes of New Business Creation in Different Organizational Settings." In *Research on the Management of Innovation: The Minnesota Studies*, edited by Andrew H. Van de Ven, Harold L. Angle, and Marshall Scott Poole, 221–29. New York: Ballinger.

Versar. 1995. *Moving Sites Faster through Streamlined Oversight*. Springfield, Va: Headquarters Air Combat Command.

Wagner, Mary. 1994. *Collaborative Planning for School-Linked Services: An Evaluation of California's Healthy Start Planning Grants*. Menlo Park, Calif.: SRI International.

Wagner, Mary, Lynn Newman, and Shari Golan. 1996. *California's Healthy Start School-Linked Services Initiative: Results for Children and Families*. Menlo Park, Calif.: SRI International.

Wagner, Mary, and others. 1994a. *A Healthy Start for California's Children and Families: Early Findings from a Statewide Evaluation of School-Linked Services*. Menlo Park, Calif.: SRI International.

Wagner, Mary, and others. 1994b. *Implementing School-Linked Services: A Process Evaluation of the First Year of California's Healthy Start Initiative*. Menlo Park, Calif.: SRI International.

Warren, Roland L. 1967. "The Interorganizational Field as a Focus for Investigation." *Administrative Science Quarterly* 12 (3): 397–419.

Weatherley, Richard A., and others. 1987. "National Problems, Local Solutions: Comprehensive Services for Pregnant and Parenting Adolescents." *Youth and Society* 19 (1): 73–92.

Weick, Karl E. 1979. *The Social Psychology of Organizing*, 2d ed. Random House.

_____. 1984. "Small Wins: Redefining the Scale of Social Problems." *American Psychologist* 39 (1): 40–49.

Weiss, Janet. 1996. "Psychology." In *The State of Public Management*, edited by Donald F. Kettl and H. Brinton Milward, 118–42. Johns Hopkins University Press.

Wheatley, Margaret J. 1992. *Leadership and the New Science: Learning about Organization from an Orderly Universe*. San Francisco: Berrett-Koehler.

Williams, David D. 1988. "The Brigham Young University-Public School Partnership." In *School-University Partnerships in Action*, edited by Kenneth A. Sirotnik and John I. Goodlad, 124–47. Teachers College, Columbia University.

Williamson, Oliver E. 1986. *The Economic Institutions of Capitalism.* Free Press.
_____. 1991. "Comparative Economic Organization: The Analysis of Discrete Structural Alternatives." *Administrative Science Quarterly* 36: 269–96.
_____. 1993. "Calculativeness, Trust, and Economic Organization." *Journal of Law and Economics* 36: 453–86.
Wilson, Edward O. 1978. *On Human Nature.* Harvard University Press.
Wilson, James Q. 1989. *Bureaucracy.* Basic Books.
Wood, Donna J., and Barbara Gray. 1991. "Toward a Comprehensive Theory of Collaboration," *Journal of Applied Behavioral Science* 27 (2): 139–62.
Yessian, Mark R. 1994. "Integrating Human Services: Lessons Learned over Two Decades." Boston.
Zellerbach Family Fund. 1990. "The Politics of Change: Issues in Providing Neighborhood-Based Services." San Francisco.
Zuckerman, Howard S., Arnold D. Kaluzny, and Thomas C. Ricketts II. 1995. "Alliances in Health Care: What We Know, What We Think We Know, and What We Should Know." *Health Care Management Review* 20 (1): 54–64.

Index